General Sir J
and Bar, MC
of THE THI
of a substan
as the forem
Australian born in 19..
stock, General Hackett might have been a don
if the imminence of Hitler's war had not
attracted him, after reading both Greats and
History at Oxford, into a family cavalry
regiment. That war brought him three wounds
and three decorations for gallantry, the last of
both when he commanded one of the two
parachute brigades at Arnhem, in a military
career that saw him Deputy Chief of the
General Staff and ended with his command of
the Northern Army Group in NATO as
Commander-in-Chief of the British Army of
the Rhine. A now famous letter to *The Times*
on the need to strengthen NATO might have
ended his career rather sooner if he had not
got around British rules about corresponding
with the Press (if only just) by writing as a
NATO general.

General Hackett's withdrawal from the Army
(he never speaks of retirement) was followed
by seven years as Principal of King's College,
London, during which he was President of
both the UK Classical and English
Associations (his Presidential Address to each
is now a classic) and set an example in a
troubled time of how a university can be run
in tranquillity. He now returns to King's as a
visiting Professor in Classics.

The Third World War:
August 1985

A Future History by
GENERAL SIR JOHN HACKETT
and others

SPHERE BOOKS LIMITED
30/32 Gray's Inn Road, London WC1X 8JL

First published in Great Britain by Sidgwick & Jackson Ltd 1978

Copyright © 1978 by General Sir John Hackett, Air Chief Marshal
Sir John Barraclough, Sir Bernard Burrows, Brigadier Kenneth Hunt,
Vice-Admiral Sir Ian McGeoch, Norman Macrae, and Major-General
John Strawson

Published by Sphere Books Ltd 1979
Reprinted 1979 (twice), 1980 (twice)

TRADE
MARK

Set in VIP Times Roman

Printed in Great Britain by
William Collins Sons & Co Ltd
Glasgow

CONTENTS

LIST OF ILLUSTRATIONS

A Soviet pilot goes out to his *Foxbat* on a Polish airfield during the Soviet preparatory 'manoeuvres' before the out-break of hostilities

Soviet *Scud* missile

Admiral of the Fleet of the Soviet Navy Sergei Gorshkov (ASSOCIATED PRESS)

Soviet *Kiev*-class aircraft carrier
(MINISTRY OF DEFENCE; CROWN COPYRIGHT)

The Soviet T-72 main battle tank
(MINISTRY OF DEFENCE; CROWN COPYRIGHT)

The USS *Ray* (SSN-653) nuclear-powered attack submarine proceeding on patrol (MacCLANCY PRESS/US NAVAL PHOTO-GRAPHIC CENTER)

US Army self-propelled 155 mm howitzer M-109 moves into position east of Giessen, 5 August, in a flank action by V US Corps (G.Z. TREBINSKI/© IAN V. HOGG)

'Target!' A NATO tank destroys a Soviet T-80 at close range in a night action on the North German Plain, 6 August (MacCLANCY PRESS/UNITED KINGDOM LAND FORCES/PHOTO BY SGT M. BUTLER; CROWN COPYRIGHT)

A fast patrol boat of the Federal German Navy and a *Sea King* helicopter on operations in the Skagerrak, 5 August (MacCLANCY PRESS/DIE BILDSTELLE DER MARINE)

Soviet motorized infantry crossing the River Weser, 7 August (MacCLANCY PRESS)

Reinforcing F-111's top up their fuel from an air tanker in mid-Atlantic on their way to Europe

Soviet tanks in an unopposed water crossing during the invasion of north Norway, 7 August (NOVOSTI PRESS)

A Soviet BMP armoured infantry fighting vehicle on the move into Holland, 8 August

A Tupolev *Backfire* bomber with its moveable wings in the forward (low speed) position (MINISTRY OF DEFENCE; CROWN COPYRIGHT)

A remarkable shot of a *Jaguar* aircraft in action as seen by the recording camera (IMAGE IN INDUSTRY LTD)

Soviet second echelon armour disembarking in Denmark (MacCLANCY PRESS)

The superlative USAF F-15 rejoining the high altitude battle after replenishment

An American F-16 aircraft with a full ground attack munitions load

A pre-war test flight of the first US Space Shuttle Orbiter being carried on the back of a Boeing 747 to altitude for launch into space

A convoy of US Army armoured vehicles rolls into a C-5 waiting to join the air bridge (US INFORMATION SERVICE)

US airborne infantry fighting to recover Bremen (KEYSTONE/US ARMY PHOTO)

Soviet casualty evacuation

LIST OF MAPS

ABBREVIATIONS

AAFCE	Allied Air Forces Central Europe
A/C	aircraft
ACLANT	Allied Command Atlantic
ADP	automatic data processing
AEW	airborne early warning
AFCENT	Allied Forces Central Europe
AFNORTH	Allied Forces Northern Europe
AFSOUTH	Allied Forces Southern Europe
AFV	armoured fighting vehicle(s)
AIRCENT	Allied Air Forces Central Europe
AIRSOUTH	Allied Air Forces Southern Europe
ALCM	air-launched cruise missile(s)
AOC	Air Officer Commanding
AOC-in-C	Air Officer Commanding-in-Chief
APC	armoured personnel-carrier(s)
A/S	anti-submarine
ASW	anti-submarine warfare
ATAF	Allied Tactical Air Force
ATGW	anti-tank guided weapon(s)
AWACS	airborne warning and control system
BAOR	British Army of the Rhine
BMEWS	ballistic missile early warning system
BMP	*boevaya mashina pekhoty* (Soviet infantry combat vehicle)
BREMCO	Branscombe Emergency Committee
BREMPLAN	Branscombe Emergency Plan
CAP	combat air patrol(s)
CASPA	Confederation of Africa South People's Army
CD	Civil Defence
CDU	Christian Democratic Union
CENTAG	Central Army Group
CINCHAN	Commander-in-Chief, Channel
CINCENT	Commander-in-Chief, Central Region
CINCNORTH	Commander-in-Chief, Allied Forces Northern Europe

CINCSOUTH	Commander-in-Chief, Allied Forces Southern Europe
CINCUKAIR	Commander-in-Chief, United Kingdom Air Forces
CLGP	cannon-launched guided projectile
COMAAFCE	Commander Allied Air Forces Central Europe
COMBALTAP	Commander Allied Forces Baltic Approaches
COMCENTAG	Commander Central Army Group
COMNORTHAG	Commander Northern Army Group
COMWAS	Commander Western Approaches South
CPR	Chinese People's Republic
CPSU	Communist Party of the Soviet Union
DEW	distant early warning
DF	direction-finding
EASTLANT	Eastern Atlantic
ECM	electronic counter-measures
ECCM	electronic counter-counter-measures
ELINT	electronic intelligence
EMP	electro-magnetic pulse
ENG	electronic newsgathering
EUROSAM	European surface-to-air missile(s)
FEBA	forward edge of the battle area
FLEETSATCOM	Fleet satellite communications
FNLA	Angolan National Liberation Front
FOSMEF	Flag Officer Soviet Middle East Forces
FPB	fast patrol boat(s)
FRELIMO	Mozambique Liberation Front
FRG	Federal Republic of Germany
FUMO	Mozambique United Front
GAF	German Air Force
GDR/DDR	German Democratic Republic/Deutsche Demokratische Republik
GLCM	ground-launched cruise missile(s)
GNP	gross national product
GS	General Staff
GSFG	Group of Soviet Forces in Germany
HDG	Home Defence Groups (of the Federal German Territorial Army)
HE	high-explosive
I (or INT)	Intelligence

ICBM	inter-continental ballistic missile(s)
IRBM	intermediate-range ballistic missile(s)
IRR	Individual Ready Reserve
JACWA	Joint Allied Command Western Approaches
JTIDS	Joint Tactical Information Distribution System
LSI	large-scale integration
MBFR	mutual and balanced force reductions
MICV	Mechanized Infantry Combat Vehicle(s)
MPLA	Popular Movement for the Liberation of Angola
MR	maritime reconnaissance
MRBM	medium-range ballistic missile(s)
MRCA	multiple role combat aircraft
MSI	medium-scale integration
MT	megaton
MTLB	(Soviet universal combat vehicle)
NASA	National Aeronautics and Space Administration
NATO	North Atlantic Treaty Organization
NBC	nuclear, biological, chemical
NEV	National Emergency Volunteers
NCO	non-commissioned officer
NORSECA	Northern Seas Environmental Control Agency
NORTHAG	Northern Army Group
OAU	Organization for African Unity
OP	observation post
OPEC	Organization of Petroleum Exporting Countries
OSS	Office of Strategic Services
OTC	Officer Training Corps
PDRY	People's Democratic Republic of Yemen
PGM	precision-guided missile(s)
QRA	quick-reaction alert
RCRIP	Reserve Component Readiness Improvement Package
RPG	rounds per gun
RPV	remotely-piloted vehicle(s)
SACEUR	Supreme Allied Commander Europe
SACLANT	Supreme Allied Commander Atlantic
SALT	Strategic Arms Limitation Talks
SAM	surface-to-air missile(s)
SAS	Special Air Service

SED	Sozialistische Einheitspartei Deutschland
SHAPE	Supreme Headquarters Allied Powers in Europe
SIGINT	signal intelligence
SITREP	situation report
SLBM	submarine-launched ballistic missile(s)
SLCM	submarine-launched cruise missile(s)
SNAF	Soviet Naval Air Force
SOE	Special Operations Executive
SOL	soldier out of luck
SOSUS	sonar surveillance system
SOUTHAG	Southern Army Group
SP	self-propelled
SSBN	submarine(s), strategic ballistic nuclear
SSM	surface-to-surface missile(s)
SSN	submarine(s), nuclear
STANAVFORLANT	Standing Naval Force Atlantic
STASS	surface-towed array surveillance system
SWAPO	South-west Africa People's Organization
TAC CP	Tactical Command Post
TAVR	Territorial and Auxiliary Volunteer Reserve
UAE	United Arab Emirates (in the Persian Gulf)
UAR	United Arab Republic
UKADGE	United Kingdom Air Defence Ground Environment
UKLF	United Kingdom Land Forces
UNCLOS	United Nations Conference on the Law of the Sea
UNFISMATRECO	United Nations Fissile Materials Recovery Organization
UNITA	National Union for the Total Independence of Angola
UNRRO	United Nations Relief and Repatriation Organization
USAF	United States Air Force
USAREUR	United States Army in Europe
VLSI	very large-scale integration
V/STOL	vertical/short take-off and landing
WESTLANT	Western Atlantic
WP	Warsaw Pact
XO	Executive Officer

PROLOGUE

The publication of this book so soon after the cessation of hostilities between major participants in the Third World War will mean that much of what it contains will be incomplete and, even more, conjectural. In the chaotic conditions prevailing towards the end, in some key centres of power, vast quantities of records disappeared. Some have since come to light. Others probably never will.

It has nevertheless seemed important to the writers, all of whom played a part in the events of 1985 and their aftermath, whether in uniform or out of it, to put on the record as soon as possible some account, however imperfect, of what took place in a time of such transcendental importance to mankind.

We write as Britons, profoundly conscious of our debt to others. The outcome could have been vastly different – and very nearly was. The world has stood on the edge of an abyss. Under providence, through a gradual but significant shift of public attitudes and the work of growing numbers of men of foresight and good sense in the last few years before the outbreak – work often done in the face of vociferous and passionate opposition – it has been held back, but only just, from destruction. The margin, everybody now knows, was a narrow one.

Much will be said and written about these events in years to come, as further sources come to light and further thought is given to this momentous passage in the history of our world. The narrative now set out in only the broadest outline and, of our deliberate choice, in popular form, will be greatly amplified and here and there, no doubt, corrected. It seemed to us sensible, however, before these events move too far into the background of our lives, to seek answers to some important questions, in the hope that this might lessen the probability of another catastrophe from which, this time, we would not so readily escape.

The questions are simple. What happened, and why did it happen? What might have happened, and why did it not?

London, Easter, 1987

ADDITIONAL FOREWORD

On page 423 the authors make clear their conviction that the only forecast which can be offered with confidence about the future is that nothing will happen exactly as they have shown it. In Chapter 2 they sketched how the world might look in 1984. This was to provide a possible model of how world conflict could come about, in order to draw attention to those precautions which the Western democracies would be prudent to take if they wish to survive it. In this political setting some of the strategic issues were raised which might exercise the minds of policy makers in both the White House and the Kremlin.

If what the authors were looking for was credible prediction no area would have presented more difficulty than the Middle East. One thing was sure, however: among the Soviet Union's persistent aims, control of both the largest source of oil in the world and the sea routes by which this oil was transported to Europe and to the U.S.A. would stand high. The U.S.A. and her European allies, for their part, would be vitally concerned to keep the oil flowing and the sea lanes round the Cape open, whatever happened.

The authors suggested in their narrative that Saudi Arabia and Kuwait might fall under the influence of revolutionary forces, while Iran would remain stable and friendly to the West. While some of the authors' suggestions about possible developments in the Third World have been borne out of events others have not. In Iran and Saudi Arabia, for example, the tables have been almost precisely turned. For illustrative purposes, however, what has actually happened does no more than reinforce the case. The oil (and the sea routes over which it must travel) have come under threat from the eastern shore of the Arabian Gulf and this is what really matters. The authors picture was one of American support for a Western-oriented Iran. What we now hear is talk of safeguarding the interests of Western oil-consumers by a military presence elsewhere in that part of the world. To all appearances it will almost certainly be needed.

The authors believe that little is to be gained by trying continually to recast the model to take account of recent events, particularly when these do more to illustrate the model than to render it less valid. Constant revision, as events unfold, would leave the story always out of date, while weakening rather than strengthening the lesson. It is more sensible to let this illustration stand. Besides, it is in and over Europe, and particularly the Central Region, that the *Entscheidungsschlacht* would be likely to take place. It was to draw attention to the defensive deficiencies of the West in general, but particularly in respect of the Central Region of N.A.T.O., that the authors embarked upon their cautionary tale in the first place. Events even of such importance as the revolution in Iran, or (perhaps more significant still) the emergence of a Polish Pope, and others as yet unforeseen, are likely to reduce the validity of the general argument – or its importance. We propose, therefore, to leave our cautionary tale as it was.

CHAPTER ONE

AUGUST DAWN:
THE FIRST BLOWS

'Black Horse One Zero, Black Horse One Zero, this is Shovel Six. Confirming Charlie One's sighting as follows: large armoured formation passed through inter-German border Zero Three Zero Five Zulu approximate brigade in size. Composed of Papa Tango 76s, Bravo Tango Romeo 62s, and Tango 72s. Inform Black Horse Six that Shovel is engaging. Out.'

Captain Jack Langtry, Troop Commander, Troop L, 3 Squadron in 11 Armoured Cavalry Regiment was speaking into his microphone early on the morning of 4 August 1985 as he stood on hill 402 at Wildech, looking across the border zone over the hills rolling towards East German Eisenach. In the dawn light he saw scores of armoured vehicles moving rapidly towards him on both sides of the autobahn. Langtry knew what this was: the advanced guard of an attacking Soviet formation. It could not be anything else.

The 11th Cavalry formed the main strength of the V US Corps covering force, whose job was to give the Corps maximum time in a delaying action. To the north was Kassel, out of the Corps area. To the south the Fulda Gap opened up, dangerously close to the border only 15 kilometres away.

Langtry's fifteen *Shillelagh*-firing *Sheridan* light tanks were in hull defilade along the high ground overlooking the autobahn that ran from the border to Bad Hersfeld, directly behind him. His three platoons had practised engaging an enemy on this same route many times. Today it was for real. He gripped his microphone and heard his

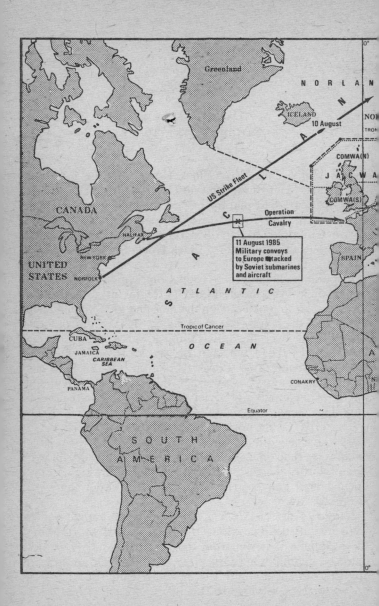

Greenland

NORLAN

NORTH

ICELAND

10 August

COMWA(N)

US Strike Fleet

CANADA

Operation
Cavalry

COMWA(S)

HALIFAX

NEW YORK

11 August 1985
Military convoys
to Europe attacked
by Soviet submarines
and aircraft

SPAIN

UNITED
STATES

NORFOLK

ATLANTIC

S A R G A S S O

Tropic of Cancer

CUBA

OCEAN

JAMAICA

CARIBBEAN
SEA

PANAMA

CONAKRY

Equator

SOUTH

AMERICA

voice give the command, 'Shovel, this is Six. Engage at will. Out.' Almost before his hands relaxed on the mike switch he heard the roar of *Shillelagh* missiles leaving fifteen tubes, guided on their way to targets silhouetted in the sad grey August morning.

The Black Horse Regiment were once again carrying the cudgel for their country as they had in the Philippines, Mexico, Europe and Vietnam.

Beside Langtry, Trooper Earl Waite suddenly exclaimed, 'Man! Look at that!' Nine of the fifteen missiles had found their targets in sudden shattering fountains of red fireballs and flames.

The *Sheridans* were already moving to their alternate firing position when hill 402 seemed to crumble with the impact of Soviet artillery fire. Waite was killed instantly and two other members of the TAC CP were wounded. Langtry, unhurt, quickly moved the command party to an observation post 500 metres further west near Spitzhütte.

The Soviet armoured formation, after pausing for a moment, was now oriented in his general direction and a unit could be seen breaking off in an attempt to outflank L Troop. Langtry knew that this would run into the seventeen XM-1s of the Squadron Tank Company. That was their misfortune. He saw one of 2 Platoon's *Sheridans* fly apart when hit by a Soviet anti-tank missile and said aloud, 'Why the hell did he have to silhouette himself on the skyline? Haven't I been harping about tactical driving for eighteen months now?' He then heard the telltale wop, wop, wop of helicopters over the din of battle as the twenty-one *TOW* carrying ATGW *Cobras* of the Black Horse Regiment began a hide-and-seek battle with the T-72s swinging off the autobahn in the direction of Heiringen.

Somehow, Langtry felt completely detached from the surrounding battle. He gave his orders as though this was only another field training exercise. His little tactical Command Post functioned exactly as it had so many times before when practising for the battle they all hoped would never come.

'Shovel, this is Six. Execute Alpha 3.' This was the command to fall back to the next delaying position, the high ground overlooking Lauterbach.

The first platoon was soon on the move and already halfway to their next position as the second began to disengage. Langtry waved his arm and the three M-113s of the TAC CP started to move. As the first vehicle crossed the bridge over the Lauter, there was a tremendous flash. The bridge disappeared. Langtry felt himself thrown into the air, hitting the ground with a searing pain in his left shoulder. Two of his three command vehicles were on fire and the third rushing down the track on the other side of the stream in search of cover. Langtry sat up and muttered audibly, 'Oh God. I hope the XO takes command in a hurry or the troop will be SOL.' He felt himself passing out. It was 0447Z, 4 August 1985.'*

'It was not yet three a.m. on Sunday 4 August and still dark when the commander of C Squadron of 8 Royal Tank Regiment in I Br Corps covering force in the Central Region received over his radio the order to stand-to. The daily routine for stand-to was just before first light. This was clearly something special.

The line of the low crest 1,000 metres away to the east was dimly visible against a sky beginning to grow paler. He stood in the turret of his tank glued to the radio, heedless of the ordered bustle about him as the fourteen other tanks of the Squadron, with their supporting vehicles, started up to move out into daylight dispersion.

He took the mug of coffee handed up to him but did not want to eat. It was impossible in this time of waiting not to speculate on what might lie ahead. He did manage to remember, however, his promise to make sure that the TV newsmen were alerted if anything special turned up.

* Taken from *Black Horse and Red Star: American Cavalry at War* by John S. Cleghorn, Col. US Army (retd), Houghton Mifflin, Boston 1986.

The voice from Headquarters came in again. 'Enemy reported on the move,' it said. 'Stand by at three zero minutes' notice for Bravo.'

All his tanks and other radio outstations would have heard that transmission; there was nothing for him to add.

'Bravo' was the move to the Regiment's emergency deployment position, 1,000 metres over the crest, almost on the Demarcation Line. Most of them knew it already from cautious reconnaissance on foot, with the tanks left back out of sight to avoid the frontier incident Division was so frightened of.

In less than ten minutes the voice came up again. 'Move out now,' it said. There was a note of urgency in it.

The light was growing as he promptly gave the word to move, on the internal radio channel, with the order to load, prepare for action and be on the alert.

The tanks lurched once again into life.

His own was approaching the crest, bumping over stumpy ground, once forest, now felled to open a field of fire, as his Commander's voice came up on the radio again.

'Enemy's closer than we thought,' it said. 'Expect early contact. Report first sighting immediately.'

His tank topped the crest on the last words, and there opened up before him the most frightening sight he had ever seen. The open ground below, stretching to a faintly seen line of trees about 2 kilometres away, was swarming with menacing black shapes coming fast towards him. They were tanks, moving in rough line-abreast about 200 metres apart, less than 1,000 metres off and closing the range quickly. Another line was following behind and a third just coming out of the trees. The world seemed full of Soviet tanks.

'You might have told me,' he said into the microphone: 'Am engaging now. Out!'

He gave quick orders to the Squadron and to his own gunner, but already a sudden huge flash seen through his periscope head, followed at once by a great black cloud of smoke with a heart of flame, like a volcano in eruption, showed where a forward anti-tank missile launcher from somewhere behind him to the left had found its first target.

In the same moment he was stunned and deafened by a thunderous blow, as from some titanic hammer, outside the tank low down to the right, and was thrown hard against the side of the cupola as the tank slewed round and shuddered to a violent halt. At the same time a gigantic clang, which seemed to rend his skull, told of a solid shot skidding off the sloping front plate without penetrating. The tank's main armament, its gun, was useless now.

The thing to do was to get the crew out, all three of them miraculously still alive, before the next projectile brewed them up.

In a daze, trembling like a leaf, he found himself on the ground, not quite knowing how he had got there, crouching for shelter in a shallow ditch. Roaring aircraft filled the sky low overhead, hurtling by at lightning speed with rockets crashing as they passed. Tanks he knew as Soviet T–72s came charging by in what seemed endless streams, the ground shaking under them and the air throbbing with the shrill clamour of their tracks. Squat BMP armoured infantry-carriers followed, guns blazing to their flanks. Flames were soaring into the sky with rich black clouds of smoke from burning tanks with their ammunition exploding in them. He could see no sign of any of his Squadron. His own tank crew had vanished. This was the war they had expected, not knowing really what to expect. For him, unhurt but alone, helpless and desolate, it already seemed as good as over.'*

The following impression of operations of the German and US Air Forces with *Tornado* and F–15 aircraft, on the first day of the invasion, is taken from *Parameters*, journal of the US Army War College, Fort Carlisle, Fall 1986.

'The first wave of German *Tornados* was back at base at

* Taken from an article 'Sketches of the Eighth at War' in *The Royal Armoured Corps Journal*, Autumn 1986.

Norvenich; only one was missing. It was 0930 on 4 August. The second wave from the same wing of the GAF should now be well over East Germany, attacking three Warsaw Pact airfields, while the first wave prepared for a further counter-air mission.

Oberleutnant Karl von Marschall was both exhilarated and relieved that their first mission of the war had gone so well. He was taking a breather at the entrance to the hardened aircrew bunker while his *Tornado* was being re-armed and refuelled. He had led eight of them in attacks at first light, his target the East German airfield of Zerbst. He could not say for sure how effective it had been because it was done before full light at 60 metres with the target shrouded in dawn mist. But his navigator, who played a key part in the run-up to the target and co-ordinated release of fire-suppression and denial weapons, had caught a glimpse of the airfield through the mist and was bubbling with confidence about the accuracy of the attack. They had gone at high subsonic speed hugging the ground at 60 metres over the Harz mountains.

Von Marschall felt that perhaps it was as well that the outward part of this first mission had been flown blind and automated, as they had so often practised under simulated conditions. The second mission flying the same sort of profile in clear conditions and full daylight might be finding it a bit hair-raising as they rushed very low over trees and houses they could actually see. He felt that having done it once blind, and with all the stimulus and excitement that battle brought, he could now face it in clear conditions with confidence, and he was eager to get off the ground and lead another attack. On the way home they had seen plenty of MiGs above them as they skimmed the trees but none of the Soviet fighters had been able to bring their guns or missiles to bear on the fast flying *Tornados* skimming the ground below. On this first evidence it certainly looked as if the ultra-low-level mode of operation was going to pay off in the penetration of heavy air defences. No doubt things would get tougher as the enemy got the measure of them – but so far very good.

The crash tenders had taken up ready positions by the runway which meant that some aircraft must be trying to approach under difficulty. He looked up to see an aircraft quite high to the east making a very steep descent and a few seconds later an American F–15 pilot smacked his fighter down on the runway very fast and very hard on one wheel. As he braked a tyre burst and the F–15 swung off the runway, missing von Marschall's *Tornado* shelter by only a few feet before slewing round with a collapsed undercarriage.

The aircraft did not burn and Karl ran over to see if he could help. The pilot was unhurt and climbed out with a cheerful grin as he pulled off his crash helmet.

'Hi – Major Dick Gilchrist. I'm from Bitburg. This bird won't fly for a while. I want to get back up there again where the action is. Can we get through to Base Ops Bitburg?' Karl nodded.

'What do you guys do here?'

'Counter-air on *Tornados* so far,' said Karl.

'Great – keep at it. We're doing fine up top but there are so many MiGs it's like putting your head in a beehive. I downed three and I guess that's a fair average, but there are so many that someone's got to turn the tap off on the ground – I guess that's you guys and the RAF in that low-level act of yours.'

They were both eager to swap experiences of the first few hours of the battle. As they rode in the crash tender back to Wing operations Karl told him of their attack on Zerbst.

Then it was Gilchrist's turn. 'I was leading the second section out of Bitburg. Our ground briefing gave us the area of build-up to the north and the scramble message was the last thing I heard on the radio. Just white noise, and if you could get a channel free then it was jammed even worse with voices – so we went visual on hand signals. Believe me, brother, we didn't need ground control – the sky up there is just full of MiGs and F–4s and F–15s. My three went down, just like that' – he mimed it with his hands – 'and then something hit my ship hard. The sonofabitch flashed across me slightly low – it was a wide angle shot and I just hit the gun button and he rolled straight over. Back at gunnery school they'd be proud of me, but,' he added ruefully, 'not here I guess. As he went down I saw his tail markings and it was a Belgian F–16 with a MiG 23 right on his tail. I guess it was the MiG that shot me up. Anyway my left engine was out and my power controls had gone so that's what got me in here on such a lousy landing.'

Karl smiled encouragingly as Gilchrist went on. 'I felt really bad doing Ivan's work for him but I had my own troubles. I sure hope that Belge got out all right – but – hell, those F–16s aren't meant to be this side of the SAM belt anyway. If this is the way it's going to be, and no radio either, you've got to stick in your own air space or ride down on the silk.'

It was time for von Marschall to join his squadron for briefing. They wished each other luck. As the airfield defence alert state was still only Amber he left Gilchrist in the Wing ground-training room. The walls were pasted with aircraft recognition silhouettes. There were some good ones of the F–16; he thought that might be helpful.'

'146 Air Defence Battery Royal Artillery had deployed its twelve *Rapier* detachments that night along the Hotenberg ridge and out on to the plain to the east. The task of these detachments was to defend I British Corps Headquarters which had established itself in the village of Nieder Einbecken. Each detachment had a launcher, loaded with four slim, matt-green *Rapier* anti-aircraft missiles, a target tracker and a complement of four soldiers commanded by a sergeant.

There was no sign of battle – no smoke, no noise other than a muted organ-swell to the east and north. Sergeant Edwards swung his eye across from the four dark-green

missiles on the launcher to the camouflaged pile that was
the tracker, with Gunner Henry buried in the rubber eye-
piece. His gaze turned to the ripening asparagus field
below: hadn't someone called this the season of mist and
mellow fruitful . . .

Alarm! The cry from Henry made him swivel and run to
the tracker. He dived into the camouflage as 'Target seen!'
was bellowed into his ear. With a curse he disentangled his
head from the netting and looked out over the plain. There
was an aircraft approaching, but far too slow and far too
low. Something was wrong.

'It's not hostile,' called Edwards. A *Tornado*, trailing
a white stream of fuel, was making an erratic course
westwards. Uncharitably Edwards swore at the pilot, for
he was way outside any safe lane and too close for comfort
to the headquarters. As the *Tornado* scraped over the
Hotenberg he suddenly felt apprehensive and with an
urgency that surprised him ordered the rest of the detachment to stand to.

Low out of the eastern horizon four silent dots were
approaching at high speed. 'Targets seen and hostile!'
burst from the tracker. In the far distance two flashes
appeared from the ground. The left-hand Soviet aircraft
disappeared in a ball of brilliant yellow flame but the
second missile soared fruitlessly into space.

'In coverage!' yelled Henry. Edwards ordered him on to
the centre aircraft of the remaining three and immediately
a *Rapier* left the launcher. The missile curved gracefully
towards its target and with tremendous elation the detachment watched a second *Fitter* scatter itself over the plain
in a brilliant burst of fireworks. Simultaneously the port
wing of the right-hand *Fitter* burst apart and the aircraft,
spiralling downwards, covered the asparagus field with a
sheet of oily flame. Before Edwards could react a second
Rapier had left its rails towards the survivor of the sortie
but with a thunder of afterburners the Russian pulled
sharply to the left, frighteningly close to the detachment,

and skimmed at tree-top height along and over the ridge. Their second missile had been wasted.

The action had taken just over two minutes. A quarter of an hour later Edwards was wondering why the four aircraft had not gone for Corps Headquarters when he noticed that, low out of the eastern horizon, four more *Fitters* were approaching fast.'[*]

This account of an action of an ATGW section in a brigade of Guards battle group was given by its commander and only survivor to R. J. McLintock, who has reproduced it in his book *Micks in Action: With the Irish Guards in Lower Saxony*, Leo Cooper, London 1986:

'. . . about thirty T–72s and at least twice that number of BMP now west of the obstacle, sounds of a large force following them – over,' crackled the headphones into Sergeant Patterson's half-deafened ears beneath the hood of his sweat- and dirt-stained NBC suit. He had been awake for more than forty-eight hours; his last real sleep had been in his quarter near the barracks three nights before. He silently prayed that his wife and baby daughter had got back to England safely and jerked his mind back from nameless fears to the present, to the section of *Milan* anti-tank guided weapons he commanded in the Irish Guards battle group.

They had deployed and dug for the last two days and this morning the Soviet attack came in. The war that everyone had said could never happen had begun. They had been in position on the edge of the now deserted village all day while Soviet aircraft roared overhead and the sounds of war from the east grew closer, like an approaching thunderstorm. They had watched pitiful, horrifying remnants of the covering force withdrawing – vehicles loaded with wounded grinding back up the main route, always under strafing and bombing. Grim reminders

[*] Taken from *A Civilian in a Short, Hot War*, reminiscences by A. E. Arnold, Chatto and Windus, London 1986.

of an overloaded APC which had exploded 100 metres to their right now hung on the fence outside the once neat German *Gasthaus*.

Then came the shelling. For twenty minutes the earth shook and the sky darkened as tons of explosives crashed around Patterson. One direct hit and his brother, cheerful young Sean, with Guardsman Nevin, ceased to exist. Nos. 1 and 4 posts had survived. The men at No. 3 post were alive but wounded, with only three missiles left. With growing disbelief he watched through the dust and smoke the ragged lines of Soviet armour coming across the battered cornfields – fields which in the sunshine that same morning had reminded him so much of the Sligo farm of his youth.

With a black hatred he followed the tanks through his sight – watching and waiting for the command tank. They had been taught to recognize it, with little difficulty, by the way it moved. He picked it up as it passed, and with a muttered prayer fired. He cursed the sweat that ran into his eyes but held the crosswires on his target while he counted . . . 8–9–10. A huge flash and the T–72 lurched to a halt, smoke billowing. He tore his eye from the sight and saw nearby another tank explode. No. 4 post had scored too.

The next minutes lasted for ever – reload – aim in the thickening dust and smoke – fire – down on the belly and crawl with gasping lungs to another position – then reload again – fire. After ten minutes No. 4 post was gone; then Flynn, his No. 2, was ripped from wrist to shoulder by a splinter.

Only three missiles left now. Patterson looked wearily through the sight and saw a tank halted, its turret facing him. He dropped with Flynn behind the stones in the ruins of a barn. The world blew up and went black . . ..

Hours later he came to, the only member still alive of Number One Section, *Milan* Platoon, 1 Battalion Irish Guards.'

The report given below of a battery of M–107 175 mm
self-propelled guns in action appeared in the *Daily Mail*
on 8 August 1985. It is based on an account given to the
Mail's reporter by one of the gun detachment.

'The six guns of 1 Medium Battery Royal Artillery were
well camouflaged. The Soviet aircraft thundering overhead
showed no interest, apparently intent on what lay further
west. The silence that followed their passage was uncanny.
Over the gun position lay the stillness of expectation – of
what, no one knew.

Earlier that morning the Battery had deployed in and
around the deserted village and had been immediately
called upon for fire by their OP with the covering force.
They fired continuously, each gun pumping three or four
rounds a minute, every minute. For what had seemed
eternity Gunner Wilson's world had been a bucking gun,
the surrounding clouds of dust and smoke and a stench of
cordite so intense that he could taste it. The concussion
and the noise no longer registered on his numb body. He
had become an automaton, very tired, more tired he
thought than at any time in his life. The war was still only
three hours old. Now there was this terrible quiet broken
only by the staccato sound of clipped speech on the gun's
radio.

Tell-tale signals from the Battery Command Post's radio
must have been picked up by Soviet direction finders and
the location of their emitters passed to the artillery.
Sixteen kilometres to the east two rocket batteries were
loaded and trained. Within two minutes 9 tonnes of high
explosive destroyed the silence of Wilson's village.

Wilson and his friend Mackenzie moved to hump the
last of the ammunition. Mackenzie never reached it, as the
village burst into flame, smoke and crashing noise around
them. A more terrifying concussion followed, then a hot
blast carrying flying metal and debris along like feathers
threw them to the ground. Driven by the most primitive
of instincts Wilson clawed his way between the tracks of

the gun and pressed himself to the ground, his eyes shut tight; at least its bulk offered some protection against the inferno outside.

It took him time to realize that there was no noise any more, no guns firing, no shells exploding. Then he became aware of a persistent gurgling animal wail from close by. Slowly he lifted his head and with a shudder saw that the sound must be coming from what was left of Mackenzie, disembowelled by a shell splinter, dying quickly but noisily. Alone with this frightfulness his fear turned into unreasoning panic.

The clang of a hatch and the No. 1's voice penetrated his loneliness: 'Quick, lad, into the gun. We're moving. We're not hanging around to cop the next lot.' Hands clasped his wrists and dragged him into the warm, oily belly of the self-propelled gun. With a clatter of tracks they moved on west to a new position to get into action again.'

The following appeared in the German magazine *Stern* during the second week of August. It was based on a report given by one of the survivors of a tank unit of the *Bundeswehr* in action:

'Unteroffizier Gunther Klaus was standing in the turret of his *Leopard* II tank, eating his breakfast. He found it unattractive. A hunk of brown bread with some cheese on it, a slice of *Blutwurst* and a hard-boiled egg had just been handed up to him by his gunner. A canteen of coffee followed. He did his best to eat.

Half an hour before, at 7 a.m., the order had come from the *Kompaniechef* to be prepared to move at 0800 hours, but to remain meanwhile in positions of observation. These were on the high ground south-east of Wolfenbüttel, and Klaus was a *Zugführer*, in charge of his own and three other *Leopards* in 16 Battalion of 3 *Panzeraufklärungs-regiment*.

There had been reports that a Soviet motorized division,

having crossed the border during the night, was moving in their direction. This morning's first-light helicopter reconnaissance had not confirmed this. All Klaus had seen was retiring groups of British and German light vehicles; none had come close enough to be asked for news. Two of his tank commanders were scanning the arc of observation for which his platoon was responsible, and shortly he would take over from one of them.

Just as he was raising the canteen of coffee to his lips, a sharp order came through his radio headphones.

'Prepare to move in ten minutes.'

He acknowledged the order, passed it quickly to his three tank commanders, and ordered his crew to prepare for action. Luckily there was still time to finish his coffee. Ten minutes is a long time in war.

Half an hour later, the position was very different. The whole of his company was advancing, in the usual tactical order, with two platoons moving to the next tactical feature about 1 kilometre ahead, supported and covered by the other two in fire positions. When the leading platoons were in position they in turn would help the next two forward. No shooting yet – there had been nothing to shoot at – but every tank was ready to fire as the leapfrogging went on.

'Ganz schnell! Vorwärts!' came a sharp radio order to him as his four tanks moved carefully forward to the ridge half a kilometre ahead, jinking from side to side as they went so as to provide a difficult target.

Suddenly the world was full of express trains shrieking past. Enemy armour-piercing shot! He fired his smoke protective shells at once and changed direction, telling his platoon to conform, to seek the cover of a small copse ahead to the left. The sky appeared to fill with huge predatory helicopters bearing strange markings and, worse, with rockets issuing from their undercarriages. The *Leopard* next to him stopped, smoke pouring from it. One crewman scrambled out, another got to the turret and fell back, a shattered trunk. Of all absurdities, there occurred to Klaus at this very moment a phrase which had been hammered home to him and his classmates at the *Panzer-ausbildungsschule* so often and so emphatically. 'The great thing about the *Leopard* tank, which makes it superior to all other Allied, as well as Soviet, tanks, is its agility. It gives you protection through speed.'

'Speed up,' he yelled through the inter-com to his driver, 'and jink for your life!'

Far from speeding up, the tank slithered to a halt as a shuddering jar smashed it sideways. Klaus glanced down into the turret. It seemed to be full of blood and roughly butchered meat. There was an ugly smell of burning.

'Protection through speed, eh?' thought Klaus. '*Was für Quatsch ist das!*' What rubbish! He jumped to the ground and ran. A moment later the whole *Leopard* exploded in a shambles of twisted metal, equipment, human wreckage and the indescribable mess of war.'

Accounts such as these show how powerful was the impact of the thunderbolt which came down in the early morning of 4 August on NATO ground forces in the Central Region of Allied Command Europe, and the fury in the air. It was so violent as to leave on most of those who first had to meet it a very deep feeling of shock. Its effect was stunning. Some of the ground troops who came through the first day unscathed were by evening as dazed and disorientated as the survivors of a savage traffic accident.

Very few of the men now engulfed in the volcanic eruption of ground action on a modern battlefield had ever before been exposed to anything remotely like it. The thunderous clamour, the monstrous explosions, the sheets and floods and fountains of flame and the billowing clouds of thick black smoke around them, the confusion, the bewilderment, the sickening reek of blood and high explosives, the raw uncertainty and, more than anything else, the hideous, unmanning noise – all combined to produce an almost overpowering urge to panic flight. To men in forward units the enemy seemed everywhere. Their roaring aircraft filled the sky, ripping the earth with raking cannon fire. Their tanks came on in clanging black hordes, spouting flames and thunder. The fighting vehicles of their infantry surged into and between the forward positions of the Allied defence like clattering swarms of fire-breathing dragons. It looked as though nothing could stop the oncoming waves. There seemed to be no hope, no refuge anywhere.

Panic here and there was only to be expected. Some lately recalled reservists – and even long-service regulars – found this sudden exposure to gigantic stress more than they could bear. Occasionally, under the swift contagion of uncertainty and fear, NATO units simply broke and melted away – but not often. Men adjust quite quickly, even to the appalling conditions of the battlefield, particularly where there is a job to be done which they know how to do and for which they have the right tools, and above all when they do it under competent direction in the company of their friends. The first day was a nightmare – but it was far from a total disaster.

But why was all this happening? What had brought it about? How had the course of events developed to this point – and what was now to follow?

CHAPTER TWO

THE WORLD IN 1984

By the inauguration of the fortieth president of the United States in January 1985, the world was in transition from the old-fashioned conflict situations, based on military and political competition for power, towards the newer ones involving urban guerrilladom and a 'Third World manufacturing revolution' -- though in some places this was going erratically wrong. North–South had begun to overshadow East–West.

There were 180 governments in the world. As in 1977, at the time of President Carter's inauguration, only about thirty-five of these could realistically expect their leaders to be replaced by a process of election. The most common way to change a government was by *coup d'état* or by dictatorial succession.

But the frequency of coups was growing, and they were often bloody. Bureaucrats in some communist countries had reason to fear that the habit might spread to them. The more fearful *apparatchiks* included some in the Soviet Union, a country which had for so many decades normally changed its government not by violent overthrow but by cosy dictatorial arrangement. China, by contrast, was concentrating on becoming 'a new Japan' through economic expansion. There was already talk of a China–Japan co-prosperity sphere.

The new President-elect of the United States, Governor Thompson, was a southern (and therefore conservative) Republican. He had been quite unknown nationally two years before his election in 1984, just as his two-term predecessor, President Carter, had been two years before his own election in 1976.

Mr Thompson had campaigned energetically against the

19

'soft-centred international liberalism' of the Democratic candidate, Vice-President Mondale. The President-elect was, however, worried by his own relative lack of knowledge of international affairs, and called two prestigious advisers in this field down to his South Carolina home the weekend after his election. One adviser was the director of the new United Universities Think-Tank. The other was a previous Secretary of State, always known as the Ex-Secretary.

The two were asked to set down a summary of their views about the main challenges that would face the Thompson Administration over (as it was assumed) the years 1985–93, and to compare these with the challenges that had faced the USA on President Carter's Inauguration Day in 1977. The Think-Tank's report was to concentrate on the 'poor South' of the world, the Ex-Secretary's report on the Soviet Union and the 'rich North'.

During the week after the election of November 1984, and therefore eleven weeks before his Inauguration Day in January 1985, Governor Thompson received these two reports.

The Think–Tank's report displeased him. It seemed, he told his wife, to be 'written by a computer with a bleeding heart'.

THE THINK-TANK'S REPORT
ON THE
'POOR SOUTH', NOVEMBER 1984

On President Carter's Inauguration Day in January 1977 there were 4 billion people in the world, of whom two-thirds (or 2·7 billion) lived in countries with a median income below $300 a head, while one-third lived in countries with median incomes above $3,000 per head. About 55 per cent (or 1·5 billion) of the 2·7 billion people in very poor countries were below the age of twenty-one. That, indeed, is a major reason why they were such poor countries. They were, in 1977, nations of children, who produced pretty well nothing, and of teenagers, who produced little but riots.

The main change on your Inauguration Day in 1985 will be that those 1·5 billion people will be eight years older than they were in 1977. The main change on your retirement day in 1993 will be that they will be sixteen years older. As the 1·5 billion have moved up into the main childbearing age groups, world population has inevitably risen somewhat (to 4·5 billion), although fertility rates have luckily continued the decline they were already showing by the early 1970s.

The poor countries of 1985–93 are no longer nations of children and of teenagers, but of under-employed cohabiting couples in potentially the most productive (and militarily effective) age groups, the twenties and early thirties.

The great majority of this unprecedented addition of 1·5 billion people to the world's labour force since 1977 are non-white, and are as literate as, for example, the Turkish workers in Germany in 1977, when they had an earnings level of around an annual $5,000 in 1977 dollars. There is no reason why with a proper techno-structure the additional population should not attain earnings of something like the same standard, bringing from those 1·5 billion young workers by far the biggest sudden increase in real gross world product the world has ever seen. The tragedy is that the technostructure is not in most places being provided.

The poor South of the world can today be divided into four groups:

1 A few *breakthrough* countries where real GNP is increasing at 7–12 per cent per annum, but which have also maintained social cohesion. Apart from the People's Republic of China, most of these are countries which have retained free-market economic systems: e.g. Brazil in South America; Singapore, Malaysia and the Philippines in Asia. Many of them are in East Asia, however,

and have therefore been aided by the remarkable economic growth in China since the death of Chairman Mao, even more by the coming together of the Japanese and Chinese economic miracles [see the Ex-Secretary's report below]. Most of these Asian 'breakthrough' countries will want to remain neutral in any big power struggle, and continue to make money, as the United States did in 1914–16 and 1939–41.

2   A certain number of *unstable right-wing* countries: e.g. Mexico and Argentina in South America, the richer states of the former Union of South Africa and the capitalist half of the disintegrating Indian Union. These countries have free enterprise economic systems, and have generally had quite high economic growth rates in the period 1977–84. But they have been unable to handle the social problems of the proletarianization and urbanization of a sizeable part of their labour force, so urban guerrilladom, muggings in the overcrowded cities, and corruption in the civil service and police are rife. Their governments are sometimes unlovely rich men's dictatorships, which proclaim loudly that they are loyal allies of the United States, though the United States should not always be pleased to have them.

3   A group of *unstable left-wing* countries: e.g. Egypt (and indeed most other African countries, including Zimbabwe), Bangladesh and the poorer states of the disintegrating federation of India, and also to some extent Pakistan. In these countries the governments are generally replaced by *coups d'état*, and the 'new class' of government technocrats live in constant fear of these.

4   The only Moscow-communist countries left in the poor South of the world are now in the Caribbean – led by Jamaica and Cuba. But some of the 'unstable left' countries – of which the most important is Egypt – seem to be moving towards Moscow. The former communist small countries in East Asia (Vietnam, North Korea, etc.) still call themselves communist – as does Chairman Hua's China – but with the Japanese–Chinese *rap-*

prochement they are merging into the East Asian co-prosperity sphere.

Significantly, the Asian republics of the Soviet Union itself are showing some signs of restlessness. Their peoples would gain if they could forge more independent ties with the China–Japan co-prosperity sphere and loosen their ties with Moscow, just as the states of the disintegrating Indian Union and former Union of South Africa have loosened their ties with Delhi and Pretoria.

The real GNP of countries in these four groups and their growth since 1977 clearly indicate that the 'breakthrough' and 'unstable right-wing' governments have made their peoples much more prosperous in the period 1977–84. In economic terms, the 'unstable left' countries (wholly) and the Moscow-communist countries (partly) have failed. It would be better for all the peoples of the world if more countries could be lifted out of the 'unstable left' class into either of the first two categories.

Yet the four most likely flashpoints of trouble in the poor two-thirds of the world, at this beginning of your presidency, are connected with possible attempts by either 'unstable left' or Moscow-communist countries to seize or subvert power in 'unstable right' countries. We would judge that these four most probable flashpoints are:

1 In the *Middle East*. The conclusion of peace with Israel, under the Geneva settlement during Mr Carter's presidency, has allowed the Arabs even more freedom for their internal quarrels. Since the new unstable left government in Egypt remembers the food riots with which its own supporters overthrew the former President Samdi, there is a strong temptation for Egypt to go for the oil of Saudi Arabia and the Gulf. This could be by means of internal subversion followed by proclamation of a new and immensely rich United Arab Republic (including Saudi Arabia and Kuwait) which would sponsor a new hard line in OPEC. Egypt has been angling for some time for Soviet support for such *coups*

d'état in Saudi Arabia and the Gulf, but so far this has been refused. It is quite possible that a 'United Arab' *coup d'état* would win popular support among young men in the Gulf, since many of them regard their free-spending sheikhs as effete pooves, like the rulers of the old Ottoman Empire. If a new UAR of this kind were ever proclaimed, some people would say that the consequent threat to world oil supplies would, of itself, justify US military intervention in the area. We would not advocate this, but the choice between peace and war, even nuclear war, might conceivably lie outside American hands. The only stable right-wing (indeed, 'breakthrough') country in the area – the Shah's Iran – might not sit idly by. And Iran now probably has a nuclear capability based on French technology, even though it has never tested a weapon.

2 The communist Caribbean (in which Jamaica is now the leader, rather than Cuba) and unstable governments of Central America might try to initiate a *coup d'état* in *Mexico*, whose dynamic new president deserves US support.

3 Black African forces from the 'unstable left' countries of Zimbabwe and Namibia, supported by Cuban and Jamaican and maybe even Soviet 'volunteers' landed in Angola and Mozambique, might attack those states of the former *Union of South Africa* which have developed right-wing governments, sometimes 'unstable right-wing' ones. By far the richest of these states are, of course, the three 'white tribes' homelands' of Southern Cape Province, Eastern Natal and Krugerland (Pretoria–Johannesburg). But a real prosperity is also being attained by those black-ruled states and cantons of the former Union of South Africa who have struck up successful (although so-called 'Uncle Tom') economic relations with the three white homelands. If there is an actual invasion of this area from the north, the dilemmas set for your Administration will be: (*a*) economic, because benign growth spreading from the

dynamic area of former South Africa appears to be Africa's only hope for a non-oil economic growth area this century; and (b) military-moral, because the white tribes in South Africa agreed under the Treaty of Pretoria of 1982 that neither they nor the black tribes in former South Africa should have substantial military forces, but that there would be reliance on UN troops on the northern border (most awkwardly, now Mexican, Polish and Indian troops) and perhaps some hopes, however ill based, of intervention by US troops.

4 Rival factions and states in the former *Indian Union* may start appealing separately to the Soviet Union and China. There might be civil war again in this whole area of India–Pakistan–Bangladesh.

But the biggest threat to peace may lie in the troubles of the Soviet Union and its satellites. This is discussed in the Ex-Secretary's report on the rich North of the world.

President-elect Thompson received the Think-Tank's report at the same time as he was presented with the Ex-Secretary's report, which dealt with subjects closer to his heart.

THE EX-SECRETARY'S REPORT ON THE 'RICH NORTH', NOVEMBER 1984

The principal instabilities in the rich North of the world between 1977 and 1984 have come in old-fashioned countries or blocs which have failed to adapt in time to the new basis of survival. Soviet Russia has shown the least ability to adapt to a changing world, and Moscow is now beset by crises to its west, east and south.

Poland and Yugoslavia, for different reasons, are the two most dangerous flashpoints in the West.

Poland has diverged significantly from the norms of

communist society. Comecon-decreed exports to the USSR are interfering with its standard of living, while political dogma is preventing the introduction of free enterprise systems in Polish industry. Polish workers much prefer employment by multi-national companies, when these operate in their country, to employment by the Polish state. The state, though the most powerful employer, is also the most disliked. As Poland goes tomorrow, Czechoslovakia and Hungary are liable to go the day after.

East Germany is bound to seek a greater political role, proportionate to its economic superiority in Eastern Europe. East Germany now has a GNP per head of $4,000 a year, twice European Russia's $2,000 a year. Neighbouring West Germany has a GNP per head of $11,000 a year, and the East Germans know they could have something like this too if they could ever throw off the yoke of the USSR.

The successful participation by the Italian communists in government since 1982, and a Popular Front government in France, have frustrated further advance towards European union and have weakened NATO. But the Italian experience has also bred unexpected dangers for the Soviet Union, because it has shown in practice the success of other roads to 'socialism', and thus provided encouragement for Poland.

This is a model more likely to be followed than that of the weak new régime in post-Tito Yugoslavia, which has not been able to resist the establishment of pro-Soviet cells in Serbia. But Yugoslavia is another very possible flashpoint, precisely because it is so weak. If there are near-revolts in Poland or East Germany, I do not think the Soviet Union will be eager to send in its own troops to put them down. But they might well engineer (and accept) an invitation from communist cells in Serbia to put down a so-called capitalist counter-revolution in Slovenia or Croatia.

This would be the cheapest Soviet intervention,

designed to show the Poles and others that the Red Army still can, and will, move quickly and aggressively when it must. It is therefore all the more dangerous that NATO has left its policy towards Yugoslavia so vague. At present the Russians probably feel that a re-assertion of their power in Poland might lead to reaction from the West (perhaps from West Germany?), but that a new assertion of power over Yugoslavia would probably bring no Western response more powerful than protests.

West Germany has been somewhat disillusioned by the disappointing progress of the EEC and of NATO. The CDU-led opposition is playing for power in Bonn by reviving hopes of reunification with East Germany. Internal revolts in Poland and East Germany might now bring a more positive response from Bonn – a prospect which fills the Soviet Union with alarm.

The Soviet Union itself is ruled by the last of the Second World War generation, believing in power for the régime, austerity for the masses and a foreign bogey to encourage obedience. The government in Moscow is said to be beginning to be somewhat worried about the possibility of disaffection in the Red Army; the present generation of educated youth has no great enthusiasm for three years' conscripted service under arms.

Moscow is even more worried about the growth of nationalism in the Asian republics of the Soviet Union, which are looking enviously at the increasing prosperity of Japan and China.

The fastest economic growth in the years 1977–84 has occurred in Japan, China and the countries with close trading links with them. Already in 1950–73 Japan had led the industrial growth league, and it should probably have been foreseen that China would follow it. China and Japan share many characteristics. These include traditions of subordination of the individual to the group in a search for group harmony; an incredible vitality, which is very different from the attitude in India, and owes less to material incentives than that in the West; and a capacity for hierarchical self-organization. China under Chairman Mao had already provided the groundwork for economic take-off by creating almost full employment in the countryside. Chairman Hua then opened the door to the import of foreign technology. It was natural that the main technology to flow in (including that for increased production of Chinese oil) should be Japanese.

The China–Japan economic alliance is leading to a sort of political alliance as well. Although China calls itself communist, it now looks like becoming a Swedish version of Japan. This is providing a degree of security in that quarter of the world.

There is no degree of security in the other three-quarters of the world. Some part of the blame for this must be laid on continuing Soviet–US military rivalry. Strategically, after eight years of Democratic Administration in the US and the ineffectuality of SALT, your incoming Republican Administration must decide how to react to a situation of Soviet nuclear superiority and an established Soviet capability to destroy surveillance and communications satellites. The remaining US superiority is now in long-distance intervention capability, in technology in general and in electronics in particular.

Mutual deterrence is further complicated and weakened by nuclear proliferation among the feuding Third World countries. Some of these are going to go nuclear anyway, and both the USSR and US might see advantage in providing know-how and intelligence to potential clients (e.g., 'unstable left-wing' and 'unstable right-wing' governments) in order to gain new positions of strength and in the belief that this will give a better chance to control a nuclear outbreak.

I would strongly counsel the new Administration against such proliferation, and indeed against any deliberate baiting of the worried Russian bear at this juncture. It is possible that a third world war could be started by mistake, though probably only if two or more of the main points of instability around the world become critical at the same time.

Reserves of crisis management have dealt satisfactorily with Cuba in 1963 and the 1967 Arab–Israeli War in isolation, and even with the combination of Suez and Hungary in 1956, but none of these directly involved *both* superpowers. Our present systems for containing crises could be overstrained in a multifarious mess in which the superpowers saw their vital interests engaged on several fronts at once. Simultaneous crises in, say, the Middle East, Southern Africa and Poland (or Yugoslavia) would cause just such overstrain.

It is possible that there will be such multiple crises if the Soviet empire starts to crack under its own pressures. There might even be important developments in the eleven weeks before your Inauguration Day.

The final words of the Ex-Secretary's report proved to be prophetic.

CHAPTER THREE

CRADLES OF CONFLICT:
MIDDLE EAST AND AFRICA

When asked by his major what history would say about all his comings and goings, General Burgoyne replied without hesitation, 'History, sir, will lie!' Gentleman Johnny knew what he was talking about.

Historians seem likely to fix the beginning of the Third World War as a day in 1985, but as far as the people of Africa and Arabia were concerned it had already been in progress for more than a quarter of a century. By the summer of 1985 the war was being conducted in a score of countries with a variety of motives, methods and participants which was remarkable even in a continent renowned for variety. Nowhere were the participants so divided, the results so inconclusive or the military operations so bizarre as in the Horn of Africa.

Events there hinged round Ethiopia. The Soviet Union's plan for a federation had of course come to nothing. There was too much to quarrel about. In Addis Ababa the Soviet puppet General Madkushu had succeeded in retaining power, but very little else. He presided over anarchy. He had had his greatest rival Colonel Abnatu executed and in this way had secured his position within the Dergue. But his position in the country as a whole had never been more insecure. It was no more than his just deserts. Sudden in his judgements, a revolutionary for the sake of revenge, a military leader for the sake of oppression, he was singularly well qualified to fulfil the role of dictator and devastator of his homeland. He had been given arms and assistance enough by the Soviet Union, but had succeeded in little more than the terrorization of the central area around

Addis Ababa. He had failed in the prosecution of operations against Eritrea and Sudan, and Kenya's support, more real than visual, availed him nothing. Madkushu could not even reassert the central government's authority over the dissident provinces of Tigre and Bagemder. Soviet troops, and Cuban advisers, training teams and troops might advise, train and assist, but they could not overcome sloth, indifference, tribal rivalries and sheer incompetence.

In spite of deep divisions within the various factions of the Eritrean Liberation Front, one figure continued to stand up as the only one likely to command support general enough to be able to forge some unity – the veteran leader Suleiman Salle. His strength lay in the support afforded him by the Sudan. Training, weapons, ammunition and, if necessary, refuge – these were powerful magnets. The other Eritrean separatists, while no doubt playing their own waiting games, could see no one else whom they could use to paste over the cracks. Suleiman Salle became the first President of Eritrea. Elderly he might have been, but the world abounded with encouraging instances of longevity at the seat of authority. Madkushu may have condemned him and sworn all sorts of vengeance, but the distractions of Djibuti and the further separatist movements in Tigre and Bagemder were enough to prevent his mounting anything other than murderous guerrilla sorties into Eritrea. Even after Ethiopian reoccupation the Ogaden continued to provide a threat to his security. How, Madkushu asked himself, could the Soviet Union first support Somalia against himself and then himself against President Sarrul of Somalia, when they themselves were such implacable enemies? The answer, of course, was that it was because they were implacable enemies. If you back both sides there is a better chance of winning: heads, I win; tails, you lose – it worked very well.

Once the French garrison had been withdrawn in 1977, and with the compliance of Hassan Guptidan and his Issa supporters, the Somalis had no difficulty in establishing themselves at Djibuti. In spite of disagreements, the temporary expulsion of Soviet and Cuban advisers, and capricious fluctuations of support – in spite, even, of helping Ethiopia against them – the Soviet Union had returned to Somalia in strength and had continued to supply arms and aid. In return the USSR exacted absolute security for their air and sea bases at Berbera and Kismayu. If this was an important requirement in a period of what the world called *détente*, it may be imagined with what speed and decision the Russians fastened their grip upon the Horn of Africa in war. With 10,000 of their own troops and some 2,000 Cubans redeployed in Somalia, this was not difficult. Equally total was their control of the other side of the Gulf of Aden, where we shall shortly make our way.

Apart from West and North-west Africa, the quietest part of the continent, sandwiched between two large areas notable for their turbulence, was East Africa. Kenya, Tanzania, Uganda and Malawi were enjoying not only tolerably harmonious relationships with one another, but also a degree of internal placidity unknown since the days of British guardianship. While Tanzania continued to support FRELIMO and to deploy troops in northern Mozambique, the others did not allow this harmony to be disrupted by what was happening in Mozambique or to interrupt their own assistance to the enemies of FRE-LIMO. It was a game that everyone played – on both sides. The succession in Kenya of a military council after Kenyatta's disappearance from the scene, some years before, was matched in smoothness by the skilful manipulative powers of Tanzania's ruler, who, while accepting Cuban military assistance in the training of his armed forces, resolutely refused to accept the political advice which was offered with it. Malawi went its own way, and since the demise of the tyrannical Field Marshal Omotin, even Uganda, under its newly designed federal government, was beginning to re-establish a degree of confidence and prosperity, with plentiful Western Aid.

The last rash actions of Omotin in the first years of the eighties had left their scars, of course. His decision, in a fit of pique and desire for that military glory which had evaded him in Zaire, Zimbabwe and the Sudan, to invade Kenya was disliked by all those of his senior advisers whose experience entitled them to an opinion. But such hostile unanimity did not deter the Field Marshal from embarking on his own chosen form of *Blitzkrieg*. At the same time the admirable and ubiquitous intelligence service built up by the Kenyan armed forces enabled them to bring about the dissipation of Omotin's forces and hopes alike. Omotin based his stroke on the supposed invincibility of his Soviet aircraft and tanks. The tanks were reduced to flaming dustbins by the skilfully operated *Milan* anti-tank guided weapons, the MiGs plucked from the sky by Kenya's *Rapier* and *Blowpipe* missile systems.

The crowning humiliation was the capture of Omotin himself, not by the declared enemy but by some of his own people, the Acholi and Langi tribesmen, to whom he had displayed the utmost extent of his spite and vindictiveness. Trusting his bulk to an Agusta-Bell helicopter in a supposedly morale-raising visit to his troops, the morale of both Kenya and his own countrymen was greatly raised by the news that he had fallen into the hands of his former victims after a forced landing. They had taken their revenge by blowing him from the muzzle of a 76 mm gun.

North of East Africa was the distressed and turbulent Horn; south of it lay the yet unfinished struggle for Southern Africa. One battle – the battle for Zimbabwe – was over. The white Rhodesians had gone, and in the main had been absorbed into the Republic of South Africa. The much more serious battle for South Africa itself had by 1985 not yet got properly under way, in spite of all the skirmishings and preparations and promises. In Zimbabwe itself, Bishop Zilothi of the United African National Council had triumphed. He could not have done so without the allegiance of the powerful Karanga tribe and the former régime's black troops and policemen. Nor could the help provided by Mozambique, Zambia and Botswana be forgotten. Indeed the leaders of those countries were determined that it should not be. Zambia's and Botswana's leaders, both nominal and actual, were easy to identify; Mozambique's less so.

The great issue for Southern Africa, indeed for Africa as a whole, was widely thought to be how and when the confrontation states would subjugate the remaining white power there. Three of the four states concerned, Mozambique, Zimbabwe and Namibia, had not only their own resources and experience of fighting for independence to draw on. Outside support was plentiful and urgent. In Mozambique, Soviet, Cuban and Somali troops were equipped with tanks, aircraft and missiles; in Zimbabwe were the amalgamated regular army, guerrilla forces and police; and in Namibia, Cubans, Nigerians and Jamaicans were well supported by Soviet advisers and Soviet weapons. On paper it appeared to be only a matter of time, of where, when and how, rather than whether. Soviet policy had had an unending run of success in Southern Africa. What was to stop it now?

But the white South Africans had not allowed the veldt to grow under their feet. Ever since the formation of Zimbabwe, they had embarked on the creation of a *levée-en-masse* to form a kind of *Volkssturm*, which would combine firepower with speed of movement, a proper intelligence system with security of military resources, and a rigorous training cycle. There were two big questions. How would they find weapons if the US and UK (and possibly even France) denied them? And what would the inhabitants of the Bantu homelands and the black population remaining in the white homelands do about it all?

Nor was this last the only question the confrontation states had to worry about. Their own internal problems were legion. Events in Mozambique continued to show that numerous and ruthless guerrilla forces were not the monopoly of Marxists. The Marxist President Sathela hardly knew from one day to the next whether he would be president in a week's time. The Soviet military advisers were strangely indifferent to his apprehensions. Perhaps it was because they were more concerned – and their concern was to turn into assurance with the arrival of further Cuban contingents – about the security, for their own subsequent use, of the new air base at Buzaruto, some 150 miles south of Beira, and of the harbours at Maputo, Nacala, Porto Amelia and Beira itself. This apart, Sathela was able to console himself with the thought that his own bodyguard was composed largely of East German and Portuguese mercenaries. As long as their pay was forthcoming, his own prospects were at least a talking point.

As for Zimbabwe, the patterns of power and intrigue almost defied even the Soviet passion for faction and counter-faction, revolution and counter-revolution. One principal thread was discernible – the uneasy alliance of Bishop Zilothi and the main guerrilla controllers. How long the alliance would survive raised the question to which Zimbabwe would commit itself and its forces to the struggle for South Africa. This was a matter for the High Command of the Confederation of Africa South People's Army (CASPA) to examine.

If enthusiasm for CASPA were to be measured solely by military contributions to it, Botswana would have rated low among the front-line states. Indeed, she had virtually no armed forces which could be despatched outside the country. How different was the capability, if not the intention, of Namibia.

In Namibia SWAPO (South-west Africa People's Organization) had won, though not without outside help. The intervention of strong Nigerian forces from Angola had been decisive. It had enabled a coalition between SWAPO's leader, the Chief of the Hereros, and the Ovambos, the most numerous tribe of Namibia, utterly to destroy the Nationalist Party's influence, with the result that, as in Zimbabwe, most of the white population, in this case about 100,000, had gone to South Africa. SWAPO troops had tasted blood. Admittedly supported by Angolan MPLA (Popular Movement for the Liberation of Angola) forces, Cuban troops and the Nigerians, they had turned out of Namibia a total of 50,000 South African soldiers equipped with modern weapons and aided by fighter aircraft. They were not likely to forget it. And they had got their hands on one of the world's main sources of uranium. This too they did not intend to forget. Namibia's president, SWAPO itself and the bulk of its Ovambo troops were all committed to the crushing of South Africa, and it was from Namibia and Mozambique that the main invasion forces would come.

South Africa itself was to become an important battlefield of the Third World War, outside Europe, another being the Persian Gulf and southern Arabia. But South Africa had not been softened by twenty-five years of changing opinions, by what was thought of as the treachery of the United States and the degeneracy of Europe. These years had hardened its white population, and had made them realize that unless US policy changed to the extent of a total reversal no succour was to be had there. They would have to do it with their own resources, their own people and their own pluck. They had not wasted time. From the very moment of the creation of Zimbabwe in 1979 and the loss of Namibia a year later, preparations had proceeded night and day. The independence of the Bantu homelands had made it easier, for the strongholds of white supremacy, reliant though they were on black labour for both urban and rural endeavour, had shrunk to the white homelands of the Transvaal, the Orange Free State, Natal and the Cape Province. There were nearly 4½ million white people in these provinces, about half that number of coloured, and a quarter that number Asian; the blacks totalled some 7 million.

What had been done militarily within the homeland had been done elsewhere by the Swiss and the Israelis, but by few others. All male and most female citizens underwent initial training as recruits for six to twelve months. Refresher training for up to one month each year was the rule for all up to the age of fifty. South Africa's regular armed forces were by 1985 about 60,000 strong with reserves about equal in number. The combined *Landwehr/ Volkssturm*, which could be mobilized in forty-eight hours, was nearly half a million. Of this well over 100,000 were Kommandos with their own air, armoured and communications units, organized into brigade-like formations of several thousand each. The Boers were not going to be caught napping. What is more they had absorbed 250,000 white Rhodesians and 100,000 white refugees from Namibia, who did not intend to pack their bags again. They were further strengthened by plentiful volunteers from Australia and New Zealand.

The antipathy of many in the world outside South Africa to the policies pursued there towards coloured peoples and the consequent deep reluctance of the US and British governments to give military aid to South Africa, even in a struggle against the spreading power of the USSR, meant that no forces from either country could be expected to come to help her in war, and there was little prospect of significant military aid from any other Western source. They were on their own. There was by the end of the seventies no longer even the hope of procuring military supplies in any quantity from other Western sources. Some were had from France but not enough. South Africa turned to Japan and her associates in South-east Asia. By the beginning of the eighties the trickle of military equipment which began to come in at the end of the seventies had become a flood. Compelled to rely solely on her own manpower for her defence South Africa had now no need of Western hardware to equip it.

In Angola there was the greatest Soviet presence and at the same time the greatest anti-communist activity. The battle for Angola was not yet over. Harassed by UNITA (National Union for the Total Independence of Angola), mauled by Zaire, Sovietized by Russian masters, and

manipulated by Cuban puppets, the reign of President
Ageto had stumbled to a humiliating conclusion, replaced
by a coalition of his rivals, still essentially Marxist, propped
up by the Soviet Union and Cubans. The Cuban and
Nigerian military contingents were now increased to 40,000
and 20,000, respectively, with two battalions of Jamaicans.
The Soviet advisers numbered some 15,000 and included
radar, communications and industrial technicians plus
port-operating experts. But even all this foreign support
could not alter the fact that UNITA's forces in the south
were growing in strength and now numbered about 25,000,
that Angolan National Liberation Front (FNLA) forces
were still active in the north, and that the Cabinde
Liberation Movement, with Zaire's assistance, was gaining
support. Whatever the difficulties of establishing absolute
control over the whole of Angola, however, the Soviet
Union was clearly determined to keep a grip of what she
most wanted – the ports, the airfields, the jumping off
ground for driving through Namibia to South Africa, and
a general area which could be used as a relatively secure
base for her proxy troops to go anywhere in Southern,
Central or even West Africa. In strategic terms the Soviet
victory in Angola had been of immense significance. South
Africa's Prime Minister at that time had seen it as the
whirlwind before the storm, as simply one exercise in a
series of exercises aimed at providing bases for black
guerrilla troops and Soviet proxy mercenaries to launch
their attack on the final target of South Africa.

Of all the black African countries and their leaders
which most wished to tread the path of moderation and
evolution, Zambia and President Luganda stood out from
all the others. He had wholly supported the creation of
Zimbabwe. He was not sure, even in 1985, that the time
had come to deal with South Africa, for he felt that the
African front-line states could not do it without enormous
and prolonged Soviet and Cuban assistance and that to
tolerate the presence of these in Southern Africa on the
scale required would simply be to exchange one sort of

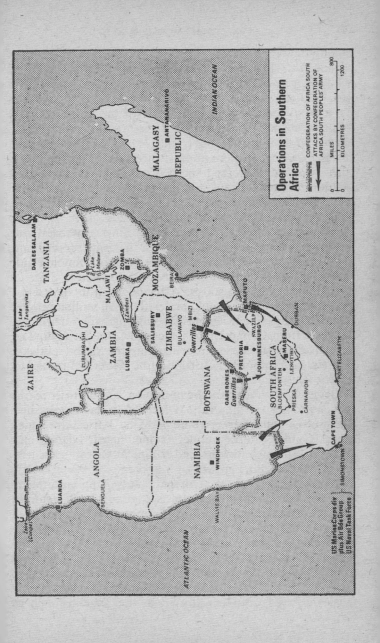

Operations in Southern Africa

→ CONFEDERATION OF AFRICA SOUTH
ATTACKS BY CONFEDERATION OF
AFRICA SOUTH PEOPLES' ARMY

0   MILES   800
0   KILOMETRES   1200

INDIAN OCEAN

MALAGASY
REPUBLIC
■ANTANANARIVO

DAR ES SALAAM
TANZANIA
Lake Malawi
Lake Tanganyika
ZOMBA
MALAWI
MOZAMBIQUE
BEIRA
ZAIRE
L'UBUMBASHI
Lualaba
ZAMBIA
Zambezi
SALISBURY
ZIMBABWE
MBIZI
LUSAKA■
BULAWAYO
Guerrillas
MAPUTO
SWAZILAND
PRETORIA■
■JOHANNESBURG
DURBAN
GABERONES
Guerrillas
■MASERU
BOTSWANA
SOUTH AFRICA
LESOTHO
BLOEMFONTEIN■
PRIESKA
CARNARVON
PORT ELIZABETH
Orange
ANGOLA
BENGUELA
■UANDA
NAMIBIA
WINDHOEK■
WALVIS BAY
Orange
CAPE TOWN
SIMONSTOWN

Zaire (Congo)

ATLANTIC OCEAN

US Marine Corps div
plus Air Bde Group
US Naval Task Force

subjugation for another. Nor with armed forces numbering a mere 8,000 and growing concern about Zambia's borders with Angola, could any troops be spared from Zambia for the great trek south.

In neighbouring Zaire, in spite of greater resources, both in raw materials and men, there was little enthusiasm for waging war outside the country's own territorial limits. Their experience of communist intervention in the latter 1970s had not endeared the Soviet Union or her proxy soldiers to the rulers of Zaire any more than the uses made by these of Katangan rebels. The former president had long since retired to his retreat on Lac Leman. The new president of Zaire had been in office for nearly five years; during this time he had reorganized the armed forces, and had turned more to France and Belgium for economic aid, shunning the Soviet Union's attempts to include Zaire in their haul of Marxist states. After all, with its diamonds, copper, oil, cobalt and zinc, and with its 30 million people, Zaire was a rich land. Frontier forays had gone on – from Angola, from Congo-Brazzaville and from Burundi. The army had not succeeded in controlling the Simba rebels on Zaire's eastern border. But all in all Zaire had reason to be content.

Soviet, Cuban and Jamaican influence and presence did not stop short in Central Africa. They had established themselves almost everywhere in West Africa. In Equatorial Guinea, Sierra Leone, Guinea itself, Nigeria and Mali, instructors, advisers and troops at once represented and encouraged the growth of Marxism.

If we leave aside the strategic value of ports, airfields and communications southwards, the principal factor in West Africa was, of course, Nigeria, with a population of some 70 million and armed forces of nearly 250,000. Her army had tanks and heavy artillery; her navy had frigates and landing craft; her air force had interceptors, ground attack and transport aircraft and helicopters. What is more they had battle experience spreading over twenty years – civil war, battle in Central Africa, the great triumph in

Namibia. Guided, equipped and encouraged by the Soviet Union and Cubans, they would be a force to be reckoned with in the coming struggle for South Africa. The head of state, formerly Chief of Staff of the Armed Forces and a declared radical, had in the end found his own presence at the summit of affairs to be preferred to a return to constitutional rule. The fact that Nigeria supplied an increasing share of US oil imports was no small factor in the situation. Nigeria may have been a long way from Pretoria. It did not intend that distance should muffle its voice or lessen its hostility.

North-west Africa was mercifully free of much of the turbulence which prevailed in the central, southern and north-eastern areas. Most North-west African states had had their struggles for liberation from the colonial powers; they had had their internal struggles for governments of their own; they had had their experiments in external fishing in troubled waters; they now wanted to be left alone. At the same time they did not wish to be totally excluded from the luxurious game of not letting others alone. Morocco was prepared to offer both advice and troops. But the likelihood of Moroccan troops being deployed as far south as the new seat of war was not great. In any event, quarrels with Algeria and Mauretania, never far below the surface, were simmering once more.

Algeria herself was the joker in the pack. She was not willing to risk a single Berber or a single dinar in a cause that could be of no direct and immediate economic or political benefit to herself. It was not for nothing that the Algerians had understudied the French for so long.

Libya was totally different again. Incredibly, Colonel Farouk, Libya's radical nationalist leader, had survived. Most of the countries in which he had attempted to intervene had shrugged off his intervention. He was always seeking out trouble but never taking up arms; always meddling and threatening, but never acting; never in battle, but never out of it.

All this was bound up with what was happening in

Egypt. President Hassan el Samdi had long wanted to have a proper hold on his paymasters – Saudi Arabia and the oil-rich Gulf states. It was not for him but for his successors to achieve this. When President el Samdi was removed as a result both of food riots and of public disillusion over the Israeli settlement he was succeeded by the somewhat unlikely coalition of the Vice-President, Ahmed Mohamed and the War Minister and Commander-in-Chief, General Aziz Tawfik.

It was almost a repetition of the Neguib-Nasser relationship. Mohamed was the comparatively respectable front man of the team, even keeping up normal relations with the conservative ruling families of Saudi Arabia and Kuwait. Tawfik, on the other hand, had the wholehearted backing of the younger elements in the armed forces and of the intelligence services. The latter, chafing at the restraint imposed on them by the previous government, came forward with ambitious plans for creating by subversion a new and grander United Arab Republic, to embrace this time not the maverick Libyans or the ungovernable Syrians, but the sources of Arab wealth in the Arabian peninsula.

There was one problem: these ambitions could only be realized with massive Soviet help, both to provide the means of military takeover and to stave off any American attempt to intervene in favour of the status quo, and to preserve the supply of Middle East oil to the West. This would be a major change in Egyptian foreign policy, but Egypt was not renowned for consistency in these matters. The adoption of Russian support in the fifties and the repudiation of it in the seventies had been equally sudden and surprising. Egypt had breathed a great sigh of relief at the ending of the state of war with Israel in 1980. But the resulting relaxation of military effort had not released enough industrial resources to match the inexorable increase in population. Moreover, with the reductions in the armed forces many officers lost their jobs and formed a discontented group, only too ready to look to new external adventure to restore the power and privilege which they had once enjoyed.

Peace had not given bread to the masses or adequate employment to the intelligentsia. Renewal of hostility with Israel seemed to promise no better results than on previous occasions, especially with the Arab world even more fragmented than before. The overriding need seemed to be to create, if necessary by force, a centre of Arab strength to which the other quarrelling factions would gradually be attracted. Then at least it would be possible for the Arab world to decide where its future lay. This glamorous objective was held to justify the risks of achieving it with Soviet support.

It is still not clear whether the Egyptian services spontaneously advocated the 'reversal of alliances', or whether it was inspired by Soviet influence, which had retained a presence in the recesses of Egyptian intelligence even when its more overt manifestation had been brought to an end. In any event, Tawfik was persuaded, by economic necessity no less than by personal ambition, and gave covert approval to a programme of subversion, provided Soviet support could be confirmed. We shall describe later the Soviet deliberations which clinched the deal.

CHAPTER FOUR

AWAKENING RESPONSE IN
THE WEST

In Western Europe the late seventies had seen something of a shift in attitudes to East–West relations. Disillusion and disappointment over the resolute Soviet refusal to make any real concession to Western concern over human rights, international agreements notwithstanding, probably did as much as anything to foster the new note of realism. The Russians began to be given more and more credit for meaning what they had now been consistently saying for a long time, that Western capitalist societies were doomed to fall before the inexorable advance of Marxism-Leninism, and that the armed forces of the socialist countries, under the leadership of the USSR, must expect to play a major part in their overthrow.

The warning was as clear as any given by Hitler before the Second World War. The steady build-up of offensive military power in the Soviet Union, at the cost of much else, was not only wholly consistent with a determination to impose Soviet-Russian ends upon other societies, by force of arms if necessary. It was hardly consistent with anything else.

There were those in the West who believed in the existence of a Soviet master plan for the achievement of world dominion, with every move at every level ordered in accordance with it. This was fanciful. Its palpable unreality, however, was not unhelpful to the Soviet interest. The derision it attracted did something to distract attention from what was really happening, which was nothing less than the preparation of a position of military strength from which any international situation could be manipulated to the Soviet advantage.

Soviet policy was one of unlimited opportunism within a wide range of possible contingencies, for very many of which quite detailed military plans were constantly kept up to date. It drew strength from two main sources. On the one hand was the dogma of the dialectic, that capitalism was bound to disintegrate under the stresses of its own internal contradictions – to which was added the somewhat puzzling injunction that though this was inevitable it was still the duty of all socialists to try to bring it about. On the other hand was the endemic thrust of Russian imperialist expansionism, owing nothing to the dialectic, constant under any form of rule.

The threat from the Soviet Union to the parliamentary democracies of the West had, in the preceding thirty years, engaged the serious attention of their governments. The Atlantic Alliance, with the supporting military structure of NATO, resulted. Public opinion in the member countries of the Alliance, however, had long showed some reluctance to support the military measures required to meet the threat. In this respect the last years of the seventies had seen something of a change, as a result of which the military defences of the Alliance began to move out of the highly dangerous conditions of weakness into which, by 1977, they had been allowed to sink.

The position of the United Kingdom, a country of critical importance to the Alliance, if only because of its geographical location, was in some ways typical of the position among the European allies in general and on both counts deserves particular consideration.

Britain had its own special problems. Withdrawal from empire had been unsettling. Swift though this had been in the twenty-five years since the Second World War, insufficient time had elapsed by 1975 to allow of complete recovery of national balance in the new role of a second-class power with negligible overseas possessions. An extraordinary obsession in the people of Britain with the redistribution of wealth, rather than its creation, had done much in the same period to cripple national enterprise. This had gone hand in hand with the encouragement of general reliance upon state-provided welfare in place of the reliance upon themselves which had previously been characteristic of the British, while there had also been an ugly and unscrupulous exploitation of the politics of envy. It began to be increasingly clear, however, even to those politicians whose hearts were stronger than their heads, that national welfare depended on national wealth, and that the state produced nothing to distribute.

At the same time the massive burden of British trade unionism began to prove unwelcome to the working people who had to bear it. Of the desirability of combination to promote and protect the interests of workers, once the Industrial Revolution had opened the door to the predatory instincts and the restless, innovatory genius of an island race of adventurers, there can be little doubt. The importance of the protection afforded to the workers by the unions, and the benefit this brought them in earlier days, can hardly be exaggerated. It was when the blind benevolence of politicians had allowed the unions to move outside the law, when a proper watchfulness on the union side had given way to unimaginative Luddism, when reaction and restrictive practices were putting a savage brake on enterprise, when activities originally intended to improve living standards were now seen to be doing just the opposite, that the majority of the nation, who did not belong to trade unions, began to be increasingly resentful of their subjection to the minority who did.

Although, as events in Britain in the mid-seventies showed, politicians in a parliamentary democracy can go on governing for some time in a manner unpopular with the people as a whole, they cannot go on doing this indefinitely. Attempts at confrontation with the power of the trade unions, made by both the main political parties, when each in turn was in power, had been total failures. Up to the mid-seventies public opinion in Britain was not yet sufficiently aware of the menace from union power to face the discomforts of standing up to it, and the attempts of both parties to diminish it were dropped.

After a few years more, however, the British public had had enough. When prudent men in politics and sensible men in trade unions, of which there were very many, saw that it was not going to be easy to push the public around much more, they gently and adroitly let some of the steam out of the situation. Trade unionism in Britain did not go out with a bang, as some had hoped, nor even with a whimper. It gradually subsided to a convenient shape and size and continued to play a very important part in its originally intended role.

What happened over the trade unions was evidence of the refreshing and welcome spirit of realism and common sense which gradually began to emerge on every side in British public opinion in the late seventies. A new political approach – which also demonstrated how politicians will inevitably in the end be guided by changes in public opinion – was before very long to become evident in the matter of defence.

These years saw slow but significant changes in Britain. A total addiction to redistributive economic and fiscal policies, which showed itself in hostility to profit-making and in penal taxation on industrial enterprise, was gradually being replaced by more sensible attitudes, which at last permitted an increase in national wealth. These changes, together with the movement of world trade out of recession and the revenue from North Sea oil, contributed to some recovery in the standard of living in Britain and, in no small measure, to a revival of national confidence.

As the United Kingdom at last began to find a new awareness of national identity in a post-imperial mode, less began to be heard of separatism in the parts. Devolution became less fashionable. Less was also heard of any suggestion that the world owed Britain special consideration, which may have at one time been justified, let alone

a living, which never was. There was less and less suppor
of what had previously been known as progressive educa-
tion. There was acceptance of the necessity for children in
school to learn, even when they did not greatly like it
Variety in educational provision almost ceased to be
regarded as sinful, independent schools were once more
allowed to flourish, as so many parents wished, and ever
the public schools, their old-fashioned discipline long
derided by radicals who so often sent their sons to profi
from it, came under less violent attack.

The instinct to voluntary service, an instinct rather
disliked by the more extreme addicts of the welfare state
was also seen to have survived, and even once again begar
to flourish. Scouts, Guides, St John Ambulance and
countless other voluntary organizations reported sharp
rises in recruiting. So did the volunteer reserves of the
armed forces. In universities it began to be quite fashionable once more to join the Officer Training Corps. There
was even a movement towards a voluntary revival of civi
defence, long neglected by government.

In this changing climate of public opinion some scrutiny
of Britain's security in the world was before long inevitable. More notice began to be taken of what threatened
it. There was more questioning of the extent to which
Britain was taking a proper share in her own defence. It
was even suggested, possibly unfairly, that it might no
longer be enough to rest on what some called abject
reliance on the United States.

The British record in the sphere of common defence
did not stand up under scrutiny any too well. At the close
of the Korean war in 1952 the proportion of the gross
national product devoted to defence was 11·2 per cent
This was possibly too much. In the financial year 1976–7
it was 4·9 per cent. This was certainly too little. Ever
further reductions were being sought by some. The
National Executive Committee of the British Labour
Party (from whose control the Labour government of the

day was content to remain free) was in 1977 demanding a further reduction in defence spending by one-third.

It is still, as this is being written, too early for a balanced assessment of where responsibility lies for the dangerously low state to which the defences of Great Britain had by the year 1977 been allowed to fall. Though historians will probably agree that no political party is free from serious blame, they are already beginning to accept that, however regrettable the economies made in the mid-seventies under the transparent guise of improved efficiency, it was in the defence policies formulated in the UK Defence White Paper of 1957 that the rot really began. It is here that the first real signs appear in the sphere of defence of a latter-day British tendency to duck responsibility and shy off into make-believe, a tendency which did much to bedevil relations with Britain's allies in the years that followed.

The basic idea behind the 1957 White Paper was that American strategic nuclear power was to be the primary guardian of peace in Europe. Britain contributed her own nuclear bomber force, but beyond that all she was called upon to do was help provide a conventional trip-wire to identify a major incursion, which would then be answered by massive nuclear retaliation from the United States. A very great saving in cost would result as well as a great saving in manpower. This is, in fact, what happened. The political party in power at the time was able to go to the country at the next general election as the party which had freed the nation from military conscription in peacetime.

The baleful spirit of the 1957 White Paper brooded over British defence policy for twenty years. When the USSR achieved rough parity in strategic nuclear power with the United States the US moved from the somewhat implausible concept of deterrence extended over her allies by the threat of massive nuclear retaliation, if any of her allies were attacked, to a rather more realistic concept of defence at any level of attack – the concept of flexible response.

To this, which became the accepted policy of NATO, successive British governments paid lip service, but little more. It was clear that what they relied upon to prevent the Soviet Union from attacking the West, even with conventional means alone, was the threat of very early escalation into a strategic nuclear exchange between the Soviet Union and the United States. Delivery systems for battlefield nuclear weapons, for which the warheads (numbering some 7,000 in the European theatre by 1977) remained under US control, were integrated into the British-commanded Northern Army Group in NATO, as they were elsewhere in Allied Command Europe. What was emerging as the basis of Allied defence planning was the concept of the 'Triad' – the combination of conventional defence, battlefield nuclear weapons and strategic nuclear action in closely coupled sequence. This was as fully endorsed in the United Kingdom as anywhere else in the Alliance. How far it was taken seriously anywhere is open to argument. There is little evidence that it was ever taken seriously in the UK.

The NATO concept of the 'Triad' envisaged the development of sufficient conventional forces in the forward areas to identify a major aggression and slow it down, while posing the threat of an early introduction of battlefield nuclear weapons if it did not come to a halt, followed, if necessary, by strategic nuclear action. No one knew exactly what would happen when battlefield nuclear weapons were released, but it was widely accepted within the Alliance that a tactical nuclear battle could hardly be expected to proceed for long without escalation into a strategic nuclear exchange. On the other hand, an observer of the British Army's deployment, equipment and training policy could scarcely fail to conclude that, whatever happened, the British did not expect to have to take part in a tactical nuclear battle at all, or indeed, it may be added (to judge by the dismantling of their civil defences), in any form of nuclear action whatsoever.

It has been pointed out elsewhere in this book that the

policy of the 'forward defence' of the territory of the Federal Republic of Germany, to which more and more attention had to be paid as the stature of the FRG among its allies grew, required, if it implied no surrender of West German soil, either enormously strong conventional forces deployed along the frontier or an immediate nuclear response. The first was impossible: Allied governments made it quite clear that they were not prepared to furnish the necessary troops. The second, an immediate nuclear release, was highly unlikely.

This dilemma in planning the defence of the Federal Republic was of not very great consequence in the southern half of it, where difficult terrain gave the Allied forces available there (under American command in the Central Army Group (CENTAG)) some chance of holding a stronger enemy. For the weaker forces deployed in easier and more open country, under British command, in the Northern Army Group (NORTHAG), there was far less hope of this. Many would say there was none, and that the only hope of countering an invasion in the north by conventional means lay in abandoning what was described as 'forward defence' (which looked uncomfortably linear) and fighting instead a battle of manoeuvre in depth.

Observance of West German susceptibilities over surrender of territory, however, obliged NORTHAG to plan for a forward battle. If the troops (some of whom were stationed a long way back in their home countries, in Belgium and Holland) could be got up in time the attack, under this concept, would be met on, or near, the Demarcation Line with East Germany. With much greater weight on the other side, as well as the initiative in choice of time and place, there could hardly be any chance of holding it there. However it began, the battle was bound to develop in depth, with the outcome being determined by the action of reserves held further back for counter-penetration operations in the first place and then for a counter-offensive.

Such reserves did not exist, even on paper. Why not?

Because, the answer would run, when it became clear that the available conventional forces could not hold the enemy the situation would be restored by the use of battlefield nuclear weapons. There was therefore no great need for conventional forces deployed in depth.

Though the forward location of special weapon stores (in which nuclear warheads were kept) meant that some would be overrun before the weapons could be used, there would still be plenty left. Delay in securing their release, however, was inevitable, even supposing a very early resolution of the agonizing dilemma which impaled the FRG, in whose territory very many of these warheads, if not most, would land. The Allied rubric, moreover, enjoined that no release could be expected before all conventional means had already been tried and exhausted – that is, in effect, before the conventional battle had been lost, leaving a situation which could almost certainly no longer be 'restored'.

The wisdom of locating stores of nuclear warheads in vulnerable forward areas was brought to question in 1977, when it was pointed out that nuclear attack was much more likely on fixed, static concentrations than on troop formations in the field, and that in consequence missile attack from submarine launchers might be more sensible than from launchers on the battlefield. By 1984 there had been some reduction in forward holdings but these were still considerable.

Accepting the declared NATO concept of the 'Triad', however, and assuming that tactical nuclear weapons were introduced, a nuclear battle would result. For this the Russians were equipped and trained. The British (and most of the other Allies) were not. No major British weapon system in use in 1978, even the newest, offered plausible protection to crewmen fighting in a nuclear environment. Training in movement over contaminated ground was rudimentary, equipment for decontamination and provision for its practice – and even for the acquisition and dissemination of radiation intelligence – was far from adequate. British defence policy, in contra-distinction to that of the Soviet Union, clearly embodied no real requirement to fight on a nuclear battlefield. It even seemed that the British contribution to the defence of Europe in the Central Region of the Allied Command contained a deliberate insufficiency, whose purpose was to force on the United States not so much an early release of battlefield nuclear weapons as an almost immediate movement into strategic nuclear attack, perhaps on the USSR itself. There could be no doubt, the argument ran, that the Soviet Union realized this too. It was here, the British seemed to think, that true deterrence lay.

To British politicians in the seventies, under pressure from some of their supporters to cut the defence vote at almost any cost, the approach was an attractive one. It was, in essence, indistinguishable from that of the 1957 White Paper. Whatever it might now be called, British defence policy was still that of trip-wire and massive retaliation, disfigured somewhat by claims that economies, which left front-line troops less capable of fighting, were in fact contributions to military efficiency. Whether this would remain indefinitely acceptable to the United States, which was clearly expected to hold the baby, was another matter.

Professional military men in the parliamentary democracies of the West are generally honest people, loyal to those they serve and reluctant to take part in politics. Many were anxious and deeply disturbed over the situation here described. But as long as the public demanded of their politicians nothing more, and showed little inclination to put up the money for anything better, there was not much that the military men could do. The difficulty was compounded in Britain where, although the Civil Service had been allowed greater freedom of political expression during the late seventies, the tradition that the military must not debate government defence policy in public was still rigorously applied. It was paradoxical that in a country where free speech was so cherished the military remained so firmly muzzled. Nevertheless, in institutes and societies devoted to the debate of public affairs, with which Britain abounded, some awareness grew up among responsible people of the real situation and, in particular, of the dangerously changed character of the air threat to the British Isles and the urgent need to repair its air defences.

The heart and core of the Alliance remained, as it always had been, the United States. There, in the mid-seventies, four tendencies began to converge. First, there was a growing awareness of the true dimensions of the threat. It was accompanied by none of the hysteria occasionally evident in the early fifties but was nonetheless impressive. Second, there was increasing impatience with the reluctance of the European Allies to take a fair share in their own defence – an impatience that grew more marked as growing prosperity left the European allies with less and less excuse. Third, it began to be questioned even in Europe whether it would be easy to persuade any American president to invite the incineration of Chicago, for example, if the Northern Army Group in Germany were broken through and there was nothing left to SACEUR but nuclear weapons. Finally, the feeling grew that flexible response should mean just what it said. This implied that a radical review of the defences of the Alliance at the non-nuclear level – including the massive contribution of the United States itself – was overdue.

The European allies did not long remain in ignorance of the trend of opinion on the other side of the Atlantic and the force behind it. In Britain, which was no bad indicator of European opinion, the public began to develop a more receptive attitude. Pressure to make better provision for the air defence of the British Isles, upon which an American effort in Europe would so much depend, now met with a more favourable response. In some of the countries whose troops were assigned to Allied Command Europe, the initiative and example of the United States began at last to be followed. It was certainly clear in

Britain that the public was beginning to take a positive interest in defence which the politicians could not forever disregard.

Quite small things often have a decisive effect. SACEUR realized that the lack of reserves in depth in the NORTH-AG area, coupled with the inability of NORTHAG either to offer a credible forward defence with non-nuclear forces or to sustain a tactical nuclear engagement, and the near certainty that a breakthrough would *not* be at once followed, as the British seemed to hope, by strategic nuclear action on the part of the United States, set up a dangerous situation. To help correct it two US brigades were deployed in the sector of the Northern Army Group (which had hitherto had no US formations under command) where NORTHAG's reserves might have been located, had there been any.

In Britain, the implications of this did not at first sink in. When it was more widely realized that the Americans were doing for the British what the British had been too idle, too apathetic or too parsimonious to do for themselves, a trace of public uneasiness was discernible which would almost certainly not have been evident a year or two before. It was by no means inconsistent with what some observers saw as a reawakening of a sense of national identity. This was to have considerable influence on British defence policy.

As the current of public concern over national security began to flow in Britain at the end of the seventies, it became increasingly clear that the reductions in defence expenditure to which all political parties had from time to time inclined – some, it must be said, more consistently than others – and which it had become part of the ritual liturgy of radicalism always to demand, no longer wholly conformed to the wishes of the people. The restoration of cuts, and even some increases, hesitantly begun in the financial year 1978–9, were seen to meet with public approval. Greater national affluence helped them to be more easily borne. By 1983 the ceiling imposed on defence expenditure five years before, regarded then by many as immutable, was already being exceeded by more than two-thirds.

The points at which improvements in provision for the national defence were seen to be most needed, and where improvements were in fact made the earliest, were three. There was a reversal of the suicidal tendency to weaken NATO on land by erosion of the British Army of the Rhine; more attention was paid to the no less critical situation of the air defence of the United Kingdom; and improvements were at last set in hand to the country's ASW (anti-submarine warfare) defences and its maritime air forces.

This outline of developments in the United Kingdom, seen as an indicator of a trend, widespread if uneven, in European countries of the Atlantic Alliance at the end of the seventies, is amplified, in some of its more important aspects, at the end of this book in Appendix 1. It is enough to say here that a sharper awareness of the threat to peace from the growing military strength and the persistent political intransigence of the USSR, on the part of some (but not all) of the European Allies, was leading, in varying degree, towards improvements in their contribution to the defence of the West. The consequent condition of NATO, as the point of decision approached, will be reviewed in Chapter 12.

CHAPTER FIVE

UNREST IN POLAND

The Third World War was said by many to have broken out in the same country as the Second, in Poland, on 11 November 1984, the sixty-sixth anniversary of the end of the First World War. It did not seem like an outbreak of world war at the time. In fact, many put the blame for the initial workers' riots in Poland on what was no more than an incident during the US presidential election campaign.

During the Thompson–Mondale television debates, both candidates had been asked whether they regarded the present Polish government as a satellite of the Soviet Union. Mindful of the Polish–American votes that President Ford had lost in Chicago and elsewhere through giving a soft-on-communism answer to that same question in 1976, Governor Thompson had been careful to keep his answer on what might be called the hawkish side of Mr Mondale's. One of his aides evidently feared that he had been too hawkish, and shortly before his press conference next day was urging an unwilling candidate to find some way of recanting.

By a misfortune which had dogged US politicians' microphones on other matters Polish, a microphone inadvertently left live passed on to waiting pressmen Mr Thompson's reply: 'Goddammit, Art, I'm not going to say that I wish to make it clear that if the brave Polish people rise against their Russian oppressors, then a Thompson Administration would most certainly leave them in the . . .' Suddenly realizing that his words were being overheard by newsmen, Thompson ended with a grin and the words, 'expletive deleted'.

There was a ripple of amused applause from the newsmen. In subsequent statements, Mr Thompson was at

Soviet forces in Europe, June 1985

SWEDEN

DENMARK
KOBENHAVN

BALTIC SEA

U.S.S.R.

KALININGRAD

HAMBURG

ROSTOCK

2 Guards
Tank Army

NEUBRANDENBURG

GDANSK

20 Guards
Army

EBERSWALDE

GERMAN

HANNOVER

STENDAL

3 Shock
Army

34 Arty Div
E BERLIN

FRANKFURT
AN DER ODER

MAGDEBURG

DEMOCRATIC

16 Air Army

COTTBUS

Oder

Viotula

WARSZAWA

POLAND

ŁODZ

8 Guards
Army

LEIPZIG

REPUBLIC

Elbe

DRESDEN

1 Guards
Tank Army

WROCLAW

WEIMAR

PRAHA

MILOVCE

KRAKOW

FEDERAL REPUBLIC OF GERMANY

NÜRNBERG

PLZEN

CZECHOSLOVAKIA

BRNO

Donau

ZVOLEN

MÜNCHEN

BRATISLAVA

WIEN

DEBRECEN

Tisza

AUSTRIA

INNSBRUCK

GRAZ

BUDAPEST

VESZPREM

L. Balaton

KECSKEMET

HUNGARY

SZEGED

RUMANIA

Drava

VENICE

ZAGREB

YUGOSLAVIA

BEOGRAD

ITALY

SOVIET ARMIES

SOVIET DIVISIONS

MILES
0   200
0   300
KILOMETRES

pains to emphasize that he was threatening nobody. Nonetheless, he was now to some extent saddled with this overheard statement – and it would have been politically damaging for him to retreat too abjectly from it. Indeed, under questioning at a meeting of minority groups in Chicago, he attempted a counter-attack. He accused the Carter Administration's Secretary of State, Zbigniew Brzezinski (himself a Pole by birth), of being 'altogether too ready to sell his native country down the river'. Nobody who analysed Thompson's statements could seriously suppose he was encouraging a Polish insurrection, but there were a good many people (including some in Poland) who feared that restless Poles who heard what he had said repeated in garbled form might suppose that that was just what he was doing.

After Mr Thompson's election as president on the first Tuesday in November, a memo from the Polish Ministry of Home Security ordered the political police, assisted where necessary by the army, quietly to round up potential strike leaders from factories in Polish towns other than Warsaw. The Ministry had heard a rumour that otherwise some sort of provincial general strike might be called to mark President Thompson's Inauguration Day on 20 January.

The rumour was untrue, but the arrests caused a crisis. The political police and the army tried to arrest workers' leaders on 11 November, and met with resistance. In some places shots were fired. In more Polish troops were reluctant to obey orders and continue with the arrest of workers.

By 12 November factories in several provincial cities of Poland were under workers' control, flying the prewar flag of Poland with the communist insignia torn out. Dramatic visual evidence of these events was provided by a group of dissidents working in Polish television. In Gdańsk, the television station was taken over and held for some hours by technicians whose sympathies were with the strikers. Though the government reacted promptly, ordering the police to storm the station regardless of casualties, the staff were able in the time available to them to beam pictures of the riots out to Denmark and Sweden. In Sweden the authorities yielded at once to the threats which swiftly followed both from the Soviet Union and from Poland. They forbade both the use of the material in Sweden and its onward transmission. The Danes, on the other hand, passed it at once to Eurovision. From there it reached stations all over the world, affording striking and ineradicable proof of the intensity of feeling in Poland against the régime. One sequence in particular, showing Polish troops standing by while strikers wrecked a Soviet cultural centre in Szczecin, was more damaging to the Soviet Union than any.

In Wroclaw and Szczecin, communist party leaders went into the factories to 'negotiate'. In both places they then tried to break the promises made in negotiations and arrest the workers' leaders. In Wroclaw they failed, and the communist mayor was shot by the strikers, who also took other communist leaders as hostages. In Szczecin the Party soon regained control.

The central government then entered into negotiations. It promised no punitive action against those who had made even the most open shows of defiance, including those who had shot the mayor of Wroclaw. This promise was honoured until mid-January. The communist government went on ruling the country, but – it seemed to some (perhaps to communist mayors especially) – in name only. In Moscow there was growing concern.

A special meeting of the Soviet Politburo was called for 14 November, together with the heads of government of all the republics in the Soviet Union. For this meeting the Kremlin leaders asked Academician Y. I. Ryabukhin, a Harvard-educated Muscovite sometimes known in the West as the best backroom Kissinger the Russians had, to prepare a position paper. This was what he wrote, in a document labelled 'most secret'.

THE RYABUKHIN REPORT

1 Although President-elect Thompson has said some regrettable things, he is unlikely ever to countenance nuclear attack on the Soviet Union, just as we are unlikely to countenance it on the USA. Both superpowers have to bear in mind the high probability of second-strike destruction.

2 Despite this, we in the governing structure of the Soviet Union now face a situation which demands attention. Of the 180 heads of government in the different countries of the world, about 100 go to bed every night wondering whether they may be shot in a *coup d'état* in the morning. Except in Stalin's day, men in the top posts in the Soviet Union have not had to fear that. Now they might well soon be doing so. After what happened in Poland there is a distinct possibility of *coups d'état* against several socialist governments in Eastern Europe. It cannot be wholly ruled out in some republics of the Soviet Union itself, especially in the Far East and south.

3 Nevertheless, we should not, at this juncture, send Soviet troops into Poland to arrest those workers in, for example, Wroclaw, who have been allowed almost literally to get away with murder. It has been thought unwise to order units of the Polish Army to open fire on the workers concerned. There are units of the Red Army which might conceivably also be reluctant to obey such orders. Only if the Polish government is overthrown by a plainly revanchist régime, or if similar events take place in other socialist countries (above all in the German Democratic Republic), should considerable Soviet forces be sent in to rectify the situation. Yugoslavia is a different matter (see note on the Yugoslav situation, below).

4 The position in Poland makes it important that we should put the Americans in a position of weakness somewhere else, and *ensure that some humiliating*

retreats have to be undertaken by the Americans during the early weeks of President Thompson's Administration. This can be called a Bay of Pigs strategy.

5   It will be remembered that in the early days of the Kennedy Administration in 1961 our agents among the so-called Cuban émigrés in America, who have been in many respects useful, helped to instigate the bound-to-be-abortive American-backed invasion of the Bay of Pigs against Fidel Castro, who knew every detail of the invasion plan in advance. This humiliation of the Americans enabled Soviet penetration of South America to continue unchecked throughout the Democratic Administration of 1961–8, except that by placing offensive missiles in Cuba in 1963 Khrushchev unwisely pushed the Americans too far.

6   Unfortunately, we cannot precisely repeat the Bay of Pigs, because the United States is not preparing to invade anywhere unsuccessfully during the early days of the Thompson Administration. We should therefore try to set up situations where President Thompson *in his early days will be forced to order or accept a retreat by America and its allies from a situation created by us.*

7   A 'Thompson retreat' of this sort should be engineered in order to check a possible 'momentum of revolt' which may otherwise begin to be felt by the Soviet Union. At risk, if there is no such early retreat, may be the lives and livelihoods of many who work within the governing structure of the Soviet Union and its allies. If a 'momentum of revolt' were to spread from Poland, many would indeed go to bed each night fearing that they might be shot in a *coup d'état* next morning. There is little likelihood that the United States will risk the desolation of the planet by nuclear action simply because we have provoked the President, and it is unlikely to allow possibly less stable allies like Iran to risk doing so either. On the contrary, as Thompson has to operate in accordance with a public opinion which will grow scared much more quickly than our own

censor-protected public opinion will do, he will order retreats at a much earlier stage than we. A straightforward threat of nuclear holocaust carries little conviction. On the other hand, to hint at escalation towards it offers great advantage to the USSR. We should make constant use of this.

8   When we have brought about one or two 'Thompson retreats', we should flatter the new president and move back towards *détente*. We should not even insist on keeping all the ground gained for our Egyptian and other allies (some of whom might become inconveniently big for their boots) during the initial Thompson retreats. *We should also play upon the President-elect's vanity by manoeuvring the lame-duck Carter Administration into taking some of the preliminary steps in preparation for a possible war before Thompson's Inauguration Day on 20 January.* Then we should proclaim on Inauguration Day that 'Democratic Administrations have always started wars in American history, while Republican Administrations have always stopped them', and make Thompson feel he is a great peacemaker instead of the weak demagogue he is. *This desirable timetable means that we need to move quickly.*

9   The five (partly alternative) plans that might be put into effect quickly are: (a) Operation Middle East; (b) Operation India; (c) Operation Central America; (d) Operation Southern Africa; (e) Operation Yugoslavia. We know from our agents in the US that Thompson's advisers − e.g., in last week's so-called secret Think-Tank report and the Ex-Secretary's report − are worried about all five of these, and are in the usual state of capitalist muddle about how to react to any of them. As will emerge, I recommend only Operation Middle East and Operation Southern Africa. I am opposed, for reasons I will state, to Operations India and Central America. I would also not yet implement Operation Yugoslavia. But let us keep the Americans worrying for a time that we may start any of them.

10 *Operation Middle East.* Some people in the Democratic Socialist Republic of Egypt have long wished to arrange *coups d'état* in the enormously oil-rich and effete states of Saudi Arabia, Iraq and the Gulf, and to proclaim a new United Arab Republic. We have hitherto restrained them from this. *We should not actively and immediately encourage it.* A Middle East planning team should be set up, and make daily reports to the Politburo each evening at 6 p.m. from now on. Primary (and attainable) objective: by Thompson's Inauguration Day on 20 January, the new president should have to take steps to restrain Iran and to safeguard America's oil, jumping humiliatingly through hoops plainly held by us. Secondary (but more difficult) objective: it will be a very great advantage indeed if thereafter Egypt remains in command of the oil of a new United Arab Republic, and we can remain in command of Egypt.

11 *Operation India.* Some of the Asian republics of the Soviet Union are frightened that the more successful (and unfortunately more capitalist) successor states of the old Indian Union may gravitate towards the China–Japan co-prosperity sphere; this is the so-called policy of 'turning India into a hundred Hong Kongs'. Our Asian comrades say this could intensify pressure in the industrializing Soviet-Asian republics to move the same way, and even 'bring a *coup d'état* in Khabarovsk', where too many Japanese businessmen are now allowed on day trips from Tokyo in connection with joint Japanese ventures for the development of Siberia. It is therefore suggested, under Operation India, that friendly socialist states of the former Indian Union be encouraged to overrun successful capitalist neighbours (especially the smaller and most capitalist and most successful ones); this is the so-called strategy of 'making those hundred Indian Hong Kongs into a hundred Goas'. I am opposed to a full Operation India at this juncture, because (a) I am not sure we would win

(we would be allying ourselves with the weakest forces in the region, not the strongest); (b) I do not want to annoy China–Japan at this time (it is vital to keep China–Japan separate from America, instead of unnecessarily promoting an alliance between them); and (c) we should not disperse our efforts in these next few critical weeks. By all means, however, make the Americans think uneasily that an operation in India may be in the wind. Perhaps we should encourage some 'trade union' strikes in appropriate places in capitalist India, and possibly some assassinations. I suggest that a second-rank KGB planning team be given this responsibility. Objective: to keep the pot boiling, but not to precipitate any actual changes of régime, except if some rotten Indian capitalist apples fall off the bough right into our buckets.

12 *Operation Central America.* Our Caribbean friends (among whom Jamaica is now rather more valuable than Cuba) say that the new President of Mexico is a dynamic and able man, who is dangerously liable to turn Mexico into a prosperous and breakthrough country. This could raise the danger of *coups d'état* against the governments of our Caribbean allies and the less successful semi-socialist governments in South America. The Jamaicans and Cubans are therefore eager to arrange a *coup d'état* in Mexico in these next few dying weeks of the lame-duck Carter presidency. I am opposed to Operation Central America on much the same grounds as I oppose a full Operation India: (a) we might not succeed; and (b) Mexico is altogether too near America, and an attempted communist *coup d'état* there might unite Americans around Presidents Carter and Thompson, possibly even leading to decisive American action, while our whole object is to find operations which will produce disunity, and where America cannot take decisive action because the outgoing and incoming Administrations will not agree. Once again, however, as with Operation India, there

might be a case for a modified version of Operation Central America. An assassination of the Mexican president could be advantageous, done by somebody who cannot be traced to us, while we express the most effusive condolences to the still capitalist but much weaker Mexican vice-president, whose vanity will be assuaged by then acceding to office. A KGB team should report on the possibilities.

13 *Operation Southern Africa*. The Jamaicans are keen that the friendly countries in black Africa should extend external and internal guerrilla war against the 'white homeland states' of the former Union of South Africa and their associated 'Uncle Tom' states. There are three reasons why we should support this action, provided it can be organized in time. First, the economic success of the 'Uncle Tom' states, and the surprising continuing prosperity of the white homelands, mean that a process of right-wing *coups d'état* is liable to spread all up black Africa – and also, which naturally worries Jamaica, into the black Caribbean. Second, the white homelands do still follow a *baaskap* policy in some respects; many Americans, especially black Americans, will not regard them as respectable allies beside whom American troops should fight. Third, the confused military set-up in South Africa should create advantages for us. We have the capability there to keep on putting the Americans in very embarrassing situations indeed. With the troubles in the Middle East because of our operation there the Americans will also be anxious about the supply lines for oil round the Cape. In addition, I suggest (for your ears only) that the Red Army 'volunteer officers' we send to Southern Africa should be those whom we could not wholly trust to put down workers in Warsaw, and whom we would most like to have out of Moscow. Instead of repeating Stalin's Red Army purges of the 1930s (which we have not the power to do), let us send the less reliable officers to lead bands of black natives wandering over the undefended

veldt! The black natives will stop these gentlemen from being too liberal. It does not matter much that there will be no time for a coherent military plan, because Operation Southern Africa will not have a coherent military objective. The political objectives will be: (a) to put the Americans in an embarrassing position by compelling lame-duck President Carter to commit American forces to unpopular pro-white South Africa action, from which President Thompson will have to retreat embarrassingly; and (b) to make it clear to the international business world that continued investment in the white homelands and in the 'Uncle Tom' states will not remain peaceful and profitable for long. At the end of Operation Southern Africa it would possibly be desirable that at least one of the three white homelands should pass over to black rule, so as to mark Thompson's humiliation.

14 *Operation Yugoslavia.* If we are to make a move in Europe, it would be better to 'capture Yugoslavia' than to 'recapture Poland' (which is not lost anyway). The arguments in favour of Operation Yugoslavia are: (a) the weak federal government in Yugoslavia is unpopular with most of the Yugoslav people, and the various state governments are all unpopular with the people of the other states; (b) if Soviet troops intervened on the side of one state against another, we would have some support from the people (while in Poland we would have practically none); (c) our communist friends in the Soviet-run Serbian Committee for the Defence of Yugoslavia want Red Army troops in Yugoslavia (after the murder of the mayor of Wroclaw, they feel quite naked and unprotected without any Russians there); (d) in Slovenia and Croatia our troops would be arresting politicians rather than storming worker-held factories; and (e) a swift overnight move of this sort would serve notice to Polish and other workers that the Red Army is in a high state of readiness and can move very quickly.

My objection to Operation Yugoslavia at this stage is

that it would be more likely than the other four operations to have wide repercussions. Indeed, an operation in Yugoslavia has been considered by the Soviet High Command in the same strategic contingency plan as a move into West Germany. If we thought that all the communist countries of Eastern Europe were liable to erupt in *coups d'état*, which would be followed by *coups d'état* in the Soviet Union itself, then I would certainly be in favour of invasion of either Yugoslavia or West Germany or both. But we have not reached that situation yet. We have merely reached a situation where it is desirable to humiliate and discredit President Thompson. Let us start on this humiliation in the Middle East and Southern Africa.

15   During the operations of the next few weeks we shall need to keep China–Japan neutral. We must also keep Western Europe neutral, possibly by intimidation.

It was going to be a far from peaceful Christmas.

CHAPTER SIX

NO PEACE AT CHRISTMAS

The Ryabukhin plan was accepted by the Politburo, and almost immediately began to move out of control. The chronology of subsequent events was as follows:

30 November 1984. Egypt, having renewed a military relationship with Soviet Russia, overthrows by subversion the governments of Saudi Arabia, Iraq and Kuwait. It proclaims a new and immensely rich United Arab Republic (including these countries) and calls a meeting of OPEC heads of government for 7 December. Iran is invited to this OPEC meeting, which is to be held on neutral territory, but the new UAR threatens that there could be immediate military action against any country which interferes in the UAR's 'proper sphere of interest' and which sends forces to the Trucial Coast and Oman. This is clearly a threat to Iran. Israel is offered guarantees which ensure her neutrality.

2 December. Rioting, led by students, in Soweto and some other townships which are capitals of 'Uncle Tom' black-ruled states or cantons of the former Union of South Africa. These are black states that have good economic relations with the three white South African states and daily send many commuters to work in them. Some of these riots are put down, with bloodshed, by the local black police.

3 December. Strikes in Madras, which appear to be politically inspired. A Pan Am aircraft is hijacked on its way to Singapore and lands in Bangladesh at Chittagong. The Chief Ministers of two capitalist states in the old Indian Union and the executives of some American multi-nationals active in Madras are aboard it. The hijackers announce that they are being held hostage until the demands of the Madras strikers are met. Two days later American marines (invited, it is claimed, by Bangladesh) try to storm the aircraft, as the Germans did in 1977 in Somalia. The Americans fail. The aircraft is blown up with total loss of life.

5 December. At a meeting in Zimbabwe the Organization of Socialist African States claims that the 'fascist police' in Soweto on 2 December used weapons that were clearly heavier than any allowed to states of the former Union of South Africa under the Brzezinski Agreement. That agreement is therefore now declared at an end. The white homelands and 'Uncle Tom' states must be dissolved and their component parts made subject states of a new black-ruled Confederation of Africa South. Military action will be taken to enforce this.

7 December. At the OPEC meeting the new UAR demands a sharp increase in the price of oil. It also announces an oil boycott against any country that does not meet its political demands. These include recognition of the proposed Confederation of Africa South. There is to be strict boycott against anybody who aids and abets the white homelands and 'Uncle Tom' states. The UAR insists that majority votes in OPEC are enforceable upon all members, and that the boycott may be policed by 'friendly naval forces', which the newspapers suggest means the USSR. Iran dissents strongly.

8 December. The Soviet Union proclaims support for the OPEC decision. It also activates its existing base and missile facilities in Aden. This may be in order to help enforce the oil boycott.

9 December. An unsuccessful attempt is made to hijack an aircraft carrying Iranian finance and petroleum ministers from the OPEC meeting home to Tehran. On the same day there is an unsuccessful attempt to assassinate the Shah.

11 December. Forays from Zimbabwe and Namibia are made into the former Union of South Africa. Poland

and some Indian states announce that they are withdrawing their forces from the UN troops on the border. Polish,
Mexican and Indian commanders on the spot declare that
they are under UN orders and will obey these. There are
signs that Polish and Indian troops in Africa are more in
agreement with right-wing dissidents at home than with
their existing governments.

13 December. Round-ups of intellectuals and some
workers' leaders are reported from East Germany,
Czechoslovakia, Hungary and Yugoslavia. These do not
appear to be very successful, and reports appear in
Western newspapers of communiqués from an organized
'underground' in these countries and what is by now
almost an open dissident movement in Poland.

20 December. Black African forces advancing, in some
disorder, from Namibia, Zimbabwe and Mozambique are
now known to be commanded by Soviet, Cuban, and
Jamaican officers. These clearly do not have their troops
under disciplined control.

24 December. The UAR announces that it has discovered an Iranian plan to send forces into the Gulf states.
It threatens that if this happens it will take direct military
action against Iran, including air attack on Tehran. Iran
threatens immediate retaliation and asks for US help.

25 December. In a Christmas message to the world,
the 'lame-duck' President Carter proposes high-level discussions with the Soviet Union in accordance with the
Agreement for the Prevention of Nuclear War of 1973,
to consider means to end tensions in Africa and the
Middle East. His proposal is that there should be a
standstill of military forces all round the globe in their
existing positions. There should also be a ban on the
export of all arms to either side in Africa or the Middle
East. He proposes that the US Navy enforce the blockade
of the west coast of Africa; meanwhile the Soviet Navy
should enforce the blockade of the east coast of Africa
and the Gulf, with assistance to be invited from the US

Navy. Both superpowers are to enforce a blockade of arms-carrying ships passing through the Mediterranean.

26 December. The Soviet Union says it will talk only to President Thompson after his Inauguration Day on 20 January. It blames lame-duck President Carter for much of the world's present ills, but meanwhile agrees that a standstill should be enforced by both the US and the USSR.

28 December. Iran declares that it is not bound by the standstill agreement. Acting contrary to US advice, it reinforces its existing troops in Oman and secures an invitation from the United Arab Emirates to send defensive forces to Abu Dhabi. Television pictures, secured by an American camera team, of Iranian troops landing in Oman, and of armoured cars with Iranian markings alongside Omani troops, are distributed worldwide, and are triumphantly used by the Russians to support their claims of Iranian belligerency. The USSR says this is a blatant breach of the standstill, and that US naval forces (which are supposed to be co-operating in preventing such breaches) have connived at it.

29 December. A Soviet submarine sinks an Iranian transport. A US intelligence ship is attacked by missiles in the Gulf of Aden.

The Soviet attacks on the 29th can with some justification be called the first shots of the Third World War. Symbolically they were fired at sea and in Middle Eastern waters. Both maritime affairs and the Middle East had been a focus of intense Soviet interest and planning for many years (see Appendix 2).

Having got over the initial shock of the submarine attack, the Iranian government set in train measures to assume complete control of the waters of the Gulf and the Strait of Hormuz. The luckless US intelligence ship, limping slowly towards Mombasa, following a friendly offer of help from the government of Kenya to the outgoing President in his last days of office, was to be joined by a US carrier group which had been on passage south in the Red Sea, on a routine relief of the standing US Navy Indian Ocean Force. Having cleared the Straits of Bab el Mandeb this carrier group was under orders to carry out an armed reconnaissance of Aden, where it located and identified beyond doubt the group of fast missile boats of Soviet origin which had attacked the US intelligence ship. Also reported was a formidable force of the latest Soviet maritime strike-reconnaissance aircraft. A request to Washington for approval to strike both fast missile boats and maritime aircraft was not approved, and the intelligence ship remained, for the time being, unavenged but still afloat.

It was possible, without too much loss of face, either domestically or externally, for the US Administration to refrain, with due public claim to be acting in the best interests of keeping the peace, from taking immediate offensive action in response to the attack upon the intelligence ship. Instead, the US carrier group made all speed to join the damaged ship and escort it to Mombasa, while strong protests were made to Moscow, coupled with demands for an international court of enquiry, apologies and compensation. Then came news that a Soviet patrol submarine of the *Tango* class had been brought to the surface in the Strait of Hormuz by Iranian anti-submarine forces and the crew taken prisoner. In short, the first essay by the Soviet Navy in the actual use of force in support of Soviet policy had misfired.

After its initial errors, the Soviet naval command (perhaps smarting under a stern rebuke from the septuagenarian Gorshkov, and acting upon his advice – as Admiral of the Fleet and even after his retirement, Gorshkov had been insisting for years on the necessity of Soviet mastery of the seas for the triumph of Marxism–Leninism) ordered the *Victor* class nuclear-powered fleet submarine which had been detailed to intercept and trail the damaged US intelligence ship to sink her by torpedo. This she did, despite the presence of the US carrier group, without being detected, let alone destroyed. The confidence of the Politburo in the Soviet Navy's capacity to act in support of their political objectives was restored. The naval staff 'Correlation of Forces' paper (see Appendix 2) was carefully read. It had become apparent that naval-air operations involving actual combat differed drastically from the peaceful penetration of ocean space with propaganda cruising which the Soviet Navy had learned to carry out in such exemplary fashion since it first took to the oceans in the 1960s.

Difficulty was experienced by the new Soviet fleet commander in establishing satisfactory relationships with the various political régimes and armed force commands in the Middle East. Hitherto the Soviet presence had been based upon political agreements drafted by the Soviet Foreign Office and covering in great detail the respective commitments of the contracting parties. Deviation from *le pied de la lettre* was strongly discouraged. Everything had to be referred to Moscow.

When events began to move fast the weakness of this situation became manifest. Proclamation by the new United Arab Republic of the Red Sea as a war zone, and the closure of the Straits of Bab el Mandeb, for example, found a number of Soviet warships, naval auxiliaries and merchant ships in situations, sometimes at sea and sometimes in harbour, requiring diplomatic intervention with the national authorities. All that Flag Officer Soviet Middle East Forces (FOSMEF) could do was report to Moscow and await guidance. From the naval point of view his authority was similarly circumscribed. Soviet naval and air units in the Middle East 'belonged' to one or other of the main fleets – the Northern, the Black Sea, or the Pacific. In suddenly transferring to FOSMEF the 'operational control' of a number of surface warships, submarines and aircraft, far away from their main bases, the Soviet naval high command introduced a number of command inter-relationship problems, the resolution of which did not come easily to a commander and staff not bred to the use of initiative in matters of administration.

Even in the operational field FOSMEF found himself somewhat isolated. He had been briefed about the Middle Eastern situation before leaving Moscow, but there had been no time to explain to him precisely what was going on in Southern Africa. He knew, of course, that Soviet advisers, Soviet weapons and equipment, and Soviet bases were contributing to the military strength of the Confederation of Africa South People's Army (CASPA). But who, precisely, was in command of all these Soviet activities and forces? What was the directive upon which Soviet actions were to be based? In desperation the Flag Officer decided to send a senior staff officer to find out what was going on. The officer, travelling in plain clothes and using civil airlines, arrived eventually in Beira, where he contacted a member of the Soviet military mission. But, alas, events had moved too fast. The Soviet Navy, having started off on the wrong foot, and then made a good recovery, had nevertheless failed to retain the control of events which effective implementation of Moscow's subtle and complex political operations called for.

As evidence built up, and could no longer be disregarded, that a state of hostilities might at any moment exist between the United States of America and the Soviet Union, contingency plans on both sides were brought out and dusted off. The difficulty for the Americans was that in addition to losing an intelligence ship they had lost the initiative. The Russians, on the other hand, though clumsy in execution, knew exactly what they were trying to do. Moreover, at this juncture, although they were deeply involved both politically and militarily in the Middle East and in Southern Africa, two additional factors favoured the Russians. First, the satellite status of their allies in the Warsaw Pact, while a prime cause of the growing dissatisfaction which had done so much to bring about the Soviet pressure on the Americans, had always had the advantage of giving them firm control over all the Pact armed forces, their deployment and operation. Not so with the Americans. Although continually justified to the American people as being indispensable to the national security of the United States, the military alliances of which she was a member, and in particular NATO, had equally been justified by the governments of their other members to *their* peoples as being indispensable to *their* national security; hence decision-making had to be shared.

The Americans, therefore, unlike the Russians, would have to consult with their allies about any military action. But this was not all. Unless the Russians chose deliberately to attack within the NATO area, they could be reasonably certain that NATO would take no action to come to America's assistance.

This inherent weakness in the provisions of the North Atlantic Treaty deserves explanation. When the Treaty was signed on 4 April 1949, the Soviet Union was not a major naval power. She had begun to establish a strong force of submarines based upon the Kola Inlet, where they would have ice-free access to the North Atlantic. But the seas and oceans of the world were not to be treated as extensions of sovereign territory. All that was needed was to include attacks upon the ships and aircraft of a member of the Alliance as cause for acting in collective defence, as with an attack across a land frontier. But surely, it was thought, there must be some geographical limit at sea. Clearly, the waters adjacent to the eastern seaboard of the United States had to be included. As to ocean limits, it was suggested that the boundary be placed at the maximum distance to which submarines operating from the Kola Inlet were likely to proceed on patrol. The Tropic of Cancer was chosen as the limit.

A number of arrangements had been made over the years to mitigate the unfortunate consequences to NATO of the Tropic of Cancer boundary. Chief amongst these was the pooling of Allied naval intelligence. This clearly could not be limited to the North Atlantic Treaty area.

After all, wherever in the world the maritime trade of the member nations was to be found, most of it would sooner or later have to pass into the North Atlantic. How could measures for its protection there be co-ordinated without full knowledge of sailing times and routes? And how could the most economical use of shipping be organized, for the support of peoples and war effort, unless a worldwide view of the available resources could be taken? NATO plans provided, therefore, that a Naval Control of Shipping Organization should be set up, and also a Planning Board for Ocean Shipping. It was through the members of these groups, acting informally as individuals and in conjunction with the worldwide shipping community, that an appropriate response began to be evolved to the Soviet Navy's activities in the Arabian Sea and the Persian Gulf.

It was the British Ambassador in Washington who first communicated to the President of the United States the urgent plea of shipowners not to over-react to Soviet naval provocation. It was pointed out that the Iranians would be bound, in exercising control of shipping in the Gulf, to ensure that the movement of oil cargoes to countries other than the United States would continue. The Japanese, for example, remained almost totally dependent upon Middle Eastern oil. Provided the oil was not cut off at source – and Iran would not connive at this – all was not lost. By switching the destinations of many cargoes already on the high seas and by relying on buffer stocks and alternative sources of supply, the United States should, it was argued, attempt to 'ride the storm'. The important thing was to determine, if possible, the political objectives which the Soviet Union hoped to achieve by bringing naval pressure to bear on the USA's Middle Eastern oil supplies, and to consider its best counters.

The Soviet naval attacks and the Iranian response had the effect of alerting NATO – already apprehensive of the consequences of disturbances in Poland and tension

in Yugoslavia – to the possibility of a direct connection
between events in Europe and those in the Middle East.
Indeed, the NATO Military Committee, in reporting
upon the blowing up of an oil well in the North Sea
shortly after Soviet ships had been in the vicinity, on 3
January 1985, drew attention to it. That the Russians had
denied responsibility and had suggested that the incident
provided 'good reason for Western Europe to keep out
of present troubles' was significant.

The fact that the oil well happened to be British had
an effect which may not have been foreseen by the
Kremlin. The action taken immediately by Britain had
the tacit approval of the Political Sub-Committee of the
North Atlantic Council, meeting in emergency session.
This was to announce the setting up of a Northern Seas
Environmental Control Agency (NORSECA) by agreement between the North Sea countries concerned, with
an executive situated at Pitreavie, the Maritime HQ of
the RN Flag Officer, Scotland and Northern Ireland, and
his RAF colleague. Already known, and well practised,
as an Air-Sea Rescue Co-ordination Centre, and accustomed to conducting operations in concert with both civil
and armed forces authorities around the North Sea, the
Pitreavie HQ was able to put into effect quickly and
smoothly the plans for NORSECA, which had been
maturing for some years. The initial phase required the
establishment of standard shipping routes through the
North Sea, adherence to which would be mandatory if
the right of uninterrupted passage through the area was
to be enjoyed. The routes led clear of oil and gas
installations, and moving fishing zones were also declared,
using the standard medium of Notices to Mariners.

The implementation of this scheme, a possibility for
some years, was facilitated by a major change in the
NATO command structure which had been put into effect
in 1983 (see Appendix 3). It had long been recognized
that the command structure, particularly as it affected
the naval and air forces in the Atlantic, North Sea and

English Channel, had ceased to correspond to strategic and operational realities. It was indeed questionable whether it ever had.

Sweden, Soviet Russia, Poland and East Germany, as individual states whose shipping and fishing vessels were regular users of the North Sea, were invited to be represented, if they wished, on the NORSECA Council, in addition to the littoral states. Meanwhile, the British naval C-in-C arranged with his RAF colleague (C-in-C Strike Command) for armed surveillance of the Soviet group which appeared to be responsible for blowing up the North Sea oil well.

Elsewhere events had been moving at an equally dramatic tempo.

31 December 1984. Riots take place in East Berlin, with West Berliners standing on vantage points near the Wall, under full TV cover, cheering the rioters on. The riots are put down by Soviet troops, taking over almost at once from the East German police, much more firmly and bloodily than those in Poland the month before.

It must be observed here that television coverage, which was to play a very important part in the events described in this book, was in these incidents of such significance as to deserve fuller treatment.

All television news coverage in advanced countries is undertaken by lightweight electronic cameras, capable of recording their images on 25 mm videotape, or of having their material beamed live from the scene. On 31 December ENG (electronic newsgathering) cameras from many countries were in position at many places along the Berlin Wall, and were able to secure – and to send out live throughout the world – shots of the rioting.

One sequence was, however, secured from within East Berlin itself. An American documentary unit happened to be working on a programme on the German Democratic Republic. The director, who had won acclaim at the time of the Vietnam War for his strongly anti-war attitude, had been given considerable latitude to move about Berlin by the East German authorities. By chance he was on his way, with his camera crew, to interview an East German trade union leader when rioters began to threaten the trade union headquarters. His camera crew, their electronic equipment readily available, had secured some particularly vivid pictures, many of them in close up, before the police became aware of their presence. When two plain clothes officers intervened to stop their recording, the East German driver of the car in which they had been travelling shouted 'Give me the tape', grabbed the roll of recordings, and disappeared into the crowd. The cameraman, his recordist and the documentary director were immediately arrested, but the next day the film, smuggled across the wall by dissidents, appeared on West Berlin screens. The pictures on it made plain, beyond any possibility of argument, that the rioters were not the usual run of urban malcontents but men of responsibility and discipline. The film also contained some ugly shots of East German police firing deliberately into the crowd, and pursuing and savagely beating the rioters.

The American crew and the director were charged with having instigated the riots, and, for good measure, with being responsible for the death of two policemen. The fact that the director had a high reputation as a left-wing sympathizer added to the irony of the situation, but did nothing to help his case.

The Federal Republic makes no move. There is now some strain between Western Europe and the United States. The stoppage of the flow of oil from the Middle East and hindrance to shipping in the Mediterranean is beginning to hit the EEC, which claims that its own interests in the dispute are not being considered. The Community asserts a right to import oil from Iran and to complete freedom of movement for the shipping of its members and insists that it must be a party to the coming summit discussions.

3 January 1985. The President of Mexico is assassinated.

9 January. The German Democratic Republic now announces the arrest of the American TV crew. They will be tried on a capital charge of instigating the riots and murdering two policemen in East Berlin on 31 December.

10–18 January. The US declares that it must have more naval forces in the Gulf in order to stabilize the situation there. A US task force is despatched to Bandar Abbas.

19 January. Egypt invites the Soviet Union to take control of the Suez Canal. The US Sixth Fleet effectively closes the northern exit.

20 January. The Inauguration Day message to President Thompson from Soviet President Vorotnikov is hailed by a frightened world as astonishingly placatory, and presaging a new *détente*. President Vorotnikov says:

a The Egyptian government has today asked the Soviet Union to take control of the Suez Canal. The Soviet government has said it would wish to do this only in co-operation with US observers on the spot, because the sole Soviet object will be to enforce the mutual standstill agreed with President Carter after his Christmas Day messages. Both the Soviet Union and the Americans may feel, in their different ways, that the other side has broken that standstill in the past three weeks. 'But from the beginning of your presidency I beg that we should work together on these difficult issues.'

b The members of the American TV crew accused of the capital offence of the murder of policemen in East Berlin are being repatriated immediately through West Berlin. (At the same time it was revealed that the driver who had carried away the film, and a number of other dissidents traced through him, had been executed as being 'primarily responsible for the murders in which the American journalists had merely been participating onlookers', and that death penalties had also been carried out 'on two Polish counter-revolutionaries who had in November brutally murdered the mayor of Wroclaw'.)

c President Vorotnikov urgently invites President Thompson to a summit meeting, which he hopes will take place 'during this very first week you are in office'.

This 'Soviet plea for a Munich *détente*', as the *Peking Daily* called it, had been preceded by the following secret communication from Soviet Foreign Minister Baronzov to the Politburo on 19 January.

THE BARONZOV MEMO

The objectives of our operations in the Middle East and Southern Africa have now been achieved. We are in a stronger position than we dared originally to hope. In particular:

1 We have now re-asserted our control in Poland and East Germany. Although we have executed counter-revolutionaries there, some American newspapers will easily be persuaded to say that, because we are returning the US television crew, we are being conciliatory. The Polish and East German counter-revolutionaries have learned that the West will not support them during a Thompson presidency; Thompson is thus revealed to them as a broken reed. If there is trouble in Poland or other Eastern European socialist states in 1985 or 1986, it will now be easier to intervene in Yugoslavia, if needed, and to implement existing plans for the invasion of West Germany. It will be clearly shown that the régime in the Soviet Union cannot be shaken by subversion and *coups d'état*.

2 We have seized a very strong position in the Middle East. The North Arabian (i.e., Saudi Arabian and Iraqi) oil supply is now in Egyptian hands. We must ensure that this continues to mean in Soviet hands. Israel has been neutralized under guarantees which should for the time being be honoured.

We can allow the Iranians to send oil to the United States and Europe, across sea lines that we should increasingly be able to command, because there will be a sufficient scarcity of it to put the capitalist countries at a severe disadvantage. Their own capitalist laws of supply and demand mean that the price of oil will stay very high. This will speed the march of these countries towards reliance on nuclear energy, though we can agree with, stimulate and support the many sincere environmentalists in those countries who say that this form of energy is dangerous and immoral. They will argue that it is especially dangerous and immoral for nuclear technology to come to poorer countries, so these poorer countries will have to rely increasingly on those who control the North Arabian oil supply, that is, on the Egyptians and the Soviet Union. We can also use the oil weapon to increase our control over the economies of socialist countries in Europe, especially Poland and the German Democratic Republic. We should be highly conservationist, and not allow anybody to have too much oil from Arabia. One of our main objects in the summit negotiations with President Thompson should be to try to extend our hold over Arabian oil: if possible, not just Saudi Arabian and Iraqi oil, but oil from some of the Lower Gulf states as well.

3 The settlement in Southern Africa is much less important. From a political standpoint we could make concessions to the Americans there, and leave the Cubans and Jamaicans in the lurch. This is a matter for the Politburo to decide in consultation with the Ministry of Defence.

The Soviet Foreign Office wishes, through me, to put on record its appreciation of the efficiency and daring shown by the Soviet armed forces in the past three difficult weeks – in the Middle East, in Africa, in the North Sea and in East Berlin. The heavy expenditure on the armed forces in the past decade has made Soviet foreign policy much easier to implement at this critical time; it has therefore been fully justified.

In this last sentence Minister Baronzov had a point.

CHAPTER SEVEN

SUMMIT AND AFTERMATH

Preparations for a summit meeting continued, but, by tacit mutual consent, at a rather slower tempo than that originally demanded by Moscow. As a first step the US and Soviet Foreign Ministers visited their respective allies in Europe. The Secretary of State found Western European opinion torn between two opposing anxieties. In spite of the North Sea, West Europe was still heavily dependent on Middle East oil. From this point of view, therefore, they hoped that the United States would secure the reopening of the oil route by firm action in the Gulf, the Indian Ocean and Southern Africa. But they were reluctant to advocate this too openly because they feared the obvious American rejoinder: 'If you want the oil as much as we do, come and help us get it.' Very few of them had any significant capability for military action outside Europe. Most of them pleaded the old argument that NATO's area of responsibility was limited to Europe and a defined area of the North Atlantic – north of the Tropic of Cancer – and that the action was likely to lie outside those limits. They were faced, not for the first time, with this basic inconsistency between the terms of the Alliance and the real situation on the ground. The line of demarcation on the continent of Europe was better defined and had a history of thirty-five years of stability, due to the concentration of NATO defence on the maintenance of that line as inviolate. But if the causes of tension were outside, where no clear lines existed, and if the tension spread around the world until Europe was encircled by conflict, could the states of Western Europe afford to stay in their tight little *laager*?

Alternatively, the question was put with some irony

85

from the American side: if the Europeans can't or won't help to keep the oil producers free and the sea lanes open, will they do more in Europe and the Atlantic so that US reinforcements can in some part be diverted from Europe to other areas more immediately at risk?

At this point the other latent anxiety of the Europeans began to show itself more clearly. If the US, with direct or indirect help from Europe, took a strong line with the Soviet Union or its Middle Eastern or African supporters, and if this action were successful, would not the Soviet Union be tempted to restore its overall situation and acquire a major bargaining counter by attacking in Europe? This might be particularly tempting if US forces in Europe were to be reduced, or if it was known that fewer US reinforcements were available.

Europe's will to win and power to make decisions were further sapped by internal developments. The Community, now enlarged to include Spain, Portugal and Greece, had taken some steps towards the common production of military equipment, but had not yet acquired the institutions necessary for the formulation of a common foreign policy or for more effective pooling of military forces in the field. Moreover, Western Europe had not yet fully decided how to live with Euro-communism. In Italy the Communist Party had gained ground by its reputation for restoring law and order, but its very success, and its participation in government, made it more vulnerable to the corruption of power. On the other hand, being now about as powerful as it wanted to be in Italy, without having full responsibility for all the country's problems, the Party was no more inclined than before to a Soviet takeover, and therefore maintained, in those uneasy years of peace, a reasonably satisfactory degree of Italian participation in NATO.

In France, on the other hand, now under a Popular Front government, the balance of political forces was more precarious. The French Communist Party was still divided between those who maintained the purity of dogma above all and those who saw a modicum of flexibility as required both to keep alive the floundering unity of the left and to win back more votes from the post-Gaullist right. France's ambivalent attitude to common defence seemed still to suit most political persuasions, but there was much greater divergence on how to handle the crisis of the early 1980s. The nuclear power programme had been limited by environmental protests, and even in its reduced form the stations were not fully on stream. Possessing very little native oil, France was heavily dependent on imported energy. With the East–West frontier now bisecting the Middle Eastern suppliers, would oil be more securely acquired by private deals with the USSR and Egypt, or by backing the US counter-offensive to re-open traditional routes? Or would a crafty combination of the two be best – *négotiations tous azimuths*, as it were?

The United Kingdom, at the peak of its oil production, was less sensitive than others to a threat to external supplies, and even the return to comparative prosperity and a Conservative government had done little to diminish the parochialism of the seventies.

In Germany the wilder excesses of the urban left had been contained, not without difficulty and with much soul-searching about the increasing power of the police. Disillusion with the European Community helped to foster a revival of the historic belief that in the long run economic prosperity would depend very largely on the development of markets and supplies in Eastern Europe. The industrial and commercial pre-eminence of the Federal Republic in Western Europe was matched by that of the German Democratic Republic in the East. Some more daring politicians were tempted by this coincidence to wonder what they might do together. The majority, while still rejecting dreams of even an economic pan-German super-power, nevertheless accepted the importance of maintaining the advantages which accrued almost imperceptibly to a people who had a foot in either camp. While it might be dangerous to envisage a removal of the barrier between them, the sharpening of its prongs by renewed East–West conflict would be decidedly uncomfortable.

So the Secretary of State did not gather a very united or determined impression of European feelings from his tour of some of the more important Western capitals. The United States would as usual have to go it largely alone in the Middle East and the South Atlantic, and would no doubt be blamed for the consequences if things went wrong – though perhaps a rather longer exposure than usual to the rough and tumble of world politics and to the shortages and privations resulting even from the present situation would encourage the European doves to grow some beaks and claws. The position papers flew thick and fast in the State Department and the options remained irritatingly open.

The Soviet Foreign Minister did not fare much better in his rather more perfunctory tour of Eastern capitals. These countries saw their painful gains in economic prosperity endangered by Soviet brinkmanship. They found it hard to believe Soviet warnings about an energy shortage by the end of the century, which could only be remedied by laying hands directly or by proxy on a large slice of Middle Eastern oil supplies – upon which was based Soviet support for Egypt's incursion into Arabia. They feared that Soviet moves towards a war footing would put further and intolerable pressure on the supply and price of consumer goods, including food. They pointed out – in vain – that while the Soviet secret police had to deal only with a handful of known intellectual dissidents, they (in Poland, for example) were faced by a movement much more widely and solidly based on the workers' expectation of a standard of living that would approach first that of East Germany, then that of West Germany. Except in most aspects of military technology and the technology of space, the gap was increasing between the inefficiency of Soviet production and the far greater technical and managerial skills of East Germany, Hungary, Poland and Czechoslovakia. Western methods and Western technology were increasingly seen as more relevant and more desirable. The example of Euro-communism in the West suggested that Party cadres could restore some of their tarnished popularity by keeping their distance from the Communist Party of the Soviet Union.

So, when the Secretary of State and Foreign Minister Baronzov met at Geneva at the end of January 1985, each had to look not only at his interlocutor across the table, but also, even more searchingly, over his shoulder at the silent ranks of his allies and supporters. A week was spent agreeing on the agenda for their meeting and a further two weeks on that for the summit. At last it was settled that President Thompson and President Vorotnikov (the offices of President of the USSR and Secretary of the Communist Party of the Soviet Union (CPSU) had by then long been firmly unified) should meet on 15 February to discuss all threats to peace and any situation likely to lead to nuclear hostilities.

Political observers and media commentators were puzzled and divided over the mood of the participants and the prospects for peace or war. Each side had stepped further into the uncharted sea of confrontation than any of their predecessors since Cuba and the Berlin blockade. The point was, did they find the temperature to their liking? Each had found a keen front man – the US in Iran and the Soviet Union in Egypt – but both were aware of the instability of such protagonists. Their more solid supporters were more than usually hesitant. In one respect each had a similar requirement: to be sure of energy supplies from the Middle East until alternative sources could be established. Public opinion in the US still felt that abundant cheap energy was a god-given right of the American people. They had elected Thompson in the belief that he would be better at getting it for them than Carter had been at persuading them they didn't need so much. Vorotnikov had other preoccupations. The Russian people could be relied on to accept what they were given, but with Eastern Europe the choice was more difficult:

either to advance more quickly towards Western consumer standards, or to restore the somewhat eroded dictatorship of the CPSU and enforce acceptance of a lower standard. The former would require more oil, the latter more Soviet troops. Both, with the growing threat from China, might be in short supply. A foreign bogey would, as usual, encourage compliance, but a bogey in the Indian Ocean might be inadequate for the purpose.

After two days of recrimination and brinkmanship, the result emerged – one that should perhaps have been more easily predictable: peace with honour. The standstill was confirmed; the control of oilfields remained as it was, that is, Saudi Arabia, Kuwait and Iraq stayed with Egypt and the USSR, Iran and the Lower Gulf stayed with the West. There was to be no supply of arms to either side in Africa or Arabia (significantly, there was no reference to Iran, Cuba or Jamaica); mutual notification of naval movements was agreed, with exchange of satellite photographs to confirm it; and there would be a resumption of SALT and negotiations for MBFR (mutual and balanced force reductions).

In fact no one was satisfied with what they had got, but some were more dissatisfied than others. Thompson made much of having snatched peace out of the jaws of war (with a confused memory of a Churchillian antithesis mixed with a phrase of Chamberlain's), and of the time won to build more ships and develop indigenous oil resources. He did not actually wave a piece of paper from the White House balcony, but the general atmosphere had more than a hint of August 1938.

The Soviet Union started building pipelines and oil terminals to move her new oil north instead of south, its former direction. More important in the short term, the Soviet leaders devoted urgent attention to the means of restoring Soviet authority in Eastern Europe, penetrating the communist parties in Western Europe, and guarding their frontier republics against the growing presence of China. The build-up of Soviet military strength continued.

The Chinese were perhaps the most disappointed of all. In the uneasy triangle of forces so accurately forecast for 1984 by George Orwell they had hoped for much from the sharpening of US-Soviet confrontation in the Middle East and Southern Africa. They feared little from the US. Their doctrines led them to believe in the ultimate victory of their system over capitalism. They could afford to wait for history to produce its inevitable result. But rivalry with another seat of communism was different. There was nothing in holy writ to show how this would turn out. Besides, even in an age of rockets, a land frontier seemed a good deal more vulnerable than several thousand kilometres of Pacific Ocean. The standstill agreement at the US–Soviet summit deprived China of the good fortune which had seemed to be coming its way in an intensified struggle between the two rival superpowers. The ensuing reassessment showed China still a long way behind in nuclear potential and conventional sophistication. Numbers of men seemed hardly to make up for these deficiencies. It was necessary to seek some other way of compensating for the Soviet predominance in armaments.

The home front in the USSR – or at least in the Soviet areas contiguous to China – seemed to offer a possible target. It would have been dangerous for China to invoke nationalism as a subversive slogan before Sinkiang and Tibet had been fully brought under control. Now the risk of regional insurgency was far less there than in the Soviet republics in central Asia. Moreover, there were elements from many of these Moslem people, ethnically and linguistically Turkish, living in China's far west. With a modest growth of cultural freedom and with economic development springing from Japanese investment in the new co-prosperity sphere, it should not be too difficult to create centres of attraction in China for the Uzbeks and the Kazakhs. A movement for real autonomy in the Soviet republics on the Sino-Soviet border could have enormous advantages for China, at least in providing another preoccupation for Soviet policy makers, in drawing off Soviet troops who might otherwise be threatening China, and in creating suspicion as to the loyalty of units recruited in those areas.

Meanwhile, back in the West the phoney peace was beginning to wear thin. It goes without saying that neither the US nor the USSR trusted the other enough to make any real attempt at disarmament. On the contrary, Warsaw Pact preparedness increased at the same rate as before while NATO continued to make some modest improvements. Political skirmishing was resumed. Three elements in particular contributed to the build-up of instability: oil, the Middle East and the Balkans, none of them new but each spreading its effects like secondary growths after an unsuccessful operation.

The disruption of oil supplies and the resulting shortages all over the world were like a running sore, making calm thought more difficult, leading to internal and international tensions, distorting economies and increasing unemployment. The new patterns of distribution were fragile and susceptible to political uncertainty. The control of the North Arabian supplies by the Egyptian-dominated UAR was in these circumstances hardly a guarantee of stability.

This was the sixth attempt at Arab union in which Egypt had been involved. All the previous ones had failed after longer or shorter periods. The few centres of population in Saudi Arabia could be controlled by military force. The association with Iraq was more uneasy. The age-old cry of Arab unity was tarnished by the only too visible presence of Soviet technicians at the oil fields and the ports. Even in this day and age the old hatreds between Sunnis and Shias were likely to erupt when Saudis and Iraqis were too closely intermingled. Arab unity is a dream which has inspired some of the noblest thinkers of that race, but in actual history Arab division has been more constant and more influential. The personal rivalries of Arab politicians have always fed on the discrepancies of tribe and dogma and social stratification.

The new union had stalled before accomplishing its full

purpose. With all the Arabian oil (especially if Iran had dissolved into chaos, as Arab propagandists had persuaded themselves would happen) the Arab union might have stood a chance of real independence. It might even have held the superpowers to ransom, from the moment when Middle Eastern oil was seen to be essential for their survival. But now, with Arabia only half won, and with Iran resurgent and better armed, the divisions of the Arab world were compounded by the contest between Soviet Russia and America. Imperialism was back under other names, and it was no wonder that disillusion had set in.

Assassination was not far behind. The association between the Shias in Iraq and the godless Russians provoked a resurgence of that orthodox fanaticism which had claimed so many political victims in the past. The murder of the Egyptian Prime Minister not only left a power vacuum in the Council of the Union, but caused ripples and echoes among the Moslem subject races of the Soviet Union, already wooed by China.

A new government was patched together with military participation, but the seeds of doubt had been sown in the Politburo about the viability of control by proxy in so vital an area. Plans were made and forces earmarked for a more direct Soviet intervention. Equipment, clothing and warlike stores appropriate for hot climate operations were issued, and an urgent programme of modification to vehicles and weapons put in hand. Crash courses in Arabic were undertaken and encyclopaedia articles rewritten to prove the fundamental compatibility between the social principles of Islam and those of Marxism-Leninism.

Meanwhile, a new crisis began to develop nearer home. After Tito's disappearance from the political scene Yugoslavia had survived the succession problem in the first instance with less difficulty than had been forecast. Inevitably the regions had obtained a little more power and the economic arrangements in each region had diverged a little more from the general norm, mostly leaning even further than before towards the market economy, but the basic federal organization remained more or less intact. Now, however, the general difficulties caused by oil shortages and price increases added to the latent tensions between the richer north and the poorer south of the country. The non-aligned group of countries, of which Yugoslavia and Egypt had been founder members, had been brusquely reduced by Egypt's acceptance of Soviet tutelage. As the path of non-commitment became narrower, Slovenia began slipping off to the West and Serbia to the East.

West Germany had for some time seen Ljubljana as one of the gateways to the development of the more intensive trade with Eastern Europe which its industry seemed increasingly to require. The Slovenian provincial administration responded to West German advances with an alacrity that went beyond merely commercial advantage and suggested a vision of a new Balkan Switzerland where East and West could meet on equal terms. The central government took fright at this separatist trend and sought to redress the balance by turning a blind eye to pro-Soviet groups which had always been in existence and had lately been sharpening up their capability for agitation against just this eventuality. Their danger signals to the CPSU lost nothing in transmission. The restoration of orthodox communist control in Yugoslavia was now moved up to quite near the top in the Kremlin's list of objectives.

CHAPTER EIGHT

HEIDELBERG, 27 JULY 1985

It was a warm summer afternoon in Heidelberg. The visitors from the Committee on Armed Services of the United States Senate were listening with close attention to the Chief of Staff of the United States Army in Europe (USAREUR). The press and TV crews were absent.

'As I am sure was made abundantly clear this morning in the Commanding General's opening address and the informal group briefings which followed,' the Chief of Staff was recorded as saying, 'this visit is warmly welcome in US-AREUR, from top to bottom in the whole command. It is evidence of the interest and support we have increasingly been able to count on in the United States as international tension has mounted further south and as we in this command have steadily improved our state of readiness.

'What I have to say is classified but, as you have wished, it is on the record, and I know you will bear with me if it is occasionally on the technical side.'

He turned to the map.

Dispositions in CENTAG are known to you, and I have at this stage no further comment on them. It is a matter for regret that the recommendations of the Nunn-Bartlett Report in 1977 and of the Annual Defense Department Report of Secretary of Defense Rumsfeld for the Fiscal Year 1978, could not, for reasons of finance, be fully acted on. Nevertheless, there has been steady progress since the period of dangerously low levels of readiness during which these reports were rendered – progress which is at least to some extent, if in varying degree, reflected among our allies – and the US Army in Europe is today in better shape than at any time in the last ten years. Progress at this rate, other things being equal, could within two years put the Alliance in a position of unquestioned security against any conventional attack from the Warsaw Pact.

Nuclear armaments will be covered at another time. I shall deal now with conventional equipment.

The XM–1 tank, three times as effective as the M–60 it is replacing, is widely in service throughout the command. The Mechanized Infantry Combat Vehicle, whose earlier introduction would have doubled the effectiveness of our infantry, regrettably is not. Its stabilized auto-cannon for fire suppression and its two under-armor ATGW (*TOW* or *Hellfire*) with a 3,000-meter range and a 90 per cent first-hit probability would be invaluable. It has, of course, been accepted for service and we have some, but not enough.

On the other hand we have through the improved Tacfire a 50 per cent improvement in automated artillery fire direction, plus battery computers, and the extended range ammunition for 200 mm and 155 mm tube artillery, with which it can now reach out thirty to forty kilometers. This much improved counter-fire capability has helped to correct a grave weakness on the CENTAG front. The weakness I refer to is our difficulty in switching fire support laterally, given an enemy possessing the initiative in choice of attack axes and a terrain not always friendly to lateral movement on the ground.

We should have welcomed the phased array artillery-locating radars for counter-battery use, and above all a general issue of the cannon-launched guided projectiles with initial laser guidance, which are effective against tanks. As you know, however, although these items have been accepted into service, full funding for production has so far been withheld. We are rather more fortunate in the provision of artillery-delivered scatterable mines, for delivery once the pattern of an attack has been revealed. These are now coming into the theatre.

For air defense it is satisfactory that our inventory of

third generation air defense missiles is virtually complete
to scale, with *Patriot* for medium and high altitude,
Roland for medium and low, and *Stinger* for low as
well, replacing *Redeye*.

We need more anti-tank helicopters with a day-and-
night and a 3,000-meter stand-off capability. There are
some, but we need more. We also need, as has often
been pointed out, many more ATGW, to be mounted on
special purpose vehicles and preferably under armor on
MICV [Mechanized Infantry Combat Vehicles], in order
to withstand the enemy's suppressive fires, which we
understand are certain to be very intense. What we
really need in US divisions in the Central Region is an
aggregate of at least 1,000 major anti-tank weapons in
each, made up of 300-plus mounted in tanks and 700
ATGW to be otherwise deployed. We have the tanks. We
do not, in these numbers, have the ATGW.

At corps and division level we have been greatly in
need of much improved intelligence, reconnaissance
and target acquisition systems. Improvement in these
last two years there has been. Signal intelligence has
benefited from better methods and much better equipment. We have a good range of remotely-piloted vehicles for surveillance and target acquisition, together
with some provision of airborne moving target radars,
both helicopter and fixed wing, and radar locators. The
degree of visibility we now have over the battlefield will
greatly help the interposition of our smaller forces on
the main axes of enemy effort and the development of
effective battlefield interdiction operations.

The effectiveness of our intelligence on the battlefield
has sharply increased with the introduction of the Joint
Tactical Information Distribution System [JTIDS]. We
are still running this system in. It has never yet taken a
full operational load and we shall not know how best to
exploit it until it has. But in this, as in other fields where
electronics are of vital importance, we are conscious of

an enormous potential which is a powerful source of confidence at every level.

I am glad to be able to report improved operational procedures and capabilities for joint air-land warfare. Joint action is now effective in reconnaissance and surveillance operations, to a lesser extent in suppression of enemy air defenses, battlefield interdiction and electronic warfare, but above all in joint control of close air support using artillery forward observers with laser designators.

The drawdown of theater stocks in support of operations elsewhere by other nationalities (of which those by the Israelis were at one time typical) have long since been made good, as you know. Prepositioned stocks of equipment for reinforcing units are complete, and there will be little difficulty in bringing up to combat level, for example, the heavy divisions expected at an early stage. One of these is even now in process of being lifted in. Ammunition stocks are now up to scale and, even more important perhaps than that, negotiations with the FRG, actively pursued in 1980 for the re-siting of certain major installations east of the Rhine, were successfully concluded nearly two years ago, and vital stocks are now no longer so likely to be denied to forward troops by interruption of lines of communication. Similar advantages will be generated by the substitution of a theater line of communication through the Low Countries for that through Bremerhaven in north Germany, though this is not yet complete and the new air defense problem it has thrown up has not yet been completely resolved. Movement towards fuller integration of Allied logistic systems has made progress. We are fortunate in having fewer problems here in CENTAG in this respect than they have in NORTHAG.

I have further to report continual improvement in command and control systems, in air defense and control, and in measures to avoid surprise.

Finally I have to report, in answer to two questions

raised by Senators, that although, of course, French national policy is still to remain outside NATO, the participation in our own planning of command and staff of II French Corps with its two divisions and supporting troops stationed in the FRG is close, if highly confidential. The two US brigades that were deployed in north Germany to make good weaknesses in depth in NORTH-AG have now been redeployed because NORTHAG has recently taken encouraging steps towards the remedying of the weaknesses there. Each of these US brigades is the basis of one of the reinforcement divisions which will form a very important element in the regional reserves now being developed by AFCENT [Allied Forces Central Europe].

The Chief of Staff came to an end and stepped aside.

The Commander-in-Chief, the Commanding General of the United States Army in Europe, then rose. He was a tall, good-looking man in his middle fifties, trim of figure, clean-shaven, well-groomed, with dark hair just beginning to turn grey. His manner was quiet, his speech deliberate. 'All generals are always on the stage,' said Frederick the Great, who knew a good deal about generals. The C-in-C USAREUR was no exception. He was playing a part and knew it, and because he was his own producer and was an efficient, intelligent and quite ambitious man it was a very well produced part, as well as being well played. He was also, like very many generals, a brave, sincere and selfless person. He knew what was required and he knew a good deal about how to get it done.

Your army in Europe [he began] is in better shape than anyone, I think, has realized, especially the Russians.

The Vietnam experience is out of our system. We are rejuvenated and modernized. Our indoctrination to battle has been pressed hard.

The main focus of the US Army's doctrine and training has been for these several years past the Central

Region of NATO – right where we are now. Almost every combatant member of the officer corps of the United States Army has served at least once in Germany. We know the terrain. We know the weather. We know our enemy.

US divisions have been optimized for combat in Europe against the tank-heavy forces of the Warsaw Pact. They have been trained to believe that even when outnumbered they can win.

Our tank crews have been taught to shoot first and to hit with the first shot, 60 or even 70 per cent of the time, out to ranges of a mile or more.

Combat teams of infantry and tanks, working closely together, have been trained to use the rolling terrain and hill country in our sector, with its plentiful forests and towns, for cover and concealment.

Our troops have been exercised against forces set up to represent most closely Soviet strength, equipment and tactics.

Colonels and generals are expected to fight moving, active battles, always seeking an advantage from the use of terrain, surprise and mobility.

Generals are expected to concentrate defending forces in front of the main thrusts of the enemy so that the fighting troops do not have to meet a greater ratio of strength against them than three or four to one.

Colonels have been taught to fight in forward defense alongside their German allies.

The captains and their troops have learned that modern weapons in the defense can and should inflict losses on an attacker, in comparison to their own, of well over three to one. They have learned, in short, that a successful defense against considerable odds is possible.

It is with convictions and tactical concepts such as these that the US forces in the Central Army Group are prepared to meet a Soviet attack.

Let me only add a word about our German allies. The two German corps in CENTAG are of similar strength and composition to our own. Some of their equipment is of the same pattern as ours. Most of it is of their own design. They have lately in service, for example, a new tank, the *Leopard* II. It represents a different tank philosophy from that upon which our own XM–1 is designed, or the British *Chieftain* for that matter, but I can tell you that it is very good. All their equipment is good. The German Army has also made great headway in the organizing and training of Home Defense units of the reserve. These can be expected to play a very important part in the defense of their country, particularly against internal dangers.

We are very close to our German allies. Joint German–American tactical exercises, war games, demonstrations and discussions have led to a remarkable unanimity between two national armies whose last battle experience in Europe was against each other.

There are, of course, differences between us, some small, some not so small. There is, for example, the greater reliance placed by US forces on air support. The greatest difference, whose significance only battle will reveal, is that a war here will be fought among Germans in Germany.

If the Commanding General had it in mind to say more, he did not say it. The door of the briefing room opened and a staff officer hurried in, handing to the General a slip of paper in what had become a highly charged silence.

'I am informed,' said the General, 'that Soviet troops crossed the frontier into Yugoslavia in some strength a few hours ago.'

The senior Senator rose.

'General,' he said, 'you will have enough to do without having us around here. It's about time we all got home, anyway.'

CHAPTER NINE

THE INVASION OF
YUGOSLAVIA

The situation in the early summer of 1985 was fraught with crises and uncertainties of many kinds. The year had begun with the Soviet exercise in the use of military power to achieve political ends in the demotion of the US from its world role. The resulting instability had, however, shown up at least as many weaknesses on the Soviet side as on the American. And the Russians had to fear that all these sources of anxiety might culminate together in some way – Chinese pressure in the central Asian republics, the collapse of the Middle Eastern house of cards, Yugoslav tendencies to move closer to the West, and the cumulative effects on the Soviet-controlled régimes in Eastern Europe of an oil shortage, higher food prices and increased military effort at the expense of civil consumption.

The comparatively cautious policy hitherto pursued, which might be described by the slogan 'proxy and periphery', had not yet produced the promised results. The attempt to turn the Eurasian landmass into a base for worldwide naval operations had suffered the inescapable setbacks of geography and temperament. The choice now lay more clearly between accepting an unwelcome and even humiliating return to previous spheres of influence, and making violent and rapid use of the remaining real Soviet assets in the shape of its truly formidable conventional attack capability in Europe and its ruthless ability to suppress dissent wherever the Red Army was present.

The West was not wholly unaware of the debate now

being conducted in the Kremlin. The belief that one of the Soviet options must be war in Europe, including the recapture of Yugoslavia, had led at last to a real effort to make good deficiencies in the conventional forces available to Allied Command Europe in NATO and in the all-important air defence of the United Kingdom as the bridgehead for US reinforcements. (For the action taken to improve the UK defence capabilities, see Appendix 1.) Means of counter-action in Yugoslavia were depressingly small, but at least from the Western political point of view conditions were more favourable. The Italian Communist Party, whose general allegiance to NATO had remained somewhat qualified, could be relied upon (it was hoped) to support the defence of an independent communist régime finding its own way to socialism against the forcible imposition of Soviet control. Yugoslavia was historically a prototype of Eurocommunism and geographically a bastion against Soviet pressure to conform. Some preparations could therefore be made by US forces in Italy to counter a possible pro-Soviet coup supported by Red Army troops from Hungary.

In the final stages of the Soviet debate, opinion varied as to whether Yugoslavia should be dealt with in isolation or whether there should be a Soviet advance on a broad front in Europe. Those advocating more general action not only emphasized the importance of prosecuting Soviet foreign policy as a coherent whole but saw this in particular as bringing a series of advantages. Acquisition of the greater part of Western Europe would extend still further the glacis hitherto provided only by the communist states of Eastern Europe. It could remove, perhaps for years, the possibility of US action on the Western flank. It might be best to do this before China was ready, before the Soviet position in the Middle East deteriorated too greatly, and before improvements in NATO defences went much further. It would allow, and indeed necessitate, strong measures against those in Poland and Czechoslovakia who were now demanding not only freedom of expression but also cheaper food. The destruction which war would cause in both Germanies would buy a further breathing space before the German problem once more posed a threat to the Soviet Union. In a major conflict with NATO Yugoslavia would be unimportant and could be dealt with *en passant*. Limited Soviet action in response to an appeal for help from within the country was in any case attractive. Effective US counter-intervention was unlikely, but if it took place it could be used to justify a more general attack upon the West through Poland, East Germany and Czechoslovakia.

In the end events as usual took control. The Soviet-inspired Committee for the Defence of Yugoslavia staged an abortive foray into Slovenia, precipitating a collision between the Slovenian provincial government and the federal government in Belgrade. The Committee called for Soviet help. At the same time some bakeries closed in Gdansk and Dresden due to diversion of fuel to factories producing military transport, and the result-ant riots threatened to get out of hand. Soviet reaction was seen to be unavoidable. The hard-liners won the day.

Meanwhile, the manoeuvre season had arrived. The Soviet command was staging two major exercises, one in Hungary and one of unprecedented size in East Germany. The Final Act signed at the Conference on Security and Co-operation in Europe required the noti-fication of manoeuvres over a certain size and encour-aged states holding them to invite observers from other countries. The Russians played this in two ways. On grounds that they were of relatively little importance they failed to notify the Hungarian manoeuvres, believ-ing that these might be the first to be converted into the real thing, but notified the German exercise through the normal channels.

On 27 July 1985 a Soviet airborne division in an

unopposed landing secured the approaches to Belgrade. At the same time a Soviet motor-rifle division from Hungary crossed the Yugoslav border on the Budapest-Zagreb road, followed by another. The pro-Soviet Committee was recognized as the provisional government of Yugoslavia, and Yugoslav frontier forces, after a short engagement, were quickly obliged to withdraw towards Zagreb. The Soviet plan was to occupy Zagreb and thence link up with the airborne troops east to Belgrade and fan out west to Ljubljana. Meanwhile, the exercises in East Germany intensified, with more formations moving forward from the Western Military Districts of the Soviet Union through Poland.

The NATO side, in spite of many warnings, had failed to make specific provision for this kind of threat in Yugoslavia. That country had remained the 'grey area' par excellence. It was not covered by the NATO commitment to automatic defence. But equally the West had not renounced interest in what happened there, as they had by implication in Hungary in 1956 and Czechoslovakia in 1968. The continued neutrality of Yugoslavia was obviously a Western interest of prime importance. But it is difficult to guarantee a country whose foreign policy is based on non-commitment, as Britain and France had found with Belgium prior to 1939. Therefore greyness was made a virtue: the very uncertainty of Western reaction was made a principle of deterrence.

The grey chicken now came home to roost and NATO had to decide – or rather the USA decided, with reluctant Italian acquiescence, while NATO tagged along. In the hope of favourable Yugoslav reaction, and in view of all the long history of Italian-Yugoslav conflict, it was vital to avoid the use of Italian forces. But after some days of furious diplomacy in Belgrade, Zagreb and Ljubljana, US marines and airborne forces from Italy were able to make unopposed landings at Rijeka (Fiume), Ljubljana and some of the Dalmatian islands. What was much more serious, within twenty-four hours they were in action against Soviet airborne and armoured units.

At this stage the US government still harboured a final hope that they might be able to isolate events in Yugoslavia from the wider European scene, and above all that they might be able to limit the impact upon American public opinion of any fighting there. They called for an immediate meeting of the Security Council. They ordered their commanders in the first instance not to move beyond the boundaries of Slovenia, and, to prevent the inflaming of opinion in the United States, to put an immediate ban on all television coverage of their operations.

But they were too late. They had counted without the enterprise of a resolute Italian television cameraman Mario Salvadori. He was not employed by the official Italian television service, RAI, but by an international newsfilm agency. He had at one time lived in the States. In Italy he had made good friends among the American marines, whose peacetime manoeuvres and parades had provided him with useful material when other news was scarce. He happened to be at their base when the alert began, and his friends took him along 'for the ride' when they were airlifted to Ljubljana.

It was thus decreed by chance that one of the first encounters between Soviet and US forces in the Third World War took place under the eye of a television camera. With his portable and lightweight electronic equipment, Salvadori was present at the first contact when Soviet forces thrusting into Slovenia came face to face with American marines on the outskirts of Kostanjevica, between Ljubljana and Zagreb. Three Soviet tanks, moving forward in the confident belief that no US forces had yet reached the area, were surprised by a unit of US marines whose armament included *Milan* anti-tank weapons. All three tanks were very quickly put out of action by first-shot strikes, and a company of Soviet infantry on a hillside beyond the town was swiftly recalled to redeploy in a stronger position immediately to the rear. At the same time Soviet strike aircraft carried out a rocket attack on the Americans, causing some very ugly casualties.

Much of this Salvadori, a daring and intelligent cameraman, recorded on tape. It was action material of extraordinary drama. The high quality of the ENG pictures gave a sense of reality and vividness greater than any in film pictures of Americans in action in the now distant Vietnam War. The destruction of the Soviet tanks, one of which blew up within 100 metres of the cameraman's position; the shocked, drawn faces of Russian prisoners being escorted to the rear; and the spectacle of the Soviet infantry suddenly withdrawing, so that the whole of the small hillside seemed to move, conveyed in sharp, almost exultant terms the information that the Red Army was far from being invulnerable. The trained military eye might have noted that the Soviet infantry, in their sudden rearward move, were providing a model of how to carry out the very difficult operation of a withdrawal in contact, under fire. A military observer would certainly have recognized that three tanks do not constitute a significant force. But this small action, if only because it was small and readily grasped, came over as a clear US victory. Only the pictures of the mutilated victims of the rocket attack, one screaming in agony, were a reminder of the cost.

Salvadori was not only a skilled cameraman. He had had long experience of outwitting officialdom. He quickly made his way to Ljubljana, without disclosing the contents of his recording, and managed to get a lift on an aircraft back to Italy. There, through his agency, the material was transmitted by satellite throughout the world. It was in the hands of the American networks before the White House or the Pentagon were even aware of its existence. The networks, moreover, knew that the material had already been circulated widely, not least to the Iron Curtain countries, who had helped themselves unhesitatingly to the satellite transmissions of the agency. So into the homes of the American public went, unplanned, uncensored, almost unedited – except for one peculiarly hideous shot of a marine whose face had been blown away – these scenes of the first clash between the Russians and the Americans.

With acute anxiety the United States authorities awaited the reaction of their own people. To their relief and also to their surprise – as indeed to that of most commentators in the press – the result was not one of dismay or fear, but of anger and pride. There was anger at the sufferings inflicted by the bombing, seen so close upon the screen, but there was also an upsurge of pride at this spectacle of Soviet troops being held in check and even withdrawing. In an instant, without formal declarations of war, the American public felt themselves to be at war, and some fundamental instinct for survival welded them together. The battle of Kostanjevica was a minute operation in the huge waves of fighting which were to follow; Salvadori's pictures were to be outdone by miles of more dramatic, more terrible coverage. But few recordings of this first television war were to have such an influence. There could be no doubt now, not only in the minds of the American public, but in the world at large, that the Soviet Union and the United States were involved in a shooting war. And the first recorded glimpse of it had been a glimpse of Soviet troops on the run.

This incident was easily presented to the Warsaw Pact countries as what some at least of the Soviet hawks had been waiting for, the 'attack' by the West on a communist state. It was the momentum of events, however, much more than the actual incident itself, that now took charge. Soviet forces were joined in battle with troops of the United States. This was the stupendous, almost unbelievable event that brought into brutal reality what had so long been feared. The Soviet Union and the United States were in combat action against each other on a battlefield. The chocks were out. The huge military mass of the USSR was already beginning to move down the slipway. There could now for the Soviet Union be no possible alternative to the launching of the full invasion, already well prepared, of Western Europe, and the advance to the Rhine, for the destruction of the Atlantic Alliance, and the removal of the threat from US 'imperialism', operating from the forward base of Federal Germany.

CHAPTER TEN

SOVIET PLANNING

The year 1984 had seen some difference of view in the Kremlin on the most profitable method of exploiting the USSR's very considerable position of military strength. The difference was in the last resort no more than a matter of emphasis, but it had been evident for some time and was not without importance in the subsequent development of events.

The older men, all with experience of the Second World War, continued to see in Germany the most persistent and dangerous threat to the long-term security of the Soviet Union. They fully recognized the enormous strength and influence of capitalist America, the other great super-power, and the potential danger it embodied. Unless the United States disintegrated under the stresses of capitalist contradictions, of which it had to be admitted there was at present little sign, there would at some time have to be a reckoning with her. But the danger from a re-armed, industrially powerful West Germany, eager for revenge, was both more immediate and more real, both in itself and in its catalytic influence on the countries of the West. These older men tended to see external problems more in terms of Europe and its extension in North America than of the outer world. They were at least as much Russian as Marxist-Leninist, and in some cases more so.

The younger men, none of whom had been old enough to take any part in the Second World War, thought more in terms of the rest of the world than of Europe, and even there, though they were fully alive to the danger from Germany, did not regard it as the whole core of the external problem. They were uncompromising Party men, born and brought up under the system, completely devoted

A Soviet pilot goes out to his *Foxbat* on a Polish airfield during the Soviet preparatory 'manoeuvres' before the outbreak of hostilities. This picture was taken by one of the Allied observers permitted under the Helsinki agreement.

Soviet *Scud* missile

Admiral of the Fleet of the Soviet Navy Sergei Gorshkov

A Soviet *Kiev*-class aircraft carrier

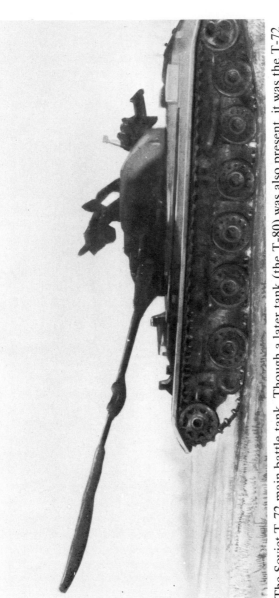

The Soviet T-72 main battle tank. Though a later tank (the T-80) was also present, it was the T-72 which was the hard core of the Soviet armoured attack on the European battlefields of the Third World War

The USS *Ray* (ssn-653) nuclear-powered attack submarine proceeding on patrol

US Army self-propelled 155 mm howitzer M-109 moves into position east of Giessen, 5 August, in a flank action by V US Corps

'Target!' A NATO tank destroys a Soviet T-80 at close range in a night action on the North

to it and wholly conscious that it was the sole condition of their being who and what they were. They were at least as much Marxist-Leninist as Russian, and in some cases more so.

Such difference as there was, it must be repeated, was only one of emphasis. There was no disagreement on the persistent threat to the system from the capitalist-imperialist world, with West Germany playing a major role under the leadership of the United States. Nor was there disagreement on the high probability of a future threat from China, on the dangers of heresies in national communism, on the absolute need to keep the Party supreme and watertight, or on any other fundamental issue. There was also complete agreement on the inevitability of the ultimate triumph of the system everywhere, on the necessity to exploit every external opportunity to advance the Soviet interest, on the wisdom of tactical manipulation in the short term to secure greater gains in the long, and on the paramount necessity for a dominant position of military strength abroad – at the cost if necessary of damping down progress at home – as a fulcrum for the lever of Soviet political power.

The differences lay chiefly in the choice of areas of exploitation. The old guard were inclined to look towards the centre, towards the manifest contradictions of developed capitalist societies and the unstable relationships between them. The younger men looked more to the periphery, to the opportunities offered among developing societies and the relations not only between these societies but also between their own developing world and more developed countries.

There was no shadow of disagreement on the necessity to neutralize West Germany at some time, by military force if necessary. Centralists put this higher on their list of priorities, perhaps, than the others, and might have been more inclined to pre-emptive action. It was agreed policy to impair the coherence of the Atlantic Alliance wherever possible; to reduce or offset the military strength of NATO by any means that offered; and to maintain a military capability at sufficient strength and readiness to ensure that any crisis in central Europe, up to and including full-scale warfare, could be managed to Soviet advantage.

Politically the years since the re-arming of West Germany (which had to be recognized as a major setback) had seen considerable improvements to the Soviet position. The departure of France from NATO was a great gain. The Vietnam War had been a useful distraction. There had been advantage in the existence of some movement in the United States towards a degree of disengagement in Europe; in the financial and economic difficulties of the United Kingdom, particularly where balance of payments and budgetary difficulties had combined to reduce troop deployments in continental Europe – and also, peripheralists might say, in the British withdrawal from the East; in the strong growth of left-wing elements in the politics of every one of the Atlantic Allies; in a general decline among Western democracies in public interest in defence; and in certain other developments. The pursuit of détente had been helpful to the Soviet interest, and negotiations on arms limitation and force reductions had brought small but useful gains.

A very highly classified planning document, given a strictly limited circulation in the Kremlin in October 1983, which fell into Allied hands after the fighting was over, throws a sufficiently clear light on Soviet policy in relation to NATO to justify the inclusion of a summary of it here.

Subject: *Removal of the threat from NATO to the security of the USSR in Europe.*

This could be achieved in the following way.

Rapid military defeat of AFCENT, with the simultaneous elimination of AFNORTH and AFSOUTH, followed by an advance to a voluntary stop-line: Hook of Holland–Nijmegen–Maastricht–Saarbrücken–Trier–the Rhine–Basel. The intention of the USSR to stop on this line without entering French territory will have been made abundantly clear worldwide. It is assumed that a government of the Popular Front will continue to be in power in France when the action takes place and that, in spite of not unimportant differences between France and the USSR, there will be sufficient reluctance on the part of the French to become involved in hostilities with the Soviet Union to ensure an adequate response to the pressures that can be brought to bear. It can therefore be expected, though of course not guaranteed, that French forces will not participate in these operations.

Once the FRG has been totally occupied its neutralization can be put in hand on the usual lines under accepted procedures. The complete collapse of the North Atlantic Alliance can be confidently expected to follow from its failure to prevent this from happening. Bilateral negotiations can then be opened with the USA. Other ex-allies can for the time being be ignored.

A firm decision to act along these lines will only be taken in the light of the prevailing situation and in relation to all other relevant developments, though complete military plans will be kept up to date for this contingency in itself. Nevertheless, certain factors bearing on choice of time should be kept in mind.

A resounding military victory over the West, followed by the dismantling of the FRG and the collapse of the Atlantic Alliance, will reinforce Soviet hegemony within the Warsaw Pact and weaken divergent national socialist movements outside it. Current tendencies suggest the advisability of achieving this fairly soon. It might be unwise to delay it beyond 1987.

NATO countries have recently initiated some improvements in 'defensive' preparedness. These are at present modest, but the maintenance of the same rate of expansion will in time set constraints on Soviet freedom of action. In five years' time the achievement of the military objective will be considerably more difficult.

Although it has been consistently and warmly denied in the West, we think there are plans to open offensive operations at some time against the Warsaw Pact with an attack on the German Democratic Republic. The Federal Republic is clearly having considerable difficulty in overcoming the reluctance of some of the Allies but might still succeed in staging an attack not later than 1986. The policy of 'forward defence' makes no sense from a military point of view unless it involves action well to the east of the frontier, and it can be taken as no more than a cloak for the planning of an invasion of the GDR, possibly already far advanced.*

China does not yet present the major military threat which can be certainly expected to develop later. NATO must be reduced before this. What requires urgent attention now, however, is the Chinese action, with powerful US support, to stimulate dissidence in the Asiatic republics. This is sharply on the increase. It would appear that unless the question of NATO can be resolved before the autumn of 1986 a deteriorating security situation in the Military Districts of Central Asia and the Far East, and possibly in those of Siberia and the Trans-Baikal as well, might offer distraction from Europe and considerable temptation to the FRG to exploit the position.

There would thus clearly be advantage in action to eliminate the FRG and ensure the collapse of the Atlantic Alliance not later than the summer of 1986. The course of events, particularly in the light of a possible requirement to intervene in Yugoslavia, may compel earlier action, and arrangements for mobilization will, of course, be kept under constant review.

The greatest relative advantage to the West, as NATO studies confirm, will be if the Warsaw Pact can spend

---

* It is probably unnecessary to say that at no time was there any planning in NATO for an invasion of the GDR. The suggestion had some propaganda value in the USSR, and among Soviet sympathizers abroad.

fourteen days in the mobilization process as against seven days for NATO. It should not be difficult to use summer exercises to conceal the first seven days. The utmost use will have to be made of deception arrangements, nevertheless, to indicate, once we are seen to be mobilizing for a possible attack, a date for it later than any that might be chosen.

In spite of some recent improvement in NATO's state of readiness, including arrangements to deploy two to four additional divisions in an emergency, further reinforcing formations cannot be expected to arrive in the European theatre, once hostilities have started, before D+16 at the earliest. Naval and air interdiction can be expected to reduce, but not entirely destroy, their effectiveness. It will be important to secure the stopline before the arrival of major reinforcements.

Even more important, in the matter of duration of operations, is the question of nuclear release. The USSR will make it clear beyond any possible doubt that use of radiation to any significant degree in offensive weapons of war will be regarded as an open invitation to discard all restraints on nuclear warfare. Escalation into strategic exchange, to use the Western mode of expression, will certainly follow battlefield applications.

There will unquestionably be doubts and hesitations in the Alliance over the initiation of nuclear release. Widespread unwillingness to allow the use of battlefield weapons on Federal territory can be counted on in the FRG, for the effect of battlefield weapons there would only differ in degree from that of strategic attack on the homelands of the USSR and USA. The USSR can count at the outset on a high superiority in non-nuclear capability. This would be largely offset if battlefield nuclear weapons were introduced. It would therefore be foolish in the extreme for the USSR to resolve NATO's doubts on their introduction by introducing them first.

The earlier that military operations in Europe can be

brought to a successful conclusion the lower will be the probability of the neutralization of Warsaw Pact conventional superiority by the arrival of major reinforcements or the introduction of nuclear weapons. The conclusion from a close study of all these considerations is that the stop-line should be reached not later than the evening of D+9. The military plan will be framed accordingly.

The essence of the military plan to implement this policy, which can now be recognized as of quite unique importance in the study of the Third World War, has been distilled from captured documents and is summarized below. It deserves careful consideration.

Invasion from a standing start from normal locations, though attractive, is for ground forces of the Warsaw Pact not practicable. Even with exercise cover, and with an excuse for military movement in the shape of real or imaginary internal security difficulties in satellite countries, it would not be possible to count on complete surprise. Some degree of precautionary preparation on the part of NATO would have to be counted on. This could be expected to include the flying-in of the personnel of certainly one heavy division from the United States to marry up with its pre-positioned equipment, and possibly of two, and the partial deployment to its emergency positions of much of AFCENT, including the Dutch and Belgian corps in NORTHAG and some of the entirely new II British Corps. It would also include the alerting of air defences. NORTHAG continues to offer the most attractive point of decisive entry, in spite of the lack of depth in the CENTAG sector, because of the inadequacy of reserves to fight the battle in depth which will inevitably develop in the NORTHAG sector. Forward deployment (adopted in the FRG for purely political reasons) has made a main thrust against NORTHAG particularly inviting.

The cover plan must firmly indicate a date for the opening of the offensive not earlier than D+9 or 10. The actual offensive on D-day will thus catch the defence not yet prepared for it.

On the night D−1 there would be widespread attacks by undercover forces (some 400 KGB-controlled cells are already deployed) on suitable targets in the FRG, stiffened by expendable Soviet airborne units. Shortly before first light on D-day airborne formations, making the best use of undercover forces, would seal Hamburg, make good Bremen airfield and seize crossings over the Weser; if possible, over the Rhine as well. The securing of Bremen airfield as an airhead would be indispensable. The success of other airborne operations would be a bonus.

Just before first light on D-day, and synchronized with the widest possible interference with US space reconnaissance satellites, an air operation of the very highest intensity, using both high explosive and chemical munitions, would be launched simultaneously against the Allied air force bases and control systems and the movement of AFCENT's land forces to their main defensive positions. When the full shock of this had taken its effect, and a favourable air situation had been achieved, the weight of air effort would be shifted to direct support of a general offensive along the entire AFCENT front, exploiting both normal mass-attack tactics and deep penetration action, the latter intended primarily to pre-empt NATO anti-tank suppressive action. In ground action chemical weapons would be employed at army commanders' discretion, with the emphasis on nerve gases, persistent or non-persistent. Airborne assaults on suitable targets, especially airfields, air defence sites, headquarters and obstacle crossings would continue. All ground force operations would have maximum tactical air support.

2 Guards Tank Army with two Polish divisions and some GDR troops would attack on the north of the

NORTHAG sector, 3 Shock Army in the south of the same sector, followed by 20 Guards Army, with two GDR divisions under command.

8 Guards Army would attack on the CENTAG front, objective Frankfurt, 1 Guards Tank Army further south, objective Nürnberg.

One Polish and two Soviet divisions would move northwards through Schleswig-Holstein into Denmark, supported as necessary. The main thrust into AFNORTH would be out of the Leningrad Military District through Kola in the first instance. The follow-up would be by rail through Finland. All effective resistance in AFNORTH should cease by D+6, though difficult country may delay the southward advance in Norway.

By first light on D+1 armoured columns in the north must reach the Dortmund-Ems Canal, making good all Weser crossings north of Minden soonest thereafter. In the CENTAG area Giessen must be secured, to develop an attack on the Frankfurt-Mainz complex, already under heavy pressure from the east.

Air-portable formations operating on the ground out of Bremen airhead should secure river crossings into Holland for rapid consolidation by following armour. Airborne troops will be used to extend the depth of the penetration in Holland. It is imperative to seize the Hilversum radio and television complex *intact* at the earliest opportunity. By D+2 resistance in Holland is expected to be minimal. All Holland is to be occupied as far south as the River Waal by D+6.

While strong pressure continues on CENTAG from the north-east and east, the main effort will now be in an offensive north to south along the west bank of the Rhine. This is expected to be decisive in the outflanking of CENTAG and destruction of AFCENT.

There must be maximum exploitation of refugee movement everywhere. Civilian casualties are wholly irrelevant and may even be advantageous. Towns and cities are to be bypassed wherever possible for subsequent attention.

Berlin will be contained. Its early capitulation can be counted on when AFCENT breaks.

Resistance can be expected to continue in difficult country, such as the Harz, Spessart, Schwarzwald and Thüringer Wald and the Bavarian high country. This can be masked and ignored. It is also likely to continue in Rhineland and Ruhr cities. Here it must be ruthlessly eliminated.

NORTHAG can be expected, when its forward defences have been penetrated, first of all to take up positions roughly east and west along the Teutoburger Wald, no doubt hoping to deny crossings across the Lower Rhine by a manoeuvre battle in depth. They will have insufficient troops for this, and there is no hope of their succeeding.

When the north–south offensive begins to develop NORTHAG can be expected to regroup, in an attempt to check it, on an east–west position west of the Rhine, between Bonn and Maastricht. No chances can be taken here. There will unquestionably be sufficient fresh Warsaw Pact formations and air resources to break through. At least three hitherto uncommitted divisions from 20 Guards Army will be available for a start. Success in this operation will lead to the rolling up of CENTAG from the rear and the collapse of the NATO defence of the Central Region.

This must be complete by D+7, at which time the only permissible pockets of continuing resistance (disregarding Berlin, if it has not yet been ordered to capitulate, and Hamburg) will be in the Bavarian Alps.

On D-Day three Soviet divisions, from Hungary and Czechoslovakia, will start moving through Austria into Italy. No Italian resistance is expected. This force may also, if necessary, furnish means of opening a flank attack on CENTAG through Bavaria.

It is to be assumed that political pressure on the

French government, with the guarantee that Warsaw Pact action will proceed no further than the stop-line, will cause France to refrain from hostile action and withdraw II French Corps from Germany.

The collapse of AFCENT (as well as the elimination of AFNORTH and AFSOUTH) will reduce Allied Command Europe to impotence and cause the disintegration of the Alliance. The United States will accept a ceasefire on or very soon after D+8, after which discussions can be initiated.

The neutralization of the Federal Republic of Germany, with the liquidation of hostile elements among the people and such population transfer as may be necessary, together with the dismantling of industrial plant for removal, or its destruction in situ, for all of which instructions have already been prepared, will proceed forthwith.

The plan for the invasion of the Central Region of NATO by the Warsaw Pact, of which this is a summary, assumed as a necessary condition a high degree of continuing control over the countries and peoples of Eastern Europe. This was quite likely to be threatened.

CHAPTER ELEVEN

OVER THE EDGE

I: Dispositions in CENTAG

By 2 August 1985 the four corps comprising the Central Army Group in the Central Region of Allied Command Europe were already in their forward position in the CENTAG sector. This ran from near Kassel in the north, at the junction with I Belgian Corps on the right of the Northern Army Group, to the Austrian frontier south of München.

The four corps of the Central Army Group lay from north to south as follows: III German, V US, VII US, II German.

II French Corps, stationed with some supporting army troops in south-west Germany, was still not under command to Allied Command Europe. It was not even certain how the French government, given its pronounced left-wing orientation in the recent past, would, in the event of hostilities with the Warsaw Pact, regard its obligations under the Atlantic Treaty. Relations between the French General Staff in Germany and CENTAG, however, were close and cordial, and communication between the two, though discreet, was fairly free.

At the end of July the personnel of an armoured division, the first of the divisions earmarked for US-AREUR, had been flown in from the United States. By nightfall on 2 August it had almost completed the drawing of its prepositioned combat equipment, including more than 300 XM-1 tanks. Some of its units, at least, had fired-in their guns at Grafenwöhr before dispersal in the area north-west of Würzburg, under command to V US Corps.

It was V US Corps' sector, running north and south

through Fulda, which was considered critical in CENTAG. The Demarcation Line with the East bulges out here in a bold westward curve towards the bend in the Rhine near Frankfurt-am-Main, at its closest no further from Frankfurt than 100 kilometres, with only another forty kilometres to the Rhine. Furthermore, in the hill country of the Thüringer Wald there is an important gap around Fulda itself, with the terrain becoming ever more readily negotiable as it opens down into the Rhine-Main plain. The distances are all short here. There is not much ground to trade for time and little opportunity for mobile operations.

The area forward of the Fulda valley favoured the defence, offering ample choice of good positions for tanks and ATGW, with considerable depth to their fields of fire. Unfortunately the distance from the Fulda valley to the frontier is no more than fifteen kilometres.

Behind the Fulda valley to the west is the high mass of the Vogelsberg, to the north the wooded country along the autobahn through Bad Hersfeld to Kassel, to the south the inhospitable terrain of the Hohe Rhon. As a good example of the course of events in a critical sector we shall be giving considerable attention to the action of V US Corps. Its commander's mission was simple: to keep the Soviet forces east of the Frankfurt plain and as close to the border as possible.

Lieutenant General Harold J. Selby, Commanding General of V US Corps, was an old hand. Just too young for service in the Second World War, he had got into the Korean campaign right at the end. Later on he had seen plenty of service in armoured cavalry in Vietnam. His total of seven years' service in Germany had included, besides a tour on the operations staff in HQ AFCENT, command of a regiment and of a division before he was given the command of V Corps in 1983.

Each of his two original US divisions had been increased in strength to 15,000 men with over 300 tanks each and nearly 500 ATGW. In addition to the armoured cavalry regiment deployed along the border in the corps sector there was a further squadron of armoured cavalry in each division. Besides the self-propelled 155 mm and 8-in divisional artillery, each division also had an additional artillery group and nearly fifty anti-tank helicopters. His third division, newly arrived in Germany but containing many officers and men with previous experience in the theatre, was at lower strength and had not yet shaken down, but it was by no means without promise.

The two forward divisions knew their areas well. Each was so disposed as to take care of one of the two most likely axes of attack – to the north of the Vogelsberg through Bad Hersfeld and Alsfeld into the plain north of Frankfurt, and south of the Vogelsberg through Fulda and down the Kinzig river valley through Hanau towards Frankfurt. The corps commander expected action on both axes but was convinced that one or the other would be chosen for the main effort. He knew that his overriding task was to establish the direction of the main thrust before the smaller force opposing it was overwhelmed.

Intelligence here was critical. Since his arrival in the corps the Commander had made a minutely detailed study of the terrain and planned a very thorough intelligence operation covering every approach. What he could not cover with his own sensors he asked to have covered for him by CENTAG. To help him find out what he wanted he relied on the reconnaissance, surveillance and intelligence resources available at every level of responsibility, from intelligent young men with binoculars and a radio in a hole on a hill far forward to the input from highly sophisticated satellite systems in space. The Joint Tactical Information Distribution System (JTIDS) had been designed to handle a vast volume of intelligence material coming in from sources as varied as satellite systems, reconnaissance vehicles, both manned and unmanned, ELINT (electronic intelligence), SIGINT (signal intelligence) and battlefield surveillance of all kinds, and to funnel it all into processing centres for analysis, correlation, assessment and distribution. The corps commander, however, was too old a hand to place exclusive reliance on processes not within his total control and on systems vulnerable to counter-measures. His principal instrument for the assessment of the enemy's intentions was to be the strong engagement he intended to fight in the covering force area up against the border, forward of the Hanau and Fulda rivers. His final judgment, which, like all fighting soldiers, he knew must in the last resort be purely intuitive, whatever aids he had, would depend on his interpretation of that action.

The armoured cavalry regiment on the border was a powerful brigade-sized armoured force in its own right, basically of light tanks, now reinforced by a medium tank battalion and a mechanized infantry battalion, together with self-propelled artillery and attack helicopters. Commanders in the covering force had been ordered to destroy leading elements in engagements which should either be opened at extreme range or be held down to very short-range ambush; to force the enemy to commit strong reserves and deploy his artillery; and to give no ground at all except to avoid the imminent certainty of encirclement and total destruction. Small armoured task forces had reconnoitred and in many cases prepared some hundreds of excellent battle positions before the battle began. The Commander was entirely convinced that in the action of the covering forces lay the whole key to success in his main battle. If this action was conducted as he intended, it would in his view both identify the main thrust and give him a little time to organize his response to it. At the same time it would slow down the Soviet surge just enough to cast doubt on the invincibility of the total armoured offensive. This, he thought, could pay a big dividend.

The course of events was to suggest that he was right.

II: The View from Rheindahlen

The G3 (General Staff – Operations) Duty Officer in Headquarters, Northern Army Group, still in its peacetime location at Rheindahlen in northern Germany, finished entering in his log the routine call at the half hour to AFCENT, while his two juniors in other corners of the map room were already putting together material for the next, and turned again to the letter to his wife. It was just after three o'clock on the morning of the first Sunday in August 1985. The night had been warm and thundery; a brief rainstorm about midnight had done little to freshen it.

There had not been much to report to AFCENT. Most of what was important had gone earlier in the night – reports on the army group's state of readiness, the dispositions at last light of its five component corps,* tank and gun states, arrival of reserve units and of reinforcement personnel, the intelligence SITREP, and so on.

The general alert ordered in Allied Command Europe on the news of the airborne invasion of Yugoslavia and the follow-up by two Soviet motor-rifle divisions out of Hungary, resulting in an almost immediate clash with US marines, had done curiously little to change things in the Central Region. Events had been moving towards a general alert for some days, though the weight of evidence suggested that an attack by the Pact in the Central Region, if it ever came off, would be most unlikely before the beginning of September and scarcely possible much before mid-August.

A good deal of intelligence material had been coming into the Ops room during the night from the 'I' staff of the British Army of the Rhine (whose C-in-C was also Commander Northern Army Group) but not a lot of it was new. Reports continued, of a sort that had now grown

*I Belgian, I German and I Netherlands Corps and I and II British. The last, formed largely from reserve units during the previous year, had been deployed for the first time in Germany a month earlier.

familiar, of preparations in clandestine cells (of which some hundreds were known to exist) for strikes at military and civil communication centres and at other key points throughout the Federal Republic, and for the giving of help to Soviet parachutists coming in on Rhine and Weser bridges. There was the usual wild disagreement on target date and wide discrepancy in detail.

What had not been in doubt for several weeks now, even since before the Yugoslav crisis, was that if the 'exercises' of the Group of Soviet Forces in Germany, now in progress on a scale far larger than any yet seen, were not in fact a full mobilization for war they were a very passable substitute for it. There had been the usual notification through the head of the Soviet Military Mission to C-in-C BAOR (NORTHAG, as a NATO command, was not recognized by the Russians) of the intention to hold manoeuvres, and of the area in the GDR that would be closed, but the areas were of quite unusual size and the exercises were to be of exceptional duration. It was explained by the Soviet Mission that these were 'readiness exercises', normal, but gone through only at long intervals.

The crisis in Yugoslavia and the Soviet intervention there, though neither could be described as entirely unexpected, now threw a clearer light on events. To bring the whole Warsaw Pact gently and unobtrusively, as far as this was possible, to a war footing before an initiative in Yugoslavia (now seen to have been planned some time before) made very good sense. The response of the West to a Soviet attempt to force a disintegrating Yugoslavia back into the system might not be easy to predict, but it was unlikely to be accepted as tamely as the subjugation of Czechoslovakia seventeen years before. Of all the possible reactions, an invasion of the Warsaw Pact by NATO could hardly be seen as likely, however useful the possibility of it might be to the USSR for propaganda purposes. It would be important, all the same, for the forces of the Pact to be fully prepared, whether for defensive action against a Western attack or for the more likely contingency of a pre-emptive offensive.

It was in June that the rumours reaching Western intelligence of increasing activity among undercover left-wing groups in the FRG began to receive some confirmation from more trustworthy sources. It was clear that plans existed for sabotage on a considerable scale, and even for operations that made little sense unless they were to be supported by military action from the other side.

In early July the evidence began to harden. An action date some time in mid-September was being indicated. But though it was still doubtful whether much could be achieved by sabotage cells acting on their own, there was still no firm indication that a major initiative by Soviet armed forces was intended, the 'readiness exercise' notwithstanding.

The Federal Republic of Germany was not unnaturally the first major Allied power to take the aggregate of these reports really seriously, considered in the context not only of current military activity in the Warsaw Pact but also of the confused and threatening situation in Yugoslavia. The United States began to do so at about the same time, and so did Belgium.

The United Kingdom was rather harder to persuade. There had been no alert for several years – not, in fact, since Tito's departure from the scene – and the British did not entirely believe what they were being told, largely because they did not want to. The false *détente* had had its effect. Enough had recently been done within the Alliance, it was generally thought, to prevent the Russians trying anything on. Whatever modification there had been of recent years in British public opinion, the habit of self-deception, persistent for so many years in Britain, was clearly hard to shake off.

The Dutch were even more reluctant to believe anything so uncomfortable. The Norwegians and Danes flatly rejected the evidence, while the French, still members of the Atlantic Alliance though not, of course, of NATO and now under a government of the Popular Front, kept their own counsel.

Troop movement by the GSFG (Group of Soviet Forces in Germany) into the designated manoeuvre area began in a spell of good summer weather in the first week of July. Information coming out of East Germany to the West was, as usual, plentiful, and it soon became apparent that these exercises were going to be conducted on a very massive scale indeed – much larger, even, than had been expected. The Red Army and Air Force certainly seemed to be playing it, as the saying goes, for real. Ammunition, fuel and warlike stores were being moved up in actual tonnages. At the same time, in the Soviet Union itself, the arrangements for recall of reservists seemed to be getting a complete work-out and the men were joining their units. The same thing appeared to be happening in all the Warsaw Pact countries.

It was the *New York Times* that first aroused really widespread misgiving in the West by reporting that what was going on in the Warsaw Pact looked mighty like a mobilization. Two days later the *Frankfürter Allgemeine* came out bluntly with the statement that that was just what it was. On the same day a journalist regarded by some as the bane of Whitehall and by others as its only hope, a man called Jardine Snatcher, told the world under banner headlines that he was defying D-notices to let it be known that the British Chiefs of Staff had exercised their constitutional right of access to the Prime Minister in order to call on Mrs Plumber in No. 10 Downing Street and tell her precisely that.

Meanwhile, outside Europe, disquieting developments, referred to elsewhere in this book, were causing increasing concern throughout the Western world – above all, not unnaturally, in Washington. Relations between the United States and the communist bloc in the Caribbean were more than usually strained and getting worse. Events in Southern Africa and the Middle East seemed to be moving towards not one crisis but several. In all three areas Soviet

activity was open, marked and increasing. One-third of
the Soviet submarine fleet was known to be at sea. Units
of it, with support vessels, had been reported not only off
Cuba and Jamaica but also at Alexandria and in North
African waters, as well as off Malta and in the Arabian
Gulf. Units of the Black Sea Fleet were known to have
been moving in some numbers through the Straits into the
Mediterranean. What was no less significant was that
Soviet combat aircraft were widely deployed in the Caribbean, as also in Libya, Malta, East Africa and Syria, while
there was much movement of transport aircraft.

In the USSR the harvest was expected to be even more
disastrous than those of the previous two years and critical
foodstuffs were known to be scarce. The measures which,
in the recent past, had produced waves of unrest in Poland
and Romania and even in parts of the Soviet Union itself
– in the Ukraine, for example, and in Georgia – were likely
to be repeated. Yugoslavia, meanwhile, was on the brink
of civil war.

Kremlin-watchers were pointing out the propitious
opportunities for Soviet Exploitation that were opening
up in many different places at once. They were also adding
gloomily that if ever there was a time when the Soviet
Union needed foreign adventure as a distraction from
domestic discontent this was probably it. Of the two prime
potential adversaries, moreover, China was not yet ready
for a major military enterprise and NATO, though something had been done in the past few years to remedy some
of its better known defects, had still not recovered from
more than a decade of neglect. Kremlin-watchers had said
all that, of course, before. One thing at least was clear:
time was not on the side of the Soviet Union.

Looking back on events, it became clear to Western
observers later that, with the less noticeable preliminaries
embarked on a good deal earlier, full mobilization in the
Warsaw Pact had begun on or about 14 July. Though no
public announcement had been made in Moscow the
indicators were enough for the Secretary of State to advise

President Thompson on 18 July that Soviet mobilization must now be accepted as a fact. The same advice was given to heads of government in all member states of the Alliance at about the same time. In the three major partner countries in NATO, the United States, the United Kingdom and the Federal Republic of Germany, defence chiefs urged mobilization at once. Only in the Federal Republic was there immediate agreement.

The President of the United States, terribly aware of his unique responsibilities, was reluctant to raise the temperature. He got through on the hot-line to the head of government in the USSR (with some delay – it was several hours before the Soviet President could be brought to the instrument) to make emphatic remonstrance and to urge the cancellation of all further warlike preparations. Surprise was expressed in response to such concern. What was happening in the GDR was only an exercise, of which appropriate notice had been given. Practice mobilizations – carried out only rarely because of the cost – were indispensable to the efficiency of armed forces. When this one was over it would not need to be repeated for a long time. It was hoped that the President of the United States would not encourage panic reaction. The best service to the cause of world peace would be to quieten the manic howls of fascist revanchists in West Germany. These were increasing daily and causing growing concern in the USSR.

Under mounting pressure from the National Security Council and the Joint Chiefs of Staff, and with clear indications that public opinion was moving strongly in favour of mobilization, the President gave the order on 21 July. The Federal Republic had begun its own mobilization the day before. The United Kingdom did not follow until the 23rd, and even then with some reluctance. It was not at first clear whether the trade unions – no longer the dominant force in the governance of Britain they had been in the seventies, but still powerful – would co-operate. There was the expected chorus of left-wing disapproval; a good deal of hard bargaining and wheedling was needed before the go-ahead could be given. Even then only a modified form of mobilization was ordered in the first instance. Parliament, hastily recalled from recess, quickly passed a short enabling Act to make possible certain preparations (such as the embodiment of voluntary reserves) constitutionally dependent on full mobilization. The reserves began to be called up.

Following an emergency meeting of the NATO Council, mobilization in every other member state of the organization was ordered at about the same time. It had long been a structural flaw in NATO, becoming increasingly apparent in the seventies, that there was no general agreement on the timing of response to alert measures by individual governments. Each retained a high, if varying, degree of discretion. It was fortunate that there was now too little cause for doubt to permit procrastination.

The position of France was uncertain. Though still a signatory to the North Atlantic Treaty she had not been for some twenty years a member of the military organization. Her Popular Front government was unlikely to welcome the possibility of hostilities with the Soviet Union. SACEUR (Supreme Allied Commander Europe) tried in vain to discover what orders would be given, in the event of hostilities, to II French Corps in south-west Germany. At least, with reservists being recalled in France, deficiencies in personnel and equipment were being made good here, as they were elsewhere, while the relations between the French command and staff in Germany on the one hand and CENTAG on the other continued to be close. Elsewhere, Switzerland, Sweden and Austria were also recalling reservists and bringing their forces to a higher state of readiness.

Almost as difficult for the Americans and British, and for the Canadians too, as the decision to mobilize was the question of whether to order the repatriation of dependants of service personnel in Germany, and other civilian nationals, and, if this was to be done, when to do it. This had always been seen as a critical indicator of whether hostilities were expected. London and Washington both gave forty-eight hours' notice of evacuation on 23 July. Movement of civilian nationals began on the 25th – in part directly by air to their home countries, in part by road, in the first instance to staging areas, in Holland for the British and in Belgium for the Americans and Canadians. Evacuation was everywhere complete by the 30th.

Meanwhile, throughout the whole European theatre NATO formations were on the move to their operational positions. The headquarters at their different levels – of CENTAG with its American commander at Heidelberg, of NORTHAG under British command at Rheindahlen, of AFCENT with its German commanding general at Brunssum in Holland, and of SHAPE (Supreme Headquarters Allied Powers in Europe), with its American Supreme Commander (SACEUR) and his British and German deputies, itself at Mons in Belgium – were all due to move to war locations, with staggered timings, in the next few days. Advance parties had manned these locations already and tested communications.

Main headquarters were still in their peacetime locations only because of the exceptionally heavy administrative load in the build-up period. This was a great burden on communications and staff alike, and was best handled through permanent signal channels, with normal staff accommodation and office facilities. There was still thought to be time, if not a great deal. D-day, if the Russians really meant business, was not expected before the second half of August at the earliest.

The Allied air forces were, of course, able to respond quickly by the very nature of their medium. The increasing period of tension and general mobilization had given ample time for the Central Region air forces to assume a full war posture. They had had years of experience under the stringent conditions of SACEUR's periodic tactical evaluation tests. These tests, called at no notice in peacetime, required the bases to go to a full war footing as if under threat of conventional and chemical attack. The time taken to raise the whole force to a full combat state was monitored and evaluated by an independent team of inspectors. What they had to do now was therefore well rehearsed and would be carried out to a less demanding timescale. From their war headquarters the commanders of 2 and 4 Allied Tactical Air Forces had been monitoring, with not a little satisfaction, the progress as the bases told-in their generation rate of combat-ready aircraft and the tote boards on the walls steadily filled.

By midnight 3 August 90 per cent of the aircraft of Allied Air Forces Central Europe were serviceable, armed, and protected in hardened shelters. During the last week reactivated UK bases and US airfields in 4 ATAF had been receiving a continuous stream of reinforcement aircraft which had been flown across the Atlantic, usually refuelling in the air. So far, very good; but General Donkin, the Commander Allied Air Forces Central Europe, had much to ponder.

He was well satisfied with the success of the aircraft generation and the reinforcements – but then he had expected all that to go well because it had so often been rehearsed in peacetime exercises and training. His mind was now turned to the adverse factor which had always existed in the military balance: namely that when at full war strength the numerical advantage still favoured the Warsaw Pact in the ratio of approximately 2:1. Tactical surprise had been sacrificed by the Warsaw Pact it was true, but they would nevertheless enjoy the initiative in calling the first shots. Furthermore, SACEUR had ordained that 20 per cent of the nuclear-capable aircraft must be held back and preserved for the time when nuclear strike operations might be necessary. The Air Commander was sanguine about the superiority of his airmen, aircraft and weapons. He knew they would give the highest account of themselves if called to battle. But the uncertain factor, and the critical one, was what the losses would be and whether there would be the numbers left after several days' fighting to hold the line until the ground forces were reinforced and able to take on the full brunt of the land battle.

Out of the window of the Joint Headquarters building housing HQ NORTHAG and HQ 2 ATAF, which also held HQ BAOR and HQ RAF Germany, both soon to run down and become base organizations, the Duty Officer looked down into the brightly lit forecourt. Blackouts, such an important feature of the Second World War in the defence of large and important targets, had little significance in an age of precision-guided weapons.

Long lines of vehicles stood partially loaded in readiness for the move to the operational location the following night. The Duty Officer watched a Dutch sentry moving slowly down one of the lines. His hair was rather long, the Duty Officer observed, even for a Dutch soldier.

It was only a month or two ago that a parade had been held here to celebrate the thirtieth year of use of these admirably designed buildings, built, like the agreeably laid-out cantonment around them, out of Occupation Costs not long after the Second World War. The comfortable married quarter in which the Duty Officer was now living by himself stood among trees already well grown.

He had sent off the rest of the family's belongings the day before, to where his wife was staying in her mother's house in Surrey. They would be thinking about the eldest girl's eighth birthday, only a week away, for which, as a special treat, she was to be taken to London to see *The Mousetrap*. He had been taken to see it on his own eighth birthday. Later on in the day he would be sleeping in the strangely empty married quarter for the last time, before moving out to join up with the headquarters in its operational location. He knew those caves only too well from exercises and had always disliked them.

He picked up his pen to go on with his letter, first filling in the date he had left out before. It was 4 August. There were signs in the sky of a new day.

The telephone rang.

He answered it and heard the familiar voice of the British Liaison Officer at I German Corps.

It was urgent and agitated.

'Parachutists!' it said, 'Russian parachutists on . . .'

The voice abruptly died.

Several direct-line telephones were jangling in the Ops room at once. He heard shouts in the building. There were shots outside, the noise of helicopter rotors, a violent explosion.

He threw the switch of the alarm system and unhooked the direct line to AFCENT and in that moment looked up.

A Russian soldier was standing in the doorway.

The Duty Officer was getting to his feet and reaching for the pistol lying by the gas respirator on the table before him when the Russian shot him dead.*

---

*It has been possible to put together the account here given of the personal experience of the G3 Duty Officer, who was one of the earlier fatal casualties of the fighting in Germany, on the basis of evidence of others present in the Ops room at the time, and the preservation of the officer's letter to his wife. This story is told by one of the present writers. who was a close friend

CHAPTER TWELVE

NATO FORCES

The structure and strength of the forces of the North Atlantic Treaty Organization, as they stood against those of the Warsaw Pact in the summer of 1985, must now be examined.

Attempts on the part of the Atlantic Council to prescribe to Allied governments, in the early days of the Alliance, what force goals they should meet had long been abandoned. Member states had always, in fact, put up no more than what they thought they could afford, usually claiming in self-justification that nothing more was necessary.

In actual structure NATO was still in 1985 much as it had been for the past twenty years. Except for some adjustment in the matter of naval and tactical air command (to which detailed reference is made in Appendix 3 and on pp. 143–5 respectively) there had been little change.

At the head of the Alliance of the fifteen signatory states stood the North Atlantic Council, meeting at ministerial level in normal times at least twice a year but with permanent representatives at ambassador level meeting constantly. The senior military authority in the North Atlantic Treaty Organization, the peacetime military structure which was such an important and unusual feature of the Alliance, was the Military Committee, composed of an independent chairman and a Chief of Staff of each Allied country except France, which had withdrawn from it in 1966, Iceland, which had no forces, and Luxembourg, which was represented by Belgium. The Military Committee was in permanent session with its own military staff. There were two Supreme Allied Commanders, SACEUR for Europe and SACLANT for the Atlantic, both American, and the Cs-in-C of the Joint Allied Command Western Approaches (JACWA) who were British. Under SACEUR were three regional commands: the northern, AFNORTH, with a British Commander-in-Chief; the central, AFCENT, under a French C-in-C until France's withdrawal from the integrated military organization in 1966 and thereafter under a German; and the southern, AFSOUTH, under an American admiral.

In peacetime there were under AFNORTH, which took in Schleswig-Holstein, Denmark and Norway, the assigned forces of Norway and Denmark and one German division. There were plans for reinforcements from the UK, Canada and elsewhere, if they could be got there in time, in an emergency.

Under AFCENT were the Northern and Central Army Groups, NORTHAG and CENTAG, the first under a British, the second under an American, commander. Also under AFCENT was AIRCENT, which provided centralized control of the two Allied air forces supporting NORTHAG and CENTAG.

Under AFSOUTH, commanded by a US admiral, came the assigned Italian and Turkish forces (and, as long as she remained a member, the forces of Greece) with the US Sixth Fleet in the Mediterranean also earmarked, though not assigned. There was an overall air command (AIRSOUTH) but two subordinate naval commands and separate commands for ground defence in Italy, under an Italian general, and, in the south-eastern part of the area, including Turkey, under an American.

In spite of the great importance of the flanks the critical area of NATO on land was clearly the Central Region, covering the Federal Republic of Germany up to (but excluding) Schleswig-Holstein and the Federal frontier with the Low Countries. It was in the Central Region that NATO's greatest concentration of ground and tactical air forces was gathered, facing those of the Warsaw Pact across the Demarcation Line which separated West and

East Germany, then followed the Czechoslovak frontier down to neutral Austria on the south-eastern flank.

All the regular forces of the Federal Republic (organized in three corps and twelve divisions, with sixteen armoured and fifteen armoured infantry, two mountain and three airborne brigades) were assigned to NATO in peacetime. The six Territorial Army brigade-sized groups established for Home Defence were not, until a lengthy argument came to an end in 1985; then these too, with the three Territorial Commands of five Military Districts, came under SACEUR. They were to play an important part in the war, though they could have been even more effectively used if they had come under Allied command rather earlier. Two German corps (II German and III German) were under command to CENTAG, the other (I German) to NORTHAG. About half the Federal German Army (the *Bundeswehr*) of some 350,000 were conscripts on a fifteen-month term of service.

Germany had, however, paid considerable attention to the problems of mobilization and of making reinforcements speedily effective. In the mid-1970s a Standby Reserve had been created, which the Defence Minister could call up in emergency without prior recourse to Parliament, and plans had been made for a number of cadre formations to be quickly expanded to war strength. The Territorial Army of about half a million men not only provided the Territorial Commands referred to above, but also defensive, support and communications units throughout the country, relieving the regular forces of all but the forward tasks. The training of reserves was reasonably good, taking advantage of the local and professional knowledge possessed by reservists and of the fact that the more difficult combat posts requiring highly skilled men could be filled by regular personnel, with reservists to assist them. Equipment was also good. Over half the *Bundeswehr*'s tanks were the new *Leopard* II with Chobham-type armour, giving much better protection against ATGW, and the advanced, smooth-bore, 120 mm

gun. New ATGW were issued widely, to the Territorial
Army as well as to regular forces. Artillery was modernized, and included new US SP (self-propelled) guns and
the FH–70 medium gun jointly developed with Britain and
Italy, thus providing for largely standardized ammunition.
Helicopters provided ATGW support and battlefield mobility. New multiple rocket launchers enabled minelets to be
sown in the face of advancing enemy tanks. All in all, the
Bundeswehr was a well-found force, with the advantage of
being on its own ground and highly motivated to defend
its own homes.

The United States Army in Europe numbered some
200,000 men, all but 10,000 of these in the US Seventh
Army in Germany, whose C-in-C was also COMCENT-
AG. The reintroduction of the draft in the United States,
to which reference is made elsewhere (see Chapter 14),
had by 1985 rescued the US Army from a highly dangerous
position in relation to reserve manpower. If we do not
count the Berlin Brigade the US Seventh Army was
organized in two corps, V US and VII US. The four
divisions and three additional brigades on station in the
late seventies had been augmented by two more brigades,
upon each of which the balance of a complete division
could be built up in an emergency. The tank strength
available to US forces in the Central Region (including
tanks in the stockpile) approached 3,000, of which the
greater part was by early 1985 the new XM–1, a remarkable
tank, with a low silhouette, Chobham armour and advanced
new armour-piercing ammunition.

As early as 1978 the United States had taken steps to
build up its air reinforcement capacity, so that by 1983 five
divisions (two to be built on the brigades mentioned
above) could be airlifted to Europe within ten days, to
join up there with their already stockpiled equipment.
Plans were put into operation at about that time to
disperse stockpiles, so as to reduce their vulnerability and
make ammunition and other stores more quickly available
to forward troops.

The XM–1 was typical of the advanced equipment that began to reach the US troops in Germany in the late seventies and early eighties. At the same time new ATGW began to come into service, including 'fire and forget' missiles, with fully automatic terminal guidance, for use from helicopters. The US Army had always laid great emphasis on the use of helicopters, which fulfilled a variety of roles, not least the provision of battlefield mobility. Artillery had been strengthened by the introduction (if only in small numbers) of the cannon-launched guided projectile (CLGP), which gave it a real anti-tank capacity. To the greatly increased firepower were added improvements in target acquisition through the use of RPV (remotely-piloted vehicles) giving instantaneous information. Close air support, with the emphasis on anti-tank action, was much improved with the deployment of the A–10, which began in 1978. The equipment of other tactical aircraft with PGM (precision-guided missiles) gave a much enhanced stand-off capability against land targets. Finally, the air defence of troops in the field was steadily thickened with the introduction of new SAM (surface-to-air missiles) and automatic guns.

The British forces assigned to NATO and stationed in Germany were embodied in the British Army of the Rhine, whose C-in-C was also COMNORTHAG. Excluding the 3,000-strong force in Berlin, they numbered 52,000 at full peacetime strength and were now organized in four armoured and one artillery division with an additional brigade-sized formation (5 Field Force), all under I British Corps. Earmarked for deployment from the UK in an emergency was the newly formed II British Corps, adding another 30,000 men.* Main battle tanks, including those in stockpile, now numbered 1,000, all *Chieftain* with the improved engine, though not all with Chobham armour.

Other equipment, though initially introduced very slowly, enabled most major weapons to be modernized by the early 1980s. ATGW, built jointly with France and

* II Br Corps was moved to Germany in July 1985.

Germany, spread throughout the regular and TAVR forces of the UK after a rather hesitant beginning. At long last the air defences of British troops in the field became as good as those of the *Bundeswehr* and US forces in Europe. Improved reinforcement arrangements, made possible by the increase in the availability of equipment and reserves, gave commanders the additional advantage of being able to replace battle casualties quickly. With the new equipment and new organizations and tactics to match, morale in the British Army of the Rhine, not at its highest in the 1970s, was now fully restored.

Of the Dutch forces in the Northern Army Group (I Ne Corps) only one armoured brigade and one tank and one reconnaissance battalion were located in Germany, the rest being held back in Holland. Of the 75,000 men which constituted the whole strength of the Dutch Army, more than half (43,000) were conscripts, doing no more than fourteen months' service. It had long been hoped in NATO that the Netherlands would be persuaded to station more of its assigned forces further forward, nearer to their emergency defence positions. The international tensions of late 1984 succeeded where previous arguments had failed and, though the false *détente* of the following spring tended to put the movement into reverse, the centre of gravity in the deployment of I Netherlands Corps in the summer of 1985 was further forward than it had ever been before.

The position of the Belgians was not dissimilar, though the conscripted element in the army (23,000 out of 62,000) did only eight months' service if posted to the Federal Republic of Germany, where there were stationed in peacetime one corps and two divisional headquarters, with one armoured and two infantry brigades, as opposed to ten months if serving in Belgium. I Belgian (I Be) Corps, with some 300 *Leopard* I tanks, like I Netherlands Corps, with some 450, was under command to NORTH-AG. Both corps had received a good deal of new equipment, notably APC, ATGW and air defence weapons.

In both cases, however, the supply of new weapons to the reserve formations and battalions that would reinforce them was limited, as was the training carried out by reservists.

In addition to the major national formations Allied Command Europe also included the Canadian Brigade Group which had become by late July the equivalent almost of a small division.* An all-regular force, its quality was high. Old hands in other Allied countries (particularly among the British), who recalled their experience with Canadian troops in the last world war, saw with satisfaction that in their technical skills and their robust and disciplined approach they were, in the changed circumstances of today, as good as ever. The Group was stationed in the CENTAG area, not far from the French divisions.

Though France had not been a member of NATO since 1966 II French Corps, of two divisions, with corps and some army troops nearly 50,000 strong, continued to be stationed in Germany, with close military liaison with CENTAG. Three mechanized divisions in France formed the balance of the First French Army, to which the French divisions in Germany belonged. The equipment of the five divisions in the First French Army was modern and good and included battlefield nuclear weapons held inside France, under French control. Little of the equipment was standardized with NATO however, raising potential problems in supply. In addition to the *Forces de Manoeuvre*, of which the First French Army was part, France disposed of Territorial Defence Forces (*Défense Operationelle du Territoire*, or DOT) some 50,000 strong. These had a very important role, among others, in the defence of key points in metropolitan France against disruption by sabotage and against civil disorder.

On the southern flank, Italy (twelve months' service for 120,000 conscripts in an army of 218,000) disposed of

* Armoured infantry, 3,500 strong, together with a regiment of sixty tanks, an artillery regiment of 155 mm SP howitzers, anti-tank and anti-air missiles, support troops and a tactical helicopter squadron.

twelve divisions (three armoured) with a mixed inventory of tanks. Though Greece's membership of the integrated military organization had been somewhat conditional since 1974, she continued to have some military links and had modernized most of her mainly conscript army (28–30 months' service) of twelve divisions (one armoured), largely with French equipment, and, it must be admitted, with an eye on Turkey rather than the forces of the Warsaw Pact. Turkey (twenty months' service) could field twenty-two divisions (one armoured and two mechanized) in an army of 375,000. Differences between Greece and Turkey over Cyprus, sharpened by competition for Aegean oil, had by the beginning of the eighties grown somewhat less than in the years before. The curtailment of military aid from the US to which this had given rise (it was resumed in 1982) had inevitably reduced the war-fighting capability of both countries, though this had latterly begun once more to improve. Turkish equipment was generally somewhat elderly and in an indifferent state; mobility was limited and it had not been possible to reach a high level of training.

To this brief account of NATO ground forces must of course be added something of how the tactical air forces stood, since in any battle their operations would be indivisible. Here not only the aircraft stationed alongside the ground forces have to be reckoned with, but also those that could operate in a given sector from immediately outside it, as, for example, from the United Kingdom or the western Soviet Union, or from aircraft carriers that might be in the vicinity, or – though this applied more to Soviet forces – medium bombers that could be flown from relatively distant airfields.

An accurate tally of air strength is therefore not easy, because of its inherent flexibility, but, taking ground-based fighter aircraft as the main yardstick, NATO deployed for operations in the critical central sector – excluding French forces – some 2,800 aircraft, compared with approximately 4,500 deployed by the Warsaw Pact. This numerical disparity had long presented a problem and still did. It was a problem compounded by the relative ease of reinforcement enjoyed by the Warsaw Pact, by an insufficiency of forward airfields on the Allied side, and by some difficulties in inter-operability, caused by the variety of different aircraft in use in NATO air forces.

There had, however, been a marked all-round improvement in NATO tactical air strength in the previous few years. Several first-class new aircraft had been introduced, embodying the most up-to-date technology. For the air superiority role the American F–15 was better than any other fighter, both in its performance and in its armament. It was admirably complemented by the lighter F–16. Both were greatly assisted in their task by the ability of AWACS (airborne warning and control system), belatedly introduced in the 1970s, to detect intruding aircraft and control the operation of our own. For strike missions the *Tornado*, with its ultra-low flying capability, presented the Warsaw Pact with severe problems, as did the *Jaguar* and the smaller *AlphaJet* and *Hawk* ground-attack fighters. The adoption of increasing numbers of aircraft developed and built in co-operation by two or more allies was beginning to give more flexibility to NATO air operations, with a higher degree of inter-operability.

The quality of the new aircraft was more than matched by the weapon systems they carried, tailored to what were seen to be the essential tasks of stopping the Soviet tanks and cutting off the flow of immediate reinforcements to the battle area. Precision-guided weapons, cluster munitions and the all-important electronic aids were given great emphasis.

The decision by the United Kingdom to provide once more a proper defence of its own airspace, described in detail in Chapter 19, helped the tactical air forces to solve two of the problems mentioned above: first, it provided protected airfields that enabled aircraft to be diverted to as well as based in the United Kingdom, thus easing the operational difficulties posed by an insufficiency of airfields; second, it enabled reinforcement by fighter squadrons from the United States to be carried out more safely, taking advantage of the steps that the United States had put in train to make her large reserves of aircraft rapidly available.

The Soviet Air Force had, of course, been increasing its own ground-attack and deep strike and interdiction capability for some years, which posed severe air defence problems for the NATO forces, ground and air. Furthermore, the Soviet Union's own dense air defence made the task of NATO aircraft much more difficult. Despite this, NATO air commanders had some confidence that the quality and versatility of their aircraft, the edge that their weapon systems and electronic warfare capability gave them, and the higher training standards of NATO airmen, would all go a long way to redress the numerical imbalance with which they had to contend.

A very important change in the command structure of NATO air forces had been the setting up, under the Central Region, of a Commander Allied Air Force Central Europe (COMAAFCE) in 1976. This greatly increased the flexibility of the Allied air forces and enormously enhanced their effectiveness.

It was technology, however, that was the principal key to the marked improvements made to NATO forces in the late 1970s and early 1980s. Weapons systems were now more effective and more versatile than they had ever been and tactical concepts and organizations had been improved to make the best use of them.

When the new NATO strategy of 'flexible response', introduced in the middle to late 1960s, was first discussed, it signalled the wish by the United States, in the face of her own increased strategic nuclear vulnerability, to have more defence options in Europe than an early recourse to the use of nuclear weapons. Her European allies were initially reluctant to downgrade the nuclear element in deterrence – seeing this as the important link between the United States and the European battlefield – and unwilling to improve their conventional forces to the level that the new strategy demanded. This reluctance persisted generally until nearly a decade later, when concern at the steady and continuous increase in Soviet military capacity slowly began to make itself felt, first among conservatives, then almost right across the whole spectrum of public opinion. The steady erosion of the military balance in Europe, coupled with an assertive and opportunistic Soviet foreign policy, notably in Africa, led by the late 1970s to the growth in almost every Allied country of a political climate more receptive to the claims of defence spending.

This new mood of caution towards the Soviet Union (following as it did one of rather euphoric expectations about *détente*, now disappointed) had coincided with a sudden surge in military technology, both nuclear and conventional. In the field of theatre nuclear weapons, the enhanced radiation weapon (the 'neutron bomb') offered the West the possibility of suddenly nullifying the Soviet tank advantage while inflicting less civilian casualties than would be caused by nuclear weapons in the existing armoury. At the same time new, very-small-yield nuclear weapons ('mini-nucs') began to be introduced and others were modernized. The possibility of basing deterrence primarily on nuclear weapons once more began to find adherents – though not, it must be said, among governments, who were treading warily. This was partly because there had also been rapid advances in conventional weapons technology. Dramatic improvements in accuracy of attack and miniaturization of components and vastly increased explosive yields (such as from fuel-air weapons – the so-called concussion bombs) made it possible to contemplate engaging with conventional weapons targets (such as aircraft shelters) that could hitherto only have been destroyed with nuclear weapons.

The debate over strategy – and with it over the allocation of resources – continued to a varying extent for some years, and in a sense a compromise was gradually adopted: the strategy of flexible response was retained and new technology was used to enhance the strength of the conventional forces, but the theatre nuclear armoury was modernized as well, on the theory that if the new nuclear weapons were known to be more effective and thus more usable the Soviet Union would be less likely to provoke their use. So both aspects of deterrence, conventional and nuclear, were strengthened.

The maintenance or restoration of the Western technological edge was accepted by all Allied governments as the primary means of stopping the military balance from deteriorating further. The ability of the NATO defences to hold against attack from massive Soviet tank forces, possibly able to attack with warning measured in hours rather than days (sometimes termed a 'standing start', to denote an attack that could be made without the need for reinforcement), was also seen to be reliant on the use of technology, but to require improvements in readiness as well. With this increased readiness should go an increase in the number of reinforcements available, largely through making better use of reserves.

With the assistance of a judicious push from the new Carter Administration in 1977, the NATO Allies began to stir themselves. Some weapons, such as ATGW and SAM, had proved so effective in the October War of 1973 in the Middle East that the need for them was self-evident. They began to come out of factories in Europe and the United States in increasing numbers and to be bought by every Allied country. More advanced weapons, such as PGM (precision-guided missiles) for air attack against a variety of targets, found their way first into United States air forces, then into others. The cruise missile, with its astonishingly accurate guidance and relative cheapness, caught the imagination, both for its possibilities in the theatre conventional role and as a potential nuclear weapons carrier, perhaps – in some cases – instead of existing QRA (quick-reaction alert) aircraft. Besides all this, great efforts went, with rather less publicity, into esoteric electronics such as ECM (electronic counter-measures) and ECCM (electronic counter-counter-measures). The miniaturization of electronic components made possible improvements in weapons and techniques (in command, control and intelligence gathering and dissemination, for example) that had been unthinkable a few short years before. In the innovative capability of the Western electronics industry lay the ability to keep technologically ahead of the Soviet Union, which was handicapped by its more cumbersome system of development and the absence of commercial competition in a collectivized, state-controlled industry.

Hand in hand with interest in new weapons went thinking, both evolutionary and revolutionary, about the new tactical organizations, or changes in old ones, that would be needed to get the best out of them. All the major Allies experimented with new divisional establishments. The United States and Germany made them larger; Britain and France made them smaller. All aimed to get more firepower for less men. Similarly, studies were made of the possibilities of using the new small but powerful weapons to give reserve forces a strength and mobility they had never had before, so that they could be deployed to give defence in depth and backing to the heavier regular forces in the forward area.

Thus, in the late 1970s the overhauling of the NATO defences so long sorely needed was put in train at last. It was often done hurriedly, sometimes reluctantly, occasionally without sufficient thought, and was not in the event enough wholly to deter the Soviet Union. But it happened, and was to prove the West's salvation. The spur was the lengthening shadow of the Soviet forces in Europe. As so often before, the Soviet Union proved the best recruiting officer for NATO.

There were, of course, still weaknesses. Two of the most serious lay, as always, in the overall numerical superiority of the forces deployed against the West, and in the low level of standardization in the equipment of its own forces. The first, giving the Warsaw Pact an overall advantage in the Central Region which (though it can be variously calculated) was certainly not less than two and a half or three to one, was made more serious by the ability of the attacker to choose his own points of attack and develop there, at will, a very much greater relative advantage. The second stemmed from the understandable tendency of free and independent countries both to consult their own economic interests in the procurement of military hardware and to reflect their own military philosophy in its design. The *Chieftain* and the *Leopard*, for example, were both very good tanks, but of different kinds. The XM–1, newer than either, was different again.

Ideally all armies should have had the same type of tank or truck or gun. Such a solution was rare. Instead the Alliance put its immediate efforts into what it called interoperability – the ability to operate with each other; to have common radio frequencies, for example, if it were not possible to have the same sets; to have the same calibre guns and rifles, using the same ammunition, if not the same weapons. Much was achieved in this direction, notably with artillery and tank guns, in fuel and in other supplies. Operational procedures were not as difficult to harmonize as policies in the procurement of hardware, and NATO had gone far, in spite of language difficulties, in developing a common practice. But they were still, in this very important respect, some way behind their enemies.

CHAPTER THIRTEEN

THE WARSAW PACT FORCES

In the Soviet Union at the end of the year 1984 there were rather more than 4½ million men and women under arms. The ground forces furnished 170 divisions, of which half were now always in the category 1 state of readiness, that is to say, not less than 90 per cent complete in personnel, fully armed and equipped up to field service scales, and with a complete provision of all supplies (including fuel and ammunition) for four days' sustained action. Forty-five divisions (twice as many as in the sixties, though not all in category 1) were deployed close to the Sino-Soviet border and some thirty more in the southern regions of the USSR.

Of more immediate concern to NATO were the thirty-two Soviet divisions – sixteen tank and fifteen motorized, with at least one (and perhaps more) airborne, all in category 1 – stationed in European countries of the Warsaw Pact. These formed four groups of forces – army commands, in effect – one each in the German Democratic Republic (Group of Soviet Forces in Germany, or GSFG), Poland (the Northern Group), Czechoslovakia (the Central Group) and Hungary (the Southern Group), containing in total over half a million men and 11,000 tanks, with some 8,000 artillery pieces and over 1,000 integral aircraft. The Sixteenth Air Army, also deployed in the GDR, represented no more than the spearhead of the available tactical air resources. In the western USSR were seventy more divisions (a third of them tank divisions), of which only a few were kept constantly in category 1, but from which further reinforcement was readily available.

In addition to the Soviet forces in Central Europe, the Warsaw Pact countries in the Northern Tier (the GDR,

Czechoslovakia and Poland) deployed a dozen tank and a core of motorized divisions of their own, all organized, armed and trained on the Soviet model, while in the Southern Tier (Hungary, Bulgaria and Romania) the one tank and five motorized divisions of the Hungarian Army were also available. The military importance of Hungary in the Pact, it may be said in passing, had recently lain mostly in its exclusion from the Central Front in any discussions with the West on theatre force reductions. Forces to be withdrawn from the Central Front could therefore be conveniently retained intact by simply moving them into Hungary. It was in large part this (among other reasons, which suggested that there was little point in continuing so unprofitable a dialogue) which had caused discussions on reductions eventually to be allowed to lapse.

Although the armed forces of the Pact satellites were organized on Soviet lines and similarly armed and equipped, with an identical operational doctrine, there existed in the Pact something less than the 100 per cent standardization and inter-operability which was sometimes, not entirely correctly, envied in the West. There were language difficulties for a start, but perhaps more important were divergences in equipment. These became more marked as newer types were introduced into Soviet divisions but by no means always into those of other Pact countries. There was also no universal mobilization system in the Warsaw Pact, any more than there was in the Atlantic Alliance. It must also be emphasized that the Warsaw Pact, as such, embodied no war-fighting structure comparable to that of NATO, and thus lacked both some of NATO's strengths and some of its weaknesses. The forces of component countries of the Warsaw Pact were regarded – and used – as integral parts of the forces of the Soviet Union.

Up to the outbreak of hostilities the question of the political reliability of the forces of the satellites was much debated in the West. It was to become clear from the outset, however, that there could be no doubt at all as to

the loyalty to Moscow to be found in Warsaw Pact force
at the higher and medium levels of command. The attitud
of the non-military masses in these countries and th
response to higher military command at lower levels o
responsibility, not least among the rank and file, was t
prove a different matter.

The quantitative level of forces facing the Centra
Region of NATO in 1984 had not greatly increased ove
the past few years. Nevertheless, even with the recen
increases in the strengths of Allied in-place forces, ther
was still an immediate superiority in Pact divisions o
almost three to one. There was also on the Soviet side, i
need hardly be added, the capability to concentrate swiftl
with little warning, resulting in a very marked superiorit
at chosen points. This, according to Allied expectation
could be as high as twenty or thirty to one in each of fou
or five separate thrusts. A critical element in the battl
was to be, as had been expected, the comparative succes
rate of Pact penetration as against the speed of Allie
regrouping to meet the main thrusts once these had bee
identified. In the north of NATO's Central Region i
northern Germany, where Allied forces were weaker
lateral movement was easier. In the south, where Allie
forces were stronger, it was more difficult. In both sector
the choice of thrust lines for the attacker was to som
extent constrained by the nature of the ground. The threa
of an overpowering concentration of strength by a
assailant with the initiative nevertheless continued to be
as it had been from the beginning, a major preoccupatio
on the Allied side. It was here, in Allied thinking, that ai
power had a crucial part to play.

More important than any recent increases in Warsav
Pact strengths were innovations and improvements i
equipment and important development in warlike prac
tice. These went hand in hand and should be treated
together.

In the mid-sixties Soviet military thinking, while recog
nizing that warfare would continue to be dominated b

nuclear weapons, began to move away from the concept of land operations as inevitably and inescapably nuclear from the outset and to consider the possibility of an initial conventional phase. There thus began the study of what has been described as the non-nuclear variant. At no time had it been accepted in the USSR that nuclear and non-nuclear operations could be distinguished in kind and that a 'firebreak', as some called it in the West, could be conjured up between them. All operations of war, in the Soviet view, lay in a continuum. The concept of a nuclear 'deterrent' which could 'fail', with its 'failure' followed by active warfare, was foreign to their thinking. All known weapons of war were available for use as policy dictated and occasion demanded. Nevertheless, it began to be accepted that a major war might open on conventional lines and that non-nuclear operations could easily be prolonged.

In any case, the massive application of armoured strength remained for the Soviet Union the primary means of resolution on the battlefield. Up to the mid-sixties the tank was still the trump card, whether the game was to be played with nuclear weapons or not. But a new complication developed. As early as 1964 Khrushchev was shocked to see how vulnerable the tank had become to guided missiles. Within a few years it was clear that Soviet generals had acknowledged a qualitative change in armoured warfare. The Arab–Israeli War of 1973 aroused a great concern for the future of the tank and triggered off an urgent search for means of neutralizing anti-tank defences. The Minister of Defence, Marshal Grechko, himself took a leading part in it.

The greatest weakness in armoured formations lay in their infantry component. The introduction into the Red Army of a new and very much better infantry combat vehicle, the BMP, was an important step towards its correction. This was not only a personnel-carrier but also an armoured fighting vehicle of considerable firepower, mounting an ATGW and a 73 mm anti-tank gun in the turret and carrying RPG–7 anti-tank grenades. But the BMP, intended to bring forward the infantry for the neutralization of anti-tank defences, was itself vulnerable to anti-tank fire from the sort of weapons likely to be deployed against it in depth. This could be expected even on the nuclear battlefield for which the BMP was designed. The solution was sought in a combination of suppressive artillery and air attack, on the one hand, with high-speed manoeuvre in deep penetration – the so-called 'daring thrust' – on the other.

The concept of 'daring thrust' – bold action in depth by a force of combined arms – though similar to that of German *Blitzkrieg* in the Second World War, was not, it was claimed, modelled on it but harked back to Tukachevsky and the officers purged with him by Stalin in 1937. Up to 1975 it was generally accepted that high-speed operations in depth, whether the battlefield was nuclear or not, would be mainly used to exploit openings blasted out by massed frontal attack. Since then it had been increasingly taught that the openings could themselves be created by high-speed manoeuvre, which would also furnish the means of suppressing, by pre-emptive attack, the threat from guided weapons and anti-tank guns to the following tanks. Surprise and swift manoeuvre were the twin keys to unlock the defence and, though the Russians never lost their respect for mass, the tendency in the late seventies was more and more to relegate the massed frontal attack to second place.

The premium placed on surprise implied that an attack on NATO would be so timed as not to allow the deployment of NATO anti-tank defences at their maximum density. Thus, though it would not necessarily be carried out solely by in-place theatre forces, it was unlikely to be preceded by a long period of deliberate full mobilization. There was also heavy emphasis on battlefield mobility to exploit tactical surprise to the maximum.

What had for a long time been described in Western terminology as the 'encounter battle' – and latterly by some as the 'meeting engagement' – now began to take a very important place in Soviet military teaching. A critical part would be played by anti-tank weapons offensively deployed. These would be introduced by combined arms groups based on motorized infantry regiments in BMP, which would open the way for the entry of heavier forces of armour to decide the issue. This required resolute action by relatively small combat teams of combined arms operating with a greater degree of independence, and with more organic and 'on-call' fire support, than had hitherto been normal in the Red Army. The self-propelled gun began, at least in part, to furnish what was required: direct fire, as called for, controlled at a lower level than that of division.

Something of a tactical revolution was now taking place, associated with changes in organization and equipment which were in part cause and in part effect of what was happening. The divisions facing NATO in the Central Region had all been furnished with BMP exploitation regiments by the late seventies, and it was at this level of command, the regimental, that the integration of different arms increasingly took place instead of, as hitherto, at divisional level or even higher.

The Red Army now faced several unfamiliar problems. Integration of different arms at lower levels for fluid operations made unusual demands on command, control and communications. Even more important in its longer-term implications was what was likely to be required of junior commanders. Now that the battle could no longer be pre-planned higher up, with all foreseeable tactical situations resolved in stereotyped battle drills, qualities were needed at quite low levels of command which it had never been the business of the Red Army to develop. The boldness of initiative and independence of judgement demanded in junior commanders by the new tactics were possibly quite common in the competitive societies of the capitalist West; they were not qualities intentionally developed among subordinates in the USSR.

The methods of any army reflect the patterns of its parent society. The Red Army was moving into a war-fighting method demanding patterns of behaviour quite sharply at variance with those prevalent in the parent system. It was to face here a growing difficulty.

Logistic support also posed problems. Soviet practice had long rested on the principle of offensive action in mass to seek a swift tactical resolution. Formations would be replaced as necessity dictated. When exhausted and depleted they would be withdrawn for fresh ones to take their places; they would not be replenished and reinforced for further sustained action, as in Western practice.

Warfare in the Middle East had shown that intense operations with modern equipment resulted in an unprecedentedly high rate of consumption of stocks. For category 1 divisions in the GSFG, stocked to combat readiness, there was now provision for two to three days' further fighting, dumped in forward positions. This would have to be brought forward if a frontal assault on the NATO defences carried attacking formations through into any significant degree of penetration. As for 'deep thrust' operations, these demanded an altogether different kind of logistic support – in swiftly moving self-contained columns, capable of keeping up with the advance and looking after themselves in a fluid battle. At the beginning of the 1980s logistic tactics rather like those being practised in British armour in BAOR in the fifties (before the blanket of massive retaliation (see Chapter 4) had fallen over the last sparks of armoured experience from the African deserts in the Second World War) were being studied – on exercises of course, in the Soviet mode, rather than in the conference room, and with an input from more recent combat experience in the Middle East. The BMP was modified as an armoured logistic vehicle, and, in the three years preceding the outbreak of hostilities, the handling of armoured replenishment columns, protected by a highly mobile anti-tank and air defence, became an important feature of Red Army manoeuvres.

Meanwhile, the offensive capability of Soviet armoured and motorized formations continued to improve. All category 1 and many other armoured divisions had been re-equipped by 1980 with the 40-tonne T-72 tank, with its high velocity 125 mm gun and laser rangefinder, its low silhouette, rugged construction and NBC protection. A newer and better tank, the T–80, with spaced armour, ATGW and an improved 125 mm smooth-bore gun, was also beginning to come into service. The T–62, whose gun had so disconcerted Israeli armour in 1973, was now being finally phased out.

In the motorized infantry of which each tank division now had one regiment to three of tanks, the proportion in motorized infantry divisions being reversed, the mechanized fighting vehicle BMP–76PB – fast, quite heavily armed and NBC-protected – had completely replaced the earlier models of personnel-carrier. A still newer infantry combat vehicle than the BMP began to appear in the GSFG in 1977: the MTLB, with improvements which included a 76 mm gun. Seven new infantry regiments appeared in that year in the GSFG, at first mounted in trucks, soon to be replaced by MTLB. By 1982, ten regiments had been similarly converted. Self-propelled artillery in 122 mm and 152 mm calibres was widely in service for forward deployment, though there was still some inclination towards the traditional Soviet use of massed artillery (now strengthened by the 180 mm piece, in answer to the American 175 mm M–107) for indirect fire controlled from further back. Saturation fire was effectively thickened by an improved version of the well-tried BM-21 122 mm rocket launcher, throwing missiles of fifty-five kilograms sixteen and a half kilometres from forty tubes on one vehicle.

Air defence organic to the division now incorporated large numbers of the new SA-8 surface-to-air missile launcher for very low-level defence, in addition to SA–7, SA–9 and SA–10, together with SA–6 and SA–3 for medium-level defence and SA–4 and SA–5 against high-level attack, as well as a liberal provision of guns, of which improved ZU–23s were the backbone.

In the anti-tank inventory, now of even greater importance in the offensive concept of the deep thrust, the 76 mm SPG–9 had replaced earlier recoilless weapons, though the familiar RPG–7 anti-tank grenade launcher, somewhat improved, was still in service. So were the wire-guided ATGW, though early models of more sophisticated weaponry, aiming at matching the 'fire and forget' systems already considerably advanced in the West (in which preset guidance and terminal homing removed much of the combat pressure on the operator), were now coming into service.

Offensive thrust had been increased by improved assault engineer resources, more and better bridging, and more effective amphibious vehicles and ferries. Mine clearance and swift automatic mine-laying capabilities, either on the ground or from the air, had developed greatly as the implications of fluid operations in depth were more fully explored.

Operations of this sort, indeed, had come more and more to dominate Soviet tactical thinking in a time of unprecedented experiment.

In a very wide area of debate on the conduct of the land battle one single issue stood out as more important than most. It concerned the basic organization of field formations.

Was the division moving towards a uniform grouping of all arms, from which task forces could be quickly thrown up appropriate to the task in hand? Many senior officers advocated this. Or should the distinction be maintained between divisions heavy in tanks with an infantry component and motorized infantry divisions with integral armour?

This was no mere arid question of military organization. Behind it lay, as is often the case with matters of military organization, a further question of profound political importance. The supporters of the more conservative approach (and they were very numerous) included those who recognized most clearly, however disinclined they might have been to say so explicitly, that the qualities demanded of junior leaders in fluid operations in depth were simply not those inculcated under the Soviet system, that such qualities were in fact actively discouraged. It deserves reiteration that independence of higher authority in a subordinate, and reliance on his own interpretation of a situation and his own initiative, instead of on the rule book and superior guidance, were completely alien to the system. Such an approach, too widely spread, could endanger the whole political structure of the Soviet Union. The Red Army was scarcely the right place to foster it, even in the most carefully chosen juniors. The thought was one which many senior officers found disturbing.

Whatever problems of command may have been emerging in the Red Army, the centralized organization and control of air forces that air power classically demands really fitted in rather well with the Soviet political and social system. Nevertheless, if land forces were to operate with flexibility and initiative from quite low levels of command, depending on how the battle developed, the air forces might need to be able to act similarly and to learn to switch rapidly to autonomous reaction. This, they knew, Allied airmen were well able to do. Certainly, they realized that in a massive offensive the ether would be heavily jammed and that close control from headquarters a long way further back, where the situation in the air and on the ground could not be known from minute to minute, might not work too well. Their aircrew, moreover, were the cream of the military technocracy. There was perhaps even more cause for unease on their account than in ground forces in the long term if there should ever be a military need to take their blinkers off. For the time being, however, pre-planned targets for a setpiece offensive were the order of the day, and the generals and their planners had more tangible and appealing matters to contemplate.

In the last ten years the Red Air Force had achieved an entirely new order of air capability. From about 1970 onwards it had become apparent to uneasy Western observers that the men in the Kremlin had woken up at last to what air power was really about. A trend had been started which was quite as significant for NATO as the emergence of the Soviet Union as a global naval power. The Alliance's counter to the numerical superiority of the Warsaw Pact ground and air forces had always rested to a large degree on the high quality of its air power, chiefly in the ability of NATO air forces to bring heavy concentrations of fire to bear with extreme rapidity and accuracy at any point in the battle. Even if the Allies had had sufficient reserves to match an all-out Warsaw Pact offensive on the ground, the problem of the defensive alliance was that those reserves could not arrive in time to conduct a coherent forward defence against a surprise, or near-surprise, attack. In Allied strategic thinking air power filled this gap, offering as it did the ability to strike hard and repeatedly at the choke points along the frontier of the two Germanies through which a Soviet land offensive would have to squeeze. At the same time tactical air power would be projected strategically, in the sense that large numbers of American tactical aircraft would fly into Europe from the United States in times of crisis. The concept of Allied air power holding a front against an offensive in this way, provided there were enough aircraft to do it, was valid and reassuring, especially since the performance of modern Allied tactical aircraft, and the effectiveness and accuracy of their weapons, had climbed exponentially on the back of commercially competitive Western technology to achieve a capability undreamt of in terms of the Second World War.

In the Alliance this superiority had long been comfortably thought of as a state of grace that would endure forever, almost irrespective of the effort that the Western world put into it. But now things were beginning to look rather different. Soviet combat jet aircraft had made their first appearance in the Korean War. By 1970 all of this first generation had been withdrawn from service except for a handful operated by the satellite countries. The second generation originating in the late fifties and early sixties reached its peak front-line strength in the early seventies. By the beginning of 1985 only about 10 to 15 per cent remained in service as the third generation took over. This generation had made its debut in 1970 and its numbers had risen steadily ever since. The Soviet Air Forces now had aircraft of broadly comparable performance to their Allied counterparts, although the latter were still reckoned to have the margin in detailed capability in all circumstances, especially where this was dependent on electronic and weapon technology. Numerically the Warsaw Pact air forces had for long outstripped those of the Allies; now a broad parity in performance was also in sight. But that was not the end of the matter. With more research and development effort devoted to military technology by the Soviet Union than by all the Western powers put together, there was plentiful evidence of a fourth generation of aircraft coming along, to include specialized air-superiority fighters to match NATO's F–15s and F–16s and land-based V/STOL aircraft. Nothing very much was known of these in detail except that they were waiting in the wings. They seemed likely to appear on stage from 1986 onwards.

By the beginning of 1985, Western analysts concluded that the strength of the Soviet tactical air armies in western Russia alone had increased since 1970 by over 30 per cent. The Naval Air Force was climbing on a similar curve, and there had been a vast increase in both strategic and tactical airlift, the number of attack and assault helicopters attached to the infantry having been almost trebled since 1970. The Soviet Air Force generals could look back on their own successful programme with every bit as much satisfaction as Admiral Gorshkov could look back on that of the Soviet Navy. In truth, it rather irritated them that the Admiral and his navy got so much of the limelight when the record of the air force was every bit as spectacular. In. twenty-five years their unremitting efforts had increased the range and war-load capacity of the Soviet Air Forces by a staggering 1200 per cent.

This meant that Soviet aircraft could now range into the Atlantic and attack targets throughout NATO Europe's rear areas, including the United Kingdom – targets that hitherto the West had considered immune from serious air threat. Moreover, they had the combat range for evasive and tactical routing, and for feint attacks. The air generals had been the architects of a vast, balanced air arm that had now significantly narrowed the West's previous qualitative superiority. It almost goes without saying that in numbers it went far beyond what could conceivably be needed purely for defence. If things continued to go its way the generals could look forward to a not too far distant time when they could confidently challenge Allied air power and its ability to protect the strategic deployment of NATO's reserves in an emergency. This would be a war winner. It was a professionally satisfying prospect.

With equal satisfaction they watched and listened throughout the seventies as military men and informed commentators in Western Europe tried to warn their countries about the critical part that air power had to play in defence of Allied security and the way the reassuring margin that had so long shielded the Alliance was all the time being narrowed. 'None so deaf as those who will not hear' might well have been their cheerful comment, until 1979 when the United Kingdom embarked on major measures to expand the Royal Air Force and especially to increase its air defence component (see Appendix 1). Most of the Allies were similarly engaged in stepping up their defence effort, but the RAF air defence interested the generals particularly because the United Kingdom had a special place in their strategic plans. Its expansion programme was not welcome to the Kremlin or to the Soviet air generals, but they consoled themselves with the thought that they had really had a splendid run while the West, of its own deliberate choice, was looking the other way. Furthermore, their own experience, over many years, of the huge industrial and training effort needed to build up or increase a modern air force, caused them to wonder if the British government might not be in for a surprise when it found how long its plans would take to mature.

In the realm of space the Soviet Air Forces had recognized the military application of space vehicles for communications and reconnaissance from the earliest moments of their space programme. The USSR–USA competition initiated by the Soviet *Sputnik* some thirty years earlier had been a long-playing space spectacular for all the world to watch. Although the engineering approach of the superpowers was often different, and US reliability was always superior, in general terms the Soviet Union had acquired capabilities which matched those of the USA. These had proved very valuable in peacetime and it now remained to see what their importance would be in war.

There was another vital matter, upon which little of much significance was said in the Red Army, perhaps because so very little was known about it. It concerned the very nature of nuclear warfare. Though the recent tendency in Soviet military thinking had been to accept that a major war might open with non-nuclear operations, and that these might even be prolonged, it must be emphasized again that nuclear and non-nuclear warfare had never been regarded in the Red Army's philosophy as alternatives. Each fitted in as an element in a total war-fighting capability, to be exploited as policy and occasion demanded. As we have clearly seen, the Western concept of 'escalation' out of conventional warfare into nuclear, and of further 'escalation' from battlefield nuclear action into strategic, had no real equivalent in the Soviet Union, still less the notion of a 'firebreak' between successive steps. Though a non-nuclear variant had been studied and fully prepared for, it had never ceased to be widely expected that a major campaign against NATO would probably open with massive attack in depth by nuclear or chemical weapons, or both, to be followed by swift and violent exploitation by formations (which would be largely armoured) attacking off the line of march. With nuclear weapons, penetration was expected to reach a depth of some 120 kilometres in a 24-hour period. Equipment in Red Army divisions was designed for action on an irradiated or chemically dangerous battlefield. Outside the combat zone, if a strategic response from the other side brought the homeland under attack with nuclear weapons, there was at least provision – not total but far greater than any until quite recently seen in the West – for the protection of some of the more important elements in the population, for the maintenance of essential services and for the continuance of the war.

If, on the other hand, advantage were to be seen in a non-nuclear offensive, if Western battlefield nuclear weapons could be smothered or blinded and important results could be obtained even before NATO, without the stimulus of their use on the Warsaw Pact side, could reach inter-Allied agreement on the release of such weapons, this possibility too would be considered. Apart from the reduction in scale of the threat to the homeland and the absence of collateral nuclear damage in the theatre (which might or might not have its advantages), the principal effect of a non-nuclear opening to the land battle would be a slowing up in the rate of advance. Instead of covering 110 to 120 kilometres in a day the assaulting formations would be doing well if they managed forty.

But whatever was said, planned or done about nuclear operations of war, whether by hard-headed realists in the East or by commentators in the West ranging from homespun tacticians to far-out philosophers, one thing was universally true. Nuclear weapons of war had never yet been used on the battlefield and nobody, anywhere, knew what would happen if they were. Even within an integral concept of total war-fighting, using all means at choice, the decision to use this one would need very careful consideration indeed. The harder-headed the realists having to make the choice, the more carefully would they be inclined to reflect on the possible – but completely unpredictable – consequences. The West's increasing preparedness to defend itself was throwing an even harsher light upon this very important consideration.

CHAPTER FOURTEEN

THE STAGE IS SET

Shortly after 0400 hours on Sunday, 4 August, it became clear to the Supreme Allied Commander in Europe, and was at once made known throughout a world waiting in an agony of suspense, that the Warsaw Pact had opened a general offensive against the forces of the Atlantic Alliance. The invasion of Western Europe had begun.

To some the news brought a curious sense of relief. At least the uncertainty was over. For many others, particularly in the governments and armed services of Allied countries, it raised the anxious question as to whether enough had been done for NATO's defences since the seventies to repair the damage of the locust years. Could the West, in fact, survive? To most who heard the news, at least in Europe, it brought only grim and unhappy forebodings.

The Soviet intervention in Yugoslavia, and the swift and forceful response to it from the United States, that conjunction of miscalculation and mischance in which could now be seen the spark which set off the general explosion, seemed almost to be forgotten. More important things were at stake. The very future of the human race might now become the issue.

From the outset the world was swamped with Soviet claims, flooding through every possible channel of communication, that this was no more than defensive action, to which the Warsaw Pact had been driven by neo-Nazi ambitions supported by capitalist imperialism.

'It has long been clear,' the announcement proclaimed, 'that the new Nazis are set on the reunification of Germany by force and the subsequent domination of Europe as an early step to world supremacy. The policy of "forward defence", which is self-evident military nonsense if it does not mean action by the FRG east of the Demarcation Line, has never been more than a thin cloak for the firm intention to invade the GDR as a first move towards the dismemberment of the Warsaw Pact and the destruction of the USSR. The change of name from *Vorwärtsvertei-digung* (Forward Defence) to *Vorneverteidigung* (Frontal Defence) has done nothing to disguise the nakedness of an essentially aggressive policy. Plans for the invasion are now, in total authenticity,' as the announcement put it, 'in Soviet hands, and their authors will in time be brought to justice. Meanwhile, it has become abundantly clear that there is no time to lose in cutting out the Nazi canker. Otherwise all hope will vanish of a lasting peace in Europe.'

The Soviet message to the world went on to give assurances that the purpose of the Pact's action was first to restore peace in Yugoslavia, where troops from the capitalist West had invaded a socialist country, and at the same time to suppress the true source of disturbance to world peace. This would necessitate the occupation and neutralization of West Germany but no more than that, except for such other action as military security demanded. The integrity of French territory would be especially respected, and the French government was urged to allow its military forces no part in resisting those of the Warsaw Pact. The Italian government was ordered, in rather more peremptory tones, to consult its socialist conscience and permit no resistance to Soviet troops compelled to enter Italy.

'It is very much hoped,' the announcement proceeded, 'that the United Kingdom will see the unwisdom of supporting its old enemies against its former allies, and above all that the United States will recognize the dangers on the one hand from a revival of Nazi adventurism and the fervent hopes for an enduring peace cherished in the Soviet Union on the other.'

Reference was then made to nuclear weapons. The

Soviet Union, the statement said, saw no need at present
to make use of its very powerful armoury of nuclear
weapons in the prophylactic action now going forward.

'Any significant use of radiation as a weapon of war,
however,' the statement went on, 'either against troops of
the Warsaw Pact or against their homelands, from whatever source, will result in the abandonment by the Soviet
Union of all restraints in the use of nuclear weapons and
full-scale counter-attack to any depth found necessary.
The cities of the NATO countries will face in that event
a dreadful end.'

Such was the Soviet message to the world, put out first
at 0400 hours, Central European time, on 4 August 1985,
and continually repeated in the days that followed. It was
made known in many different ways, in many different
lands and in many different languages. It was heard with
feelings varying from rapturous hope to blank despair, and
greeted with responses ranging from warm welcome, which
was rare, to raucous derision, which was not.

In Europe, on 4 August 1985, even after only a week of
NATO mobilization, the Allied Command was in a far
better condition to meet an emergency than could have
been possible a very few years before. Several months of
spurious *détente* in the first half of the year had certainly
done something to slow down the rate of improvement in
NATO's preparedness; indeed in some respects it had
almost brought it to a halt. Illusory hopes that the leopard
had this time changed its spots had been freely aired.
There had even been repetition of the whimsical claim, so
often heard in left-wing groups in Britain, that there could
never be any question of changing spots, for the animal
had always been in fact immaculate, and that the enormous
offensive capability of the USSR had been developed
simply to protect its own progressive way of life and the
freedom of the peoples it had liberated.

The voices raised for so long among the British left
wing, and from their ill-assorted allies among the die-hard
disengagers in the USA, urging a sharp reduction in

military spending and the withdrawal of troops, had recently been listened to with growing scepticism. It was therefore possible, even in the months of false *détente* in the spring and early summer of 1985, to proceed, against this chorus, at least with those defence programmes whose suspension would increase domestic unemployment. Improvement in the air defences of the United Kingdom, for example, went on. It was even possible in the USA, though only by the narrowest of margins, to retain the Active Forces Draft.

There is no need to dwell here on the political and social stresses generated in the United States in the years 1979–81 over the reintroduction of the draft, nor to recapitulate the stormy history of the passage of the appropriate legislation. We are more concerned with its consequences, as seen in Allied Command Europe in 1985, and with the sobering reflection that without it no book like this, placing on record as it does the manner of the free West's survival, could ever have been written.

It is just worth recalling, however, as a helpful reminder, that the US Army was in 1977 facing a critically dangerous position in the virtual disappearance of its reserves. When public disenchantment with the Vietnam War resulted in the end of the draft and the creation of an all-volunteer army, a sharp decline in paid-drill personnel (i.e. personnel actually carrying out reserve training) set in. By 1977 the Army's National Guard and Reserve were 100,000 under peacetime strength. The Army's Individual Ready Reserve – the pool of trained men to fill up units and replace combat losses – was dropping so fast that by 1982 it would at this rate have been 360,000 short of mobilization requirements. The back-up Selective Service System was in such 'deep standby' that training of drafted personnel could not start until four months after mobilization and no trained men to replace combat losses could be expected to reach Allied Command Europe until three months after that.

A scheme produced by the US Army to spend $750

million a year on a Reserve Component Readines
Improvement Package (RCRIP) was rejected. Scheme
for a Reserve Component Draft, or for an Individua
Ready Reserve (IRR) Draft, were found to be unworkable
The only real alternative was an Active Forces Draft, with
exemption for Reserve Components and IRR volunteers
Without it, within a few years, the US Army would only
have been able to go to war when the war was over.

American public opinion in 1977 would not have
accepted reintroduction of the draft. A Gallup poll in that
year showed that 45 per cent of all Americans were against
it, with a count as high as 82 per cent of all males between
eighteen and twenty-four years of age.

Gradually, however, as elsewhere in the Alliance, the
realization began to spread that the Russians meant what
they had so often said and knew exactly what they were
doing. In spite of the most strenuous efforts of those who
refused to recognize the threat, or argued that if there
were one it did not matter, or even claimed that they
welcomed the chance of living under a Marxist dictatorship
(whether anyone believed them or not), the awareness
grew in the United States that a time could come when
truly vital decisions would have to be made, and that it
would be very foolish for the nation to surrender in
advance all power of choice.

Soviet international diplomacy, uncompromising and
unconciliatory as ever, was not unhelpful to those in the
West who sought to make the danger better known. The
Active Forces Draft was introduced in 1982. By early 198
the reserves, though with some way still to go, had passed
above the crisis level. The US Army in Europe was no
longer in such a state that, in the event of a military
showdown with the Warsaw Pact, it would face early and
unavoidable disaster because of a lack of trained man
power.

The position of France, critical to the whole question of
the survival of the Alliance, must now receive attention
In the long history of Soviet maladroitness and miscalcu

lation since the Second World War nothing – not the free
elections so rashly allowed in Austria in 1946, or the swift
re-arming of West Germany by the USSR's recent allies
in response to Soviet threats, or yet the alienation of
Marxists outside the Soviet Union or the antagonization
of China or the ineffective meddling in the Middle East –
nothing at all in an impressive record of political ineptitude
proved to be a more spectacular and costly failure than
the confident attempt by the Soviet Union to persuade
France to renounce her obligations under the Atlantic
Treaty.* The II French Corps, stationed in Germany,
embodying two enlarged divisions now, with supporting
troops, up to full strength, was put by the French government at SACEUR's disposal even before the Soviet
announcement. In fact, it came under command to
AFCENT at midnight on 3–4 August. The corps was to be
followed in a matter of days by the first of three further
mechanized divisions from the First French Army. From
4 August the French Tactical Air Force was ordered to
support French forces on the ground as SACEUR might
determine. French ports, communications, military installations and, above all, airfields and airspace were at the
same time made available to the Allies.

If France had stayed in Nato, or come back in good
time, a French army group located in southern Germany
and fully integrated into AFCENT might so have
strengthened the whole Central Region as to deter in real
terms – without nuclear shadow-boxing – a Warsaw Pact
invasion. It was too late to think about that now. What
gave real cause for satisfaction and solid ground for hope
was the very active unofficial contingency planning which

---

* Article 5 of the North Atlantic Treaty lays down that in the event of
armed attack on any signatory each member will assist the country so
attacked by taking 'such action as it deems necessary including the use
of armed force'.
  The earlier Brussels Treaty, to which France also still belonged, was
even more categorical about affording military aid to a victim of attack.

had long been a feature of relations between the French General Staff in Germany and CENTAG.

The onset of war in Europe posed a particularly cruel problem for Turkey. She was recovering from deep economic gloom, but her armed forces had been weakened by the restriction on equipment supplies from the US. This ban had been imposed by Congress, contrary to the wishes of the US Administration, on the occasion of the Turkish action in Cyprus in 1974. Some partial mitigation had occurred in the late seventies but full re-supply had only been arranged three years before the present outbreak. Turkey had for some time been making it clear to the US and to the other Allies that the performance of her Alliance responsibilities would have to be made proportionate to her reduced capability. It said much for the steadfastness of the Turkish character, as well as for their historic fear of Russian aggression, that they did not go further in their reaction to Congressional displeasure. Relations with Greece had begun to recover from the low point reached at the time of the Cyprus affair and the argument over sea-bed rights in the Aegean, and it was largely the progress made in patching up this quarrel which finally led Congress to authorize the resumption of full equipment deliveries. But three years was a short time in which to make good the deficiencies and catch up with the new types of weapon systems which had meanwhile become available.

The growing threat during 1984 of Soviet action from the north and Soviet influence in Egypt from the south had further helped to cement the improvement in Greek-Turkish relations, and thus paved the way for Greece to resume active participation in NATO planning and co-operation, which had also been interrupted in the aftermath of the Cyprus affair.

The circumstances leading to the actual outbreak of war in Europe proved particularly unfavourable for Greece and Turkey, however. Egypt's move into Arabia had disrupted some of their oil supply and emphasized the

Soviet presence in Syria and Iraq, which were Turkey's neighbours to the south and east. The outbreak of hostilities in Yugoslavia brought increased Soviet troop concentrations into the Balkans and enhanced Bulgaria's role as a potential jumping off point for a drive to the Straits or the Aegean.

Nevertheless, Soviet policy also faced a dilemma. The rugged terrain of the Anatolian plateau was not of much use to them, but passage of the Bosphorus and Dardanelles might be crucial to their success in driving America out of the eastern Mediterranean. No doubt sufficient forces could be concentrated in Bulgaria to force back the Turkish First Army from Edirne and open the way to occupation of Gallipoli and the Bosphorus approaches – even if Istanbul itself, now peopled by 4 million Turks, would be a most indigestible mouthful. But any such moves, even accompanied by airborne landings, would give plenty of time for the blocking of the Straits by demolition, mines and blockships. Even with control of the shores of the two waterways these obstructions could take some vital weeks to clear. Since this was intended by the Soviet planners to be the period within which the whole European operation would lie, the disadvantage of armed attack on the Straits loomed rather large.

Soviet planners were necessarily aware that the Montreux Convention, which since 1937 had regulated the right of passage through the Turkish Straits, almost totally forbade this right to the warships of belligerents. After the beginning of operations in Europe they would hardly be able to claim not to be in this category, even if no formal declaration of war had been made. Some of them were inclined to assume that, faced with the threat of overwhelming force, the Turks would have no alternative but to accept a bending of the Montreux rules and allow Soviet warships continued passage. Others, who knew Turkey better, argued successfully that this could by no means be relied on and that Turkey was fully capable of living up to her obligations even at great cost to herself. They pointed out that it would do the USSR little good to be in Istanbul if the Bosphorus was blocked. Moreover, apart from Turkish action, it would not be difficult for US aircraft even from the western Mediterranean to make passage of the Straits by Soviet warships exceptionally hazardous.

It was therefore finally accepted by the Soviet command that the only safe course was to get their ships out first from the Black Sea into the Mediterranean. Once there they would have shore facilities in Alexandria again since the Egyptian volte-face. They could hope for the use of Malta and the seizure of a harbour in the course of the Yugoslav operation. There might even be a chance to settle old scores with Albania and re-occupy the submarine base at Valona, from which they had been rudely ejected when Albania joined the Chinese in 1961. The ships would thus not be as dependent as formerly on periodic return to Black Sea ports for refitting and supply. Civilian merchant shipping from the Black Sea could no doubt fill up the supply gaps, and their passage through the Straits would pose much less risk of Turkish reaction. In the spring of 1985 there was, therefore, an unusual amount of Soviet naval tonnage leaving the Black Sea for the Mediterranean, for manoeuvres, trials and transfer to other stations; by the outbreak of hostilities in Europe all the units required for naval operations in the Mediterranean had already passed through.

There was of course a risk that these movements would seem to imply a Soviet intention to prepare for a European war and stimulate precautions in the West. By routing almost all the ships first of all to Alexandria, however, the Russians strove to give the impression that they were still concerned primarily with the Middle East and the Indian Ocean.

When finally hostilities began and the Russians succeeded in penetrating Italy, causing the removal to Spain of all that was possible of AFSOUTH's infrastructure, as well as its headquarters, the possibility of active participation by Turkey and Greece was drastically curtailed, since only long-distance US air support with help from the Sixth Fleet would for the time being be available.

It was not the first time in Turkey's history that she had been left almost alone to face her great neighbour in the north. As so often in the past, the Turkish government made it quite clear that while their intentions were not aggressive, no Turkish territory or Turkish rights would be conceded without fierce resistance and if necessary sacrifice. Frontier forces were reinforced and preparations ostentatiously made for blocking the Straits should this prove necessary. Local animosities were forgotten in the face of greater danger, and Turkish and Greek forces linked up in Thrace to confront Bulgaria, while the remaining Greek forces strengthened their northern border against any possible incursions from Yugoslavia or Albania.

The threat of attack from the Warsaw Pact side was a very real one and gave rise to deep apprehensions. In the end, however, the Russians did not find it worth while to divert forces for this purpose, believing no doubt that if all went according to plan in the centre and west they could complete their mastery of the Balkans and of Turkey at greater leisure thereafter. The political and military weaknesses of NATO's south-east flank had been repaired just in time to make it possible for the flank to hold, even in considerable isolation. It was rash of all concerned to have left the remedial measures so late.

Since the central issue was in the first instance to be the survival of the Federal Republic of Germany, and since the first great land battle would take place on German territory, it is important to take a further look at the Federal Republic's land forces.

The three German corps embodied sixteen armoured brigades (each with three battalions of tanks, one of armoured infantry and one of armoured artillery), fifteen armoured infantry brigades (each containing two tank and two armoured infantry battalions, one of *Jäger* infantry and one of armoured artillery), with units mostly organized broadly on US models, together with two mountain and three airborne brigades. They were on the whole in very good shape, well officered and well equipped. In an army in which roughly half of its regular strength of 350,000 were conscripts, the general level of troop training was not as high, or as even, as that of an all-regular long-service force like the British. Units had on the whole been kept up to strength rather better than the British, however, and there had been fewer reorganizations in the interests of economy (always presented politically in Britain as improvements in military effectiveness) and a more realistic approach by the Federal government to the provision and maintenance of equipment. The *Bundeswehr* had thus suffered less from its politicians than its brothers-in-arms in Britain, where cynicism and insularity had long traded on a depth of good will and loyalty in the country's armed forces that few governments of any party had done much to deserve.

Of two major improvements brought about in the army of the FRG in the five years before the outbreak of war, one was structural, the other operational.

The first concerned reserves. Three Territorial Commands, each of five Military Districts, had been created. In these commands six Home Defence Brigades formed the fighting core of a reserve force with a peacetime strength of some 63,000 (including 30,000 conscripts still working out their reserve service) and an ultimate full mobilization strength for the Territorial Army of half a million. The Federal government was not at first inclined to place these resources under NATO command. They represented, it was argued, the last armed forces available to the Federal Republic as a sovereign power and should remain at its disposal alone. Arguments for undivided command in time of war proved more persuasive. Events were to show the wisdom of assigning these reserve forces, at least on mobilization, to SACEUR.

The second improvement reflected a change in outlook on the best method of defending Federal territory. 'Forward defence' *on* the frontier could hardly mean in military terms anything other than a defence *forward* of the frontier, a point Warsaw Pact planners were not slow to take. The clearest alternative was defence in depth, trading ground at the best possible rate for the time needed to set up a counter-offensive. This, though it made good military sense, was hardly popular with politicians publicly dedicated to the total defence of the integrity of Federal territory.

The rapid development of anti-tank techniques, the increasing urbanization of much of West Germany and the growing size of the FRG's military reserves suggested another approach. A network of squads of reservists, locally drawn and armed with ATGW, was incorporated into the operation of the covering forces along the frontier.

A concept had been gradually gaining favour in the Federal Republic since the end of the seventies under which a defence against attack from the East would be organized into three tiers. These would comprise a frontier defence almost entirely composed of *Jagd Kommandos* (tank-hunting and skirmishing units), with powerful counter-penetration forces in depth in what was described as *Raumdeckende Verteidigung* (spatial defence) and an area of *Heimat Schutz* (so-called Homeland Defence), depending mostly on territorial forces, in further depth behind that.

The covering forces deployed by AFCENT would still be expected to fight a delaying battle forward. In the late seventies the proportion of troop strengths in forward corps assigned to fight the covering-force battle had been some 30 to 50 per cent of the whole formation, all along the front of the Central Region. New tactics in NORTH-AG, appropriate to the terrain, had enabled forward corps to reduce this to some extent. The full covering-force concept, however, was still to prevail in CENTAG where lack of depth made it important to give away as little ground as possible.

In NORTHAG, British experimentation was proceeding

on lines closely related to the new concept now under discussion in Germany, with light anti-tank defences exploiting the possibility of ATGW deployed far forward. The system of frontier defence thus created, with counter-penetration forces deployed in further depth, was beginning to be thought of, by many British and some German officers, as a possible replacement for, or at least a modification of, the full doctrine of 'forward defence', however the term was interpreted, which had hitherto prevailed. It was still largely experimental, but over several years of continuous exercises it had been showing considerable promise.

Where the most important advances had been made in preparations to defend the Federal Republic, however, was without any question in the organization of home and civil defence – including the protection of vulnerable points and attention to the problem of refugees – and in the better use of reserves.

Of the other Allied forces deployed in the Central Region on 4 August 1985 (in addition to their most powerful component, those of the United States), I Belgian and I Netherlands Corps in NORTHAG were almost up to strength (though the training of reservists in some units gave little cause for confidence) and were already, at least in part, deployed forward. Pressure within NATO over the years to increase the long-service content in these formations, thus placing less reliance on reserves, and to deploy a higher proportion of them within the Federal Republic near their battle stations (and less in their adjacent homelands) had met with incomplete success. I Belgian and I Netherlands Corps were not the strongest links in the NATO chain.

The embryonic II British Corps, composed in part of reserve units manned by former long-service regulars and in part of regular units, had been due this year, as it happened, for the first time to carry out a full formation exercise, with troops, in BAOR. It was building up in north-west Germany. Its equipment, stockpiled in advance but not yet fully up to scale and, where reserve units were concerned, not always of the latest type, had already been drawn. Its personnel embodied a considerable level of experience, fortified both by a leaven of regular units and by judicious cross-posting from I British Corps. The morale of its reservist soldiers was high.

The much strengthened Canadian Brigade Group, in the rear of the CENTAG area, was held in the Central Army Group reserve.

CHAPTER FIFTEEN

THE STORM BREAKS ON THE CENTRAL FRONT

Active hostilities opened first of all in inner space, very shortly before 0400 hours, Central European time, on Sunday, 4 August 1985, with widespread and clearly very carefully prepared attacks on US communications and surveillance satellites. The Soviet interference capability was known to have developed considerably since the resumption of a programme temporarily discontinued in the USSR in 1971. The extent of its development came as an unpleasant surprise. Airborne relay stations of the US Air Force, already deployed, took up some, at least, of the communications load, though with a high initial degradation of efficiency. The sudden removal of large areas of satellite surveillance cover, however, was to be much more acutely felt than reduced communications capability. The latter could be largely replaced at short notice by other means. Satellite surveillance could also be restored in time, but that would take longer.

A few minutes later, at about 0400 hours, massive air and missile attacks, using both high explosive and chemical munitions, on airfields, headquarters locations, logistic areas and *Hawk* and *Nike* air-defence sites, heralded the opening of a major Warsaw Pact offensive on the Central Region of NATO. At the same time under-cover parties, as many as 300 or 400 in number, moved in to attack civil and military communications centres, government offices, fire, police, railway and generating stations, and key road and railway bridges. Almost simultaneously NATO forward troop locations came under heavy air and artillery attack along the whole length of the forward edge of the Central Region's battle area.

Surprise was nowhere complete: NATO troops in forward positions were already alert. The expectation that an attack, however likely, would not take place just yet had some effect, at least initially, in reducing the effectiveness of protective and defensive measures in rear areas, but even here the numerous, widespread and carefully prepared strikes by under-cover parties met with gratifyingly little success. It was just not possible, as Kremlin planners had very sensibly realized, to prepare a sudden attack on so many points at once with complete surprise. They had therefore sought concealment in deception planning, particularly in terms of timing. It proved to be ineffective. A few discoveries of under-cover attacks on the very verge of delivery, together with other unmistakable signs of what was imminent, served to set off a general alert among Federal German police and territorial forces already standing by at short notice. Damage there was, even serious damage, but the first armed clash between the Warsaw Pact and the territorial defences of the Federal Republic resulted in at least 75 per cent failure and something of a boost to civil morale. (The attack on HQ NORTHAG noted on p. 114 was, in spite of initial penetration of the HQ building and some casualties, a total failure, like very many others.)

Though Allied forces everywhere were already dispersed, as far as possible, in an anti-nuclear posture (with all its inconveniences), no nuclear attack was anywhere reported. Warsaw Pact forces, on the other hand, confident that nuclear release by the NATO defence was at this stage most unlikely, were able to operate with only that degree of dispersion required against conventional air attack, which was much less.

Chemical agents were used in the attack from the start, but only on some sectors of the front. They were not used against the two US corps, perhaps because USAREUR possessed integral and effective chemical offensive weapons of its own. US policy had consistently been that US troops would retaliate in kind if attacked with chemical agents but would not use them otherwise. The Soviet commanders seemed to have taken this threat seriously and did not use chemicals against any formation in CENTAG.

In the NORTHAG sector none of the national corps possessed a chemical offensive capability. This position had persisted in the 1980s despite the growing strength of the argument that possession of a retaliatory capability would be a relatively unsophisticated and economic means of discouraging recourse by the Soviet Union to chemical weapons, whose use of them would further add to the Warsaw Pact's non-nuclear superiority. There was now widespread use by the enemy of chemicals to support attacks against NORTHAG, principally launched in BM–21 rockets. These equipments operated in battalion groups of eighteen which, when fired in unison, were able to land 720 rockets on a square kilometre within fifteen seconds. The warm weather was ideal for the use of non-persistent agents such as HCN. This has a hazard duration of only a few minutes at 10°C in moderate wind conditions with rain, or at 15°C in sunny conditions with a light breeze. Soldiers not wearing respirators within the target area died within a few minutes of inhaling the vapour. The agent evaporated so quickly that Soviet assault troops would be able to move through the target area with only minor precautions. Despite peacetime training, Allied casualties in forward areas as the offensive opened were considerable.

At the same time, major airfields were attacked with chemical agents (usually mustard, or G- or V-type nerve gases) delivered by missiles, each one of which could put down sufficient of a persistent agent to cause severe disruption over the whole airfield complex. Ground crew were forced to wear full personal protective equipment to carry out maintenance and aircraft refuelling and re-arming. This severely handicapped their performance and increased aircraft turn-round times significantly.

Major logistic installations and communication points, where large numbers of the civilians operating them had no protective equipment, received similar treatment. Physical removal of persistent agents was virtually impossible while further missile attacks maintained a high level of lethal contamination. Such attacks upon airfields and logistic installations caused more prolonged disruption than sustained high-explosive bombardment.

Even a minute quantity of a highly toxic agent such as HCN, either inhaled or absorbed through the skin, was capable of causing death within a few minutes unless prompt medical attention was available. Medical services soon overloaded with battle casualties were severely taxed to cope with casualties caused by chemicals as well.

Constant precautions and the wearing of appropriate personal protective equipment quickly reduced the casualty rate. Excellent personal protective equipment had been available to I British Corps since the middle 1970s and had been rushed into service by other European NATO countries just in time to prove its value. Without it, very heavy casualties would have resulted from chemical agents delivered against forward troops not only by rocket launcher and *FROG* missiles but also by conventional artillery and from spray tanks mounted on ground-attack aircraft.

The Warsaw Pact attack had also been preceded by very extensive ECM and anti-radar activity from the Eastern side. This was initially by no means ineffective, but was very soon seen to be quite dramatically inferior to the resources in electronic warfare available to the West.

In rather less than an hour after the opening of initial preparations for the land offensive, four powerful armoured thrusts, each on a divisional front led by an advanced group of mixed arms in regimental strength, had moved through swiftly prepared gaps in the frontier defences into the territory of the Federal Republic. The form of the attack, when it came, was by no means unexpected. Preceded by light forces operating as far ahead as the

errain allowed, the first wave in the main assault on each axis was made up of the T–72 tank regiments of the armoured divisions, operating on divisional fronts never more than eight kilometres wide and sometimes as little as two, depending on the nature of the ground. The leading tank battalions were closely followed by motor-rifle companies in their BMP armoured combat vehicles (sometimes no more than 100 metres or so in rear), whose chief purpose was known to be to suppress the opposing anti-tank defences. Following closely behind the tank divisions were the motor-rifle divisions, each consisting of one armoured regiment and three motor-rifle regiments, which were prepared to exploit the breakthrough which such a heavy concentration of armour in the lead could hardly fail to achieve. Turning off the line of march into encounter battles their purpose was to sweep opposition out of the way and thus allow the tank and motor-rifle divisions in the next echelon, piling on into the battle, to maintain the impetus of the advance.

The general offensive in Europe opened in accordance with the subsequently recovered plan whose substance has been given on pages 116–20. Though this plan was not, of course, known to Allied intelligence in detail until after the war, the pattern of the offensive caused no great surprise. SHAPE expected, for example, that heavy pressure would initially develop along the whole front, followed by major concentrations to break through at selected points as well as very numerous probing operations to find and exploit opportunities for deep penetration. It was realized that the verification by NATO commanders of the main axes of thrust at a very early stage would be of the greatest importance. Where, for example, would 3 Shock Army be directed? South-west, to follow through behind the initial onslaught by 8 Guards Army, in a drive for Frankfurt? This would tax CENTAG severely. Or westwards against NORTHAG? This could be more dangerous still. The considerable loss of satellite surveillance was a severe blow, even if in part offset by intelligence from other sources. Reconnaissance in any depth in such a hostile environment was difficult enough for special unmanned air vehicles relying on their small size and radar reflection to evade enemy defences. For manned aircraft, operating singly on deep penetration missions without the benefits of defence suppression and adequate electronic counter-measures, it was an extremely difficult and dangerous task. But the strategic importance of identifying the main axes of the thrust was such that it had to be tried, tried, and tried again, no matter what the cost.

The Allied tactical air forces and air defences, already on full alert, had responded to the opening of the offensive at once. They concentrated initially on both defensive and offensive counter-air operations to reduce Soviet air activity, and to strive for a tolerable air situation over the battle and behind the battle area in AFCENT airspace. COMAAFCE's (Commander Allied Air Forces Central Europe) assessment of priorities in the first few hours of the conflict is discussed in detail in Chapter 20 on the air campaign.

The picture that began to be clarified in HQ AFCENT on the late afternoon of 4 August, out of the flood of information coming in, can be described as follows.

At the northern end of the Central Region Bremen airfield, so recently, ironically enough, protected by a US brigade, was in Soviet hands. It had been seized by one of the very few fully successful fifth-column actions, followed up by airborne infantry. A Soviet air-portable division under very strong air cover, was now building up on the airhead thus formed. Three divisions out of 2 Guards Tank Army, slowed down but not stopped by the action of covering forces which had been furnished by the Americans to strengthen the forward defences of the Dutch. were fighting their way towards the Bremen airhead through I Netherlands Corps. One Soviet division out of 2 Guards Tank Army had turned up northwards in the direction of Kiel, followed, it appeared, by two Polish divisions, one armoured, one motorized. The 6 Polish Airborne Division was also known to be concentrated in the north, with special deep penetration troops from Neuruppin, units from the East German Willi Sänger Special Services organization and naval specialists.

The city of Hamburg, masked by a strong Red Army force to the south of it across the Elbe, was apparently being bypassed for the present. The Hamburg *Senat* had urged strongly that the Allies declare Hamburg an open city, which meant that no troops of any origin would be allowed to enter and, since its use was denied to both sides it would not be attacked by either. Under strong pressure from the FRG, this was soon agreed by the NATO Council. The Soviet attitude was not made known.

Refugee movement from the relatively thinly populated areas of north Niedersachsen was already considerable. There was here an unwelcome forestaste of what lay in store further south.

In the centre of the NORTHAG area a strong armoured column from what was almost certainly 3 Shock Army had been launched on a two-divisional front, with four more divisions in the follow-up. It was moving westwards, in the direction of Hannover. Movement behind it along the same axis was observed from 20 Guards Army.

On the Central Army Group front to the south of NORTHAG an armoured column from 8 Guards Army with two divisions up was driving at Frankfurt, which lay only 100 kilometres from the Demarcation Line, but with difficult country in the Thüringer Wald to be crossed on the way. Four more Soviet divisions were known to be following up the first two.

Further south on the CENTAG front another column, again with two divisions up and four following, almost certainly from 1 Guards Tank Army, was pressing towards Nürnberg.

Chemical attack, heavy in NORTHAG, not used in CENTAG, had a varying impact: the Americans, who did not have to face it, were, with the British, technically best

prepared to meet it, the Germans and the British stood i
best, the effect on the Belgians was mixed and that upor
the Dutch on the whole rather bad.

The main result of chemical attack was less the infliction
of casualties, which were never intolerably high after the
initial attacks, than the severe constraint on physica
activity occasioned by defensive precautions, particularly
the wearing of respirators and cumbrous protective clothing. The performance of combat infantry was degraded
under full precautions by as much as 60 per cent. Mobility
was reduced in avoiding contaminated areas. The requirement for chemical reconnaissance took time and units
were frequently forced for lack of it to fight in a contaminated environment. Similar constraints applied to headquarters. Staff officers under threat of attack had to work
in protective equipment, including gloves and respirators
with a significant degradation in command and control.

On the opening day of the offensive Soviet ground-
attack aircraft also used napalm against forward Allied
units. Fortunately most were well spread out and casualties, where they occurred, although gruesome, were smal
in number. Attacks were also mounted against tanks and
some tank losses resulted. Allied tank commanders had
been taught to drive straight through any napalm attack
and, generally speaking, tanks which continued to motor
on in this way drove themselves out of trouble. The target
against which napalm was used to greatest effect was soft-
skinned, that is unarmoured vehicles, which stood a poor
chance of survival against it. Quite heavy casualties were
sustained in soft-skinned transport in the opening days of
the offensive.

Although Allied formations had no answer to napalm
attacks other than to redouble their vigilance against low-
flying aircraft, such attacks tended to lessen in frequency
and intensity as the Russians found that the damage being
caused, particularly against Allied tanks, did not warrant
the high cost in aircraft. Although sporadic attacks con-

inued throughout the following days the use of napalm was
ot regarded by the Allies as offering a major hazard.

No nuclear weapons, by the end of the first day, had as
et been used on either side. The Soviet declaration
otwithstanding, SACEUR had felt obliged by the uncer-
ainty of the situation to withhold some of his strike
ircraft – chiefly F–111s, *Buccaneers* and *Tornados* –
rom the battle for possible nuclear action. Their absence
esulted in a slight but significant increase in Soviet
umerical superiority in the air.

Whether in the air or on the ground, it was chiefly forces
f the Soviet Union which had been so far engaged. Three
olish divisions with some East German specialists were
nown to have moved into Denmark. One tank and two
notor-rifle divisions of the East German Army had been
n action against NORTHAG. No troops from any country
ther than Poland and East Germany in the Warsaw Pact
ad yet been identified in action.

Without any doubt the most important development of
hat first morning of open hostilities in Europe was the
leclaration by the French government of its intention to
arry out to the full its obligations under the Atlantic
Treaty. France was now, therefore, in a state of war
gainst the Soviet Union and its allies in the Warsaw Pact.

II French Corps in Germany, some 50,000 strong, when
ssigned to Allied Command Europe and placed by
SACEUR under command to the Commander-in-Chief,
Central Region (CINCENT), was in the first instance put
nto regional reserve, with a warning to be in readiness for
a move forward in Bavaria. Three further French divisions,
f the smaller size which had resulted from a reorganiz-
tion at the end of the seventies (8,200 men in armoured
livisions, 6,500 in infantry), were under orders to move in
rom France forthwith. The mobilization operation, which
vould in due course produce fourteen divisions more, was
lready under way. Particularly welcome was the addition
f the eighteen fighter-bomber squadrons of the French
Tactical Air Force, even if only to be used – on the first

day at any rate – in support of French formations. More important than anything else for the immediate future however, was the availability of French ports and airfields and the massive and quite invaluable increase to the theatre's depth, particularly in the matter of airspace.

The French nuclear capability was retained firmly and exclusively in French hands.

Though the intervention of the French gave a degree of encouragement to the Allies whose importance it would be hard to overestimate, the situation on the ground in the Central Region at nightfall on the first day was far from promising (see Situation Map p. 197). The covering forces along the entire forward edge of the battle area, with the exception of those to the east of Frankfurt between Alsfeld and Bamberg, had been driven back. In the north, sheer weight of numbers had enabled the enemy to push regiment-sized groups of all arms, very strong in tanks and armoured infantry, almost invariably moving mounted, with powerful tactical air support, round centres of NATO opposition that had been effectively pinned down south of Hamburg. These groups were now driving on to link up with the air-transported Soviet units which were deploying out of the Bremen airhead. Soviet airborne infantry units with light support were in their turn feeling forward to seize crossing points over the River Weser against determined but not always well co-ordinated opposition from units of I Netherlands and II British Corps.

In the North German plain armoured units from German and I British Corps, extricated with some difficulty from encirclement, were now regrouping north of Hannover to face the main threat pressing down upon them from the north and east. The North German plain was no longer the wide open tank-run it had still been held to be (perhaps even then no longer correctly) a decade or so before. Villages had become townships, offering opportunities for anti-tank delaying action which the Germans and the British had been quick to seize.

developing tactical practices already referred to which had much in common. Operating in small and inconspicuous detachments, with *Milan* ATGW and the recently introduced (and long overdue) replacement for the *Carl Gustav* recoilless rifle, the British had shown a special aptitude for what they called 'sponge' tactics. It was remarkable how regularly distributed the villages and small townships of Niedersachsen were, with groups of habitations separated from each other by some 3,000 metres. The British practice, which was very like that of the German *Jagd Kommandos*, was to install a platoon of infantry, organized to man two *Milan* ATGW and otherwise armed only to protect itself, in the last houses of the village, with another village similarly garrisoned, very little further away than the effective range of a *Milan* missile, which was about 2,000 metres. The leading tanks of a Soviet column would be allowed through unmolested. The third, or fifth, or seventh would be attacked and destroyed with the first shot. If BMP were far up with the leading tanks, several of these would be sent up in flames as well. Before an effective clearance operation could be mounted against it the NATO platoon would then be withdrawn, perhaps by a previously reconnoitred route, for similar action in the next village. It was here that the German *Jagd Kommandos* were particularly effective, for most of the men in them were local resident reservists.

Both in the urban development of the North German plain and, with appropriate adjustment, in the hill country of the Harz, these tactics began to show promise, even on the first day, of a significant capacity for the absorption of armoured impetus. The depth of the enemy's penetration by nightfall on the 4th had certainly not been as great in the NORTHAG sector as he must have hoped. It was still great enough, nonetheless, to put the army group's ability to retain its balance in some doubt.

In the NORTHAG sector, as elsewhere in the Central Region, another serious problem was emerging. An immense, sprawling swarm of civilian refugees from the towns and villages of Niedersachsen was already beginning to cause the difficulties that had long been foreseen – and feared. It was greatly to the Soviet advantage to increase disorder wherever possible, while trying to keep clear the main axes of their advance. Ground-attack aircraft maintained a ceaseless rain of machine-gun fire along these axes, with small anti-personnel fragmentation bombs, the Soviet intention clearly being not so much to cause casualties (though they minded little about these) as to drive refugee traffic off any roads they intended to use. Armoured engineer equipment moving with leading tanks swept derelict civilian vehicles to one side without noticeable loss of momentum to the advancing columns. The tanks themselves were driven without hesitation through groups of people vainly struggling to get clear, charging on at high speeds over human wreckage already pulped by vehicles ahead of them. Some side roads soon became jammed, and Allied troops were being seriously impeded by a chaotic mass of pedestrians and vehicles which it was nearly impossible, in spite of heroic and efficient work by German police and Home Defence units, to control.

In the CENTAG sector, with III German Corps on the left under pressure and pinned down, it had become clear by early afternoon on the 4th that a major thrust directed towards Hersfeld was developing on the left of V US Corps, with a secondary effort through Fulda towards Hanau, along the Kinzig river valley and the ridges running south-west to the Rhine-Main plain. The covering force of reinforced US armoured cavalry had used its anti-tank weapons and artillery admirably from first light onwards, making good use of favourable terrain to slow the enemy's advance. It had even been found possible to turn the great numbers of the enemy's vehicles to his disadvantage by blocking defiles which it then took time to clear. In this the F–15 aircraft of the US Air Force, having already established a clear superiority in air-to-air action, were particularly effective, operating in a secondary ground-attack role.

In the CENTAG sector, too, very good use was being made of German *Jagd Kommandos*, deployed far forward in well-sited localities. In CENTAG, however, the emphasis was laid more on the actual stopping – or at least delaying – power of the armoured covering force. The terrain, for one thing, was in general closer, more thickly wooded and more up-and-down than in the north, and thus more favourable to the defence. For another thing, it was dangerously short of depth. There was no ground here to be traded for time.

Time-consuming actions had been fought, with very considerable loss to the enemy, before Fulda at Hunfeld, in front of Schlitz, and south-east of Hersfeld. Fortunately for the defence the weather was clear and the maximum range of ATGW could be exploited. The covering force on this part of the CENTAG front exchanged losses with the attackers at a rate in their own favour of nearly five to one, but they were obliged in the process to yield some fifteen to twenty kilometres.

With III German Corps on their left fighting hard and giving very little away, the brunt of the attack on 4 August in the CENTAG area was met at about 1600 hours by the armoured division on the left of V US Corps. Four Soviet tank regiments ploughed into the two brigades on the left of the division, the motorized infantry companies, mounted in their BMP, coming along close behind the leading tanks. Another tank regiment and a motorized infantry regiment followed up. With nearly 100 T–72s leading, the Soviet attack ran into a network of anti-tank fire which the enemy's heavy artillery preparation for nearly an hour before, and the best efforts of his tactical air support, had been unable entirely to suppress. The leading US battalions were forced back several kilometres through their own anti-tank defences, but as these reduced the impetus of the assault it was possible to regain some, at least, of the ground lost. By nightfall the two leading Soviet divisions had gained, in the event, a few kilometres, but with very high losses. Pressure continued through the night. When the attack was resumed with a new ferocity at first light on the 5th, by two fresh Soviet divisions which had passed through the first in the hours of darkness, it was met by the combined strength of two US divisions, of which one was from those most newly arrived, and brought to a halt, at least for the time being, after relatively shallow penetration, just forward of Alsfeld. The V US Corps front now extended from Alsfeld in the north to Schluchtern in the south.

On its right, further south, VII US Corps had faced a major attack on the opening day, following exactly the same pattern, on the Meiningen-Schweinfurt axis along the River Main near Würzburg. Again, ground had been lost, but the effectiveness of the anti-tank defences had prevented a decisive breakthrough.

Further south still, II German Corps was fighting a stubborn rearguard action in the area of Nürnberg, giving away no more ground than was absolutely necessary in the expectation of the early arrival of the French. There was little enough they could do. The action of covering forces in the Bayrischer Wald had gained too little time to prevent the Russians from bouncing a crossing over the Danube. As night fell powerful armoured columns of the Soviet 1 Guards Tank Army were bypassing München to the north. The next hope of stopping them, at this southern end of the Central Region, would be along the River Lech.

In spite of the splendid news from France, with the First French Army moving eastwards to strengthen the southern flank and the French Tactical Air Force already in action ahead of it, the day, 5 August 1985, ended in uncertainty and gloom.

It was by now clear that at any one of half a dozen points at once, on either army group front in the Central Region, the Russians could develop a high degree of local superiority in armoured and armoured infantry attacks, under massive artillery and air-to-ground support, and would press any advantage with the utmost vigour and complete disregard of casualties. Soviet momentum was maintained by heavy concentrations of armour and firepower on narrow fronts; flanks were largely ignored. With the weight of the attack and the determination – even the recklessness – with which it was pressed wherever it took place, penetration at one or more points was inevitable. Swift exploitation by troops of the second echelon would then follow hard on the heels of the first. Immediate counter-attack from the Allied side was in the early stages rarely possible. The Russians made no attempt to consolidate ground. It was hard to find a moment, however fleeting, when they could be caught off-balance. Counter-attack often simply ran head-on into the armour of the next wave and was smothered almost before it had got under way. Even the concentrated fire of Allied divisional and corps artillery could for the most part only attenuate somewhat the force of attacks pressed with such violence and in such numbers, with so high a disregard for loss. Air-to-ground attack, in this first forty-eight hours, was nothing like as plentiful as the corps and subordinate commanders would have wished, but the Allied air forces were, on CINCENT's express order, being used to counter the enemy's air forces both in the air and on the ground in an endeavour to establish a tolerable air situation in addition to their continuous pounding of 'choke points' now in rear of the main battle.

It was only rarely that the attacks of Soviet tanks and armoured infantry could be stopped. Tanks would almost always get through, and fresh waves of attacking armour would move in behind them. Equipment for equipment, sub-unit for sub-unit, man for man, the NATO defence was by no means inferior to the attacking forces. In one important respect at least, that is in almost every aspect of the whole field of electronic technology, NATO was already showing up better. On the first day, however, the defending formations were simply being swamped by numbers, dominated and driven on by blind faith in the doctrine of the total offensive.

But even on the first day weaknesses began to appear in

the way the Russians fought their battle. The handling of armoured infantry provides an example which deserves attention, for it was to be of critical importance.

The BMP, improved but still essentially the same machine, had originally been evolved as an armoured infantry combat vehicle for use in exploitation of nuclear action. Its chief purpose was to move in swiftly to overwhelm, by mainly mounted attack, whatever NATO defences still survived the nuclear attack, travelling in close company with the tanks whose further action would resolve the battle. To maintain the impetus of the armoured advance some protection of the tanks by infantry was indispensable. But the BMP was itself highly vulnerable to anti-tank attack. The precision-guided missiles now deployed by NATO in very considerable numbers showed that mounted attack was often suicidal. The toll of BMP on the first day was heavy.

The Red Army had long recognized that in the non-nuclear battle mounted action for motor infantry was not always feasible, though it was certainly worth trying, particularly in the first assault. The alternative was to dismount the infantry for an attack on foot against such NATO anti-tank defences as survived the suppressive fire of artillery and air forces. In the event, well-located Allied missile launchers survived, even on that first day, in considerable numbers. Dismounted infantry had no hope of keeping up with tanks moving at their best speed. When motor-rifle infantry were prevented by anti-tank fire from going in mounted, therefore, the whole attack slowed down.

We have seen how Soviet tactics for the penetration of hostile defences in the non-nuclear variant of the land battle had latterly come to depend upon manoeuvre at least as much as on massed frontal attack. Manoeuvre by mounted infantry demanded both tactical surprise and effective suppression of anti-tank defensive fire. In the battle of the Central Region neither, for the Warsaw Pact, was complete, even on the first day.

Situation,
1800 hrs 4 Aug 1985

TERRITORY OCCUPIED BY
WARSAW PACT FORCES

Professor J. Erickson, one of the best informed and soundest observers of the Soviet military scene, had said in 1977: 'Above all the Soviet command will pay the closest attention to the loss-rate in the *first 10–15 km of the advance* . . .' These were prophetic words.

A battle drill to deal with the differing requirements of each combined arms tactical engagement had proved, for the Red Amy, impossible to find. When should the infantry dismount? How were the varying *speeds* of tank, BMP, SP gun and foot soldier to be related? How was the *fire* of tank, BMP, SP gun, divisional artillery and helicopter gunship, with tactical air support thrown in, to be co-ordinated? The command responsibilities formerly held in the Red Army at division now devolved in greater measure than before on the regiment, which was akin to the Allied brigade, but the heaviest load of all lay on the battalion commander. In a reinforced motor-rifle battalion with a minute staff of four officers, one NCO and eight men, he would be attempting to control a force some 700 strong, with a company of thirteen tanks, a battery of six guns (or even a battalion of eighteen), a mortar battery, anti-air weapons, an ATGW platoon, reconnaissance and engineer elements, thirty BMP, sixty light machine guns and 356 assault riflemen. It was a tall order.

The Allied maxim was a simple one, even if to follow it demanded fortitude: stay put, keep your head down, and go for the commander. He was not all that difficult to locate. The information coming in from many sources, processed in JTIDS and almost instantaneously disseminated, could often pinpoint centres of command at divisional and regimental level. They had then to be attacked, which was rather less easy.

At lower levels the problem was simple. Junior commanders on the NATO side had been taught to look for the command tank. Its behaviour pattern at company level, for instance, gave it a quite unmistakable signature. The temptation to take the easiest shot first was one to be resisted. Take out the command tank; this would not stop the attack but it would at least blunt the follow-through. Battalion command was harder to break, but to take that out was even more rewarding.

Few junior commanders, in the heat and confusion, the clamour and horror, the fear and growing weariness of those battles on the first days, would perhaps have thought of putting it quite that way, but what they were trying to do was to uncouple the parts of an interdependent whole. This would not stop the onrush. To do that in the case of 3 Shock Army would have meant the elimination (or at least the neutralization) of some 120 artillery batteries and 2,800 armoured fighting vehicles (AFV). To hold a single breakthrough on one axis would have meant accounting for some thirty batteries and 800 AFV. What was already just beginning to happen, however, if not on the first day at least towards the end of the second, was the emergence of a hope in those Allied commanders whose nerves were strongest that, if wedges could be driven between the main elements of the Soviet combined arms operation, the enemy might just be prevented from breaking all the way through to the Rhine. There was also now a growing awareness on the other side that to reach it in nine days might not be easy.

What was also beginning to emerge was that a battle seen superficially at the outset as a mainly armoured offensive against an anti-tank defence was becoming more and more a contest between firepower and counter-measures. In an older terminology it would have been called an artillery battle between battery and counter-battery; in newer terms it was seen as a battle between rival arrays of electronics.

On the 5th, after a night in which the pressure had been hardly less than by day, the advance went on. In the north the enemy secured crossings over the Weser north of Minden and leading elements were reported moving west towards the Netherlands. I Belgian Corps had been pushed back west of Kassel; I British Corps was still fighting in the outskirts of Hannover and, in the built-up areas and the hill country of the Harz, exploiting with German reservist *Jagd Kommandos* the advantage of the 'sponge'; I German Corps was established east and west along the Teutoburger Wald; II British Corps was extending its left westwards to the Dutch frontier, behind which reserve formations were hastily preparing defences in low-lying country now being flooded.

On the CENTAG front the first of the newly arrived US divisions, which had already fought such a valuable action, had been withdrawn from V US Corps to join the strong Canadian Brigade Group in army group reserve. The First French Army, taking II German Corps under command, had now assumed responsibility for that sector of the region which ran from Nürnberg south to the Austrian frontier, coming for the time being under command to CENTAG, with which French ties, as has been seen, were close.

By the evening of 5 August further enemy attacks had opened a salient on the left of III German Corps, in the extreme north of the CENTAG sector on the Corps boundary with the Belgians, and a Soviet thrust was developing towards Giessen. This was checked by flank action from the V US Corps between Alsfeld and Schluchtern. It was perhaps significant that the leading divisions in the enemy's assault were now more often motor-rifle than tank divisions, and powerful probing for weak points was tending more and more to replace the massive armoured assault of tanks in the first wave. The Allied tactic, at unit level, which was essentially a matter of striving wherever possible to separate the tanks from their supporting infantry, was clearly paying off.

Further south the anti-tank defences of VII US Corps, with strong artillery and increasing tactical air support, had just been sufficient to contain a major attempt to break through south-east of Frankfurt where pressure was again building up. From Nürnberg southwards the situation was confused, but what information was available suggested that the First French Army with II German Corps was still more or less in control along the Lech.

Over the next five days of bright, clear weather, as growing French strength in the south did much to stabilize the right flank, it became increasingly clear that the main effort would continue to be made in the north. The boundary between the two army groups had been moved up to give the Kassel area, with command of the much weakened I Belgian Corps, to CENTAG. After very hard fighting had held up a determined attempt to push down to Frankfurt through Giessen, COMCENTAG now believed that he had a good chance of holding an area whose forward edge would run from Kassel down through Alsfeld to south of Würzburg. If the Soviet 3 Shock Army had been put in behind 1 Guards Tank Army the outlook would have been different, but it had been committed to the attack in the north.

By 7 August the continued enforcement of chemical defensive measures upon NORTHAG was beginning to cause concern, and pressure from field commanders for some form of retaliation grew. In theory a nuclear response had always been considered a possibility, at least by the British, but at this stage SACEUR was in no doubt that such a response would be an irrational risk. He was, however, prepared to see chemicals used in retaliation; indeed, authority for their use had already been delegated to local US commanders. SACEUR thus felt able to offer some chemical support to NORTHAG. It presented no problem to COMAAFCE to allot a squadron of US Air Force F–4 *Phantoms* equipped with spray tanks to 2 ATAF, while a quantity of US 155 mm chemical ammunition was released to the gunners of the British and German divisions of NORTHAG. This capability was put to immediate use.

The *Phantoms* attacked second echelon and reserve Soviet divisions with extensive and heavy concentrations of persistent lethal agents. These attacks forced Soviet units into unplanned moves. The personal protective

Situation, 1800 hrs 8 Aug

TERRITORY OCCUPIED BY
WARSAW PACT FORCES.

equipment used by Soviet soldiers was not suitable for prolonged wear and under continued attack by persistent gases grew almost intolerably irksome. It was less easy for NORTHAG formations to use the US 155 mm chemical ammunition. It only slowly became available, for the logistic problem in drawing the ammunition from US locations caused delay, while Allied forces were unskilled in its technical and tactical use. The overall effect of the use of chemical agents against the Soviet offensive was nonetheless welcome. Protective clothing and equipment taken with Soviet prisoners was found to be rougher, clumsier, worse-fitting and considerably less effective than that of the Allies – which was itself a great improvement on what had been available only two or three years before. Red Army troops suffered in consequence more serious casualties from the same weight of attack. Their less flexible command and control procedures were more easily impeded. On balance, Soviet commanders considered a chemical exchange to be to their disadvantage, and since the Allies adhered to the rule of only using chemical agents in retaliation their use on the battlefield, as distinct from the rear areas, soon declined.

Refugees were posing an acute and growing problem in the south, as in the north. Large numbers of people from Augsburg and Ulm had moved in the direction of Stuttgart, and a rapidly increasing mass of frightened people was building up in the vicinity of Karlsruhe. The same sort of thing was also happening where crowds fleeing from Nürnberg and Würzburg, augmented by refugees from smaller places, were bearing down on Mannheim. From the Frankfurt area there was a good deal of movement in the direction of Wiesbaden and Mainz. The general picture was one of a widespread and virtually uncontrollable flow from east to west, much of it on foot with possessions piled on vehicles drawn by animals or pushed or dragged by hand, with a chaotic jumble of motor vehicles of every description, more and more of them abandoned as petrol supplies gave out. At the Rhine crossings the pressure was tremendous; to keep the bridges open was putting increasing strain on Federal German police and territorial troops. Disorder was increased by determined Soviet air attack, both at low and medium levels, of which some at least always got through the defences. The importance of maintaining freedom of movement across the Rhine for the Allies, and of blocking it for the Warsaw Pact, was fully realized on both sides. By the fourth day some success began to attend the strenuous efforts of Federal German police and territorial troops to establish control over refugee movements and divert them into areas of open country east of the river. This did much to relieve pressure on the Rhine crossings but could not prevent serious interference with the movement of troops and other essential military traffic.

To the north of the Central Region AFNORTH was proving a tougher proposition for the Warsaw Pact than many in the West had expected, perhaps because few had much experience of the very great difficulty of movement from north to south in Norway. By 4 August the Allied Command Europe (ACE) Mobile Force of seven battalions with supporting troops had been put in by air and deployed north of Narvik. A Royal Marine Commando came in from Britain by sea and other Allied reinforcements arrived by sea and air to strengthen and support Norwegian national forces deployed in north Norway.

Advanced elements of a Soviet motor-rifle division crossed into Norway from the Kola peninsula on 4 August. A second was already moving westwards through Finnish Lapland, directed on Narvik. The fact that the Soviet and Finnish railway systems were integrated meant that no movement problem hampered the early follow-on of eight to ten more Soviet divisions. Soviet air superiority was complete.

The relative strengths of ground troops in AFNORTH did not, however, give a true measure of the Warsaw Pact advantage. It was less than it looked. The strength of the defence lay in the very great difficulty of deployment for offensive action, even with a favourable air situation. It was, in fact, only the action of a Soviet amphibious force in effecting a landing south of Bodo on 10 August that was to compel a southward redeployment of Allied forces to protect the land line of communication through north Trondelag and Nordland. By 15 August a firm Allied defence was based on Trondheim, which was unlikely to be seriously threatened so long as a delaying action continued to be successfully fought in the north.

To the south of the Central Region, HQ AFSOUTH, with a hastily put together Italian government in exile, had moved on 6 and 7 August to Spain. The Italian peninsula was now entirely under Soviet control, though with no great strength in Red Army troops.

The Italian and US air elements based in Italy constituting 5 Allied Tactical Air Force, after their initial operations, found themselves overtaken by the virtual disintegration of the NATO Southern Region. The wings and squadrons were faced with a fleeting chance and those aircrew who had serviceable aircraft took it by flying to Spain and the south of France where they were subsequently used as a general reserve of tactical air power for the central battle, chiefly in the south of the Central Region.

Holland came under Soviet occupation as far south as the River Maas by 10 August, the seat of government having removed to Eindhoven. The last remnants of a Dutch defence of the frontier had been dispersed in an action near Lingen on the 8th, and thereafter only floods caused by the opening of the dykes and an active civilian resistance had stood in the invaders' way.

On 10 August the right-hand corps of the Northern Army Group, I British, was still in being, though battered, in the area round Paderborn. Its anti-tank defences had been its salvation. The tactics of the 'sponge' had been highly successful. Small infantry detachments manning ATGW were still lying up in built-up or hilly country, waiting for the vulnerable flank, always trying to reduce the impetus of the enemy's advance by hampering the follow-up and interfering with supply. The concentration of attack at all levels, by every means, on communications, command and control was paying off handsomely. One guided missile could destroy one tank. A single hit on a divisional command post could impose confusion and delay upon a hundred. Even where physical disruption was not possible (and, with the methods currently in use, nodal communication points could quite often be located and destroyed) interference with communication almost always was. It was remarkable how far such interference could reduce the effectiveness of an enemy accustomed to close control by superiors.

To the left of I British Corps, I German Corps was still established along the Teutoburger Wald, offering so great a threat to the enemy's advance from east to west as to invite a major effort very soon to push it out. On its left, in turn, stood II British Corps, forced back to positions south and west of Münster, with one US brigade under command on the west bank of the Rhine. The remnants of I Netherlands Corps, which had taken very heavy punishment in the past few days, were strung out further west towards Nijmegen.

By the evening of the 11th, I German Corps had been put under such severe pressure from the south and west as to be no longer able to hold the high ground on either side of the Minden Gap. NORTHAG's main preoccupation was now the defence of the Ruhr and Rhineland and the prevention of a breakthrough on the west bank of the Rhine in the area of Venlo.

In the Central Region the Warsaw Pact invasion had not, it is true, achieved the swift and overwhelming success planned for it. If it had not been completely successful, however, the shortfall so far lay only in the timetable. Allied Command Europe was facing a serious position which was now growing critical.

It was on 13 August that SACEUR made known two decisions which can now be seen, among the many difficult problems before him in those momentous days, to have been truly critical to the outcome of the war in Europe. The first was a final refusal to endorse any of the urgent requests of his subordinate commanders for the release of battlefield nuclear weapons. The second concerned the commitment of reserves,

Speculation would be idle on how long any Warsaw Pact offensive into the Central Region of Europe could have continued under the thunderous threat of national revolt, soon to be looming, as we shall learn, in the Red Army's rear. What is beyond doubt is that the Allied counter-offensive, shortly to be opened by the forces of the Central Region northwards towards Bremen, was to set up a completely new operational situation for the Pact to face on the land battlefield. To bring this under control was clearly not impossible for the Pact forces. Of the huge military resources available to the Warsaw Pact, relatively little had as yet been lost. But regrouping would be needed on a considerable scale. There was already a growing uncertainty in the rearward political infrastructure, with increasing threats to the security of lines of communication, and a discernible decline in confidence in the reliability of non-Soviet formations. Divisions expected to follow up for the maintenance of offensive momentum were more and more being kept where they were, to safeguard the very lines of communication along which they should have moved. These and other related factors were to combine to render less and less stable the basis on which the operation of containing the Allied counter-offensive and regaining offensive momentum, once this had been lost, would have to rest. A real check to the forward impetus of the invasion of West Germany could not therefore be regarded as only a temporary setback. It was likely, in all the circumstances, to mark the beginning of something much more important.

It was the Supreme Allied Commander's decision, at a time of great uncertainty, to commit his theatre reserves that made this all-important check possible.

The Allied position in the Central Region at nightfall on 12 August was not very good (see Situation Map, p. 209). The French command in the south – now the Southern Army Group (SOUTHAG), with II French Corps and II German Corps under command, together with a division's worth of Austrian troops – was under heavy pressure along the line of the Lech. Here and there it was losing ground. North of the present boundary between SOUTHAG and the Central Army Group (CENTAG), which now ran from Karlsruhe through Bayreuth, with its three corps and some eight divisions, was in a similar situation. It was just holding on to an area whose forward edge ran from west of Kassel to Würzburg and was hourly expecting attack by fresh formations.

A great blow to CENTAG during the day had been a direct hit from a missile on its Main HQ in the field. The mobile tactical HQ further forward was unharmed, but unhappily the commanding general was in Main HQ at the time and was killed outright. He was replaced by the commander of V US Corps, whose vigorous defence in the Fulda area on CENTAG's left, the hinge of the whole army group's position, had been of such vital importance.

The new Commander of the Central Army Group and Commander of the United States Army in Europe was already a familiar figure on television screens on both sides of the Atlantic. It was an appointment as popular with the American public, to whom he had in a few short days of intense exposure become something of a folk hero, as it was in the command he now took over.

To the north of the Central Army Group NORTHAG was deployed in a great bow, with a position running first of all northwards from west of Kassel to within twenty kilometres of Hannover, which was now in enemy hands. Thereafter, the forward edge was much as it had been for the past few days, running south-west along the Teutoburger Wald to Osnabrück, then westwards to the Rhine near Wesel. It was here on the left that most ground in NORTHAG's sector had been lost, in spite of a deter-

Situation, 1800 hrs 12 Aug

▨ TERRITORY OCCUPIED BY
WARSAW PACT FORCES

DENMARK

NORTH SEA

Kiel Canal

HAMBURG

Elbe

NETHERLANDS

AMSTERDAM

S.GRAVENHAGE

ROTTERDAM

Waal

NIJMEGEN

OSNABRÜCK

MINDEN

Teutoburger Wald

BREMEN

HANNOVER

GERMAN

DEMOCRATIC

I Ne

EINDHOVEN

VENLO

WESEL

MÜNSTER

FEDERAL

I Ge

PADERBORN

II Br

Ruhr

XXXX

I Br

KASSEL

LEIPZIG

BRUXELLES

NORTHAG

KÖLN

AACHEN

BONN

XXXX

I Be

REPUBLIC

BRUNSSUM

LIÈGE

Rhine

H e s s e n

BELGIUM

II Ge

REPUBLIC

FULDA

Rheinland

FRANKFURT

V US

LUXEMBOURG

MAINZ

CENTAG

XXX

Main

WÜRZBURG

BAYREUTH

CZECH.

LUXEMBOURG

VII US

MANNHEIM

XXXX

OF GERMANY

KARLSRUHE

II Fr

STUTTGART

Donau

STRASBOURG

SOUTHAG

XXX

FRANCE

II Ge

MÜNCHEN

MILES   100

0

KILOMETRES   150

BASEL

SWITZERLAND

BERN

AUSTRIA

Meuse

Maas

mined defence by II British Corps, disposing of one US
brigade and some Dutch units in addition to two divisions
of its own. West of the Rhine the key Venlo position was
still holding. There was no doubt at all that it would soon
come under very heavy pressure.

In theatre reserve SACEUR was holding the heavy US
division withdrawn in pretty fair shape from V US Corps
on the second day of the battle, the second US reinforcement division now less one brigade, two more US divisions
married to their prepositioned equipment in the first few
days of August, one fairly strong German division, one
rather weaker British division, the Canadian Brigade
Group of almost divisional strength, and some other troops
amounting to about a division all told.

These, adding up in the aggregate to only some seven
divisions' worth, were all nominally under command of
the Central Army Group, but with the firm instruction
that none must be committed by CENTAG without the
Supreme Commander's authority. They were located
largely in Hessen and the Rhineland. Most lay east of the
Rhine. The main Rhine bridges, surprisingly enough, were
still in service, though only through a major effort on the
part of Allied air defence and truly heroic work by army
engineers.

Pressure on the Supreme Allied Commander from
subordinate commanders to release troops from this
reserve had already been considerable, and was now
growing. To all requests, however pressing, SACEUR had
invariably replied that army groups must manage with
whatever local reserves they could find. Inevitably there
had followed urgent insistence on the release of battlefield
nuclear support, as the only possible way of preventing
collapse, if no reserves were to be made available.

The Supreme Commander knew the mind of his Commander-in-Chief, the President of the United States. The
President would go to almost any lengths to avoid nuclear
attack on the cities of the United States. It was not easy

to see how this could be avoided once the battlefield nuclear exchange had begun.

Among the European Allies, opinion on the use of battlefield nuclear weapons in this confused and highly dangerous situation was divided. Understandably the Federal Republic was against it. The United Kingdom was in two minds. The Belgians were in favour, the Dutch against. The French reserved absolutely the right to decide their own nuclear policy but undertook not to use any of their considerable nuclear armoury, battlefield or strategic, without prior consultation.

Meanwhile, Warsaw Pact air attack, conventional and chemical, on the home countries of the Allies, begun on 4 August, continued unabated, though with varying intensity. In the Federal Republic and to a lesser extent in the Low Countries it was hardly to be distinguished from tactical interdiction. In France and the UK it was more strategic in character.

French ports, communication complexes and military installations had suffered considerably from it, though not to the same extent as targets in the UK, which were more important to the US war effort and more readily accessible. There had been no bombing of French cities and it seemed probable, for the present at least, that France would not use her strategic nuclear capability unless there were. But the United Kingdom, in spite of the best efforts of its air defences, was taking a pounding as the battle in the Central Region approached a climax.

It was perfectly clear to SACEUR that if there was any possibility at all that the military position could be held back from total disaster without nuclear weapons it was his plain and compelling duty not to press the President for their use. He was also aware that if he did press for nuclear release his request would almost certainly be granted.

SACEUR was alone and on the spot, and he knew it.

Shortly before midnight, Central European time, on Monday 12 August, the President came up on a voice channel. Satellite communications had not yet been fully restored and visual channels were still far from reliable, but it may also have been that the President preferred an exchange by speech alone.

'Can you do it?' he asked.

The question was a very simple one but nothing more was necessary.

There was a momentary pause.

'It all depends,' the Supreme Commander answered, 'on what is happening in the Atlantic – and whether the air bridge holds.'

'The air bridge still seems to be holding,' was the response. 'We shall know what has happened in the Atlantic in a very few hours.'

What was known already was that four transatlantic convoys bringing from the United States almost the entire heavy equipment and the remaining personnel of two complete corps, already largely lifted in by air, had set out on 8 August and had very soon run into persistent and determined Soviet attack, both from submarines and from the air. Losses were already heavy. Nearly a fifth of the transport shipping had been sunk, with considerable loss to escorting naval forces. Many survivors had been rescued but the sum of the equipment lost – the XM–1 tanks, SP guns, APC, soft-skinned transport, electronic equipment and, above all, munitions, especially for air force weapons and anti-tank and anti-air missiles – represented for the time being a quite serious, if happily only temporary, setback to the Allied war effort.

The personnel for these reinforcing formations, numbering in all some 70,000 officers and men, had already for the most part been moved in over the air bridge to the United Kingdom and north-western France. Considerable use had been made of impressed civilian air transport, and here too there had been losses. Nearly a tenth of the passenger-carrying aircraft bringing over US military reinforcement personnel had been brought down into the sea. The rescue rate of survivors had been high, but this nevertheless represented a setback too.

Troops on the ground in Western Europe were now waiting for the equipment, in all its huge complexity – from a main battle tank to some tiny triumph of electronic micro-processing – without which they could not even approach the battlefield, let alone fight on it. How much of what was wanted would arrive, and what formations SACEUR would be able to put into the critical battle now being fought for the future freedom of the Western world, depended largely on how soon the shipping making its way eastwards across the Atlantic could be brought under land-based air cover from Great Britain and France, within the UK Air Defence Region.

CHAPTER SIXTEEN

SEA POWER

The course of events at sea, immediately following upon the Warsaw Pact incursion into NATO territory on 4 August 1985, is not easy to follow in detail. The overwhelming need to preserve secrecy about their intentions, and the full exploitation of surprise, were reflected in the sparseness of Soviet and Warsaw Pact records, when these became available. On the NATO side it was all that the exiguous staffs could do, once war seemed imminent, to begin to put into effect the complex Alliance plans which had been prepared for just such a contingency. The detailed record disappeared with the miles of telex tape which had to be disposed of as quickly as it accumulated; critical decision-making by telephone and closed-circuit TV was also lost to the record; only the main features of the naval and maritime air operations can be established with reasonable certainty.

From the start-line of 2 Guards Tank Army, on the Elbe near Lübeck, to Flensburg, at the Baltic Exits, is 150 kilometres. By dawn on Monday 5 August, the Russians were there, and the Kiel Canal was in their hands.

The reorganization of the main NATO naval command structure (see Appendix 3) had been the occasion for a thorough review of the maritime aspect of NATO strategy, its concept of operations and its plans. The NATO Joint Allied Command Western Approaches (JACWA) had called for reaffirmation by the NATO Military Committee, the NATO Council of Ministers, and finally the NATO governments, of three cardinal elements in NATO strategy. First, that there would be

change in the determination of NATO to offer the
outest possible resistance on land, as far forward as
ossible. Second, that NATO would remain flexible in
gard to the use of battlefield nuclear weapons. Third,
at the primary maritime task of NATO would be to
isure the safe and timely arrival in Europe of seaborne
inforcements and supplies from North Africa and
sewhere.

JACWA, in developing their plans, had to bear in
ind certain considerations arising from the new com-
and structure and relevant to NATO strategy. These
ere:

1 The fundamental purpose of NATO, as a military
lliance, was to preserve the territorial integrity, politi-
al independence and economic strength of its member
ates.

2 The major member of the Alliance, the United
tates, had national security requirements of critical
nportance besides those of NATO. In particular, her
rategic nuclear weapons were not, except for a few
sBN (submarines, strategic ballistic nuclear), committed
NATO.

3 The British *Polaris* ssBN force, though it was
ommitted to NATO, could in certain circumstances
evert to British national control.

4 The major problem of command and control (apart
om disruption of the electronic environment in war-
me) would be to conduct operations effectively across
he interfaces between JACWA and SACLANT to the
est and north, and between JACWA and SACEUR to
he east and south.

5 It had become glaringly obvious that if the margin
f Warsaw Pact numerical superiority over NATO
ontinued to increase in all arms, accompanied by
echnological equivalence and even advantage in some
ases, the initial shock of Pact aggression in Central
urope might well carry its forces to the Baltic Exits

and the North Sea coast. The lack of depth in th
NATO defensive position on land, therefore, woul
necessitate, in the early stages of a conflict, the inclusio
of the British Isles as the 'rear area' for the Centr
Front. Later, Britain would become a springboard fo
the counter-offensive. The closest possible understandin
between command at sea and on land, between JACWA
SACLANT and SACEUR, would therefore need to b
established and maintained.

6 In order to get the essential seaborne supplies an
reinforcements from North America safely to Europ
when required, SACLANT and JACWA would have t
co-ordinate their strategy and operations closely, an
give each other full support at all times.

7 The special character of the Western Approache
command, comprising naval forces (surface, air an
submarine), maritime air forces and UK air strik
forces, would have to be continually borne in mind.
was to be a 3-D team. The key point was that warship
move at about 500 miles per *day*, aircraft at about 50
miles per *hour*; but whereas aircraft can stay on task fo
a few hours only, ships and submarines can stay at se
for weeks.

8 It was forty years since there had been a majo
war at sea. How would the complex array of weapo
systems, counter-measures and counter-counter-measure
work when the shooting started? There would be surprise
The fog of war might well obscure valuable lessons to b
learned from the first engagements with the enemy. Th
Operations Analysis teams would have to be given ever
opportunity to find out exactly what had happened. Ther
would probably be heavy casualties on both sides. It woul
be just as important to know why we were successful a
why we had failed.

It had been the usual practice, in drawing up NAT
plans, to consider first 'the threat'. JACWA decide
instead, to begin by looking in some detail at what th

Command would have to do, first of all during any period of warning that NATO might have of an impending Soviet or Warsaw Pact attack, then during the first two or three days of hostilities. As far as the opening phase of a war was concerned, they considered how SACLANT and JACWA could achieve sufficient ascendancy over the Soviet Navy, in the Atlantic and elsewhere, to ensure the safe and timely arrival in Europe of the seaborne military supplies and reinforcements essential to sustain SACEUR.

Turning over in their minds the broader aspects of maritime strategy, JACWA recalled a useful division of the maritime task which the British naval and air force staffs had once jointly set down in a War Manual. It contained lessons learned in the UK from the Second World War, not all of which had been applied. Maritime warfare, they had written (the word 'maritime' had been introduced in order to include the naval tasks of the RAF), comprises two separate but complementary functions:

1 *The management of sea use:* the organization and movement of shipping; the loading and unloading of cargoes; the control and defence of ports; and the manning, training and maintenance of naval forces.

This is predominantly a naval responsibility.

2 *Combat with hostile naval and air forces:* offensive and defensive operations of all kinds in support of the maritime aim, including direct support of land forces.

This is predominantly a joint naval and air responsibility.

As to strategy, what were the forces involved? The naval and air general-purpose forces immediately available to NATO and the USSR, for operations in the North Atlantic and Western Approaches (to which the contribution of non-Soviet forces would be negligible), would normally be of the following order:

	Category	NATO	USSR
1	Carrier strike fleet	1	–
2	General purpose support groups	3	2
3	Escort groups	4	2
4	Fleet (nuclear-powered) submarines	44	60
5	Patrol (diesel-electric) submarines	40	40
6	Escort and patrol ships (other than those included in 1, 2 and 3 above)	52	64
7	Maritime strike aircraft (two-thirds carrier-borne)	300	250
8	Maritime patrol aircraft	50	50

Both sides would have a number of logistic support ships; amphibious ships and craft; mine counter-measure ships and auxiliaries. The Soviet Northern Fleet would also include upwards of twenty-five fast missile craft.

There were, of course, in addition, the large Soviet and Warsaw Pact naval and naval air forces in the Baltic, which the naval and air forces of the Federal German Republic and Denmark would have to oppose. In the Mediterranean there were the United States Sixth Fleet and a large part of the French Navy. The Italian, Greek and Turkish naval forces were also earmarked for NATO and would, provided their governments remained staunch, fight the Soviet Navy effectively.

The attitudes of the various governments in North Africa, as well as their capability to support Soviet naval operations, would be of critical importance. The relinquishment by the British, in the 1970s, of a naval presence in the Mediterranean, to be replaced partly by the US Navy, partly by Allied Forces South (AFSOUTH), had proved to be a weakening step.

Considering strategy, therefore, first of all during the

hoped for warning period, JACWA foresaw five main tasks:

1 To put the Western Approaches command on a war footing.

2 To step up reconnaissance of Soviet and Warsaw Pact naval and naval air activities.

3 To inaugurate measures to control and protect shipping.

4 In conjunction with CINCNORTH, SACEUR's major NATO commander in Oslo, to protect the oil and natural gas installations in the North Sea.

5 To ensure the safe and timely movement of all sea traffic between the UK and the Continent in support of SACEUR.

So far, little in the way of strategic thinking was needed. Once hostilities began, however, the options for decision would open up, as, under the impact of enemy action, the demands upon inadequate forces began to come into critical competition.

In the 1914–18 and 1939–45 wars JACWA's predecessors (with the warm approval of the British Admiralty) had proceeded at once to sea with their fleets 'to sweep the enemy from the seas'. Many thousands of miles of largely unproductive steaming had worn out both machinery and men. Valuable ships had been torpedoed, or sunk by air attack, without inflicting even equivalent losses on the enemy. JACWA, as a team, had a most compelling reason for rejecting this precedent. With so few forces at their disposal, and no reserves from which to make good losses, the only offensive operations which could be justified were those which promised to reduce, at once, the level of the threat to NATO's aims.

It was evident that the most potent enemy forces were the sixty nuclear-powered general purpose submarines (SSN) of the Soviet Northern Fleet, together with the

250 *Backfire* maritime strike aircraft also based in the
Murmansk area. JACWA's first two offensive operations, therefore, were as much SACLANT's as JACWA's.
But the system of integrating functional commands
ensured clarity of purpose, of command, and of control.
The British Flag Officer Submarines was, in the NATO
structure, both Commander Submarines, Eastern Atlantic, and Commander Submarines, Western Approaches.
His RAF equivalent, the Air Officer Commanding 18
Group, was Commander Maritime Air, Eastern Atlantic,
and Commander Maritime Air, Western Approaches. The
deployment of NATO submarines on anti-submarine
patrol was therefore to be carried out without delay.
And the launch of a powerful maritime air strike against
aircraft on the ground and air installations in the
Murmansk area was planned to take place at the very
earliest moment possible after the outbreak of hostilities.

The British naval contribution to NATO had been
augmented, during the period 1979–85, following a
sudden, eleventh-hour awakening of public opinion to
Britain's extreme vulnerability to attack upon her seaborne trade and supplies – a vulnerability now felt
almost as much by the other NATO countries in north-
western Europe. The most important elements in the
emergency naval programme were:

1   Three escort carriers. These were container ship
hulls fitted with 'ski-jump' flight decks and containerized
aircraft control and operations modules. Carrying a mix
of V/STOL fighter-strike-reconnaissance aircraft, and
ASW helicopters, these 28-knot ships, built to merchant
ship specifications, were good value for money.
2   Four additional improved *Sheffield*-class fleet
frigates.
3   Twelve corvettes of a new type, for fast patrol ship
duties.
4   Six additional mine counter-measure ships.
5   Five small patrol (diesel-electric) submarines.

This naval construction programme was feasible, despite Great Britain's poor economic performance in the 1970s, because her shipbuilding industry, other than in designated warship building yards, was very short of orders and the extra jobs were warmly welcomed. It seemed a preferable alternative to building merchant ships, at a loss, for Soviet satellite countries, to be employed in cut-throat competition against the merchant fleets of the United Kingdom. The shape and size of the Royal Navy in the mid-1980s was appropriate, therefore, to the two main functions of the UK maritime task, namely, sea-use management and combat with hostile forces. This pattern had become accepted, also, in the other NATO navies, so that the mix of forces achieved overall had gradually moved towards the optimum.

The strategy of SACLANT, as it had evolved under a series of most able incumbents of the post, by 1985 comprised three main elements: first, to maintain in readiness the US Navy's strategic nuclear forces, and ensure that no Soviet operational development could upset the strategic nuclear balance; second, to act, with his conventional forces, as vigorously as possible to reduce the threat from Soviet conventional forces to NATO's seaborne supplies and reinforcements; third, to give direct assistance, as appropriate and feasible, to both SACEUR and JACWA in their operations.

SACLANT's assessment of the combat capability of various types of naval and air force had led him to base his concept of operations on the judgement that the supersonic homing, guided or programmed missile, whether launched from land, surface warship, submarine or aircraft, was the main danger to naval forces and shipping at sea. But it was a danger to which some effective counters were already in operational service. The hoary 'axioms of action' – above all surprise, concentration and economy of force – had to be borne in mind. Owing to the inability of submarines to operate submerged in large groups, in the way, for example, the

U-boat 'wolf-packs' were able to operate on the surface in the Second World War, it would today be difficult for a submarine attack to saturate the anti-missile defences of a well-ordered escort or support group. Maritime strike aircraft, on the other hand, could carry out a heavily concentrated attack, which might temporarily overwhelm the defences.

It was with these considerations in mind that SACLANT's operations were planned. It was essential, as a basis for them, to exploit two capabilities, which had been developed in recent years, to provide early warning of impending attacks. The first of these concerned submarines. The knowledge of Soviet submarine dispositions and movements painstakingly built up in peacetime had been augmented by the use of the surface-towed array surveillance system (STASS), operated in a number of suitably stationed patrol ships. These monitored the noise made by submarines underway, especially when they exceeded modest speeds. The information so obtained could be fed into the total submarine surveillance system, with corresponding improvement in its reliability and comprehensiveness. The second important system was the airborne warning and control system (AWACS), operated in large patrol aircraft. This could provide long-range warning of low-flying aircraft or missile attack, and hence help to offset, to some extent, the danger of defences being overwhelmed by the weight of a surprise missile onslaught.

The Soviet Naval Staff, in planning the naval operations which would support 'defensive action' by the Warsaw Pact, if that should prove necessary, were quite clear in their minds about what had to be done. The Soviet Navy had to show that its contribution to the achievement of the Soviet Union's political goals could be more than just supportive of the ground forces' campaign. By concentrating upon the isolation of the north-west European battlefield, it could not only help the Red Army directly but also do much to weaken the commitment of the United States to Western Europe. The main tasks of the Soviet Navy, therefore, during the first ten days of hostilities, would be to:

1 Maintain the Soviet Navy's strategic nuclear forces intact and at readiness, whilst limiting as much as possible the damage which could result if NATO were to unleash strategic nuclear warfare or tactical nuclear warfare at sea.

2 Help the ground and air forces to seize and keep open the Baltic Exits, and the Kiel Canal.

3 Support the ground and air forces in the invasion of Norway from the north.

4 Destroy as many NATO warships, submarines and naval aircraft as possible, in the Arctic Ocean, Norwegian Sea, North Atlantic, North Sea, English Channel and Baltic. Outside these areas, in the Atlantic south of the Tropic of Cancer and elsewhere, NATO forces, or the forces of NATO member states, would only be engaged when hostile action seemed to be inevitable, or had already begun.

5 Interdict all sea traffic between the United Kingdom and the Continent.

6 Neutralize or destroy the North Sea oil and gas installations.

7 Maintain freedom of movement for Soviet submarines in the Greenland-Iceland-UK gap, whilst denying this to NATO submarines.

8 Prevent shipping, and especially military transports, from reaching NATO's European ports.

9 Get all Soviet and other Warsaw Pact ships, including fishing and research vessels, into friendly or neutral ports before their capture or destruction.

NATO's warning of imminent attack by the Warsaw Pact had been brief. Much reliance had been placed upon detection of the increased deployment of submarines from the Soviet Northern Fleet, based on Murmansk in the Kola Inlet, into the Atlantic. The Soviet naval command was aware of this. Although, under reasonable excuse, there was a movement of surface shipping from the Black Sea through the Bosphorus and the Straits (see p. 174), no change was permitted in the pattern of submarine movements during the three weeks prior to D-day, 4 August 1985. There was, in fact, no need for it. Of the sixty nuclear-powered general purpose and forty diesel-electric patrol submarines in the Northern Fleet immediately available for operations, about one third were always at sea on a variety of tasks. They were primarily concerned with surveillance – of the US and UK strategic nuclear submarine forces, and of major US naval force movements and exercises. The submarines invariably went on patrol ready in all respects for war. They could remain on task, once hostilities broke out, until they had used up all their weapons, or were running short of food and (in the case of the diesel-electric submarines) fuel. What did happen, on 4 August and during the next few weeks, showed that, although the efficiency of the Soviet submarine force had improved a great deal since the Second World War, the anti-submarine measures of the Atlantic Alliance had done so too.

The situation at sea was uncannily reminiscent of the early months of the Second World War. Something like a *'Blitzkrieg'* in Central Europe, accompanied by supporting naval operations; submarine attacks on shipping in the Western Approaches; sporadic attacks, submarine, surface and air, on Allied shipping worldwide; the bottling up, capture or destruction of the merchant shipping of the continental power, the Warsaw Pact, by Allied naval forces.

There were differences between then and now. These were, first of all, politico-military. Unlike Germany in 1939–40, the Soviet Union in 1985 was firmly established in the Middle East, and in both West and East Africa. On the other hand, the United States in 1985 had not stood aside, as in 1939–41, when Great Britain and the Commonwealth stood almost alone against Nazi Germany. The United States was now, from the very outset, at the head of a great alliance of countries formed for the purpose of supporting each other if attacked on land or – but here was the rub – if any of their ships or aircraft were attacked in the Atlantic north of the Tropic of Cancer (the southern limit of the NATO area) or in the Mediterranean. Outside these specified sea areas, unfortunately, the Alliance could not operate as such.

The rapid growth in the number of independent nation states since 1945, most of them with sea coasts and maritime interests both commercial and naval, had added correspondingly to the complexity of war at sea.

The best that NATO could do had been to set up NATO Shipping Councils at the world's main ports. These consisted of representatives from the shipping and forwarding agents of NATO countries, as these existed in each place, together with diplomatic representatives of the nations concerned. Communication between the NATO Planning Board for Ocean Shipping and NATO naval authorities made it possible for NATO to organize and protect its shipping outside as well as inside the NATO area. This was no substitute for the worldwide system of naval commands and shipping control officers by means of which Great Britain and her maritime allies had conducted the 'sea affair' in 1939–45, but it was better than nothing. Better, indeed, than the over-centralized Soviet system. The advantage of flexibility and initiative enjoyed by the NATO Shipping Councils was in stark contrast to the difficulty the Soviet Union's representatives had in obtaining permission to act, as they so often felt that the situation demanded, in the light of local knowledge of rapidly changing circumstances.

The second set of differences, in the general conditions of the war at sea, between the Second World War and the Third, was technical. The most important new factor was the advent of nuclear-powered submarines. Able to go two or three times round the world without having to refuel or replenish, and not having to show any part of themselves above water (except momentarily for navigation or communication purposes), these were potent instruments of sea power. That is to say, they were potent instruments of sea power in the negative sense, namely, of the power to deny the use of the sea to a hostile country or coalition. To the positive side of sea power, submarines could contribute a good deal less. A French naval officer had aptly described nuclear-powered, missile-armed submarines as 'myopic and brutal'. In placing such reliance upon a huge submarine force as the main instrument of her putative sea power, the Soviet Union underlined, one might think, its own 'myopic and brutal' character. For the quintessence of sea power, exemplified *par excellence* by the British Empire in its hey-day, is the positive contribution which it can make to peaceful and growing international trade. Maritime strike aircraft, although the reverse of myopic, were if anything more brutal than submarines. The latter at least could operate, in certain circumstances, with due regard for humanity, using minimum force and helping survivors to safety. This a shore-based aircraft could never do. In 1985, therefore, the Soviet Union at last had to face certain facts. The possession of enormous ship-sinking power, together with a huge merchant marine directly controlled from Moscow, was no substitute for the carrying power of the West's ships, freely co-ordinated, under the protection of the Allied navies of the maritime governments whose flags they flew.

This realization did not come easily or quickly to those members of the Politburo and the CPSU who had backed Admiral Gorshkov's line for so long. Why is it, they demanded to know, that every single Soviet or Warsaw Pact ship has been ordered into port? What is the Soviet Navy doing? Supporting the Red Army's operations in central and northern Europe, yes. Supporting 'fraternal' wars in the Middle East, yes. But what about the seaborne supplies needed by our socialist brothers in East and Southern Africa, in West Africa and the Caribbean? As to the Mediterranean, why is it that our shipping, and that of so-called neutral and friendly governments, remains immobilized?

'Do not be impatient, comrades,' replied the Commander-in-Chief of the Soviet Navy. 'Once our gallant Red Army has imposed peace in north-west Europe, and the Americans have come to the negotiating table, you will see how Soviet sea power can become paramount, even as our armies have triumphed on land. You will see that it will be the Soviet Navy which has gained the victory.'

CHAPTER SEVENTEEN

THE BATTLE OF THE ATLANTIC

The first naval action of the Third World War was between two submarines, one British and the other Soviet. They met in the Shetland–Faroes gap, which, with its extension to Iceland and beyond to Greenland, would be the main naval battleground of the war. The following account of what happened, which sets the scene for the war at sea, is taken from *Submarines at War* by J. Heller, published by Sidgwick and Jackson, London, in 1987.

' "Up periscope." Commander Peter Keene, Royal Navy ("P.K." to his fellow submariners), grasped the handles and began to sweep another sector of the horizon. A clear, blue sky. Calm sea. Nothing in sight so far. It would not be true to say that P.K. was nervous, let alone uneasy. But he was keyed up. He had been in command of HMS *Churchill* for nearly a year. The nuclear-powered boat had been in refit when he was appointed in command. He had brought her through the comprehensive post-refit trials and "work-up" programme. She was in good shape, with a first-rate crew. But now he, and they, and the *Churchill*, were facing the ultimate test. It was 5 August 1985. When they had sailed from Faslane two days before, Great Britain was still at peace. Now she was at war. P.K. felt his mind working overtime. Surely he should be feeling, not just keyed up, but different in some way. He must think. Has everything – but *everything* – been done to make ready? There must be no mistake. It is them or us.

"Down periscope – sixty-five metres." It had taken P.K. some time to get used to ordering the depth to keep in metres. But it was over ten years since the Admiralty charts had been made metric and the fathom had dropped out of the language.

P.K.'s orders were to establish anti-submarine patrol in an area between the Shetland Islands and the Faroes. He would be well clear of other NATO submarines. Because of the prevailing water conditions he had decided to remain in the "surface duct"; this would also enable him to come quickly and quietly to periscope depth to classify any sonar contacts there might be. There were still some trawlers at sea, and possibly other surface vessels.

"Control room – Sonar." The watchkeeper's voice came over the intercom. "Red three two, sir – contact."

"Action Stations, Number One," ordered P.K. "Bring all tubes to the Action State. Periscope depth." The boat angled slightly upwards and levelled off. "Up periscope."

Keene gazed intently, moving the periscope a little to and fro either side of the bearing. Then he clicked the handle to give "low power" magnification and swung quickly right round and back to the original bearing.

"Down periscope."

In the Control Room men had moved to their Action Stations. As nuclear-powered submarines spent almost all their time dived, the hallowed cry "Diving Stations" had been discarded in favour of the more descriptive "Action Stations". But to a submariner the "dangers of the sea" were always more to be feared than the "violence of the enemy" . . . or were they? The next few minutes would tell.

"All tubes at Action State, sir," came the report from Jake Bond, the Torpedo Control Officer.

"Bearing Red three oh, sir, diesel H.E.," from the Sonar Room.

"Up periscope." P.K. looked on the bearing, then, as before, a few degrees either side. "Nothing in sight on the bearing. Could be a submarine 'snorting'. He may have just begun to. Could be close. Number One, pass the word that we are attacking an enemy submarine. Down periscope."

Tom Richardson, the First Lieutenant, called, "D'you hear there?" on the intercom and passed the word.

"Bearing Red two eight, sir. H.E. increasing. Classified submarine. Diesel. Two forty revs, sir. Eight knots if it's a *Tango* class." It was the Chief Sonar Operator now. Gordon. An excellent man.

"Port twenty. Stand by One and Two tubes. Pilot, let me have a range as soon as you can. Steer three zero zero."

The Coxswain repeated back the order. The Control Room was very quiet now. Everyone was at his post. The tension was building up.

"I'll take another look," said the Captain. "Up periscope."

"Bearing Green four three," came from the Sonar Room. "Moving right."

"Range five thousand two hundred, sir," said Harry Clay, the Navigator.

The Captain aligned the periscope on the bearing. "Bring her up, Number One, I think there's something there . . . YES! By God, and she's close. Down periscope, sixty-five metres. Switch to sonar. Range three thousand. Number One tube – Shoot!" P.K. moved to the Fire Control Panel.

"Torpedo's running, sir," said Jake Bond.

"Good," said P.K. He had carried out scores of dummy attacks on friendly submarines in the course of his training. He had seen many *Tigerfish* anti-submarine torpedos fired, for practice. Some had run badly. He gazed intently at the illuminated panel, ready to guide the torpedo if need be. He could hardly believe it. There was his torpedo – a homing torpedo – moving straight out towards the target. A minute went by. It seemed eternal. Half a minute more and then from the Sonar Room:

"Acoustic contact!" Followed, after an agonizing pause, by, "Tonk!" A faint metallic thud was heard.

"Damn!" said Keene, in an agony of dismay. "Something's wrong. The torpedo hit but didn't explode . . ."

"Control Room – Sonar," Gordon's voice broke in, 'H.E.'s stopped, sir! I think we got him. That *was* an explosion! Last bearing Green five seven."

"Good," said P.K. "Periscope depth. Up periscope." Once again P.K. examined the bearing. "Bring her up, Number One." The Captain swung right round, examining the horizon, then came back to the original bearing. 'There's nothing there. That *Tigerfish* did its stuff, after all. It didn't sound like it, though. Pilot, get a report ready: Have sunk *Tango* class submarine in position so-and-so.' We'll check for survivors or wreckage, or any other evidence. But I don't think there's any doubt. That's one down and three hundred and two to go." '

Churchill reports torpedoing a submarine – a *Tango* – twenty miles north west of Herma Ness, sir!' was the first bit of heartening news of the war for the Joint Allied Command Western Approaches. It was given to them, in their capacities as Cs-in-C Eastern Atlantic and Commander Maritime Air, Eastern Atlantic, at the first morning briefing' of the war, deep underground at Northwood, Middlesex. The Flag Officer Submarines, who since 1978 had been located at Northwood, was, as they said, 'somewhat chuffed' as his Chief Staff Officer made the report. Are you quite sure that it wasn't one of ours?' was the question asked, simultaneously, by the Admiral and the Air Marshal. They were greatly relieved to be assured that it was not. 'No doubt at all. It was a diesel-electric boat, and there were no NATO ones anywhere near.' The discussion which ensued, regarding Soviet and NATO submarine dispositions, revealed that the avoidance of mutual interference between NATO's own submarine forces, and between NATO surface and air anti-submarine forces and NATO submarines, would be a serious problem. This had been expected, but its resolution would continually govern the operations of all NATO naval and air forces.

Turning to current operations it was reported that the

First Support Group (formerly STANAVFORLANT – Standing Naval Force Atlantic) was on its way, at best speed, towards the Norwegian coast. In about twelve hours it would reach the limit of shore-based air cover from the UK. The fast transports, carrying reinforcements for the northern flank, had sailed from the Forth and were expected to rendezvous with the First Support Group shortly.

The air strike planned against Soviet installations on and around the Kola peninsula on the outbreak of hostilities was launched from UK bases, and timed to achieve a co-ordinated on-target time of 1100 hours GMT. The force consisted of thirty-six *Tornados* and sixteen *Buccaneers*. The latter, venerable though they might be, had been retained, refitted and re-armed, in the maritime role as they were superseded by *Tornados* in the more complex and demanding Central European overland role. They were well respected for their performance, handling qualities and robustness – 'Not built, carved out of the solid!' noted one pilot with affection.

The targets were four Soviet Naval Air Force (SNAF) airfields on which were based the bulk of the Northern Fleet *Backfire* force. 'Destroy the aircraft and close the airfields' was the objective, and a tall order at that. The flight profile was straightforward: to fly with tanker support as far towards the Lofoten Islands as prudence (with regard to tanker survival) would permit, then to carry out an overland low-level penetration. The *Tornados* would recover to Britain with tanker assistance, the *Buccaneers* would refuel at Bodo. The attacks would open with anti-radar missiles fired at stand-off ranges by the *Tornados* to damp things down a little, and would then be pressed home with area weapons against runways and aircraft installations. Gun and rocket fire would then, it was hoped, finish off any unscathed aircraft.

And so it went, broadly. Remarkably, the Russians seemed, if not unprepared, at least surprised. Although no firm evidence has come to light, it has been suggested that they had assumed some form of tacit *quid pro quo* with the Americans, whereby neither would launch an attack upon the homeland of its adversary until escalation was approaching strategic levels. If so, it was an expensive assumption. A calm analysis – the immediate claims exhibited the usual optimism of war – showed a score of sixty-one *Backfires* destroyed and many damaged, which was certainly more than had been hoped. But there had been a cost: five *Buccaneers* and nine *Tornados* were lost during the attacks. Sadly, all but one of the remaining *Buccaneers* were caught on the ground at Bodo during their recovery by a massive Soviet attack on that airfield.

The three maritime radar reconnaissance squadrons of RAF *Vulcans* had been occupied in routine surface surveillance of the North and Norwegian Seas and the Eastern Atlantic for weeks. The scale and intensity of their operations now increased, co-ordinated with sea surveillance squadrons of USAF working in WESTLANT and the Greenland–Iceland gap. The loss of satellite surveillance of the Atlantic at the outbreak of hostilities placed an increased burden on their activities. Their first major customer appeared on the evening of 4 August, when a *Vulcan* detected what seemed most likely to be an amphibious landing group rounding the North Cape. One *Vulcan* squadron was now devoted to a round-the-clock surveillance of this group, working in co-operation with Norwegian fast patrol boats.

Anti-submarine operations in EASTLANT to clear the sea for Strike Fleet, particularly the vital gap between Greenland and the UK, for long a major role of the Royal Navy, had also been under way, on a surveillance basis. Now they were in earnest. Three ASW (anti-submarine warfare) groups of the RN, supported by Dutch and Norwegian surface units, combed the ocean, co-ordinating their operations with the RAF, USAF and Royal Norwegian Air Force maritime patrol aircraft based in the UK, Iceland and Norway. Air defence cover was provided by an escort carrier, land-based fighters from the UK supported by tankers, and AEW (airborne early warning) *Nimrods*. Further west, Iceland-based F–15s would cover the operations. Whatever their quarry, Strike Fleet or convoys, the Soviet submarines had to be detected, and hopefully destroyed, here in the gap.

As far as sea management was concerned, the proclamation by the British government of a state of emergency, a week previously, had been indispensable. It had enabled the Naval Control of Shipping to be instituted, the reserves to be mobilized, and a large number of dormant appointments to be activated, setting up Naval Officers-in-Charge at all the major ports. Mine counter-measures had been started, on the pathetically small scale which was all that could be done with the derisory forces available.

The first JACWA briefing, which followed that of EASTLANT, was dominated by reports, many of which came in by telephone and teleprinter during the meeting, of heavy fighting in northern Germany and the Baltic Exits. A desperate message from the Commander Allied Forces Baltic Approaches (COMBALTAP), at Karup in Denmark, was typical:

'To CINCNORTH, for information to JACWA:
'1   Soviet ground forces with air support are attacking Aarhus.
'2   Minelaying in Great Belt and Langeland Belt 50 per cent completed.
'3   All operational naval forces ordered to sea. Submarines will patrol in Kattegat. Surface forces are to engage hostile surface forces as opportunity offers, retiring on Stavanger for replenishment. Operational control now with Allied Commander Naval Forces Scandinavian Approaches.
'4   Understand Danish government now en route to UK by air.
'5   COMBALTAP with elements of staff expects to leave Karup by air shortly for Kolsaas.'

It soon became clear, from Soviet declarations, that the political aim of Warsaw Pact military action was to overrun and neutralize the Federal German Republic, then call a halt and seek negotiations with the United States. Pact operations in the northern area of the Central Region had certainly gone according to plan. Despite spirited resistance by NATO forces, most of the Soviet's territorial objectives had been gained. Sheer weight of numbers saw to that. The Baltic Exits were to all intents and purposes in Soviet hands, though the main channels had been closed by mines; the North Sea coast as far west as the Hook of Holland was also under Soviet control; and sea traffic between the United Kingdom and the Continent was under constant and heavy attack from large numbers of Soviet light forces. These had been sent through the Kiel Canal (an attempt to block it was too late) and operated night and day under strong fighter cover.

Western approaches naval and air combat forces vigorously opposed this threat to vital cross-Channel communications. German and Dutch frigates, and a few Danish fast patrol boats (FPB), transferred by SACEUR to JACWA's operational control, made many successful attacks. The handful of FRG Naval Air Force *Tornados* which had been evacuated to the UK bolstered those few RAF *Tornados* and *Buccaneers* that could be spared by JACWA from operations in the Norwegian Sea. At this point the RAF *Hawks*, now liberated from their training tasks and armed with guns and rockets, came into their own and were launched into the war. Over this mixed force presided one squadron of *Vulcan* MR (maritime reconnaissance) aircraft, withdrawn, after long debate, from the Norwegian Sea, to feed the vital target information to the attackers, seaborne and airborne. The Soviet forces suffered heavy damage in the intense struggle, but again their numerical advantage was taking its toll: as far west as Boulogne the *Grishas, Nanutchkas* and *Osas* of the Soviet Baltic Fleet were joined on the bottom by more and more NATO ships.

On land the NATO forces were fighting back desperately, and the decision of France to play her part in the Alliance had given rise to some hope in the councils of NATO that the Soviet intentions might, at the eleventh hour, be frustrated. The anguished debate over the use of nuclear weapons and the decisions taken have been recounted elsewhere. Recent improvements in NATO's defences had allowed SACEUR to stem the flood. But if the tide was to be turned, all would depend on the safe and timely arrival of the seaborne reinforcements. The prospect of successful ocean transit could to some extent be assessed in the light of certain naval and air operations which had been taking place in the Atlantic and the Norwegian Sea simultaneously with the *débâcle* in the southern North Sea and the English Channel.

The First Support Group had, since the 5th, been supporting the attempt to reinforce northern Norway, where the airlifted ACE Mobile Force had been engaged since late on the 4th in resisting the powerful Soviet invasion through Finmark. Bodo had been rendered unusable, first by Soviet attack and then by the Norwegian response to the invaders, and the Allied forces were struggling to hold the line at Trondheim.

The Soviet amphibious group detected on the evening of the 4th had since been subjected to a vigorous assault by Norwegian naval and air forces and JACWA *Tornados* from the UK. By the 7th it was a much depleted Soviet support group that moved on south to reinforce their paratroop comrades.

But the fortunes of war turned again to the Russians that morning when their fighters, now operating from Norwegian airfields in the far north, destroyed first one, then in swift succession two more, of the *Vulcan* MR aircraft providing the vital surveillance of the Norwegian Sea. The Russians were quick to exploit the confusion which gripped, albeit temporarily, JACWA's coverage of the surface scene.

On the night of 7 August a NATO submarine reported

hat, in about the latitude of Trondheim and near the meridian of Greenwich, it had attacked with *Harpoon* missiles a Soviet force of fast transports escorted by surface ships, on a course which would take it to the Faroe Islands. A V/STOL *Harrier* III aircraft, one of four carried by the new escort carrier *Argus*, which had recently joined the First Support Group, had been flown off for a search to the north and west and the Soviet force had been relocated. The NATO submarine, having used up all its missiles, had been unable to destroy more than three of the Soviet ships, one of which was a troop transport. ACWA therefore ordered a strike, with six *Tornados*, the most that could be mustered, against the Soviet force. This succeeded in damaging another transport and an escort ship. The Soviet force then turned back towards Norway. The battle for the Greenland–Iceland–UK gap had been joined, and NATO had won the first round.

One feature of the action was the interruption of ship-to-shore, aircraft-to-ship and aircraft-to-shore communications, both Soviet and NATO, resulting from interference with communication satellites. Secondary channels had been used, but a certain amount of luck, on both sides, had proved effective. There might well have been complete loss of control by the respective shore-based HQs.

Soviet reaction to the failure of their operation against the Faroes was not long in coming. They had already observed by satellite, and confirmed by air reconnaissance, the approach of the First Support Group and the Norwegian reinforcement convoy. On D+5, therefore, twenty *Backfire* maritime strike aircraft were sent to attack the NATO force. Fortunately, owing to Bodo being out of action, these bombers had had to fly from airfields near Murmansk, and their transit had been reported. Some fighters from the UK were therefore able to intercept the second and third waves of *Backfires* and a total of five were destroyed. Three ships of the NATO troop convoy were hit, one of them sinking, and two ships of the First Support Group were put out of action, including the escort

carrier *Argus*. In consequence, the organic ASW capability
of that force, mainly consisting of helicopters, was much
diminished. Maritime patrol aircraft were hurriedly transferred from their relentless beat in the Greenland-UK gap
but two Soviet submarines supporting the amphibious
group were able nevertheless to get in attacks on the
damaged ships, all of which were sunk. A NATO submarine similarly dispatched the damaged ships of the Faroes
raiding force.

Rather more one-sided was the Soviet attack on the
North Sea oil and gas installations. Appreciating that the
most vulnerable, and least easily defended, elements in
the supply from wells to shore were the pipelines on the
sea-bed, the Russians had decided to cut these. It was no
difficult to do this, except in the southern North Sea, which
initially was not readily accessible to the attackers. In the
north, six diesel-electric submarines, approaching via the
deep water off the Norwegian coast, were deployed to
predetermined positions, where they released special
underwater manned vehicles, to locate and destroy the
twelve most important pipelines. By using delayed action
charges, the submarines were able to withdraw without
detection. Three of them, operating in the shallower areas
also laid mines in the vicinity of the pipelines, where the
destruction would occur. Two NATO patrol ships, sent to
investigate the explosions on 8 August, struck mines and
sank. In order to distract attention from the submarine
operations, sporadic air attacks, using stand-off missiles
were carried out on some of the oil and gas rigs themselves
The UK air defences took a heavy toll of the elderly
Badgers used by the Russians for these attacks.

The final major event of the war at sea, during the
opening phase of the Warsaw Pact onslaught, was the
declaration by the Soviet government on 9 August that
the Western Approaches was a War Zone, into which
shipping of any kind entered at its peril. The only neutral
countries within the War Zone were Sweden and Finland
The Swedes were told that the inconvenience they would

A fast patrol boat of the Federal German Navy and a *Sea King* helicopter on operations in the Skagerrak, 5 August

Some men attained relief from monotony in the Pacific. War (?)

Reinforcing F-111s top up their fuel from an air tanker in mid-Atlantic on their way to Europe

Soviet tanks in an unopposed water crossing during the invasion of north Norway, 7 August

A Soviet BMP armoured infantry fighting vehicle on the move into Holland, 8 August

A Tupolev *Backfire* bomber with its moveable wings in the forward (low speed) position

A remarkable shot of a *Jaguar* aircraft in action as seen by the recording camera

suffer would not last long and that the action had been forced upon the Warsaw Pact by the aggressive intentions of NATO. The Soviet objective of neutralizing the Federal German Republic would soon be achieved. The correlation of forces made this inevitable. As to Finland, it was hardly necessary to seek her compliance.

The declaration of the War Zone was not regarded by the Soviet Union as sufficiently emphatic of itself. Certain of her submarines, which had been ordered to take up patrol positions and at all costs to remain undetected, were therefore ordered to attack with tactical missiles, after careful identification, certain important ships – oil tankers, container ships and dry cargo ships belonging to European NATO countries. Sailing weeks earlier from distant ports, along standard ocean routes, these ships had been ordered to continue at full speed, some towards the North Channel and some towards St George's Channel, where they would be met and escorted into harbour. Ships which were more than five days' steaming from Western Approaches coastal waters had been turned towards the nearest NATO friendly or neutral port or anchorage, to await further instructions.

Late on 9 August reports reached JACWA that two large oil tankers, two container ships and two dry cargo ships had been attacked without warning with submarine-launched missiles. The positions given, four in the Bay of Biscay and two west of Ireland, could not immediately be reconciled with the plotted positions of any Soviet submarines, as deduced from the various anti-submarine detection or surveillance systems. If ever the gravity of the Soviet submarine threat to shipping had been doubted, such doubts were now speedily removed. Against nuclear-powered submarines, aided by satellite and aircraft reconnaissance, even the fastest merchant ships were sitting ducks.

The first thing to do, having established that Commander Western Approaches South (COMWAS) was organizing the search for survivors and sending tugs to the damaged

oil tankers (neither of them had yet sunk), was to order
any other NATO merchant ships approaching the declared
War Zone to turn back. The next was to consider, with
SACLANT, the implications of these attacks. The situation which now faced the maritime commanders, in the
Atlantic and the Western Approaches, was critical. It was
quite obvious that unless SACEUR could be certain of
being reinforced by fresh combat forces from the United
States by 15 August, he could not throw in his final reserves
on the Central Front within the next four or five days, and
thus stand some chance of holding up the Warsaw Pact
advance to the Rhine.

A group of military convoys, with a speed of advance of
twenty-three knots, had sailed from Halifax NS on 8
August. They could be disembarking troops and equipment in northern French ports by the 14th. But there were
strong indications that a wave of Soviet submarines, which
had sailed from the Kola Inlet on 4 August, was now
crossing the Greenland–Iceland–UK gap. Denial of the
Faroes to a Soviet raiding force had fortunately helped to
maintain NATO anti-submarine surveillance of the key
area, and three more Soviet submarines were known to
have been destroyed, two by NATO submarines operating
independently and one by a combination of air and surface
forces. On the other hand, at least one NATO submarine
had failed to report on leaving her patrol off the North
Cape. In two days' time, it was estimated, there would be
twenty-four Soviet nuclear-powered submarines in the
North Atlantic.

Had time permitted, at least some of the vital initial
convoys could have been routed south of the Azores
where they would have been beyond the reach of *Backfire*
maritime strike aircraft from Murmansk. The effective
radius of these aircraft was about 4,000 kilometres. As
things were, there was really no choice but to assemble the
most powerful escort and support forces available, and
fight the convoys through by the shortest route across the
Atlantic. It was expected that NATO submarines oper-

ating to the north of the gap would further reduce the number of Soviet submarines reaching the convoys. Most important of all, US Strike Fleet Atlantic, supported by maritime aircraft based in Iceland and northern Scotland, would cover the whole operation. If Soviet *Backfires* could attack convoys in mid-Atlantic, the US Strike Fleet could pulverize the Soviet Northern Fleet base from a position in the Norwegian Sea. Its approach, plumb through the middle of the gap, could not of course be concealed from Soviet reconnaissance. Nor could it be ignored by the C-in-C Soviet Northern Fleet. The battle of the Gap would be quite unlike Jutland, or Midway. But battle there would be.

Once again, the question of 'to use or not to use' nuclear weapons in the war at sea had to be faced. It was the opinion of the naval commanders that, on the 'form' so far, the use of nuclear depth charges or nuclear warheads or torpedoes would by no means show gains commensurate with the risk of escalation. As to nuclear strikes on the Soviet bases in the north, only if nuclear weapons had finally been resorted to on the Central Front would these be carried out.

SACLANT had been under less pressure from minute-to-minute, hour-to-hour and day-to-day events since the war broke out in Europe on 4 August than his Western Approaches colleagues. The departure from Halifax NS four days before of the group of fast military convoys which formed part of Operation CAVALRY could not possibly have gone unobserved and unreported; and the route which the convoys took could not be varied much. It was not surprising that a fierce battle was taking place, the outcome of which would be critical for events on the Central Front. Operation CAVALRY *had to* succeed.

SACLANT had been under no illusions about the losses which the Soviet submarines might inflict, with their horizon-range and stand-off missiles. Measures had been taken, therefore, to limit the effectiveness of the Soviet

ocean surveillance satellites and air reconnaissance. Since
the destruction of three of the Conakry-based reconnaissance *Bears* on the 4th – old models, but carrying a
somewhat rudimentary and hitherto unsuspected air-to-
air capability – three more *Super-Bears* had been removed.
But indications of increased Soviet submarine movements
had been reported by the four STASS ships on patrol. It
looked as if the Soviet Submarine Commander had
ordered his force to concentrate ahead of the CAVALRY
convoys. Each of these consisted of twelve ships, stationed
in three columns of four, with an escort group, including
an escort carrier, disposed appropriately in the vicinity.
Some distance away was a powerful ASW support group,
consisting of a light aircraft carrier (with V/STOL fighter-
strike-reconnaissance aircraft and anti-submarine helicopters embarked), two anti-missile cruisers and four ASW
frigates. It had been intended that a second ASW support
group should take station astern of the convoy formation,
because submarines can attack with missiles from any
direction – unlike in the days of torpedoes, when 'limiting
lines of approach' for effective attack put a premium upon
the submarine pelting ahead and then 'lying in wait' for
his targets. But a submarine attack upon a support group,
as it formed up in Hampton Roads, had seriously damaged
the carrier and sunk a frigate. The remainder of the force
had been told to 'get that goddam'd submarine' and were
still hopefully and energetically pursuing one or two sonar
surveillance systems (SOSUS) reports which could have
been the culprit.

For the first two days of the transit, US and Canadian
MR aircraft operating from Newfoundland would support
the convoys. For the last two, RAF MR aircraft based in
south-west England would take over. For the perilous two
days in mid-Atlantic, the best that could be hoped for from
the shore would be spasmodic cover from the already
over-stretched US Navy Air Force *Orion* MR aircraft at
Lajes in the Azores.

The Commander Strike Fleet Atlantic, entering the

Iceland–Faroes gap on 10 August, was extremely thankful to have had the protection, during this transit, of fighters from Newfoundland and Iceland. These were maintained by air-to-air refuelling, and operated with the AWACS aircraft in continuous attendance. There had been a strong westerly wind, and the need to operate fixed-wing aircraft from the carriers would have slowed him down. As it was, he had made a speed of more than twenty knots. What worried him was the absence of submarine contacts. Several Soviet submarines had been plotted, according to STASS and shore-based intelligence reports, in the general area of his advance. He had hoped to detect at least some of these with his helicopter searches and bring them to action. How else could he carry out his mission of reducing the submarine threat to the convoys, now en route to Europe?

But the Soviet submarines were under strict orders to concentrate on the troop convoys. They had no time to lose. There were in any case other forces waiting to engage the US Strike Fleet. By 11 August, therefore, no less than eleven Soviet submarines were within 150 kilometres of the CAVALRY convoys and disposed on their line of advance. Then came the first attack, with salvoes of horizon-range supersonic cruise missiles. Sixteen missiles arrived over the convoys, fired within twenty minutes by two *Charlie*-class nuclear-powered submarines. Eight of the missiles were decoyed away from targets. Of the other eight, two hit one of the transports and one hit another; two more hit one of the escort carriers, which blew up and sank at once; and three more each hit one of the frigates in the same escort group. The Soviet submarines which would be first to engage the convoy formation had orders to attack the escorts and support groups. Half an hour after the submarine attacks one of the leading support group's helicopters was quickly joined by a second and, taking it in turns, the pair between them dropped four anti-submarine torpedoes, to be rewarded very quickly by an explosion in the sea beneath them. Just as this occurred a frigate at the far side of the formation was struck by a Soviet missile and lay dead in the water. The next attack took place four hours later. Once again sixteen missiles arrived in salvoes of four, within a few minutes of each other. Once again half of them found a target. Another transport and two frigates were hit, and badly damaged. It seemed that, owing to the very high speed of advance of the convoy, the screening helicopters with their dipping sonar could not give adequate coverage far enough from the main body of the convoys. The next two attacks, again each consisting of salvoes of four missiles, came within two hours. They were again directed at the support group and succeeded in putting the light carrier temporarily out of action and sinking one frigate. This ship had the misfortune to be struck by a missile which had been successfully decoyed from another target. It was satisfactory, however, from SACLANT's point of view, that a number of missiles had been destroyed by the *Aegis* antimissile system with which the entire support group was equipped. Furthermore, both the attacking submarines were being hunted, and one of them was soon sunk.

The progress of the CAVALRY convoys across the Atlantic was of course being followed by C-in-C Soviet Northern Fleet, and by Soviet Naval Headquarters in Moscow. Although reports were incomplete, it was evident that heavy attrition of the NATO escort and support groups had been achieved. It was now time to launch the air strike, planned to coincide with the attacks of a third group of submarines, this time under orders to concentrate fire on the convoys themselves. Unfortunately for the Russians, the US Strike Fleet Atlantic was now approaching the Norwegian Sea. A Soviet surface striking force, together with its anti-submarine support group, which had sailed from the Kola Inlet on 10 August, would not be able to engage the US Strike Fleet for another twenty-four hours. By that time heavy air attacks could have been launched against the Soviet northern bases. C-in-C Northern Fleet therefore proposed to despatch an annihilating

Backfire strike against the Strike Fleet. He was overrruled by Moscow: 'We do not expect Strike Fleet Atlantic to use nuclear weapons at this stage. Our primary aim is to destroy the CAVALRY convoys. Two-thirds of available *Backfires* are therefore to be launched against the NATO troop convoys. Our submarines in the Norwegian Sea must be concentrated against the Strike Fleet Atlantic, with diversionary air attacks only, until our surface striking force can come into action.'

The forty *Backfires* consequently sent by C-in-C Northern Fleet to attack the CAVALRY convoys were routed individually to a rendezvous point midway between Newfoundland and the entrance to the English Channel. The approach of the *Backfires* to their targets was not detected in time for a fully effective air defence disposition to be taken up by the CAVALRY convoy escorts, several of which were busily engaged in prosecuting submarine contacts. The *Backfire* attacks, with AS–6 air-to-surface missiles, therefore caught the NATO force at something of a disadvantage. The *Aegis*-fitted support group was racing to position itself with the main body of the convoys. The casualties were heavy. Seven transports were hit, four of which sank quickly. The loss of life was appalling. Of the eighty AS–6 missiles launched by the *Backfires*, from ranges of 220 down to 160 kilometres, no less than thirty reached a target. The escorting warships suffered as well as the transports. Only the fact that in some cases two, or even three, missiles hit the same ship limited the number of escorts sunk or damaged to five. Fifteen *Backfires* were destroyed.

Within two hours of the *Backfire* attack, the next submarine attack took place. This was less successful than the Russians had hoped. Owing to the timely arrival of a British support group, a drastic alteration of course by the convoys during the air strike, and harassment by maritime patrol aircraft, the Soviet submarines were unable to co-ordinate their attack either with each other or with the *Backfires*. During the next twelve-hour period three Soviet submarines were sunk, for the loss of only one more transport.

The number of Soviet submarines now in position to attack the convoys was less, in fact, than either C-in-C Northern Fleet or SACLANT had expected. There were several reasons for this. First, four Soviet submarines in transit, at high speed, had been destroyed by ASW operations in the Greenland-UK gap, unknown as yet to the Soviet commander-in-chief. Second, signals to certain Soviet submarines, ordering them to take up new patrol positions, had not been received. This involved mainly the submarines which had been sent on anti-shipping patrol prior to the declaration of the War Zone. Third, two diversionary fast convoys had been sailed twenty-four hours before the CAVALRY convoys, one along a more northerly route and another along a more southerly one. Each had attracted a group of Soviet submarines towards intercepting positions. The diversionary convoys, being free to follow highly evasive courses, which were carefully judged, had succeeded in reducing by a quarter the number of submarines which could be brought into contact with the CAVALRY convoys, once the Soviet command had realized what was going on. Finally, the use of unusually high speeds by these submarines, under orders to intercept CAVALRY at all costs, had led to several of them being detected by various means and attacked by maritime aircraft from Iceland and the Azores.

In addition to the most welcome reinforcement of the sadly depleted CAVALRY escort force by the British support group, of which the anti-submarine cruiser HMS *Invincible* formed part, two of JACWA's escort groups, one with a British escort carrier, and a number of Dutch and German, as well as British frigates and destroyers, had joined the convoys by 12 August. It looked as if the worst part of the ocean transit was now over. CAVALRY would soon come under the umbrella of the United Kingdom Air Defence Region.

In the Norwegian Sea, Strike Fleet Atlantic had succeeded in destroying five of the *Backfire* bombers returning from their attack on CAVALRY. NATO submarines had successfully attacked the Soviet surface strike force off the North Cape and sunk a *Kiev*-class light aircraft carrier and a *Kara*-class cruiser. Early on 12 August, within twenty-four hours of the combined air and submarine attacks on the CAVALRY convoys, US Strike Fleet Atlantic began to pound the Soviet naval bases and airfields in the Kola Inlet. C-in-C Soviet Navy, Admiral Starsky, in order to justify his decision to use the main *Backfire* force to attack the troop convoys, rather than concentrating on neutralizing the US Strike Fleet, accepted with alacrity the reports he received of the 'annihilation' of the CAVALRY convoys by air and submarine attack. He therefore ordered C-in-C Northern Fleet to send his available *Backfires* to attack Strike Fleet Atlantic. In fact, having lost only one more transport and two escorts to submarine attack, the convoys were now, on 13 August, under air cover from the UK and France. One hazard remained to be overcome. The Le Havre mine counter-measures force, working round the clock to keep the approach channels swept, detected mines during the night of 13–14 August. Possible diversions of the troop convoys were considered. Cherbourg was in any case the destination of some of the ships. But every hour of delay in getting the troops and their equipment to the battlefield would diminish the prospect of averting the use of nuclear weapons, if the Soviet advance was to be checked. It was a balance of risks.

The French Flag Officer-in-Charge of the First Maritime District had reason to believe that the mines had been laid by a small force of Soviet coastal craft, under cover of the severe fighting in the Channel four or five days previously. It had not been possible to plot all the contacts, while so many things were happening at once. He decided, therefore, having conducted a clearance sweep and reswept the main channel, to accept the planned number of CAVALRY transports in Le Havre, the remainder being sent to Cherbourg and Brest. In the event, there were no further casualties to the troop convoys. Out of the forty-eight transports which had sailed from the USA and Canada, twelve had been sunk or badly damaged. But 'the US CAVALRY had arrived in time'.

This letter written at the time gives one man's experience of Operation CAVALRY. It is from a young American serviceman.

Haslar Hospital
Gosport, England
24 August 1985

'Dear Mom,

You should have heard by now that I'm O.K. – some cuts, bruises and burns here and there, but believe me, I'm in good shape. I guess I'll be back to duty in a couple of weeks. What then I don't know. Another ship, I expect. I'm being looked after real well, though. Yeah, but how come you ended up in hospital? I hear you ask. O.K., well – you remember I was drafted suddenly to Military Sealift Command, at Norfolk Va? Next thing I was aboard a great big container ship in Boston. I'd better not give you the name. Believe it or not they censor your letters here. At any rate, this ship was loading the Army's weapons. And then they slung a whole lot of bunkhouses aboard – big containers. About 120. Then came the soldiers, 1,000 or so. My job was in the extra radio team we took for the voyage.

Things happened fast. Two days after we heard the Russians had invaded Germany we sailed from Boston. Then we waited in Halifax NS until the convoy had gathered. When we sailed there were forty-eight ships, all big and fast, and full of soldiers. We were really four convoys, each of twelve ships, three columns of four in each. Ours was ahead. We also had two aircraft carriers, but they were old ones, and full of troops. There was one at the head of each of our outer columns. My station was on the bridge. I had to pass the signals to the Skipper, or whoever was in charge of the ship – the watch officer. So I could hear and see a good deal. On the third day out things began to happen. We ran into some submarines that fired missiles. We weren't hit then, but I could see columns of smoke coming up here and there. Of course there were ships – troopships or escort ships, big and small – everywhere. We passed near where a couple of "choppers" were hunting a submarine. We didn't think they had much chance of getting a "nuke". But suddenly there was an explosion in the sea and we reckoned they'd got one.

A few hours later, when it was dark, there was another missile attack – more ships hit. Again we got away with it. Two of our convoy were hit, though. In a moment they were ablaze, and hauling out of line. The rest of us said a prayer and pressed on. Next day we copped it. I got the missile raid warnings on my radio net. This time, as the submarines opened up on us, there came the air-to-surface missiles. We were a long way from Murmansk, but these boys found us and reached right out. Suddenly there was a terrible flash and bang-crack, all at once. Then in a moment another. We were all thrown in a heap. The Skipper (I think it was) shouted, "Full left rudder! Emergency stop!" We had to haul out of line, you see. That's about all I remember till I came to in a life-raft. I said, "Where's the ship?" Some guy squatting there lifted up my head. "There," he said, pointing. "She's still afloat, but pretty near burned out." I could see the smoke. I didn't feel too good. But I guess I was very lucky. We all were, who were on the bridge, or somewhere aft. The missiles had hit amidships and killed most everyone around. Then the fire took hold. But as we turned out of line we brought the ship's stern to the wind. And as we stopped, the wind took the fire away from the after superstructure, where we were – and a good many life-rafts. Some of the solders who jumped straight overboard when the missiles hit were saved. But hundreds were lost. It was bad. We were lucky. A British frigate found us, and

that's why I'm in Gosport, England, Mom. There's a great
joke going around here that Britain's been saved by the
US Cavalry riding in – like those old movies, you know?

Hope you are all well at home.

Love,

Dan'

In assessing the outcome of the war at sea, which continued
unabated until the NATO counter-offensive checked the
enemy's advance in the Central Region, it is necessary to
consider the aims of the respective naval commanders, the
extent to which these were achieved, and at what cost. In
the first place, it may be said that in failing to interdict
more than 25 per cent of the immediate seaborne
reinforcement sent from North America to Allied Command Europe, the Soviet Navy failed to support the Red
Army decisively. SACLANT and JACWA between them
had for their part decisively supported SACEUR. As to
the war at sea in general, the losses of warships, aircraft
and submarines on both sides, during the first phase, had
left the balance little changed since the outbreak of
hostilities, although at a lower level. Losses had been
heavy, and there were virtually no reserves. Replacement
by new construction would take years.

NATO did enjoy one advantage over the Russians,
however. It remained a good deal simpler for the NATO
navies to redeploy their existing surface forces than for
the Soviet Navy to do so. Several important US units from
the Pacific were soon on their way to the Atlantic, to
replace elements of the Strike Fleet which had been sunk,
some by air but more by submarine attack, during the
withdrawal of the force from the Norwegian Sea. But the
Soviet Baltic and Black Sea Fleets, despite the seizure of
the Baltic Exits and the transfer of Black Sea units to the
Mediterranean, were unable to support each other. NATO
maritime strike aircraft in Britain, 'the unsinkable aircraft
carrier', and NATO submarines in the Mediterranean,
were a constant discouragement to Soviet naval move-

ments. Soviet naval and air forces in the Middle East did succeed, for a time, in dominating the Red Sea and the Arabian Sea. But a combined US, British and Australian force, operating in the Indian Ocean, eventually neutralized them. Again, losses on both sides were heavy.

The movement of oil, food, raw materials and war equipment to north-west Europe was strongly opposed by Soviet submarines and maritime strike aircraft. But attrition of the Soviet forces was such as to wear down gradually the weight of attack. In 1974 Admiral Gorshkov had made this point: 'The underestimation of the need to support submarine operations with aircraft and surface ships cost the German high command dearly in the last two wars.' Now his own country had made the same strategic error. Had the submarines been capable of operating submerged in large groups, as the German U-boats had done on the surface in the Second World War, there is little doubt that their campaign would have succeeded. As it was, the submarines could be dealt with in ones or twos – though nearly always with the loss, to missile attack, of one or more anti-submarine vessels. The escort carriers, frigates, patrol ships, helicopters and maritime aircraft had been built, as a matter of great urgency, during the period 1979–85. Of critical importance to JACWA had been the contribution of the Federal German Navy, which, with the strong support of the NATO Council, had been greatly strengthened during the period. The Federal German government, recognizing the supreme importance of the safe and timely arrival of the convoys bringing US and Canadian reinforcements to the Central Front, had increased its light naval forces and naval air forces in the Baltic. This had permitted the release of frigates to work with the additional UK escort carriers.

When the outcome of the 1985 war as a whole can be assessed, it may be that the downfall of the USSR will be attributed, ironically, to Gorshkov, the greatest Russian admiral of all time, whose forceful and successful advocacy of ever-increasing Soviet sea power led the comrades to disaster – when the seas got too rough the Bear drowned.

Even on land the Soviet Union appeared to have overreached itself. In the all-important central front of Western Europe, the Red Army had counted on very early and decisive success. This success had eluded its commanders. Instead they were faced with a check to their offensive and serious misgivings about support at home.

CHAPTER EIGHTEEN

THE WAR IN INNER SPACE

In 1957 the world ran into its gardens and out into the streets to watch *Sputnik* streak across the sky. Later they were to be glued to their TV sets watching men walking on the moon. Then came the link-up of the US *Apollo* and Soviet *Soyuz* spacecrafts, the politics of that misleading handshake in space engaging the world's spectators more than its technology. As Congress cut back the funds for NASA's (National Aeronautics and Space Administration) space programme the earthbound mortals with their daily lives to lead rather lost interest. Films like the record running *Star Wars*, first screened in 1977 and still showing in London at the outbreak of the war, and books about inter-stellar wars in deep space, fascinated and absorbed the public while real men and their machines performing tasks as they orbited the world, no further away than London is from Manchester in England, seemed of no particular account. That was not, of course, true of the small scientific-military groups whose task it was to think about and manage these things; especially so in the Soviet Union. It was this inner space from 300 to, at most, 32,000 kilometres that occupied their attention. The military applications of this extended area of man's domination over his environment were seen as precisely those first sought in aviation – namely, reconnaissance and communications.

By 1985 the superpowers had developed astonishing capabilities in those directions. Especially dramatic was space photography of such high resolution that soldiers marching on earth could be counted in their columns. In the event of war, the Russians would be especially interested in seeing what was going on in the Atlantic and on the eastern seaboard of the United States. The US, on behalf of the West, had a prime interest in observing military developments and deployments in the heartland of the USSR by photography and electronic eavesdropping, particularly during periods of tension or actual war, but also in routine times of peace. Communications satellites acting as relay stations in space had not only enormously increased the extent of available facilities, they had enhanced the reliability and quality of radio transmission and reception out of all recognition. They had also provided remarkable navigation assistance, with an accuracy down to a few metres, to ships, submarines and aircraft.

Just as this inner space was now a quite readily accessible extension of the atmosphere, so its military opportunities proved to be, in the main, extensions of existing earth-based facilities, considerably enhanced but not unique – and therefore never wholly indispensable. There was just one activity, of critical interest to the Allies, where the time advantages in war might be so great that it was perhaps in a special category and an exception to that general rule. That activity was electronic reconnaissance. As noted elsewhere in this book, the West enjoyed a decided advantage over the Communist East in ECM, and for that reason the Soviet Union in peacetime shrouded its communications with every possible veil of secrecy. If the West was to exploit its electronic advantage to the fullest extent it needed to know from the outset of hostilities just which parts of the frequency spectrum, and in what modes of emission, the Soviet forces would operate. This information was urgently needed as soon as the battle was joined; the Soviet cloak of secrecy had to be torn aside. This could all be done very much more quickly and comprehensively from space reconnaissance satellites than would ever have been possible by monitoring the communications networks in the war theatre on the ground.

After the early scramble to catch up with the Soviet

Union, when spurred into competition by the success of the *Sputnik* shots, the USA soon took the lead. Their vehicles and systems were demonstrably more capable, more reliable and more durable than those of the USSR. Out of that technological and engineering success came a difference of approach that was to be of fundamental strategic importance: the Americans invested their resources in complicated long-life, multi-purpose craft designed to function in orbit for periods as long as a year. The Russians, under *force majeure*, went for frequent launchings of simple, single-purpose, short-life payloads. The corollary to this in 1985 was that the Soviet Union had a high launch capability – they had put no less than thirty-two photo-recce satellites in orbit in the previous twelve months, and on 3 August they had more than twenty launchers ready at Baikonur and Plesetsk with a variety of satellites ready as their payloads. The USA, on the other hand, had no more than a few giant *Titan* II rockets designed to put the thirteen-tonne *Big Bird* II satellites into space, and five Orbiter aerospace vehicles developed for their space shuttle system.

In the late seventies the US programme seemed to have reached a plateau of development, while the USSR continued with frequent manned launches on research tasks, the exact purposes of which were not always evident to Western observers. It was, however, pretty well authenticated that they were developing a counter-satellite capability employing, in addition to jamming, certainly lasers and other high energy beams. In 1985 both sides had some counter-satellite capability, but it was suspected that the USSR was well in the lead It refrained from making use of this capability until the early hours of 4 August for fear of still further conceding the advantage of surprise but, as recorded elsewhere, as soon as the offensive was launched in the Central Region it made an all-out effort in space.

This immediately degraded Allied communications, but it was a degradation that could at least in part be compensated for by switching to atmospheric systems as soon as space circuits went out. When the history of the space war comes to be written the part played by the communications managers in the US control centres will be seen to have made a remarkable and decisive contribution to the Allied war effort.

On NATO's declaration of alert in July 1985, NASA, together with the Department of Defense, urgently reviewed the launch schedules for the space shuttle Orbiter vehicles. Of the five in service, one was available. Of the others, one was on long turn-round for replacement of its thermal tiles; one was having its undercarriage renewed after a heavy landing at Vandenberg AFB; one was on a thirty-day refit and one was in orbit recovering a satellite. The European Space Laboratory was on the ground and not scheduled to be relaunched until later in the year.

At 0600 hours Eastern Standard Time on Friday 2 August the available orbiter (*Enterprise* 101) was launched from Cape Kennedy with a four-man crew and Colonel 'Slim' Wentworth, USAF, in command. It was a multipurpose mission on which priorities might need to be changed, and a manned craft was the best way of preserving flexibility. Photography and a full range of electronic reconnaissance was required from its regular passes over Soviet Russia and Eastern Europe. In addition it was ready with specially prepared tapes in over a dozen languages for propaganda broadcasts, but these would only be ordered if political developments during the mission made it propitious to do so.

As tension heightened towards the end of July the two *Big Birds* were so manoeuvred as to photograph the likely dispersal sites for the Soviet SS–16 mobile ICBM (intercontinental ballistic missiles). At the same time the Chairman of the US Joint Chiefs of Staff ordered the readying of two further *Big Birds* as replacements for any damaged satellites, with priority going to maintaining the electronic surveillance which would be so vital to the Allied ECM campaign if war broke out. He and his colleagues had also ruled that three supplementary navigation satellites should be placed in geostationary orbit 30,000 kilometres up over the Atlantic. This was the system that gave such an astonishing navigational capability and allowed USAF's F–111 aircraft to be immediately capable of reading out a ground position to an accuracy of twelve metres. It was not thought that these high satellites would be at much risk. They were very difficult to get at, and there must surely be more cost-effective ways of disrupting the system than by days of satellite manoeuvring in order to effect close-range interference. Some corroboration of that view came on 2 August when the FLEETSATCOM (fleet satellite communications) tracking and control station on the eastern seaboard suffered major damage from an undetected saboteur. The very disturbing feature of this was that the damage was done by electronic means and could only have been inflicted by someone with an intimate knowledge of the station and its technology.

The war in space was very much a matter of move and counter-move and the outcome was fairly evenly balanced. The US were all the time concerned to husband their limited number of launchers. On the other hand, their satellites had much more comprehensive and versatile capabilities in space than those of the USSR. Furthermore, with doubling and tripling up of systems they were very resilient to interference and could accept extensive damage on occasions and still usefully carry on their tasks. The key information on Soviet electronic emissions in the Central Region battle area was in fact extracted very rapidly and early on in the war to the great advantage of the Allies. Ballistic missile warning from high satellites was also preserved completely throughout the war. The Soviet system suffered heavily from US interference and from the random effect of its own inherent unreliability and the short life of its vehicles. By dint of frequent replacements the Russians kept up good coverage of the Atlantic and the United States itself, but in the event this was not to give them the same practical advantage that the Allies obtained from their own electronic reconnaissance.

None of this accorded very closely with popular ideas gleaned from the bookstalls and the cinemas, and it was not to be expected that it would. However, there was one incident that came quite near to the science fiction fantasies, and for what it may presage for the future it may be worth recounting here.

Enterprise 101 had been in orbit for forty hours by midnight on 3 August. All her systems were working excellently and she had been discharging regular canisters of exposed film back into the atmosphere for recovery and processing. Colonel Wentworth had not been ordered to start the broadcasts but his spacecraft had been under close observation by the Soviet Union; her missions, on which the Russians were well informed from their own sources in the States, were highly unacceptable to them. Apart from the very real strategic disadvantages to the Soviet Union of this space mission, the Politburo and military alike found it intolerable that four Americans should be able to sweep across their country with impunity ten times a day when they were on the brink of war. But they were well prepared, and had already laid plans for putting *Enterprise* out of business if they could.

In the early hours of 4 August a *Soyuz* 49 mission was launched with a two-man crew, and on its fourth orbit the *Soyuz* craft was manoeuvred to within 150 metres of *Enterprise*. Wentworth was keeping a visual look-out at that time, and when Mission 49 made its first beam sweep across *Enterprise* the laser traversed his line of sight and blinded him. The *Enterprise* crew therefore had plenty on their hands, both in alerting space control as to what was going on and in coping with a blinded and weightless commander. Captain Jensen of the US Navy took over command and ordered an immediate check for further damage. The craft had in fact been subjected to other high energy beam sweeps and the damage check brought gloomy news: their five engine nozzles and their elevons had been damaged, and there was now no possibility of a successful controlled re-entry into the atmosphere. Worst of all, their solar cells seemed to have suffered and electric power generation had ceased. They had a large battery capacity, but Jensen immediately ordered a reduction of all electrical services to the minimum required for life support and for communication with space control.

Space control were reassuring; after a five-minute pause they announced that *Enterprise* 103, which was now safely back at Vandenberg with her recovered satellite, would be readied with all possible haste and sent up to recover them. Jensen and his crew knew very well that it normally took several days to get one of the orbiters ready for flight again, and they wondered quietly to themselves whether their own batteries would be able to maintain their life support functions until the relief mission could arrive.

But the war was now on, and damage and interference to US surveillance required the two waiting *Big Birds* to be placed in orbit without delay. Grimly, the Joint Chiefs decided that when *Enterprise* 103 was ready she must be held for priority satellite replacement. Colonel Wentworth and his crew had left the earth before hostilities started. They spent the duration of the Third World War orbiting in space, and their bodies were recovered on a solemn mission at the end of August 1985. They were the first casualties of the war in space and are buried in Arlington National Cemetery.

CHAPTER NINETEEN

AIR DEFENCE OF THE UNITED KINGDOM AND EASTERN ATLANTIC

For some years after the Second World War the UK maintained a high level of air defence. The Berlin crisis and the airlift in 1948, and then the Korean War in 1950, did much to offset the idealists' beliefs that all arms could be laid aside at once, and while the threat was possibly not very great in those days wartime memories of 1940 were still vivid. As a result Fighter Command's resources up to the first half of the 1950s remained considerable. Indeed, in 1957 it boasted some 600 jet fighters and a sufficiency of airfields and radars to support them.

But in 1957 there was a major shift in policy that was to leave the country denuded of adequate air defence for nearly twenty years. Evaluation of the nuclear missile threat from the USSR in the early fifties, at a time of overwhelming strategic nuclear power in the USA, had led to the contemporary strategy of trip-wire and retaliation. In 1957 it was decided, with impeccable logic, that all that was needed was a fighter shield to protect our nuclear-armed V-bomber bases to ensure that they could get into the air on their retaliatory missions just as soon as the ballistic missile warning system indicated that they must go. (For a discussion of this phase of British defence policy see Chapter 4.)

Whether or not the policy of trip-wire and massive retaliation was appropriate to the circumstances of the time, it was later to demonstrate a fatal flaw. As Soviet missile strength grew and the retaliatory strategy had to give way to the flexible response, with its emphasis on the ability to fight with conventional as well as nuclear weapons, so the basic assumption on which this minimal air defence was predicted disappeared. But by then the demands on government spending from many quarters left no room for the costly rebuilding of a comprehensive air defence system to counter the growing Soviet capability to attack the UK in a phase of conventional war.

By the time intelligence assessments had finally (and rather belatedly) recognized the conventional air threat it was not just a matter of numbers of aircraft – though heaven knows they were short enough; it was also a matter of numbers of men in the air and on the ground. Both were difficult to come by with the competing attractions of industry and commerce in an affluent society. Radar communications and control centres were also insufficient in capacity or availability for the changed situation. The shortage of airfields gave particular concern. By the end of the 1939–45 war there had been an airfield every fifteen to twenty-five kilometres throughout most of the country; now there were only a handful – all the others had gone back to the plough or had been handed over to municipalities or other users for a variety of purposes. The shortage of airfields was critical.

In the seventies it was necessary to think of air defence on an immeasurably larger canvas than that on which the Battle of Britain was portrayed. Not only did the stand-off weapons of an attacking force require the defences to be pushed out hundreds of kilometres if the launching aircraft were to be destroyed in time, but the areas to be defended now reached across the Eastern Atlantic, where it was necessary to protect shipping which would no longer have air cover from large fleet carriers in the Royal Navy. In addition to the central task of the defence of the United Kingdom and its base facilities, SACLANT and SACEUR assigned air defence responsibilities to the British in an area that extended from the Channel to the North Norwegian Sea in the north and out very nearly to the coast of Iceland in the west. It was a tall order. If the worst NATO

fears were ever to be realized then the air resource
available in the mid-seventies would be decidedly inade
quate, for in those circumstances the United Kingdom -
as a rearward base for SACEUR and a forward base fo
SACLANT, roles decided by the strategic geography o
the British Isles rather than by defence planners - coul
not hope to escape the close attention of the Soviet Ai
Forces.

To SACLANT, apart from affording air defence an
anti-submarine air patrols for shipping in the Easter
Atlantic and Channel, the UK was a critically importan
base from which to mount flank support for his Strik
Fleet as and when it had to fight its way against Soviet se
and air opposition into the North Norwegian Sea. And i
war this was assuredly what the Strike Fleet would have t
do. For SACEUR, the UK would be the mounting bas
for much of the deeper air effort behind the forward edg
of the enemy's battle area on the Continent. It would als
be to the UK that any aircraft and crews held in reserv
would be likely to be withdrawn. And then there was th
air bridge: the endless belt of heavy-lift jumbo-size
aircraft that would carry most of the human reinforcement
and much of their equipment from the USA to Europe a
soon as full mobilization plans were put into effect. Give
a rudimentary air-to-air missile system, even early genera
tion long-range aircraft could wreak havoc with this flo
if they got into that great aerial procession. They must no
do so - and it was the task of the British Air Defenc
Commander to see that they did not. If that office
appeared, with the resources available to him in the mid
seventies, a preoccupied man, no one could say he had n
cause.

Nevertheless, by 1977 things were beginning to improv
even if, in the view of the Royal Air Force, nothing lik
quickly enough. Some measurable progress had been mad
with the addition of two extra air defence squadron
provided by extending the life of some of the *Lightnin*
interceptors; the F–4 *Phantoms* were now the backbon

of an interceptor force and had greatly raised its capability at all levels, as well as its resistance to electronic jamming; *Bloodhound* surface-to-air missiles (SAM) had been reintroduced to give low-level area defence in the south-east of England, while mobile squadrons of the British *Rapier* SAM provided point defence to vital airfields in the north. More improvements were in the pipeline: the *Tornado* air defence variant was due to replace the *Phantom* in the eighties; *Nimrod* airborne early warning (AEW) aircraft were on order; and a major rationalization and modernization plan was in train to streamline the heterogeneous and unwieldy radar communications and control systems that had grown up piecemeal through the years as the RAF struggled to improve its air defence under the parsimony of British defence policy. Looking further ahead, airfields were to have hardened protection for their aircraft, while a particularly flexible and jamming-resistant new data communications system, the United Kingdom Air Defence Ground Environment (UKADGE), would link the fighters, control centres, airborne early warning systems and airfields by the early 1980s.

Once the national consciousness began to become uneasy about the danger to the UK of unchecked Soviet military expansion, the path of the air planners became easier, and it was possible to gain some political support from all sides in the House of Commons for measures now clearly seen to be needed for the defence of the homeland. Policy agreement was one thing, putting it into effect was another. The task was formidable. It is no simple matter to increase, or speed up, the production of complex aircraft and weapons, or to create their support facilities. It is more difficult still to conjure up the skilled and experienced men and women needed to operate an expanded and complex military system without mounting a deliberate programme of expansion in sufficient time to develop it in an ordered way over a number of years.

By 1985 the *Tornado* interceptors were in service in considerable numbers, thanks to increased production and round-the-clock working by all the contractors in that part of the European industry. The AEW *Nimrod* had replaced the *Shackleton*, and the numbers of SAM systems had been increased by restricting overseas sales and by purchase from the United States. Among some very promising air-to-air and ground-to-air weapons was the new EUROSAM, a collaborative project with France, of which the RAF now had two squadrons at home. A tanker conversion of the splendid old VC–10 transport was coming into service, and this, together with some Boeings bought from the United States, had greatly increased the air-to-air refuelling resources so critically important for long-range interception over the sea to the north and west.

Just as early scientific gropings with radar at Bawdsey Manor in the mid-1930s had helped to turn the tide in 1940, so perhaps the most significant process was in the completion of the new control and communications system (UKADGE). Without going into the technical details, it is sufficient to say here that it worked through mutually-supporting hardened control centres and accepted digitized data from the whole range of sensors contributing to the air defence system: ground and airborne radars, early warning aircraft, and NATO ground and sea-based sensor systems, including those of the French. This gave the Air Defence Commander, and all those concerned in the control chain, an immediate picture at any moment of the air threat and the resources available to counter it. It was to be the essential management platform from which the expected battle would be conducted.

Despite these improvements in equipment, and the highest quality of aircraft and weapons, the Royal Air Force still remained dangerously short of one vital asset: trained and skilled manpower. Political recognition in the late seventies that discontent with service pay and conditions was making a career in any armed service unattractive to young men came belatedly. The air force chiefs had long been anxious because the young men and women of the calibre they needed commanded particularly good opportunities in civil life. When substantial increases of pay were agreed in 1978 the situation quickly improved, but skilled servicemen became an even more expensive item in the defence bill than ever. The levels were raised to meet the increased front-line requirement, but not to the extent that the RAF, or indeed SACEUR in his operating criteria, considered necessary for sustained operations. If the RAF was to be engaged in hostilities in the near future, its commanders knew that through good leadership the human reserve would need to be stretched to its limits and probably far beyond.

The account that follows is taken from a personal interview with Air Chief Marshal Sir John Hazel, AOC-in-C Strike Command and CINCUKAIR (C-in-C United Kingdom Air Forces) in the NATO command chain.

At 0700 hours on the morning of 30 July the Air Chief Marshal waited in the hardened war room of his regional air operations centre at High Wycombe in Buckinghamshire, England, for the next briefing to begin. Since mobilization seven days ago he had virtually lived in the small subterranean office with his bunk set in an alcove to one side. Now his eyes were on the closed circuit television screen as the master clock ticked off the seconds to the start time for the briefing. Exactly on cue, the briefing officer appeared on screen and the routine began: weather conditions, actual and forecast, throughout his wide command; totes of aircraft and aircrew availability, and readiness at the operational airfields and the newly activated satellite fields and forward operating bases. All of this was called up direct from the resource catalogue of the Command automatic data processing (ADP) bank.

Despite the urgent refurbishment programme of the last three years, new assets of runways, dispersals and hangars were still far from what he would have wished; overcrowding, and therefore vulnerability, was exacerbated by the inflow of USAF squadrons to their war bases in his command area. The reinforcement so far had been most impressive, but one of the consequences was that there were now some very juicy airfield targets on offer, and he made a mental note to have another talk about dispersal with the Commander of USAF Third Air Force after the briefing. The transition to a war footing had really gone very smoothly, and with all the air movement that had taken place he was particularly pleased with the way the complicated airspace management task (the identification and separation of aircraft) was being conducted. He reflected on how different things might have been if the improved UKADGE had not come on line much as intended. The greatly increased capacity to track and identify aircraft was going to be worth its weight in gold once the President authorized the reinforcement air bridge to start operating at full throttle, as he must surely do very soon now if SACEUR was to get his troop reinforcements in time.

A continuous stream of heavy transport aircraft at the rate of one every two to four minutes, day after night after day, was what was called for to pump in the manpower to the Central Region in order to steady the inevitable recoil of the forward defences when the massive armoured thrust of the Soviet forces hit them. Even though many transports would fly over his air defence region without landing, their identification, safe control, separation and integration with the UK based movements, including the reinforcement shuttle traffic to and from the Continent, would tax his control resources to the utmost. On top of that, of course, there had to be scope for immediate reaction to hostile air activity, which had to be expected in his vast airspace once the war began and, perhaps, way out over the sea even before that.

The situation brief continued. *Tornados* of the Northern Interception Alert Force from Leuchars had been launched during the night in reaction to a high, fast-flying, radar plot. This was probably a reconnaissance MG–25 *Foxbat*, since it had turned away north-east and passed

out of scan at an estimated 20,000 metres and two and a
half times the speed of sound before the *Tornados*
abandoned the chase and returned to base. Most of the
ground-based radar sensors had experienced some sporadic ECM interference at the extremities of their cover but
the AEW patrols had managed to maintain a clear low-level
picture in their operating areas.

Overall his command looked in reasonable shape. All
UK-based units had completed their formal alert measures
and were now husbanding their aircraft except for essential
air tests. Civil flying had virtually ceased now that the
emergency repatriation flights for summer tourists were
out of the way, and the national airline resources were
being incorporated as a transport reserve. Liaison officers
at the reception bases for the USAF augmentation forces
were very busy briefing new arrivals. The C-in-C was
confident that the joint operating procedures hammered
out over recent years between the two air forces would
stand up to wartime pressures. The influx of men and
women from the support units and reserves to their war
appointments was now virtually complete. After his call to
Third Air Force Sir John handed over to his deputy
commander and left to visit some of his nearer bases to get
a feeling for the situation at first hand. After all, the
intelligence staffs still thought the signs pointed to another
ten days or so of this sort of waiting game.

As his helicopter approached Wattisham, he noted with
satisfaction the effectiveness of the toning down and
natural camouflage measures which had been pursued for
some seven or eight years now. You could not really hide
the runway, of course, but it was not at all easy to
distinguish the airfield from three or four kilometres away
unless you knew the area very well. The dispersal and
decoy system would also make it very much more difficult
for an attacking pilot seeking to destroy aircraft on the
ground.

"If only they were not tied to those damned runways,"
he said to himself. Being a good airman the inflexibility

and vulnerability that went with long runway airfields had always affronted his professional conscience.

Talking to the *Tornado* crews in their hardened operations room he was, as always, exhilarated by their professional competence and dedication. This squadron had less than a year's experience with the *Tornado* but they were clearly delighted with it.

"The radar is absolutely superb, sir," one enthusiastic crew member told him. "We can track them right down in the weeds if we have to."

Talking to the Squadron Commander, Hazel was reassured by the thoroughness with which the training programme had been conducted; co-operation with tankers and with AEW was obviously first class, and full advantage had been taken of the *Tornado*'s electronic navigation and weapons system to develop methods for concerted, and if need be autonomous, interception techniques between groups of fighters.

Flying on to Bentwaters, he had a talk with the USAF Base Commander who was grappling with the problems of absorbing some fifty F–15s that had just landed from the States. Overcrowding was his problem; the pre-stocking of spares and munitions seemed all right, and he was deploying the aircraft to pre-planned dispersal airfields as rapidly as he could. One thing was certain: he was not going to get caught with his birds on the ground if the balloon went up.

"They'll be up there," he said, "fighting – and shooting the hell out of the Russians."

Dropping in at Stanmore on the way back, Sir John talked at length with AOC No. 11 Group, his Air Defence Commander, and they reviewed the state of preparation together. They did not expect heavy losses in the air; after all, they had superb aircraft, and there was no reason why they should lose many in combat against intruding attackers. Losses on the ground were another matter. But the AOC's real concern lay in the limits of his human resources.

"We can't know," he said, "whether this is going to be short and decisive or drawn out by reluctance to go nuclear. My chief worry is that in any action beyond a week or two my air and ground crew will be stretched beyond the limits of exhaustion."

This was not news to the C-in-C; he shared his AOC's reservations, but there was little that could be done about it. Together they looked into the Command bunker that would serve as first alternative operations centre, with all the information available to the Command and Group operations centres duplicated there. This would be a vital facility if battle damage put out the main centres at any time – which was something that a resolute enemy was bound to try to do.

It was a thoughtful and reflective Air Marshal who flew the remaining few kilometres back to his headquarters that afternoon. Much had been done to gear up defences since the penny had dropped with the Western governments. The crucial question was whether there had been time to do enough. On the answer to that question might well depend not only the continued existence of an independent United Kingdom but the survival of Western democracy.

Five days later, as we know, the Soviet offensive opened in the Central Region. Sir John Hazel did not take much waking in the early hours of 4 August. He was not greatly surprised to learn that heavy Soviet pressure was already being exerted along the whole length of the Central Region. He knew that many of his strike-attack forces would be committed immediately to interdiction and counter-air operations, for which they were ready, in an effort to slow down the momentum of the Soviet advance. He also knew that such of his aircraft as were assigned to SACLANT would be required for a pre-emptive attack on the main Soviet *Backfire* base in the Kola Peninsula up in the Arctic Circle. This would be carried out by *Tornados* and *Buccaneers* from the UK, supported by tanker aircraft for refuelling during the mission.

Hazel thoroughly approved of this objective. Maritime air defence philosophy had long been a lively subject for debate between differing schools of thought, but he saw this attack on the source of the threat as entirely consistent with his own strongly held view that the best form of maritime air defence was to prevent as many of the enemy aircraft as possible from reaching the sea area where the targets were. In the EASTLANT area this meant an emphasis on a barrier defence across the routes that geography forced on the Soviet long-range bombers. This philosophy, which was not shared by all, did not rule out air defence forces being dedicated to the needs of a specific surface group, but resources were sparse and point defence was an extravagant way of using aircraft. He certainly would need strong arguments before he would divert significant effort from the more cost-effective tactic of hitting the enemy at or near his point of origin.

In less than an hour the radar plot started to show intruders approaching the UK Air Defence Region from the far north. In the next few days the defences were to be very hard pressed indeed as wave after wave of attacks were launched against the UK mainland. The pattern suggested that the Soviet long-range and naval air forces hoped to achieve four main objectives: the neutralization of the air defences; the elimination of nuclear-capable forces on the ground; the disruption of command and control; and the impeding of the transatlantic flow of reinforcements by sea and air.

No one as yet knew an effective way of hiding a radar aerial, but mobile equipments complicated the attacker's job and made gap-filling feasible – with the underlying strength resting in the flexibility and resilience of the new command-and-control data system which could accept and process information from any source. Radars were knocked out, AEW aircraft were shot down, and air defence ships were sunk; continental early warning was nullified quite early on by the speed of the Soviet advance on land. At no time, however, was the air defence system so bereft of data as to prevent it from reacting. In some of the worst periods the *Tornados*, supported by tankers, ran autonomous combat air patrols, providing their own raid information and directing their own interceptions until replacement AEW aircraft could come back on station or a mobile radar could be brought on line.

Airfields presented a less tractable problem. If only there had been time and money to prepare more satellite airfields and dispersals – better still, if the fighters had been less dependent on those wretched concrete surfaces. Dispersal to reduce losses on the ground increased the operating problems on bases already short of manpower and the time needed to get aircraft into the air. Cratering and mining were among the most disabling forms of attack: an airfield with its runway out meant that all the aircraft on the ground were neutralized until repairs could be effected. Rapid runway repair units had been a key feature in the improvement programme, and now paid off well. They took many casualties, especially from delayed action mines, as they courageously pressed on with their vital repair work. In one way, things turned out rather better than Hazel's men had expected. Low-level attacks did not seem to be the Soviet Air Forces' strong point. After 1,500 kilometres or more of transit flying, and of fighting their way through defences, many of them failed to locate their targets with sufficient precision. Those who climbed to 500 metres or so for a quick verification of their navigation were almost always picked off by the *Rapiers* positioned around the airfields.

As was expected, not all the attacks were at low level. Some came in at medium levels with a massive shield of electronic counter-measures and a high-speed dash to the point of release for their stand-off weapons. Against these tactics the *Tornados*, pushed well forward on combat air patrol and supported by tankers, proved the only effective counter. From the outset it was clear that the electronic war was going to be as closely and tenaciously fought as any other aspect of the air defence battle. The Soviet command of the art was clearly high, but air force thinking within the Alliance had foreseen this and the in-built counter-measures proved equal to the task when the test came. The revived emphasis that the RAF placed on tactics after the sterile years of the trip-wire strategy also paid off handsomely.

The corollary to the development of precision-guided stand-off weapons was that targets had to be selected with great discrimination. This was evident in the pattern of Soviet air attacks. Apart from airfields and vital points in the air defence system, key targets such as ports, ordnance and aircraft factories all received attention and suffered substantial damage. Whitehall was strewn with masonry. Many buildings (including, ironically, the Treasury, as well as parts of the Defence Ministry and the Palace of Westminster) were destroyed – though key members of the government and central administration were safely established at alternative and hardened centres. Civilian casualties, while not on the scale of the 1939–45 war, were nevertheless considerable, and because of the selective nature of these attacks they were often very disruptive.

As the Allied forces were pushed back in Central Europe a great hole was torn in the NATO air defence system in the northern area. This opened up new and shorter lines of approach for the Soviet Air Forces' attacks on the United Kingdom. Their aircraft could now come out through the Baltic with comparative immunity and fly across, or down, the North Sea. The response to this was to mount *Tornado* combat air patrols (CAP) and tankers forward in the direction of that area in the same way that CAP were mounted at focal points to intercept Soviet aircraft coming around the North Cape into the North Norwegian Sea. Soviet aircraft, dropping to low level, could now pose a much stronger threat to the French Channel ports which were so vital to JACWA for the reception of the massive transatlantic CAVALRY convoys. Hitherto the Russians had found it difficult to find a short, and sufficiently soft, line of approach to be able to attack with intensity. Now, if they could skim through the Channel undetected at very low level they had a chance of doing very serious damage indeed to the installations and the sea transports themselves. In addition to the barrier patrols across the Baltic Exits, the C-in-C now agreed with HQ Third Air Force, and with COMAAFCE's ready consent, that some of the recently arrived F–15s held in reserve should be dedicated to meeting this threat and protecting the French ports (in conjunction with the French Air Force). This was done, and the brilliantly versatile F–15s had great success against those attacking aircraft that managed to evade the barrier patrols to the north.

Losses in the air were well up to the levels that the peacetime analysts had forecast, but valuable fighters were more often lost on the ground than in the air. AEW aircraft paid the price for having to be far out on station and relatively unprotected, and tanker aircraft were sometimes lost for the same reason. A proportion of airfields were always unusable, but never so many that the defences were totally grounded. The problems of identification in a very active sky and of separation between missile and non-missile zones proved as difficult as exercises had always suggested that they would be. Inevitably some RAF attack aircraft returning from their Central Region targets fell victim to their own defences. The barrier patrol up to the north was there as a tourniquet around the Soviet long-range air forces seeking to threaten soft transport aircraft coming over the air bridge and the shipborne reinforcements coming across the sea. Some inevitably got through the net, but when this happened there was a second chance to intercept them in lower latitudes, though not always until after they had done damage to sea and air supplies.

As one instance, on 6 August two *Backfire* bombers armed with a massive battery of air-to-air missiles got loose in the procession of air transports wallowing across the Atlantic at 550 miles an hour. It was easy shooting. They knocked down three C–5s and four 747s before withdrawing at high speed to the north. One of them fell to a *Tornado* trap on the way home.

A system of dispersing the transports when a raider was known to be loose had been introduced, but that time, for some reason, the codeword did not get through. The air bridge had been attacked before, but this was a black day with more than 2,000 men missing from a Central Army Group formation before they even knew they were in action. But for most of the time the losses were at least militarily acceptable.

After eight days it began to look as if the advantage might be lying slightly with the defences. It was impossible to draw up an exact balance sheet, but they were certainly taking a heavy toll of aircraft in the promising ratio of around four to one. All now depended on how long the Russians would keep up the pressure and how long the UK air defences could sustain their reaction.'

The following rather more personal account of events on a day in the second week of full hostilities is taken from an as yet unpublished narrative by the former Personal Staff Officer to AOC-in-C Strike Command. It illustrates the understanding commonly found between top commanders and those who work with them.

'Late in the afternoon of 12 August there was, for the first time, nothing on the radar plot. There had been plenty of action that day. The last incident had been when a force of ten-plus aircraft had turned back as soon as they ran into the *Tornado* CAP outside the Baltic. As many of No. 1 Group's attack aircraft as they were likely to see again were now back from their early sorties over the Central Region, and it looked as if things might be quiet for an hour or so at least, while they, and no doubt the enemy, got ready for the next assault.

Sir John came up from the ground for a breather. His surface HQ had been hit several times but his operational control facilities were still working. It was a relief to walk on the grass in the Chiltern Hills on a summer afternoon. The day was clear but up in the sky a milky veil of what looked like cirrus cloud stretched from horizon to horizon. In fact it was the condensation trails of the great transatlantic airlift, each aircraft's trails being churned up and added to by the one behind it as they ploughed on to their destination airfields.

In 1940 he had been at school in Kent, and he recalled how the masters and boys had had a grandstand view of the Battle of Britain from the playing fields – watching and cheering as *Hurricanes* chased Heinkels, and *Spitfires* fought Messerschmitts. The school-boys nowadays, and for that matter the whole civilian population, must be puzzled, he reflected, as they heard bombs explode and saw the grim result, with no action going on in the sky. They would know what that great milky way was because there had been so much about it on television. But would they understand that No. 11 Group, the same group as bore the brunt of the battle back in 1940, was once again fighting day and night for the survival of the country and the West – but this time way out of sight and far from the country's shores? In due time, and if things came out right, he certainly hoped they would, for these were important matters to be understood by the public. If his reputation meant anything at the end of this war he would do his damnedest, he resolved, to see that the politicians did not forget a second time.

After the luxury of letting his thoughts stray for five minutes he went down the hole again and picked up a direct telephone to AOC 11 Group, his Air Defence Commander.

Air Vice-Marshal Bill Williams, the AOC, was a very experienced fighter pilot, but of course he was not old enough to have been in the 1939–45 war. He had a feeling, one way or the other, that this war was not going to last very long; as an airman to the core he had no wish to have to tell his children that he had spent all of it underground. So that morning he had handed over to the Group Captain

Ops and flown one of the *Tornados* on the Baltic Exits combat air patrol. The very one, in fact, in face of which the raiders had turned back. Later he remembered his telephone conversation with the C-in-C because it seemed to mark a watershed in the relentless battle that he was running.

Understandably, he was keen to give his chief a first-hand account from the front line of battle. The C-in-C, who knew most things that were going on, forestalled him.

"Hello Bill – I see you had a good trip. What were they?"

"*Backfires* we think, sir, but we didn't get a visual. They turned back as soon as they got us on their radar. We couldn't close them – not this end of the Baltic anyway – and we thought they might be spoofing."

"How are things in the Group?" asked the C-in-C.

"Well, you know our battle claims and our air and ground casualties. We're still keeping a four to one kill ratio including aircraft losses on the ground and that seems to be good. Everyone's tails would be right up now except that they're so bloody tired. The aircrew are still all right – just – and we're enforcing rest periods between sorties for them, but the ground crew have only been snatching sleep as and when they can since the first scramble. They've taken the casualties on the ground absolutely marvellously, especially in the runway repair teams. There have been plenty of medals earned by those chaps if we ever get round to that sort of thing. But they're pretty well flaked out now. I hate having to say it but I can't see how we can keep this pace up for more than a day or two. How do you think things are going, sir?" There was a pause before the C-in-C answered – he wanted to be encouraging.

"Several of their raids have turned back in the last eight hours and that must mean something. I think it's just possible that they're coming round to the idea that they probably can't win this one." He paused again. "I only hope they don't twig that they probably could if they raised the tempo and kept at us for another week or so. Bill, you've got to keep your men going and it may be quite a time yet."

As the C-in-C hung up, a Sergeant placed a folder of intelligence reports and photographs on his desk. He studied them very closely. Half an hour later he called the Air Defence Commander again:

"Bill, we're getting some very good Int stuff by satellite now about our counter-air ops. The losses of 1 Group, and of the Germans and USAF, in *Tornados* and F–111s, have been pretty heavy but COMAAFCE reckons the exchange rate is a very good one and I agree. With what they're doing, together with the cruise missiles, it looks as if we're fairly ripping those airfields to bits."

"Can I pass that round the Group?" asked the AOC, hoping for anything that would help hold back their battle-weariness.

"Of course," said the C-in-C, "but, Bill – for your ears only in case I'm being too optimistic – if these reports are as good as they look your chaps should be getting a little more rest before long." '

CHAPTER TWENTY

THE AIR WAR OVER THE CENTRAL REGION

Since the earliest days of the Alliance, ideas about the use of air power had centred, non-contentiously, on the ability of air forces to bring rapid concentrations of power to bear to redress the imbalance between Allied and Warsaw Pact numbers. Over the years, ways of achieving this had changed with the shifting balance in numbers and quality and with the continually evolving political appreciations of the times. In the late fifties the strong Allied tactical air forces were cut back as the emphasis swung to massive nuclear retaliation and the 'trip-wire'. In the late sixties, with the change to the 'flexible response' strategy, defence efforts were directed to the development of aircraft capable of undertaking both nuclear and conventional operations. As time went on, a numerical Warsaw Pact superiority in the air, as well as on the ground, looked as if it was to be a permanent feature in the balance of power. This placed a high premium on maintaining the Allied technological lead. It also demanded attention to methods of improving the effectiveness of the amalgam of national air forces through better standardization of their weapons and tactics and of their engineering and logistic support. These were not easy aims to achieve, for a variety of national reasons, and progress – though happily considerable by 1985 – had been slow and painful.

The NATO air forces in the Central Region were made up of two tactical air forces, 2 ATAF associated with the Northern Army Group and 4 ATAF with the Central Army Group. This structure was a hangover from the occupation of Germany after the Second World War. Its appropriateness came into question in the late sixties and early seventies. The problem was resolved in 1974, when an overall United States Air Commander (COMAAFCE) was established, with his own headquarters, to exercise central control of Allied air power at the highest level of air command in order to exploit the flexibility and concentration of the numerically inferior Allied air forces. COMAAFCE was responsible to the Commander-in-Chief, Central Region (CINCENT), and his two immediate subordinates were the commanders of 2 and 4 ATAF who retained, in peacetime at least, the same close contact with the army groups.

On the other side of the Iron Curtain we have seen how, during the 1970s, the Russians had developed a more sophisticated concept of air power. What had once been an air arm with very narrow aims, and an almost exclusively battlefield role, had evolved into an air force as the West understood the term. COMAAFCE saw the need to organize his air forces so as to counter this increased threat, while still being able to support the defensive land battle in the critical phase before full reinforcements arrived. He also saw the difficulties. Land and air commanders were agreed on the immediate, full-blooded use of air power in the first hours of an offensive. They saw it as a strategic task of the first importance to identify and slow the enemy's main thrusts on the ground. At the same time, COMAAFCE realized better than anyone that the success or failure of this plan would depend on the security of his air bases. In particular, his mind often dwelt on the fact that the bases from which 2 ATAF operated were uncomfortably far forward.

On the other hand, he felt confident about his assessment of the enemy's air objective. In a surge offensive with the initiative, and with an overall advantage, in numbers of more than two to one, it was dangerous and misleading to think much in terms of what the enemy's priorities might be – the Warsaw Pact would probably do

everything they could do in the air, and would do it all at
once. They would want to neutralize the Allied nuclear
strike capability in the theatre; they would aim to ward
off interference with the land battle and to establish a
tolerable, and if possible favourable, air situation; they
would need to protect their own air bases; and they
would want to put all the weight of air power they could
behind their forces on the ground. The prospect was one
of air effort, at every level, of an intensity hitherto never
experienced.

In the last fifteen years the development of the Soviet
Air Forces had stimulated hard thinking and debate
among the Allied air commanders and their staffs. This
thinking had reinforced the three classic counters to the
threat: offensive counter-air operations against the
enemy's bases; engagement in the air; point and area
defence.

There had been general agreement among Allied airmen for many years that the most effective way of
countering the Soviet air threat lay in 'taking it out' at its
point of origin – but this, never an easy task, had become
steadily more formidable as Soviet defences had advanced.
The airfields would be hardened and very well defended.
But major developments in fire-suppression missiles, in
precision-guided stand-off munitions, and in airfield-
cratering and area-denial weapons gave COMAAFCE
cause for sober confidence, though he knew that losses
would be high. Great improvements had been made in air-
to-air capability since the late seventies. Ground-controlled
long-range interceptions would still be possible and
necessary, especially in the air defence of the United
Kingdom and adjacent areas of sea, but the pressure of
geography in Central Europe and the short warning time
that this would allow, together with the confusion of
electronic counter-measures that would reign in the battle
zone, pointed to the need for a less rigid and more
general air combat capability. COMAAFCE was well
satisfied that the introduction of the F–15s and F–16s to

supplement the F–4 *Phantoms* had gone a long way to meet the requirement. These were not only very potent aircraft, but had once more the agility and manoeuvrability that had marked the earlier generations of fighters. In addition, attention had been focussed on the need for far more SAM and gun defences with a rapid rate of engagement around the air bases, while passive defence measures such as provision of concrete aircraft shelters, command bunkers, and hardened fuel and weapon storage were seen as essentials. Happily, a NATO-wide programme of such improvements had been brought to an advanced stage by the spring of 1985.

Turning from the air versus air battle to the central purpose of NATO's tactical air contribution – intervention in the land battle – COMAAFCE saw two essential roles. First he would have to check the surge of the enemy's ground offensive by hammering at the 'choke points' through which he would have to pass, then blunt the cutting edge of those armoured thrusts that did get through to the Allied area. This role called for an all-weather capability, very high sortie rates, and rapid reaction to army requests in a fluid ground situation. Second, he would have to take the momentum out of the assault by harassing and destroying the succeeding attack waves. He was completely against the so-called 'panacea targets' vaguely described in terms like 'the enemy's transportation system'. From hard practice and experience with their aircraft and weapons, the airmen were convinced that the best way of destroying armour was by area-denial and cluster weapons dispensing large numbers of bomblets. Fortunately, after the improvement programmes of the eighties they had such munitions in abundance.

On the morning of 3 August, as he mused on the characteristics of air power and the battles his aircrew might soon be fighting, COMAAFCE came back again and again to a major area of uncertainty. Twenty years earlier, as a squadron commander in South-east Asia, he had learned about electronic warfare at first hand, and he knew the sort of influence this could exert on all aspects of air war. The Allies were confident of their technological superiority, and especially so in this direction, but their closed society had enabled the Russians to shroud their electronic warfare methods and developments in such secrecy that positive identification of the best ways of countering them might not be available until hostilities were well under way.

These reflections led to thoughts on the past difference between the US and European (primarily British) approaches to the use of tactical air power. In the seventies the US, with great resources in technology and the experience of the Vietnam War behind them, had stressed the importance of suppressing the defences and of elaborate electronic command and control and communications systems. In the European view, however, this was prodigiously expensive, over-dependent on technology, and dangerously vulnerable to counter-measures. The US had seen tactical air power as a central force for the delivery of massive firepower on clear-cut targets. European airmen, on the other hand, saw it as more important to integrate the tactical air with the land battle, and they thought flexibility would be gained not by close control of aircraft at medium altitudes but from more autonomous and self-reliant procedures with very high sortie rates at very low level.

These divergences sprang naturally from differences in experience and resources, but it had latterly been seen, as in a blinding light, that this diversity in doctrine in fact had a very positive merit in compounding the problems facing the Soviet defences. Moreover, if the Europeans were wrong, they could still ride on the coat-tails of US technology, supplementing the US aerial task forces. And the Americans, realizing that they might be over-dependent on one thesis, started to pay more attention to autonomous and low-level operations as a reinsurance without departing from the main theme for the bulk of their air force.

Finally, as he thought about the human equation, COMAAFCE felt confident that, in the high standards of their training, his air and ground crews, if put to the test, would be second to none. The stringent tactical evaluation test of the NATO air forces over many years of hard practice and training gave him every cause for confidence.

The RAF Air Marshal who commanded 2 ATAF was also reviewing the state of his command – and in the main with satisfaction. The improvements in the last few years had been impressive, and nowhere was this more evident than in the RAF elements of his command. In the late 1970s Gordon Lee wrote in the *Economist* (17 December 1977): 'Man for man the RAF is the finest air force in NATO, perhaps even in the world. The finest, that is, in the sense of being the best trained and most professionally skilled.' If members of the RAF, on reading that, had felt, with justification, some pride and even a little complacency, it was short-lived; for in the next few lines he went on to say that the same unstinting praise could not be bestowed on all its aircraft and equipment. In fact, there was nothing wrong with the RAF in those days that money could not put right. Some money had been made available, and rightly the first *tranches* had gone to the improvements of the UK air defence. But by 1982 substantial improvements had also been made to the RAF in Germany.

At the time much political capital was made of the intention to increase the front-line strength of RAF Germany by 30 per cent. But as an immediate measure the air staff devoted some of the resources to the improvement of current equipment. In this way they had an eye to the likely difficulties of increasing the aircrew numbers. *Jaguar* and *Harrier* aircraft were extensively modified and improved; hardened accommodation with filtered air was provided for all airfield personnel. Six regular and six auxiliary squadrons of the Royal Air Force Regiment were raised to increase the level and quality of ground defences of the main air bases and the *Harrier* force in the field. The air bases and their aircraft throughout 2 ATAF would be a much harder nut to crack than would have been the case five years earlier.

But Air Marshal Broadwood, AOC-in-C 2 ATAF, had one matter on his mind that caused him great anxiety. In the late seventies, for reasons that have been explained elsewhere (see Chapter 19), the aircrew strength of the RAF had fallen very low. It had not been possible to recover entirely from that situation by 1985 because of the years it takes to turn suitable young men into combat-ready pilots. As a result, the ratio of aircrew to aircraft in RAF Germany in 1985 was still the lowest for any of the national air forces in the Central Region. The essential aggressiveness and skills were there in abundance; the worry was how long they could be maintained in intensive operations with high losses and insufficient rest.

The steadily increasing tension in the Alliance, followed by general mobilization, had given sufficient time for the air forces to reach a full war posture. By midnight on 3 August, 90 per cent of the aircraft of the Allied Air Forces Central Europe (AAFCE) were clocked up on the operations centre tote boards as serviceable, armed, and protected in their concrete aircraft shelters. During the previous week the US bases in continental Europe and the UK had received a continuous stream of reinforcement aircraft flown across the Atlantic. As a USAF general, COMAAFCE was delighted that the American reinforcement of Europe via the Atlantic air bridge had gone so smoothly. All the same, he still had much to ponder. He was well satisfied with the rate of aircraft generation and reinforcement, but the numerical advantage still lay with the Warsaw Pact by something in the order of two to one; and although the Pact could not now achieve tactical surprise, it could still enjoy the great advantage of calling the first shots. Moreover, SACEUR had ordered that 20 per cent of the nuclear-capable aircraft should be held in reserve. Clearly this had to be done, but it did not help him in the numbers game.

For the previous four days, NATO early warning had been affected by electronic interference from the other side of the German border. This was not unusual. It had been experienced increasingly during the current Warsaw Pact military manoeuvres and the early hours of 4 August showed no change. At 0345 COMAAFCE was woken from a fitful sleep in his command bunker in the Central Region's war headquarters to be told of threatening developments on the other side of the border. Minutes later he reached his war room where the German Air Force (GAF) general on duty had positive information of a major Warsaw Pact penetration of NATO airspace under cover of heavy ECM. The general on duty reported that he had taken the initial war measures and aircraft were already being scrambled. Within another few minutes, reports of attacks on the Alliance missile belts, air defence radars and air bases began to come in. The war had begun.

Looking back when it was all over, surviving aircrew of both sides agreed that the first hours in the air over the Central Region had been indescribably chaotic. With the exception of a few grey-haired American colonels – veterans of South-east Asia – few had ever fired a shot in anger or even heard one. The excitement, the danger and the general confusion of the air battle during the course of 4 August all contributed to what seemed utter chaos. Nevertheless, thanks to years of planning and thought there was in fact a coherent pattern underlying what was happening. A preliminary look at the records suggests that at 0800 hours on 4 August there were no less than 3,000 tactical aircraft airborne over the Central Region. Although the full story of the war must await a detailed analyis of combat reports and assessments, it is possible to describe the general trends at least in outline.

The counter-air offensive on Warsaw Pact airfields was

launched the instant SACEUR gave authority for Allied aircraft to cross the border. The first aircraft to do so were USAF F–111s and GAF and RAF *Tornados*, flying at tree-top level from bases in the United Kingdom and West Germany. The effort was concentrated against airfields in East Germany, and a gratifyingly high percentage of the aircraft got to their targets. Confidence in their ability to get through heavy defences at very low level was immediately established among aircrew and commanders alike, and the very high speeds of the attacking aircraft at heights often below sixty metres undoubtedly achieved tactical surprise. The few engagements by Warsaw Pact fighters suggested a lack of confidence at ultra-low level and possibly some shortcomings in their look-down radars. It was also evident that the Russians had not solved the vexing problem of operating missile and fighter aircraft in the same airspace.

It is not yet possible to make a quantitative assessment of the effectiveness of the counter-air offensive; but sufficient is known to say with certainty that, maintained as it was around the clock, it very seriously hindered the Warsaw Pact in achieving its main air objectives.

On the morning of 4 August, after consulting CIN-CENT and the ATAF and Army Group commanders, COMAAFCE allotted a major air effort to armed reconnaissance and interdiction of the battlefield approaches as soon as the main enemy thrust lines were identified. All the *Jaguars*, *Harriers* and *AlphaJets* in 2 ATAF were dedicated to this role, and in 4 ATAF the *AlphaJets* and US A–10s were similarly tasked. The French tactical air forces were mainly employed to the south in the 4 ATAF area, but only, on the orders of their government, in support of forces under French command.

When, later, the enemy's main effort was identified as being in the north, and the war in the south began to stabilize, COMAAFCE progressively switched a proportion of 4 ATAF aircraft to operations in the NORTHAG–2 ATAF area; by the evening of 13 August 30 per cent of 4 ATAF offensive air support potential had been transferred to 2 ATAF. The crunch point in the Central Region air war was approaching.

At this point it can be seen that three factors had a decisive influence on air activity in support of the land battle. First, the weather throughout the region was uniformly good and the picture was only occasionally obscured by dawn mist and the odd rain shower; visibility, for the most part, was excellent, and the smoke and dust thrown up by the massive Soviet mechanized forces could be spotted from as far as thirty kilometres away. This was a wonderful help to the *Harrier*, *Jaguar* and A–10 crews. Second, as our land forces were pushed back, Allied pilots found themselves fighting over very familiar ground and the reaction time to army requests for support was thereby reduced.

A combination of these factors did much to offset the enemy's superior numbers. But these operations were not carried out so effectively without grievous loss. By 11 August the *Harrier* and *Jaguar* forces of the RAF had been reduced by 50 per cent, and by 13 August the steady attrition of NATO aircraft had reached the point where COMAAFCE was seriously worried as to whether he would be able to keep up the pace. If they paused, the enemy might have time to recover his balance and redeploy his air power forward and closer to the FEBA (forward edge of the battle area), as it shifted westward. In the event, three things came to COMAAFCE's aid. First was SACEUR's decision to commit his reserves; second was his rejection of persistent requests for nuclear action. This prompted COMAAFCE to seek approval for using the aircraft hitherto held back for nuclear strike, to which SACEUR agreed with the proviso that 5 per cent must still be retained. Third was the imminent safe arrival of the CAVALRY convoys. At COMAAFCE's request, SACEUR then asked SACLANT to transfer to him the latter's *Tornado* and *Buccaneer* aircraft. This was immediately agreed, and on the night of 13 August all

these aircraft, further augmented by F–111 reinforce
ments from the United States and the Italian and Amer
can reserves from 5 ATAF waiting in Spain and France
ravaged the Warsaw Pact supply columns and dump
across the length and breadth of the North German plain
This sudden stepping up of the conflict with fresh crew
and more aircraft can be said to have regained the a
initiative for NATO.

As far as air-to-air battles were concerned, over 10,00
air-to-air engagements were registered over, and to th
west of, the battle area in the first seven days. A
COMAAFCE had predicted, the Warsaw Pact thre
their mass of aircraft into battle in successive waves an
– like the Allies – they supported their operations wit
every kind of electronic measure. Although the enemy
air offensive achieved successes and caused moments o
great concern at the War Headquarters of Allied Com
mand Europe, it can now be seen that it never succeede
in gaining complete domination of the air.

NATO's main contribution to the defensive air battl
over the Central Region was in the operation of F-
Phantoms, F–15s and F–16s. A long-standing debat
between the British and Americans concerning deploy
ment of air defences had been solved by the adoption o
a concept of defence in depth. Thus the first fighte
barrier was deployed forward of the NATO missile bel
to cover the ground forces; this was allotted to th
American, Dutch and Belgian F–16s. Behind the missil
belt, RAF *Phantoms* and American F–15s flew comba
patrols to complement the rear area point defences. Th
air defence of France remained a national responsibilit

In the early days of the war, the enemy's ECM and i
assault on the NATO radar stations seriously degrade
the Alliance's capability for close-controlled interceptio
But the weather favoured the defence, with good visibili
beneath the cloud layer at around 3,000 metres. Th
inability, or reluctance, of the Warsaw Pact pilots to fl
quite low enough offered the defending fighters man

skyline sightings as enemy aircraft crossed ridges and hills. The Russians' strong suit was their numerical superiority and not surprisingly they wanted to preserve it – so in the main their preferred tactics on interception were to evade. On balance, their air combat skills were shown up as inferior to those of the NATO pilots.

But the weight of numbers took their toll of the Allied defences. While in the first few days of the war aircraft losses favoured the Alliance in a ratio of three to one, the *HAWK* SAM belt was eventually saturated and those radars that survived the initial onslaught were soon picked off by anti-radar missiles. The air bases themselves were subjected to intense air attack – with the notable exception of the US bases in the 4 ATAF area over which the F–15s maintained air superiority throughout the war.

But although Warsaw Pact aircraft managed to achieve local air superiority on a number of occasions in the first week of the war, full air support of their ground forces proved impossible to sustain in the face of determined opposition from the F–16s and, on occasion, *Harriers* armed with air-to-air missiles. But mounting Allied aircraft losses, battle damage and fatigue often left the eventual outcome of this ferocious air fighting very much in doubt.

Although the development of the Warsaw Pact offensive in the Central Region has yet to be followed on the ground (which will be done in the next chapter), coherence and continuity make it desirable to anticipate here its course and outcome sufficiently to carry this tale of the air war over Europe to a conclusion.

COMAAFCE's first indication of a distinct trend in his favour came with a Soviet attempt to launch airborne and heliborne assaults in support of their attack on the Venlo position on 14 August. They did not achieve surprise, and their efforts to gain local air superiority lacked concentration and determination. The ensuing mêlée in the air to the north and west of the Krefeld salient was greatly enjoyed by the exhausted and hard-

pressed German and British soldiers, who afterward
christened it the Venlo Turkey Shoot.

When the NATO forces improved their command o
the air after the sudden release of reserves, local ai
superiority was exploited by precision-guided weapon
on Soviet crossing points over the Lower Rhine an
Maas, which helped to throttle the supply lines to enem
leading formations at a critical stage. With enemy divi
sions to the west of the Rhine isolated, COMAAFCI
allotted 90 per cent of 4 ATAF resources to the Com
mander 2 ATAF, leaving the remainder of 4 ATAF an
the remnants of 5 ATAF to support CENTAG. For th
next two days this tremendous concentration of airborn
firepower wrought havoc with the enemy forces west c
the Rhine.

But the air effort stood or fell on the retention c
secure bases, a fact of which Allied air commanders ha
always been uneasily aware. On the very first day of th
war some airfields were completely overwhelmed b
combinations of high explosive and persistent chemica
agents; others suffered their full share of misfortune. Bu
rigorous peacetime exercises in the flexible use of ai
power now paid dividends. Although airfields, unlik
aircraft carriers, could not be sunk, they could be overrur
and in the first days of war the enemy advance in th
north forced the abandonment of no less than six Germa
and Dutch airfields. The German *Tornados* were rede
ployed to the United Kingdom and their *AlphaJets* move
south. Dutch F–16s moved back into Belgium. Wher
four days later, the enemy crossed the Lower Rhine th
RAF had to withdraw from its airfields. Its attack *Tor
nados* and *Buccaneers* went back to the UK and th
reconnaissance *Tornados* were redeployed to the south
One of the greatest threats to NATO air bases lay i
surface-to-surface missile (SSM) attacks as the enem
advanced and deployed his mobile missile systems furthe
west. A co-ordinated missile onslaught on 2 ATAF ai
fields only just failed to catch the Allied aircraft befor

heir redeployment. It was a very narrow squeak and the esson was not lost on COMAAFCE, even though, in nounting the attack, the missile batteries gave away their positions and earned a particularly sharp and quick Allied air response.

The Warsaw Pact air forces did not achieve their objective to the full principally because they failed to gain tactical surprise and the Allied air forces were ready and waiting for them. In addition, NATO's electronic warfare was of a superior quality throughout the campaign, and the Allied aircraft and their crews, as had always been hoped, proved significantly superior in technology and skills. The Allied defence plan had required the air forces to stem the Warsaw Pact flood and hold the ring until the armies were reinforced and in battle order. In this they succeeded. The furious air actions, air-to-air, air-to-ground and ground-to-air, vindicated classical air thinking over half a century. It also qualified some of the commandments in the airmen's bible in important ways. For instance, while airmen rightly saw the need to fight the air battle above all, in the circumstances of this war they learned that there is no convenient tempo which can allow them to meet their tasks in the ordered sequence so beloved of the Staff Colleges. The airman's belief, born of Second World War experience, and so irritating to the soldiers, that the chronology of war should allow them to fight the air battle and establish air superiority before addressing the problems of the land battle, were shattered once and for all. Everything had happened together.

Given the limited resources that the West were prepared to devote to defence before the Third World War, the air forces saw the need to compete above all in qualitative terms. In this they were right; they would have been right in any circumstances – for a second-rate air force is an expensive national indulgence – but it is worth underlining the point that once the qualitative

margin narrows between opposing sides then number
become very important indeed. It was because of this tha
COMAAFCE's counter-air offensive was so importan
Happily the aircraft, weapons and electronic attack sys
tems specially designed for this task proved highly suc
cessful and did more than anything else to offset th
numerical advantage of the Warsaw Pact in the air.

Outside the European theatre, but of crucial import
ance to it, a new air factor was manifested in th
transatlantic air bridge. Despite the early lessons fror
the Berlin airlift back in the late forties, Western Euro
pean strategists had been slow to see air transport excep
in terms of an extension of existing logistic support. Nc
so with the Americans, or for that matter the Russian:
who in 1977–8 set up an air bridge to the Horn of Afric
that even in those days moved tanks to Ethiopia in larg
Antonov transports. The reality was that air transpo
had now become one of the major strategic manifesta
tions of air power. It was therefore particularly ironi
that the British, in their defence economies of the se\
enties, should have so drastically cut back their a
transport force – a cut which forced their planners to re\
on the use of car ferries and steamers to and from th
Hook of Holland in their efforts to find ways of gettin
British reinforcements to the Northern Army Grou
Such measures were more reminiscent of the Paris tax
used to move troops up to the Marne in 1914 tha
appropriate to the development of air power in th
second half of the twentieth century.

Perhaps the most vivid vindication of classical a
thinking was the organization of the command system o
the Allied Air Forces in Europe in the early 1970s. It ha
long been the claim of the airmen that if the flexibili
and capacity for concentration of air power was to b
exploited then the air must be centrally organized. Th
was indeed what happened, very much under US infl\
ence and pressure, when a single air command was set u
under COMAAFCE in Europe. When the lock w\

forced at the northern end of the region and the entire Northern Army Group was swung back like a huge door hinged on Kassel, it was this organization which enabled COMAAFCE to swing his air forces through ninety degrees to an east-west north-facing axis in a matter of hours. By the same token he was able to accept the suddenly released reserves and apply them promptly to the battle to which air power made such a decisive contribution.

CHAPTER TWENTY-ONE

THE CENTRE HOLDS

Early on 13 August it was confirmed to SACEUR that the transatlantic convoys proceeding from the United States were at last within the UK Air Defence Region under air cover operating from bases in France and the United Kingdom. Losses to personnel brought across by air (which included most of the units in reinforcing formations, together with the greater part of their light and some heavy equipment), had been high. Losses at sea to the ships bringing the balance of the heavy equipment, with considerable numbers of men and invaluable munitions, had also been heavy. Nevertheless there was now an early prospect of augmentation of the forces available to Allied Command Europe by some four divisions, together with a corps headquarters and corps and army troops. The massive build-up which Soviet action had been planned to forestall was already under way.

With a heavy concentration of air defence and, of no less importance, elaborate precautions on the part of French police and troops to avoid civil disturbance and disruption (see Chapter 22), the ships of the CAVALRY convoy could be expected to begin discharging into French ports, where US troops were waiting to take over their equipment, early on the morning of the 14th. Fully equipped units would then move by road and rail at best speed through France and Belgium into the area round Aachen.

At noon on that day, 13 August 1985, the Supreme Commander ordered the release of four divisions from the theatre reserve. They were to come under command to NORTHAG from 0001 hours, 14 August, for the purpose of opening an offensive from present forward locations in the direction of Bremen. This was to start not later than at first light the following day, 15 August. The operation, codenamed 'Culloden', was already far advanced in contingency planning.

It was known for certain, from high-level surveillance, SIGINT and deep agency reports on troop movements, that the enemy divisions now in action were from 7 Guards Army, brought up (as was also the case with 5 Guards Army) out of the Byelorussian Military District in the USSR. Behind the leading motor-rifle divisions in the first echelon of the assault force were two tank divisions. In greater depth still, but with their leading units still only some thirty kilometres in rear, were three more divisions, believed to be from the Twenty-Eighth Army out of the same military district. It was now known that the unsuccessful assault, by 103 Guards Airborne Division, had also been mounted from there.

Of the Red Army formations met in action up to a week ago there was now little sign in the forward areas, though some were known to be dispersed well in the rear. Of those which had taken part in the initial assault on 4 August, no unit at all, on the unquestionable evidence of reliable local sources, now remained on Federal German soil. The Soviet practice of using divisions for three to five days in all-out assault, to very near the point of total exhaustion, and then extracting them for replacement by completely new formations, was clearly to be seen in action. On the Allied side mos⁺ formations had already been in action more than once

At 0400 hours on 14 August Warsaw Pact forces, after very heavy air and artillery preparation, but no chemical attack, opened the expected assault on the Venlo position. Airborne attack in battalion strength on the flanks fifteen kilometres in rear, on Neuss and Roermond, proved fortunately to be of little more than nuisance value. Two German Home Defence Groups, one on each flank, each of nearly a brigade in strength, gave an excellent account of themselves in a role for which they had done much training: after some very tough opposition the German reservist and civilian soldiers triumphed over both attacks. Allied air defence entirely prevented any heliborne follow-up. The crossings over the Rivers Rhine and Maas remained in Allied hands, under the control of severely harassed engineers, open at least by night and even sporadically by day. The enemy's attempt to isolate by airborne action the forward edge of the Allied battle area was thus a total failure.

In the attack on the Venlo position the forward concentration of Allied forces, four divisions deployed between two rivers on a front of thirty kilometres, with anti-tank defences that were strong and well disposed in depth, put any use of the enemy's light lead forces on the usual pattern out of the question. The attack came surging in, at first shooting light, after thirty minutes' intense artillery fire aimed at suppressing anti-tank defences, with three motor-rifle divisions up, each led by its tank regiment, the tank companies coming in first and the motor-rifle companies following, mounted in their BMP, some 200 metres behind. Direct ATGW hits on leading BMP soon indicated that a mounted attack could only bog down. A dismounted infantry attack in great strength followed, under fire support from tanks, SP guns and BMP, with heavy concentrations from the tube artillery and rocket launchers of the enemy's divisional artillery, and air-to-ground attack pressed hard in spite of considerable losses in aircraft. The very heavy weight of the assault, with unit after unit piled on regardless of casualties, began to tell before long. Here and there NATO defences, swamped by numbers, began to crumble. The enemy, within an hour or two, was seen to be gaining a clear advantage.

At the same time as the main assault on the Venlo position, another attack was being made by one Soviet motorized division west of the Maas, southwards towards

Roermond. Heavy Allied missile concentrations on crossings over the Maas and Lower Rhine, which were being kept open with great difficulty by Soviet engineers, took sufficient of the edge off this attack to enable one US brigade, operating with two Dutch regiments under command and anti-tank defences disposed in depth, which the enemy had found it impossible entirely to suppress, just to hold its own. Ground was given, but sufficient of the network of ATGW remained in action to foil the enemy's first attempt at doing to the Venlo position on the west bank of the Maas, on a smaller scale, what the general Soviet offensive had been trying to do to AFCENT as a whole, that is, to roll it up from the rear by attack from north to south along the west bank of the Rhine.

An even stronger enemy attack than that west of the Maas developed at the same time east of the Rhine, where units of II British Corps, with a Dutch brigade and a strong and very recently regrouped German division, together with three German Home Defence Groups, the whole force under a German general-lieutenant, had up to now succeeded in preventing the movement of any but light forces across the hardly formidable water obstacle of the River Lippe. Three things had here contributed to an extremely important delay in the enemy's advance: flooding, which had done something to canalize movement from the north-east; the extensive use of mines; and close air support, exploiting the slight but growing advantage in the air the Allies now enjoyed and the evident superiority in electronic warfare which was contributing so largely to it.

Of great assistance in the battle of the Lippe, on the right flank of the critical fight for Venlo, were the heightened protection from air attack electronic techniques afforded the Allied ground forces and, above all, the survival of effective anti-tank defences against all attempts completely to suppress them. What was of scarcely less importance here was the action on the ground of Federal German reserve and territorial forces.

Even though a numerical superiority, at the chosen point of attack, of twenty or thirty to one in favour of the enemy could be greatly reduced, considerable advantage still remained to them. By nightfall on 14 August the forward edge of the Allied position east of the Rhine was back to a line from Paderborn to Duisburg. But for the tough fighting of the German territorial units, now reinforced by another complete group, even this could not have been held. What became known as the Battle of the Lippe was indeed something of a triumph for the reserve forces of the Federal Republic.

By nightfall the centre of the Venlo front, between the Rivers Rhine and Maas, had broken. The two British divisions defending the position, with one German and one Belgian division, had been driven apart, and penetrations of up to twenty kilometres had been reported.

Pressure from the enemy to exploit his advantage continued during the hours of darkness. A full-scale assault was resumed at first light. Repeated requests from II British Corps for nuclear fire support continued to be refused by AFCENT on the Supreme Allied Commander's orders, but very heavy artillery concentrations, from both tube and missile systems, together with tactical air support on a scale not yet seen on the Allied side, was having a marked effect in slowing down the enemy's advance. It had been possible during the night, moreover, to stabilize in depth a number of defensive localities, where the anti-tank network was found to have remained, to a surprising and encouraging extent, still in being. The enemy's suppressive action had been very far from fully effective. His advancing armour and mechanized infantry now found itself obliged to move through a system of interlocking ATGW positions which was still formidable.

What has been said before deserves to be said again. More and more, as the fighting in the Central Region had developed during the last few days, was the superiority of Allied electronic technology being seen on every side, both on the ground and in the air. Now is not the time to speak at length on the improvement in electronic techniques, in which the West had so very far outstripped the East over the last few years, techniques in which a dramatic reduction in the size and complexity of electronic components, as well as in their failure rate, had been accompanied by a phenomenal reduction in cost. It is sufficient to say that, almost unnoticed, the West, unhampered by industrial collectivism under state control and with the stimulus of commercial competition, had established a lead over the East. This had long been uneasily observed there but was now seen to be far greater even than had been suspected. Its results were manifest in every sphere: in the exploitation of the attack and reconnaissance capabilities of F–15 aircraft and remotely-piloted vehicles (RPV), for example; in the deadly impact of precision-guided missiles (PGM), which were immune to interference; in the netting of tactical electronic units; in the reduction of vulnerability to interference with communications by proliferation of channels; and in countless other ways. Allied electronic counter-measures and counter-counter-measures were at the same time reducing the effectiveness of hostile air and missile attacks without prejudice to their own.

The operation of carefully co-ordinated intercept and interference systems against communications was proving invaluable in the ground battle above all. The location of hostile launchers and their swift destruction by terminally-homing PGM; the jamming of hostile sensors; the diversion of missile attacks; the application of a wide range of electronic counter-measures, behind an elaborate and effective barrier of counter-counter-measures, to reduce the enemy's capacity to retaliate; and not least a policy of concentrated attack on the enemy's command and control mechanisms – all this was paying off handsomely. The Soviet system of operational command was particularly sensitive. It was too inelastic to withstand continued and determined efforts to seek out and destroy headquarters installations. The inability of regimental commands to handle a fluid situation when deprived of signals communication with divisional headquarters was now more marked than ever. Forward radio intercept of transmission from penetrating Soviet columns was picking up with growing frequency requests for fresh orders in an unexpected situation.

Anti-tank defences, well disposed in depth, and in a highly favourable electronic environment, could do a great deal to offset a heavy numerical inferiority on the ground, particularly when the Allied tactical air forces were proving more effective than those of their opponents. It could hardly be a complete substitute for adequate strength in guns and armour on the battlefield, however. The commander of II British Corps had not lost all tactical control within his area of responsibility. His corps was still an operational entity, but it was split and penetrated, and between groups now no longer able to support each other the enemy's advance went on. Though anti-tank defence detachments took a very heavy toll, missile re-supply to the launchers was proving more and more difficult. One by one ATGW crews were pinned down and overrun by motorized infantry in BMP now for the most part, in a development of high significance, attacking mounted. By the late afternoon of 14 August leading elements of a Soviet tank division were approaching Jülich.

During the preceding night, however, a French armoured division had been moving into the area around Maastricht. This was part of a French corps previously intended for the Southern Army Group, but switched by SACEUR to this location at the urgent instance of AFCENT (after hasty discussion with the French government and swift intervention from Washington) late on the 13th. By first light on the 15th, though not yet in contact, this French division was in a useful and well-balanced position. Still rather thin on the ground as its units moved up, it was nevertheless in touch on its right with the left flank of a force of two US brigades, with which German Territorial units were operating in support, deployed and largely dug-in east and west of Düren.

The peacetime location of HQ AFCENT at Brunssum, not far away, had now been finally abandoned, command having been long exercised from a field headquarters whose present location was near Liège. It was into the area of Aachen that the advanced parties of the newly arrived US Corps, the disembarkation of their heavy equipment in French ports now virtually complete, began to arrive just before dawn on the 15th.

To the east of what was now becoming known as the Krefeld Salient two British divisions and one German were fighting with their backs to the Rhine. Their fire on the enemy's flank, exploited by the timely manoeuvre of armoured squadron groups, could not stop his southward advance but did much to slow it down. On the other side of the Rhine, on the east bank, 14 August was a critical day. NORTHAG was at all costs determined to hold firm in the area south of the Lippe, to get the offensive now in preparation for the following morning off to a fair start. Against the weight of opposition pressing down from the north this was far from easy, but the battle that was now being fought, in great part by German troops both of the regular army and of the reserve, on German soil, was everywhere recognized to be of critical importance to the whole future of a free Germany. The Battle of the Lippe was above all a stand by Germans, to give the best chance of success in the counter-offensive for which Allied formations of six nations were now advancing to their assembly and dispersal areas in preparation for the attack. At nightfall the lines of approach for Allied units were still clear. They were kept clear till dawn.

Situation, 0400 hrs 15 Aug

TERRITORY OCCUPIED BY
WARSAW PACT FORCES

During the night the boundary between the Northern and Central Army Groups was moved northwards. It now ran from Koblenz to Hannover.

We have treated the operations during these few days in mid-August 1985 with a degree of detail which might seem out of place in a book so limited in scope. The reason is quite simple: 15 August was a critical day, a major turning point in the whole battle for Europe.

What would have happened if the Alliance had done as little for its defences in the past quinquennium as in the wasted years before is, as we look back today, painfully evident. The Russians would by this time have been secure on their stop-line on the Rhine, the Western Alliance would have lain in ruins, and the brutal obliteration of the Federal Republic of Germany would already have begun. The hopes of freedom in the subject peoples of the Soviet Union, both within the USSR and outside it, beginning once more to stir when war broke out, would have withered and died under a suffocating blanket of despair.

What had been done within the Atlantic Alliance was not enough to prevent war. Brought to the edge of it by miscalculation and mischance, with time not on their side, the Russians were not held back from the invasion of Europe by the clear certainty that an invasion would fail. On the contrary, the opening, even if less attractive than before, still looked too good to miss, especially as it might not come again. What the Western Allies had just managed to do, through a new surge of confidence and resolve in some of them at least, was enough to soften the blow when it came, to prevent the swift military resolution on which Soviet Russia depended, to give time and opportunity for the use of some at least of the huge resources disposed of in the West, and eventually to spark off the explosions in subject nations which were in the end to bring the Soviet Union down.

At midday on 15 August, as the units of the new US corps, fully equipped and ready for action, were hurrying under formidable defensive air cover by road and rail through France, while on the far side of the Atlantic further shipping was being marshalled into convoys to bring across the equipment for another, the welcome news reached AFCENT that the NORTHAG offensive had got off well and was making progress.

For the first time Allied ground forces were operating under conditions of local air superiority. A formidable slice of 4 ATAF's air reserves had been allotted by COMAAFCE to 2 ATAF. CENTAG and SOUTHAG were supported only by what was left of 4 ATAF, with the remnants of 5 ATAF and the French Tactical Air Force, the latter long released from the French government's insistence that it operate only in support of troops under French command. For the time being, while the main counter-offensive battle was opened in the north, this was enough in the south. SOUTHAG's turn would come.

Bremen airfield had been seized by US airborne troops and some, if not many, air-portable units had been flown in, under anti-air defences that were now proving more and more effective. The main attack, with three divisions up and two more to follow, moving across the Lippe just before first light, with elaborate deception measures to indicate an attack further west, was very greatly helped by the emergence of well-equipped and carefully hidden stay-behind groups of German *Jagd Kommandos* and British SAS (Special Air Service) left in the Teutoburger Wald ten days before. A brilliantly successful SAS attack on a Soviet divisional HQ did so much to confuse the Warsaw Pact defence that by nightfall on 15 August forward troops of a German division were once more back in Osnabrück.

Useful and heartening though the Allied riposte might be, it could by no stretch of the imagination be seen as the victory over the invading forces of the Warsaw Pact which was immediately announced, to the great discomfort of Allied chiefs of staff, by the Western press and

TV networks worldwide, above all in the United States. Little else had changed. In Norway, for example, AFNORTH, without much in the way of air support except what could be provided from the United Kingdom, and, with great difficulty, from carriers operating north of the Faroes, was still containing and harassing the Soviet advance in the exceedingly difficult terrain of Troms and Nordland. From the Skagerrak to the Hook of Holland the coast, and the hinterland to some depth, was in occupation by Pact forces under Polish command. Denmark had been overrun more than a week ago. Hamburg had been declared an open city, a declaration which the Russians had ignored. It was being left alone all the same, bypassed for attention later. The Berlin garrison, surrounded by troops from divisions now withdrawn out of the fighting in the FRG, was being almost contemptuously left alone. From the Baltic and Carpathian Military Districts of the USSR some twenty divisions were on the move to come in, as the next echelon, behind those that had followed up, out of Byelorussia, the first incursion from the GSFG.

Further south little Austria had been brutally brushed aside. Two or three brigades of good mountain troops were fighting on with the French and Germans in Bavaria, and older folk in Graz were remembering again how things had been in an occupation by Russian soldiers once before. AFSOUTH, with its regional headquarters no longer in Italy but in Spain, had fallen apart. Soviet domination of the Italian peninsula, if unobtrusive, was complete. In Yugoslavia the civil war dragged on, with US marines, once in the eye of the storm before it became a hurricane, now virtually cut off in Slovenia and tenuously supplied by air. Greece was manning her frontier with Bulgaria, alongside Turkey-in-Europe. Asiatic Turkey was under some Soviet pressure from the north, though not yet an object of major attack. The Soviet Black Sea fleet had moved through

the Straits already. That, for the USSR, was enough fo
the present in south-east Europe.

The whole Allied position could hardly be called
winning one.

In the Central Region itself there were now deploye
some forty divisions of the Warsaw Pact, fifteen of then
tank divisions. Though some, at least, of this formidabl
order of battle had felt the effect of Allied air an
missile attack, not more than half of it had yet been i
action against an enemy on the ground. By any standar
it was still three to four times as effective in firepowe
as the aggregate of Allied troops arrayed against it, an
up to now the Warsaw Pact had held the whole initiative

The Allied offensive of 15 August, nonetheless, wa
the key to changes of critical importance. In the firs
place it brought into being in the forward areas a ne
operational situation. The enemy had now to set abou
securing his flanks and rear before attempting to resum
the full impetus of his forward movement, which it wa
only prudent for the time being to reduce. But ther
was more to it than this. The operational challenge t
the Soviet High Command could, at least in the shorte
term, be met and mastered. The political consequence
of what was happening, in the chemistry of which th
military action of 15 August can now be seen as
catalyst, could not.

The Soviet plan to bring about the military collaps
of NATO's Central Region, with the occupation of th
Federal Republic and the disintegration of the Atlanti
Alliance, before there was time to mobilize the West'
superior resources, or for the Western Allies to come t
an agreement on the use of nuclear weapons, ha
already gone quite badly wrong. The intervention of th
French, and the vigour with which it was pursued, ha
been as unwelcome as it had been unexpected. Th
improvements to NATO's defensive posture in the pre
vious few years, though not such as to put invasion b
the Warsaw Pact right out of the question, had bee

ufficient to make it a good deal harder to bring off. The magnitude of the superiority in electronic technology enjoyed by the Allies, above all by the United States, and the adroitness of its application on the battlefield, had also come as an ugly shock. This, among other consequences, had prevented the suppression of anti-aircraft and anti-tank defences upon whose elimination Soviet tactical practice, both in the air and on the ground, so heavily relied. It had greatly hampered, by the severe degrading of communications which were someimes reduced almost to nil, the operation of mobile formations expected to manoeuvre in depth.

The combined arms operations, moreover, upon which the battle-fighting method of the Red Army fundamentally depended, had been anything but a complete success. The Allies had operated, as it were, in the interstices of the method, separating components whose strength lay in their interdependence. The four main elements of the combined arms concept – manoeuvre, fire suppression, organic defence and combat support – had rarely been allowed to operate together in anything like the degree of harmony required.

For all these and other reasons the strategic programme had fallen so far behind that there was now a real danger of that massive Western build-up which it had been so important to forestall. Unaccountably, troop reinforcement over the US air bridge had continued and the Soviet Navy had been unable to prevent the safe arrival of heavy equipment by sea. More reinforcements were on the way. From the military point of view the question had to be asked: how much was there now to be gained by going on with a plan which had already failed?

The political consequences of incomplete military success in Germany were to be far-reaching. The military might of the Warsaw Pact had not been defeated. Far from it. What had happened, however, was almost as important as defeat. The Red Army had been shown

not to be invincible. As awareness of its limitation
began to spread so hope began to rise in places where
up to now, only an occasional display of brave and
fruitless dissidence had relieved the grey uniformity of
a hopeless resignation.

National revolt was still a long way off but the seed
of it were already being sown as, in spite of the strictest
censorship, the news went swiftly round that all was not
well with the offensive of the Warsaw Pact in Germany.
From mid-August onwards growing partisan activity
with widespread sabotage and the disruption of rail
communications through satellite countries, began to
present an increasing problem on the lines of communication. This occurred first where, from the point of view
of military supply, it mattered most – Poland. The same
thing also began to happen in Czechoslovakia, and to a
lesser extent in Hungary and Romania.

Allied assistance to partisan forces, already some
months in preparation, was immediately forthcoming. In
the last year techniques of the Second World War, which
some had feared might be allowed to lapse entirely, had
been revived. The very large expatriate communities,
particularly of Poles and Czechs, and to a lesser extent
of Hungarians, in the United States, and of Poles born
in Britain to ex-soldiers of the Second World War who
had settled there, had been combed for recruits. Detachments of some size were already in an advanced state of
training and were now, with munitions, weapons, communications equipment and supplies, being lifted surrep-
titiously by air into their own countries. Their principal
task, in addition to the raising of now no longer wholly
unjustified hopes of future deliverance, was interference
to the maximum degree, with rail and road communications.

As the US air bridge had so dramatically shown, the
personnel of military formations could readily be replaced
by air. The Soviet airline *Aeroflot* had for years been
organized for, and practised in, the task of personnel

reinforcement, and in the 'exercises' which had preceded invasion had been fully mobilized for it. Some freight movement, too, even of heavy loads, was possible by air, but very large tonnages of fuel and munitions could not be handled so easily, still less the large numbers of heavy equipments, the tanks, SP guns and BMP, which were needed as unit replacements, and least of all the entire provision for an armoured or motorized formation moving up to relieve another which was exhausted and depleted in the battle. Road movement could help, though with all the disadvantages of wear and tear upon equipment the essential means of transport for combat formations remained the railway.

Great improvements had been made in the last few years in the rail support system within the Warsaw Pact. Gauges had been unified, equipment standardized, tracks multiplied. Long stretches of permanent way nevertheless remained open to interference, only secure under close and continuous watch, a heavy drain on military manpower. Partisan attack, over the very long stretches involved, was becoming a great and growing problem, absorbing in protective duties increasing numbers of formations which should have been moving up to the front.

The Soviet Union had always enjoyed the advantages of relatively short land lines of communication between the area of probable operations in Europe and the home base. The United States had the Atlantic Ocean to cross, involving much longer distances and less secure transit in slower and less efficient load carriers. Air transportation had modified the position and reduced the disadvantage to the US. It could not entirely remove it. This was a situation that the Soviet Union had always sought to exploit (with a success that throws an interesting light on the gullibility of some Western politicians) in any discussion on mutual force reductions. The advantage of land over sea routes would always persist, but the action of determined partisans, maintained in the face of measures of repression and reprisal whose very brutality underlined the importance of what was happening, was already doing much to reduce it.

In absolute terms, moreover, the mass and volume (to say nothing of the cost) of all that was required, particularly in fuel and munitions, to maintain an army in field operations at an intensive rate against a similarly equipped opponent, was now very great. It had taken a quantitative jump since the Second World War. Warfare in the Middle East in the seventies had shown this very clearly, if on a relatively small scale. It was just no longer possible, at the rate at which stocks could now be exhausted, to sustain intensive operations of war for months on end. Head – and equipment – counts were no longer the true measure of an army's capability. Formations in large numbers could be a liability rather than an advantage unless they could be kept effectively in action.

The Soviet war-fighting philosophy, from whatever origins it may have been evolved, was in the circumstances of the 1980s exactly right. It enjoined the initiation of total and violent offensive action, swiftly followed through to the early attainment of a valuable objective. The position of military advantage thus secured would then be exploited by political means. Speed was everything. The corollary was that failure to secure the objective in good time must result in a thorough-going reappraisal, in which to continue to press towards the same end might very well be the least sensible course.

In the operation in the Central Region, at its sharpest point in the Krefeld Salient, the Warsaw Pact advance never got any further than Jülich. The newly arrived US corps, equipped out of Convoy CAVALRY, was already by 16 August building up on the western flank. This posed a threat which, taken in conjunction with the northward offensive of the Northern Army Group, could mean nothing other than a halt to the advance and an enforced change-over to defensive action (for which the Red Army was not well suited) or to withdrawal.

The French division deployed in the Maastricht area in the emergency situation of 13–14 August was relieved as soon as US troops began to arrive in strength. It joined up with the rest of the Southern Army Group, which was now in a position, with some further switch-back of Allied air power, to open a counter-offensive towards the Czechoslovak frontier. This began on 17 August. By then NORTHAG's northwards offensive towards Bremen had regained possession of the Teutoburger Wald, but it could make no further headway against the very heavy flank defences of a rearward regrouping movement by Pact forces which could hardly yet be described as a retreat.

We have looked in some detail at the circumstances leading to the abandonment of the initial plan of the Warsaw Pact and the rearward regrouping which followed. The events of the next few weeks can be passed over more rapidly. Before we move on, however, some comment on SACEUR's handling of the battle may not be out of place.

It was a very near thing. The Supreme Commander was quite determined to avoid the use of battlefield nuclear weapons if he possibly could, in the certain conviction, shared by the President of the USA, that this could have no other result than swift escalation into the nightmare of unrestricted strategic nuclear exchange, with results which could not fail to be disastrous. As commander in the theatre he was also determined to keep under his own hand as long as he possibly could those modest theatre reserves which constituted his whole remaining capability to influence the battle. He was on the horns of a dilemma, precisely the same dilemma which had brought so much discomfort into the debate on the 'forward defence' of the FRG. To be able to hold off a very much superior attacking force, without giving ground, either additional troops were needed on the spot – or nuclear weapons.

SACEUR's subordinate commanders had been pressing him to furnish one or the other with ever-growing urgency. Counter-offensive action to relieve pressure at the vital point was most critically necessary. It was the prospect of the arrival of the transatlantic reinforcement convoy which justified him, in his own judgment, in taking the considered (and considerable) risk of releasing his only reserves for this purpose before the new formations to reconstitute them were securely under his hand. This, it may be added, greatly strengthened him in resisting any further pressure for nuclear release.

Analysts are already busy in debate on the wisdom of Soviet naval policy in the seventies. We make some comment on this in Appendix 2. What is abundantly clear in the present connection is that without the US Navy, assisted by the European Allies, there would have been no further reinforcement of Allied Command Europe by any but light formations after the outbreak of hostilities. Without Allied air power the movement of troops to the theatre and the safe delivery of essential equipment would have been impossible. Without the expectation of early reinforcement SACEUR would have been faced with a choice between surrender of his last remaining means of influencing the battle or, by securing the release of battlefield nuclear weapons, committing the world to the near certainty of a catastrophic future. Without stout fighting by the German Territorial forces, in addition to the outstanding performance of the regular forces of the FRG, the Allied counter-offensive might never have got across the start-line. Without the strength and flexibility of Allied tactical air power, and its skilful exploitation, the battle for the Central Region would have been lost almost before it began. The list of what could have gone badly wrong is a long one. It was certainly a very near thing.

The rearward movement of Warsaw Pact forces in the

Federal Republic was not the retreat of a defeated army. Though always under pressure from Allied forces which were growing constantly in strength, penetrating where they could and never failing to preserve that intimacy of contact which was always something of an insurance against nuclear attack, the forces of the Warsaw Pact were still able to develop a local superiority almost at will and to retain a high degree of tactical control along the forward edge of their battle area. They had failed in what they had set out to do, however, and the opportunity to do it could not be recreated. There was not only no point in staying where they were. It was going to become increasingly dangerous and difficult to try to do so. The wisest course was to withdraw.

We are concerned here only with the military situation as it confronted Allied Command Europe. Political developments, and particularly those within the Warsaw Pact, which were to become of paramount importance at a later stage, are another matter and are treated in Chapter 26.

In the AFNORTH area, the whole of Denmark and north Norway remained occupied. A gentle movement of the Soviet administrative elements, with security troops and guard units, which was virtually all that had moved into Italy in the first days of August, had begun to pull out of the AFSOUTH area. By the end of the month the communist-dominated Italian government was on its own, to make what reconciliation would be found possible with its former allies under the Atlantic Treaty.

In the Central Region the early withdrawal of the Soviet divisions in the Krefeld Salient, following hard upon the opening of the NORTHAG counter-offensive of 15 August, was the beginning of an orderly rearward movement along the whole Warsaw Pact front, everywhere – except possibly in the extreme south – under firm Soviet tactical control. A concentration of four Soviet divisions north of Osnabrück, facing south, kept open the southern hinge of a door which might otherwise have closed upon Pact formations moving eastwards out of the Low Countries and the westernmost parts of the Federal Republic, harassed on their way by Allied air attack and the action of II British Corps but still in being. The Allied airhead round Bremen, which might have been the hinge of the northern half of NORTH-AG's door, was firmly contained by the enemy; it would be some time before mine clearance allowed access to it from the sea. In spite of persistent pressure from the south the gap between the Teutoburger Wald and the North Sea coast was never fully closed, and Pact formations were able to move through it eastwards, if only, for the most part, at night. Allied artillery fire caused heavy losses and, in spite of the occasional temporary establishment of local air superiority by Pact air forces, Allied air attack was frequently of devastating effectiveness. A dogged Soviet screen of tank and motorized divisions, however, was able to maintain a defensive front, and this, with the help of local counter-attacks, just held off the threat from the south to the rearward movement.

The Allied purpose was less to inflict a punishing defeat on the armies of the Warsaw Pact in the field than to get them off the territory of the Federal Republic as soon as possible, with the minimum of Allied loss and collateral damage. From the junction with NORTH-AG, which was now on a line running north-east through Hildesheim, CENTAG maintained continuous heavy pressure on Pact formations moving eastwards (though with no further major setpiece battle) all the way south to the junction with SOUTHAG. By 18 August no troops of the Warsaw Pact were anywhere to be found in the CENTAG area, out of captivity, west of the Demarcation Line. It was clear, however, that an advance by Allied troops across the line into the GDR would be fiercely resisted, and orders to Allied Command Europe were for the present to hold hard.

In north Germany the position was rather more

complicated. Bremen was relieved by 20 August. On the 23rd the forces of the Pact had consolidated everywhere along the Demarcation Line except in the vicinity of Hamburg. Here the River Elbe was the front. Hamburg, its declaration by the *Senat* as an open city notwithstanding, had been occupied by the Russians. In order to avoid further harm to a city so far very little damaged and the loss of civilian life, no attempt was as yet being made by the Allies to take it back.

It was only in the extreme south that offensive operations were still in active progress. The Southern Army Group, with II French Corps, II German Corps and about a division of Austrian troops, all under French command, and a heavy concentration of Allied tactical air forces in support, had crossed a start-line between Nürnberg and München on 17 August in an advance directed on Pilsen. It had moved into Czechoslovakia on the 20th and was now making slow but steady progress. Of the troops opposing it none were Czechoslovak. Instead, SOUTHAG was now facing Soviet divisions out of 8 Guards Army and the Thirty-eighth Army from the Carpathian Military District.

On 21 August the southern advance was brought to a halt, at least for the time being, with its left flank, where II German Corps was deployed, south-west of Cheb. It has since become clear that the Central Group of Soviet Forces was concerned at the possibility of invasion of the GDR from the south and was under orders to resist it strongly if it came. It can also be safely claimed that the forward thrust of the Southern Army Group threw the operations of the Warsaw Pact in the Central Region of NATO considerably off-balance and thus helped to expedite its withdrawal in the northern plain.

Three momentous weeks had passed since that morning of 4 August when the world woke up to find itself once more with a major war on its hands. Only a pocket, if an important one, of Federal territory was still in the enemy's hands. Though still very much at war the Federal Republic was able to look cautiously around and make a first assessment of the damage. Bremen was in ruins. Hannover was very badly damaged too, particularly on the east and south. Probably on account of the speed of the action the damage in other cities was not as great. Kassel, Nürnberg and München had all suffered, and the great cities of the Rhineland had not been spared, though the spire of Köln cathedral had again surprisingly survived. But though the future was obscure and peace was not yet in sight, the worst seemed to have been averted, for the time being at least. The invasion of the Federal Republic of Germany by the Warsaw Pact had failed and the Atlantic Alliance had survived.

CHAPTER TWENTY-TWO

HOME FIRES: THE
DOMESTIC SCENE IN A
TELEVISUAL SOCIETY

Hostilities had opened in Europe after a period in which every country in the Western Alliance had, to some degree or other and each according to its own particular needs and inclinations, done something to offset the result of years of general public disregard of the possibility of war.

In the Federal Republic of Germany, the country most exposed, it had been necessary to move with circumspection. The inescapable requirement to make some provision for the evacuation of forward areas near the border with East Germany, where early fighting would be sharpest, and the need to take account of refugee movement flooding westwards, had to be met in such a way as not to diminish confidence in the policy of forward defence or in the protection given by NATO. Carefully and unobtrusively a great deal had been done. Arrangements for the evacuation of children and the provision of emergency stand-by services in depth were generally allowed to be not incompatible with an official policy which encouraged people to stay where they were in a war emergency. There was realistic, discreet and thorough planning for what was to be done if they failed to do so. The provision for the handling of a very big flow of population from the forward areas, much of it panic-stricken under air attack, for its marshalling, guidance, reception, dispersion and maintenance, was both extensive and sound. The development of the Territorial Army, which with its three Territorial commands of five military districts had made impressive progress from the late seventies onwards, furnished an invaluable supporting structure for the operation of emergency services. Its communications, engineer, police and service units, working in close harmony at Federal and Land level with civil and paramilitary border police, all under a staff and command system reflecting the usual efficiency of German military practice, proved of inestimable value. In the same years, civil defence measures – including some provision of shelters, emergency stores of food and medical supplies, hardened stand-by communications and sources of power – had also made progress. A more generous financial provision in Federal and Land budgets in the previous five years was well justified in the event.

In France there was less inclination to provide for civil defence than in the FRG. The argument was freely used that to do so would only diminish confidence in the deterrent effect of the country's preparedness to defend itself (which included a built-in nuclear capability under national control). It certainly saved the French government a good deal of money.

The French nuclear capability was never used, however. Under a Popular Front government the nuclear element in the defence programme had been allowed to fall behind, but even if it had not been, there was no question but that in a bilateral exchange with the USSR, without US intervention, France would be the loser. Soviet propaganda played upon this. The Soviet Union made it clear that there would be no area bombing of French cities but that precision attack could be expected from the air on any port or other target actively operating in an Allied military interest. A nuclear response from France would result in a rain of weapons of mass destruction upon her cities.

There was, in fact, considerable Soviet conventional bombing of French ports and communications complexes. Since, however, penetration by hostile aircraft was for the greater part of their journey over land and through several belts of air defence, the damage that was done, where it mattered most to the Allied war effort (above all in the Western ports), was not intolerably great.

Quite as much hindrance, and possibly even more, to the prosecution of the war in France came from civil disturbance. War with the Soviet Union stripped the mask from many professing Euro-communism in France, as in Italy and other countries. An impressively well-prepared Peace Movement burgeoned on the streets at once. Demonstrations, strikes and sabotage led to frequent clashes between communist and Gaullist sympathizers and a growing strain on the police, in whose support troops sometimes had to intervene. Widespread avoidance of call-up was accompanied by a sharp rise in petty crime. Food and petrol rationing, introduced on mobilization, never worked and perhaps were scarcely expected to. On the whole, nevertheless, France moved towards a war footing without intolerable upheaval, largely because the overwhelming majority of the French people were seen to be plainly in favour of resistance to the Soviet initiative.

Conditions were much the same in the Low Countries, with the added pressure of the immediate danger of invasion in both Belgium and the Netherlands, and, in the case of the latter, the burden of partial occupation by the enemy within a very few days. Resistance in Holland was slow to get under way in the Second World War, due to the habits formed over a long period of neutrality. When it found its feet it was formidable. In the Third World War there were many still in Holland who remembered how it had been before. Underground movements began to come into being as soon as the country was ordered to mobilize. From the time Soviet troops first crossed the frontier they felt the strength and dourness of Dutch resistance and replied with savagery far exceeding what was still remembered in Holland from the Germans. It was fortunate indeed for the Dutch that this occupation by a wartime enemy of a very different sort lasted only a few weeks.

Britain, once again free from invasion and occupation by an enemy, had its own problems. An account is given in Chapter 4, 'Awakening Response in the West', and in Appendices 1 and 4, of the growing awareness, in the seven years before the outbreak of war, of the reality of the danger to the Western Alliance from the USSR, of the dangerously weak state into which the defences of the United Kingdom had been allowed to fall, and of the country's exposed position as the bridgehead for US reinforcement. In the matter of civil defence, growing pressure from the public, spearheaded in the first instance by unofficial bodies such as the National Emergency Volunteers (see Appendix 4), finally compelled a reluctant government to take the threat more seriously. Government spending on civil defence (at £2 million per annum in 1978, just one-twentieth of what had been allocated ten years earlier) was sharply increased, until by 1983 it was approaching the 1968 figure. The legislation on army reserves (see Appendix 1), introduced as a result of constant pressure from Chief Constables on the Home Office, provided for the re-establishment of what was known as TAVR II – a part of the Territorial and Auxiliary Volunteer Reserve of particular relevance in the management of a national emergency – in a general increase in reserve forces. Further legislation included, in 1983, a Civil Protection (Emergencies) Act, which rationalized and extended emergency planning at all levels and introduced a phased system of alerts. A national civil defence exercise held in August 1984 led to a widespread improvement in procedures and brought out the clear lesson – borne out a year later – that law and order would provide the acutest problems.

It is now perfectly clear that but for these reforms Great Britain would have fallen into near-chaos under Soviet air attack. And no rocket attack was experienced for more than a fortnight. Until the Soviet Union was prepared to initiate the use of nuclear weapons as a deliberate act of policy, and accept the consequences, it would be taking a wholly irrational risk to allow ballistic missiles to appear on Western tracking screens. Conventional high explosive and incendiary bombing, mixed with chemicals, delivered from manned aircraft using stand-off methods, caused damage enough.

Evacuation of children, food and petrol rationing, the activation of emergency services, the decentralization of administration – all worked smoothly enough. It was the exodus from the towns, particularly from the Midlands and the north towards the west and south, that did most to tax the authorities, even with their new-found powers and resources. It was in movement, too, that there occurred the ugliest scenes of mob violence, rioting and looting.

Lawlessness was particularly in evidence in the towns. Houses left untenanted were an open invitation to burglary. Mugging in the streets, even in broad daylight, was common. Air raids offered particularly favourable opportunities for crime, though it was claimed by some that you were safer on the streets during an alert than after it. The 'all-clear' brought the muggers out again.

It cannot truthfully be said that Britain was ever near collapse as an ordered society, though life in it in those few weeks was difficult for many, and dangerous for some, while death and destruction were widespread. Much went on as before. The weather was good. In the country the hay was in, the harvest promising. Industry, the railways, coal mining, went on much as before, though North Sea gas was cut off and little oil flowed. Movement was difficult but rationing hurt very few. Food distribution worked well enough, even under the stresses of refugee movement. Cricket was played. People swam, sailed and fished. There was even some racing. The school holidays were not yet over, though when they were very many schools would not reopen in the same place. People still tended to live a large part of their lives with, and through, television – perhaps even more so than before. Indeed, since television was an aspect of life which, in wartime, at once assumed an enormously enhanced importance, the part it played in the events of August 1985 deserves closer examination.

The war brought immediate censorship to the television screens in Western Europe and the United States. In the years preceding the outbreak of fighting there had been considerable debate as to how far it would be wise to adopt open censorship, with the risk of breaking public trust in the television news, long established as the main source of news. The realities of the war swept those doubts aside. One of the most cogent arguments for censorship in the Second World War – the need to deny the enemy information which would be of value to him – was no longer valid. Soviet space satellites, with the detailed information they could afford, provided an immediate and much more accurate picture of what was happening than could be gleaned from the television screen. Had fear of informing the enemy been the only factor, risks could have been taken. But the risk which no government and no military leader in the West could accept was that of potential damage to civilian morale if the high and horrible cost in human suffering of this war were to be projected night after night into the homes of the public. This was a more important factor in the United States than in Britain and on the Continent, where the pattern of viewing had been much disrupted by air attacks, which drove people away from their sitting rooms and into cellars and shelters into which they could not usually move their televisions. Here the radio reasserted itself as the main source both of news and of guidance from the authorities. But on the Continent, too, over wide areas, particularly outside the main cities, life was able to continue nonetheless with a considerable degree of normality, and the television screen remained the centre of attention. So the authorities from the outset adopted a policy of allowing the television bodies to

cover the war as freely as they could whilst insisting on
a rigid censorship of the material which emerged. In
practice, this did not prove too difficult a task, for the
highly mechanized, rapid, highly scientific nature of the
fighting, together with the paralysing effect of chemical
warfare on all but those equipped to deal with it, limited
drastically the coverage which was possible. Battle losses
among television cameramen, even in the comparatively
short time the fighting lasted, were high.

This policy of strict censorship prevailed throughout
the three weeks of the fighting in Europe. Whether it
could have lasted in such a rigid form if the conflict had
gone on much longer is another matter. There were
already signs of restiveness by the third week. In Britain
the policy received its most severe test when Birmingham
was destroyed. For the first twenty-four hours after the
attack the authorities declared a complete ban on all
pictures from the scene – pictures which were in any
event difficult to secure. Coverage was concentrated on
the size of the rescue operation, on scenes of fire brigades
and rescue squads moving into the area, and on the
damage on the periphery. But such was the wave of
rumour and alarm which spread throughout the country
that the government rapidly reversed this decision, and
decided that only the truth would meet the situation. It
therefore allowed the full story to be told, encouraged no
doubt by the knowledge that the counter-blow on Minsk
had already done much to loosen the links between the
Soviet Union and its Eastern European satellites.

The propaganda war, which was to a large extent a
television war, was not, however, fought by the combatants for the minds of their own peoples only. It was also
a war to influence the minds of the enemy, and the minds
of the neutrals – and of *their* allies. Both sides saw
immediately that the most effective propaganda they
could make use of would be to emphasize the sufferings
of their troops, giving the widest possible exposure to
those scenes of casualties and damage which were being

so carefully censored out. Within Germany the communist bloc were able to make immediate use of the East
German and Czechoslovakian wavebands, already readily
viewable within Western Europe, to disseminate such
pictures. They reinforced this, particularly in the case of
Britain, by disseminating material from satellites, utiliz-
ing for this purpose the fourth television channel which
existed on most British sets, and which had by 1985 still
not been used for entertainment. It should be added here
that the main reason for this had, ironically, been the
decision to divert into improved defence expenditure the
resources which might otherwise have gone to financing
further television. Though the British authorities were
able to jam this wavelength, the Soviet Union were still
able to infiltrate a considerable volume of material aimed
at damaging the morale of Western audiences. It was
almost all of terrible casualties, shown in close-up, of
shocked and exhausted prisoners, of mile upon mile of
damaged tanks, smashed vehicles and the wreckage of
every kind of equipment. Many sequences showed shocked
and wounded Allied prisoners pleading, whether genu-
inely or with false voices dubbed over, for peace.

The Allied response was on similar lines. From West
German transmitters a steady volume of comparable
material was directed at East Germany, Czechoslovakia
and Poland. To begin with little effort was made to hit at
the morale of the Russians themselves. The Allies rightly
appreciated that if the crack was to come, it would be
within the satellite states. Two 'black' propaganda television stations, operating from the Federal Republic, one
beamed into Czechoslovakia and one into East Germany,
began broadcasting within hours of the outbreak of war.
These had been skilfully prepared, with the aid of exiled
broadcasters from those countries, to resemble closely
the official communist stations. They presented themselves as being Czechoslovak Television and GDR Television, operating on a separate wavelength because of
damage to transmitters on the main wavelength. They

ave a service identical in pattern to the official service,
ut with the news, and in particular the newsfilm, selected
o present the communist position in the worst possible
ght. Since the main stations were still transmitting, the
evice was readily detected, but investigations after the
var showed that these stations had commanded a sur-
risingly high audience, due at least in part to the high
uality of their transmissions. One feature was their use
f recordings of popular serials and popular music pro-
rammes which ran on the official Eastern channels,
vhich had been pirated off the air by agencies of the
federal Republic in advance, ready for re-use.

The parallel propaganda battle for the minds of people
utside Europe and the United States was also fought on
adio and television. Three areas were of outstanding
mportance: Africa, the Middle East and the Far East.
Both the Warsaw Pact and the Allied powers sought from
he outset to use television to prove one central point to
he people of these areas – that their side was winning.
There was no time to go into the question of the rights
nd wrongs of the struggle. What was going to influence
he attitudes of Africa and the Middle East and Far East
vas above all which side they thought was going to win.
oviet propaganda concentrated on constant radio reports
f the success of their attacks, supported by television
ews pictures of their forces in action – and winning.
Allied propaganda was much the same, except that the
nessage they had to convey was not one of victorious
dvances but of successful resistance. Every day that the
Russians were held away from the Rhine was a propa-
anda gain of the utmost value, for it dented the image
f Soviet invincibility.

In this propaganda struggle the Allies were possessed
rom the outset of superior resources, both technical and
uman. The addiction of the peoples of Western Europe
nd America to television in the prewar years now proved
boon. It had given Western Europe, and above all
Britain and the United States, an efficient worldwide

infrastructure for the swift transmission of televisio
pictures, via satellite, all over the globe. The structur
designed to meet the world's hunger for pictures c
European football, and news, was ideal for internation:
propaganda. Every day, in peacetime, international news
film agencies, together with Eurovision and the othe
international television bodies, had been transmitting
chiefly from centres in London, New York, San Francisc
and Madrid, a steady stream of programme materia
Thousands of technicians were trained for this work an
accustomed to doing it. The Allies could draw, therefore
on the hundreds of television camera teams, almost a
now equipped with lightweight, highly portable ENG cam
eras, who worked for the many television stations of th
West. When the fighting broke out the American ne!
works operated from their relatively secure base in th
United States as a united body, pouring out to the re:
of the world a flood of material gathered by the camer
teams of all the Allied countries.

Three aspects of the battle for Europe received par
ticularly vivid coverage. First there was the operation c
the transatlantic air bridge. Day after day the televisio
screens of the world showed the endless stream of trans
port aircraft bringing in and discharging into Europe me
and war material from the seemingly limitless resource
of the United States. Second, West German camerame
provided, with great courage and day after day, muc
dramatic footage of German resistance to the invader:
seen at its most spectacular along the line of the Rive
Lippe. Not only were there shots of close combat, at onc
terrifying and moving, but interviews with the Germa
infantry which left no doubt as to the strength of thei
morale and their great determination. Third, similar cov
erage was provided of the fighting through of the CAV
ALRY convoys at sea. No fewer than five camerame
lost their lives in this operation, for camera crews ha
been stationed on many of the escort craft and majo
transports, and others flew with maritime aircraft. Thoug

there was considerable footage of the sinking of Allied vessels, this added a note of convincing veracity to the recording of the arrival of the bulk of the convoy. Culminating, as the work of these cameramen did, in scenes of troops moving away from the quayside in France, depleted perhaps but very formidable, this highly important battle was shown to the outside world as the victory which it was. In the field of peaceful electronics, the electronics of television, the Western technical superiority was to prove almost as important as its superiority in the electronic technology of the battlefield.

In this propaganda battle the Allies had another weapon on their side – flexibility and speed of decision. The US President made one ruling of major importance immediately upon the outbreak of war. He resisted demands that a censorship board be established to guide and select the flow of television material overseas. 'We must trust the networks and the individual broadcasters,' he said. 'We must rely on them to be both patriotic and sensible.' An *ad hoc* organization of television professionals was set up and given scope to make the constant, split-second decisions on the choice of material to be transmitted throughout the world upon which television depends. They were guided – and in the last resort could have been controlled – by military advisers whose task was to ensure that no information of positive military value to the enemy was sent out. For instance, no coverage was given of the points of embarkation or the detailed composition of air loads from the US, still less of the location of their points of arrival in Europe. There was no coverage of the assembling of the CAVALRY convoys, no disclosure of their exact contents or destination. Shots which showed secret equipment in detail were excluded. But even such material as this was treated much less stringently than in previous wars, for, as has already been pointed out, it was known that the Soviet Union, by means of satellite surveillance, active prewar espionage and the early capture of much equipment in the fighting in Germany, had access to most of these secrets anyway. By and large the broadcasters were free to treat this material very much as they wished, within the general understanding that it should be fairly selected so as to give a reasonably accurate picture of the broad strategic scene. This meant that coverage of Allied losses and withdrawals was balanced by coverage of Allied resistance and counter-attack. Within this broad understanding, however, the broadcasters were left to make their own judgments.

This had two results, both of considerable value to the Allied cause. It meant that the material from Allied broadcasters reached the screens of the outside world ahead of that coming from the Soviet bloc; and that it reached those screens in a form that made it all the more convincing. It contained, if not the whole truth, at least a reasonably rounded version of the truth. Certainly it was more truthful than the coverage which came from Moscow. The communist material was not only less plentiful, there being fewer peacetime camera resources to deploy, but it was also dangerously delayed by their censorship machine. All Warsaw Pact footage of the fighting had to be screened, in both senses of the word, by Soviet officialdom. It arrived hours – and sometimes days – later than the Allied coverage. Day after day the first impression of the fighting available to television stations all over the world was that supplied by the Allies – and it was an impression of embattled countries which, whilst suffering heavy and grievous setbacks, were holding on strongly enough to enable the massive power of the United States to be brought to bear. This did a great deal to sustain the morale of key countries like Iran, a great deal to ensure the continued but friendly neutrality of the Far Eastern bloc, and a great deal, as postwar research has already shown, to raise anxieties within some African and Middle Eastern states that they might have backed the wrong side.

Within that most television-addicted society in Europe, the United Kingdom. television played a curiously sub-

dued role. By 1986 it had become in every way the main
source of information and entertainment for the public.
The various view-data systems which were then common-
place had added the dimension of a journal of record, a
development which had weakened still further the impact
of the newspapers. When war came, the public turned to
television for news, guidance and information, and for
that measure of entertainment for which the human spirit,
however closely facing disaster, still has a craving. The
first of these the television organizations were able to
supply, in copious measure. For the first few days of the
fighting the screens were given over almost entirely to
continuous news programmes, interspersed with messages
about air raid precautions or emergency services, with
administrative instructions on such matters as rationing
and evacuation. There were also frequent speeches from
government leaders.

Here the broadcasters found themselves on secure
ground. Their touch was less certain when it came to
entertainment. They fell back in the first instance on
music, played from behind a caption card. But modern
rock sounded suddenly out of place. Light entertainment
and comedy struck such a false note that, after one
channel had experimented with these as some form of
relief from the gloom, they were abruptly dropped. One
British regional station had an immediate and warmly
approving reaction from its audience when it went over
unashamedly to an abundance of frankly patriotic music.
But there were limits to the number of times which even
the works of Elgar could be played within the space of
twenty-four hours. An early answer was found in the
wide use of soap operas. Extensive re-runs of *Coron-
ation Street* and *Crossroads* proved extraordinarily
acceptable, if only because they were a reminder of
normality which had once existed, and which might, with
good fortune, exist again. And the Western, that one
indestructible standby of television ever since its early
days, also proved readily acceptable in wartime, with its

recipe of fantasy rooted in reality, and its reassuring message that in the end the good and the right always triumph.

CHAPTER TWENTY-THREE

THE VITAL PERIPHERIES:
MIDDLE EAST AND AFRICA

Almost fifty years ago General Wavell, when contemplating from the Middle East the stakes involved in an earlier world crisis, summed up the strategic balance in a statement remarkable alike for its brevity and its prescience. Oil, shipping, air power and sea power, said Wavell, were the keys to the war against Germany and Italy. They were dependent on each other. Air and sea power required oil. Oil had to be moved about in ships. Ships themselves required the protection of naval and air power. Wavell went on to argue that since the British Empire had access to most of the world's oil, as it had to most of the world's shipping, and since it was well endowed with naval power and potentially with air power – 'we are bound to win'.

To what extent did this sort of reasoning still apply half a century later? It was true that oil was still both cause and means of conflict; it was true that sea power was still largely dependent on oil and on the shipping indispensable to its transportation; it was true that air power and oil were still inextricably bound together – for use, for protection, for movement. What was no longer true was that 'we' – the Western Allies – still had a monopoly of all of them.

Every great nation which without the benefit of sea power had sought to humble others in inter-continental struggles had in the end been humbled itself by sea power. It was a lesson enviously learned by the Soviet Union and carelessly thrown aside by its once greatest exponent – Great Britain.

The equation was now a very different one. The Soviet

Union had some 8,000 registered merchant ships with a gross tonnage of 20 million; the USA less than 5,000 ships although a tonnage also of close on 20 million. The Soviet Union had 500 oil tankers, the USA 300. In reserves of crude oil the Soviet Union had some 6½ billion tonnes as against 4¾ billion tonnes. The Soviet Union was the world's leading crude oil producer, the United States the second. Yet the United States now imported 500 million tonnes of crude oil annually, nearly half of it from the Middle East, Africa and the Caribbean. The Soviet Union imported none. As if this were not enough, the Soviet Navy was the largest in the world, with some 250 major surface combat vessels and 300 submarines, of which 200 were nuclear-powered. Aircraft integral to the Soviet Navy totalled around 700. The Soviet Air Force had some 10,000 combat aircraft, including 1,000 bombers, of which one-fifth were inter-continental, 4,000 fighters in support of ground troops and about the same number for air defence. Air transports, including helicopters, amounted to more than 2,000. We summarize these resources here (though it must be remembered that a good part of them would be orientated towards China and the Pacific) as a reminder that it seemed to be the Russians, now, who had all the ingredients of Wavell's recipe for victory.

In the Second World War the struggle for Africa and the Middle East had been a sideshow. The power of the *Wehrmacht* had been broken in Russia, the power of Japan by United States sea and air power; only Italy had been knocked out by Allied efforts. Although the Middle East may have been subsidiary for the Germans in the Second World War, for the Allies it was a fulcrum. Moreover, it had been an excellent training ground. How did it appear forty years on with the Soviet Union powerfully established astride the Red Sea and in Southern Africa? Could her policy of denial seriously affect the West's ability to wage war?

The loss of all Middle Eastern oil, the oil lifeline of Western Europe, the loss of all Africa's raw materials, the loss of the sea routes – and 70 per cent of NATO's strategic materials were carried through the Cape route – the loss of a gigantic jumping-off point for naval and air operations elsewhere, the cutting of the world in half, would be a very serious matter. The West would be cut off from some 60 per cent of the world's oil reserves, available to it only from the Persian Gulf. All the mineral wealth of a continent exceptionally wealthy in minerals would be totally denied to Western Europe. The United States would cease to be able to import nearly 50 per cent of the oil it used and would lose more than 60 per cent of its imports, which travelled around South Africa. If some 8 million barrels of oil a day, 90 per cent of Western Europe's consumption, could no longer pass within a few miles of Cape Town it would be a grave situation indeed.

The Soviet Union's own policy of denial was a clear reflection of the position. For what else had the Soviet Union built up its navy? Why else had it established its influence in Yemen, Somalia, Mozambique, Namibia, Angola and Nigeria, except to deny these strategically important places to the West? No wonder they had taken such a keen interest in Southern Africa and the Horn in the 1970s. The Middle East was third only to the United States in her share of world exports, and Africa blocked the road from it. The total loss of influence in Africa and the Middle East, and of command of the sea, to be denied oil and material and to have to hand over great tracts of land to the undisputed authority of Soviet aircraft – such setbacks might not absolutely subjugate the United States, but would certainly reduce its ability to stand up to the Soviet Union. Africa and the Middle East were the key, not to winning, but to not losing a world war, as the events leading to the outbreak were to show.

We must now consider the action of the United States in two particular areas which profoundly affected the operations in Africa and the Middle East. First, the American intervention in South Africa. If the United States were not to be elbowed aside in a part of the world

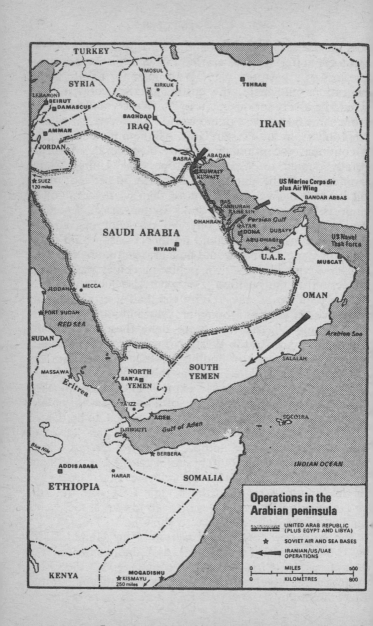

Operations in the
Arabian peninsula

▨▨▨	UNITED ARAB REPUBLIC (PLUS EGYPT AND LIBYA)
★	SOVIET AIR AND SEA BASES
➤	IRANIAN/US/UAE OPERATIONS

MILES   0 ———————— 500
KILOMETRES 0 ———————— 800

f vital importance there was clearly no alternative to the
stablishment of a firm footing and a naval base in
outhern Africa. In late July 1985 a brigade of US marines
lus an air group of forty combat aircraft, supported by an
ircraft carrier and a naval task force of twenty warships,
ositioned themselves in and around Simonstown.

The base was occupied and put in a state of defence.
The Soviet naval mission had quietly withdrawn. Whatever
hopes this may have raised, the United States had not
committed itself to the support of South Africa against
CASPA. In the months to come no US forces were to
operate in South Africa, except in defence of the Simons-
own base. This was to become the foundation for the
maritime supremacy and the ascendancy in the air which
not only contributed to the defeat of the Soviet Navy in
the South Atlantic but also played a major part in the
development of operations in the Indian Ocean vital to
the success of the American intervention in the Persian
Gulf.

When one important naval task force had positioned
itself in the South Atlantic and Cape area, another was
deployed in the Arabian Sea and the western part of the
Indian Ocean. A brigade of US marines with their naval
and air support was from the end of July at Bandar Abbas,
beginning to fulfil the United States' undertaking to Iran
and to the Union of Arab Emirates to keep them clear of
interference from either the newly formed United Arab
Republic or the Soviet Union itself. It was a timely
reinforcement, for the Soviet bases in Somalia and Yemen
had also been strengthened in the previous months of false
détente.

This United States' action on both sides of the continent
was at once condemned by the Organization for African
Unity, whose name continued as before to mock reality.
A resolution confirming the African states' determination
to establish black majority rule in the Confederation of
Africa South by force of arms – not just African arms but

Soviet, Cuban, Jamaican and Arab arms as well – was reaffirmed.

The battle for Southern Africa, without US intervention, was to be a slow and inconclusive affair. But what it was to lack in speed, concentration and decision, it was to make up for in variety, complexity and malignity.

In the Middle East things were different. United States intervention there was decisive. The nature of the country, as well as of the conflict, enabled American firepower – land, sea and air – ranging far afield in reconnaissance and destruction, by sheer domination of communications to deter any serious counter-strokes by the UAR. It enabled Iran to remain free from invasion, it assisted the Arab Emirates to hold their own against somewhat half-hearted Saudi attempts to settle old scores, it facilitated the preparation in Oman of the counter-offensive forces which would sweep the Yemenis aside after one decisive battle.

Another of the most notable differences between the fighting in Southern Africa and that in the Middle East was that whereas almost all the African participants had had recent and bloody reminders of what battle was about, in Arabia the only contestants who had any experience of war with modern weapons – Egypt, Syria and Israel – were involved either very little or not at all in the fighting.

The Israelis had been continuously in a state of general alert, with reserves mobilized and the country on a war footing, since the time of the formation of the new United Arab Republic in November 1984, but they were not, in the event, surprising as it seemed to many, involved in any fighting. A Soviet guarantee of immunity from attack by her neighbours, within her frontiers as then established, in return for a guarantee on the Israeli side of complete neutrality in any developments affecting the security of the Soviet Union, was offered in December 1984. On the advice of the United States Israel accepted. From that time on, through the world crises of the following summer and the general hostilities that ensued, Israel remained neutral.

Egypt played, in the event, in spite of possessing considerable armed forces, no more than a small and ineffective part in the fighting in the Middle East. Syria played virtually none.

In the Middle East, of course, the United States was simply allying itself with powerful indigenous forces in order to protect its own interests as well as theirs. Its firm base was Iran. Iran had 2,000 tanks, most of them *Chieftains*, an excellent armoury of ATGW, a huge infantry force which with reserves amounted to 200,000 men, more than 2,000 APC, 1,000 guns and all the paraphernalia of supporting weapons and aircraft, including 400 *Cobra* attack helicopters. Her navy boasted over fifty operational warships, including patrol boats, the air force 400 combat aircraft. Such strength enabled Iran to position in the UAE and Oman the best part of three divisions – one armoured, one infantry with APC and two special brigades – all fully supported with SAM, guns, helicopters, logistic units and tactical air squadrons. At the same time more than enough remained to secure Iran itself from the threat of Kuwaiti or Iraqi adventures, and this still left the bulk of Iran's armoured formations with 1,000 *Chieftains* in reserve – an unattractive fact for the Soviet Union's army commanders in Turkestan or Trans-Caucasia to contemplate. In addition, the Union Defence Force of the UAE was of no small size or competence, with its total of 25,000 men, tanks, SAM, ATGW, patrol craft, helicopters and *Mirage* fighters. Finally, Oman could deploy regular forces of some 15,000 including armoured cars, guns and ATGW, with ten fast patrol boats and fifty combat aircraft.

The United States contribution was designed to fill the gaps. A strong Middle East naval task force was assembled mustering a total of two carriers and a dozen surface combatants. Ashore in Iran was the best part of a division of the US Marine Corps, a US airborne division and an air wing.

On the side of the Soviet Union the New United Arab Republic's armed forces were by no means negligible in numbers. It was in their deployment and immobility that they were at a disadvantage. Egypt had a large and well-equipped army, nearly 300,000 men making up the equivalent of some twelve divisions, half of them armoured or mechanized, and ten independent brigades. Their equipment was largely Russian and included more than 2,000 tanks, with 2,500 APC and over 3,000 guns and mortars. The Egyptian Air Defence Command and the air force between them could call on 700 combat aircraft and sixty transports. The relatively small navy had a dozen submarines, eight destroyers and escorts, and fifty smaller craft. The para-military forces totalled 120,000.

But the Egyptian Army's experience of operating in distant Arab countries was an unhappy one, and the bulk of their forces remained at first in the traditional deployment areas – Sinai, the Canal, the Western Desert, the Red Sea, and Southern and Central Districts. The Field Force was organized into three armies, all stationed on Egyptian soil, one east, one west, one south.

Saudi Arabia, with her small population, had a small army – a mere five brigades, three of which were already deployed in Jordan, Syria and the Lebanon as part of the Geneva Conference arrangements; the rest, together with the National Guard, Frontier Force and Coastguard would be adequate for internal security and for looking after sea and air bases but little more.

Kuwait's efficient little army of about one division supported by some forty fighter aircraft and thirty patrol boats had neither the logistic resources nor the inclination to venture much beyond its frontiers.

The Libyan Army of 20,000 had more than enough to do keeping an eye on its own people.

To this prospect, the Soviet Union had little to add. Her sea and air bases in Eritrea, Socotra, Djibuti, Port Sudan, Suez, Jeddah, Berbera, Mogadishu, Kismayu and Dhahran were manned by some 50,000 armed technicians; her air forces including transports amounted to about 500 aircraft of all types; her naval strength in the Red Sea, the Gulf of

Aden and the Indian Ocean was not great. For the Soviet Union it would be a matter of hanging on to what she had got rather than reaching out for more. If, however, the Soviet Union appeared to be adopting a defensive strategy in the Middle East, the same could not be said of Southern Africa, for here she had powerful and more adventurous allies.

It had been laid down by the High Command of the Confederation of Africa South People's Army that the invasion of South Africa should be carried out from all four front-line states: Namibia, Botswana, Zimbabwe and Mozambique. Largely because of the difficulties of supporting logistically any more sophisticated operations of war, the forces from Botswana and Zimbabwe would be essentially operating as guerrillas, though on a very large scale. The two main thrusts would come from Namibia and Mozambique, with the backing of west and east coast ports, air bases, better equipped armies both in combat and logistic units, and the opportunity for seaborne support. From Mozambique forces amounting to nearly 30,000 would take part, made up in the first place of the recently reconstituted Mozambique Liberation Front (FRELIMO) army, now swelled by more Makonde troops from the Mozambique United Front (FUMO). Second was the Somali contingent, a mechanized brigade with tanks, APC and guns. Third, there were the main regular forces of Zimbabwe, a strong brigade, to which Tanzania had added two battalions. The Cuban force amounted to no fewer than 10,000, and it was the Cubans who were charged with directing the operation, though under the nominal leadership of a Mozambique guerrilla general, the new strong-arm ally of FUMO's head. General Chinde Inhambane (it was of course a *nom de guerre*) was a man who loved the petty details of military administration, who would have made a respectable quartermaster in a stores depot. He now determined to be not only commander-in-chief but also his own principal logistics adviser, with subsequently dire results for the whole expedition. The plan of campaign

decided on by him and his Cuban advisers was nothing if
not bold – an assault on the Transvaal aimed at Pretoria
and Johannesburg, with a substantial diversionary push
into Natal.

The expeditions from Zimbabwe itself and from Botswana were to be essentially huge distractions for the
South African security forces, to whom the excellent
communications southwards from Mbizi and Gaborone
were important. As Botswana had so few men to spare,
Namibia was to draft in a force of 20,000 guerrillas. The
Zimbabwe force would be about the same size.

The other main operation would be the SWAPO,
Angolan, Cuban and Nigerian attack from Namibia. One
force was to head for Prieska, the other for Cape Town
and Simonstown. The Nigerians had provided 30,000 men,
the Cubans 10,000, the Angolan and SWAPO armies
numbered 50,000 together – all in all a force not dissimilar
in total to the eastern armies invading from Mozambique.
Soviet 'advisers' and technicians were much in evidence.

What sort of enemy would these various contingents be
likely to meet? In the first place there was South Africa's
regular army, swelled by former Rhodesians and refugees
from Namibia – with a growing number of volunteers from
Australasia – to a force of 90,000. A US naval force at sea,
even if no US formations were involved in the fighting on
land, would in effect be holding the ring. Behind the
regular South African army there was the *Volkssturm*,
200,000 strong, confident, well-trained and utterly dedicated to the idea of winning, or dying – a hard nut for
CASPA to crack.

There was some convergence of views, but far more
divergence, between those variously involved on either
side as to what the whole thing would be about. Over-
simplified, it was this. The United States wanted to hang
on to what she regarded as two of her strategic interests:
Middle Eastern oil and the ability to bring tankers and
other shipping round the Cape. For the USSR the requirement was to keep a grip on Southern Africa, which would

give her dominance of the sea routes, and to control the Middle East and its oil. Those involved there had other ideas. The black African nations wanted to destroy the white hold on South Africa and have it for themselves, its riches, its land, its influence, its strategic potential. The white South Africans were equally intent on keeping what they had. Neither cared greatly for the broader issues beyond their own horizons. In the Middle East, Iran was concerned to preserve her own integrity and influence, an influence extending to southern Arabia; the smaller states simply wanted to continue with their well-endowed development; the new UAR wished to become the centre and controller of the whole Arab world. For the time being the convergences of policy were sufficient to allow these sets of allies to work together. Their divergences would become more apparent as operations developed.

Policy is one thing, method another. The United States' concept of how to maintain her foothold in Africa and support her allies in the Middle East was clear, simple and within her capacity. It had four main features: first, to break Soviet air and sea power in those areas whose strategic control was necessary to the United States; second, to provide those elements of defensive power which her allies in the Middle East did not possess themselves and without which they would be unable to employ effectually the military power they did possess; third, to keep these allies supplied logistically and to give further training to their armed forces when practicable; fourth, to keep US forces out of the land fighting in Southern Africa except in so far as the security of Simonstown demanded.

Everything the United States hoped to do depended on winning the war at sea, which itself demanded ascendancy in the air. The course of the battle for the Atlantic has been traced in Chapter 17. What matters here is its outcome. The Soviet Navy's defeat had two important effects on the battle in Africa. First, the severance of maritime connection with the Caribbean meant that no

Jamaican or Cuban reinforcements or supplies could come by sea to West Africa. Second, the blockade of West Africa from Conakry to Walvis Bay ensured that no support could come by sea to the belligerent countries from anywhere else. The battle for the Indian Ocean had been less intense and less costly than the battle for the Atlantic, but it had been important. The United States Navy now had a strong presence along the east coast of Africa from Mombasa to Port Elizabeth and in the Arabian Sea and the Persian Gulf, and superiority in the Indian Ocean as a whole. The Red Sea remained under Soviet domination; so did the Eastern Mediterranean.

Mastery of the sea and air, as the United States had discovered in both Korea and Vietnam, did not necessarily mean mastery on land, but it helped a good deal, particularly in the Middle East. Here there were four main areas of operations for ground forces. One was supremely important; the rest were sideshows. The first was a joint operation by the United States and Iran, supported by the Union of Arab Emirates and Oman, to seize complete control of the Persian Gulf. It involved the elimination of Kuwait and the destruction of all Soviet and UAR forces in the eastern part of Saudi Arabia. To start with, Kuwait was edged out of the game. The tacit neutrality of Iraq, whose relations with Syria had deteriorated almost to the point of military hostilities, enabled Iran to remove any threat from Kuwait without a fight. In the summer of 1985, powerful Iranian amphibious and air forces, poised for invasion, together with an unequivocal ultimatum, obliged the Kuwaiti ruling council to announce the severance of their new relationship with Egypt and Saudi Arabia. It was a *volte face* as total as that of Italy in 1943. From being the integrated ally of their UAR partners, the Kuwaitis suddenly became their declared enemies. Better, the ruling council had decided, a change of sides and a chance of survival than the certainty of destruction by Iran supported by US naval and air power. The UAR was without the means of arguing the toss.

The next phase was less one-sided and resulted in a prolonged, though not very bloody, campaign. The Soviet base at Dhahran was subjected to heavy attack by US ships and aircraft. A US marine force then captured and occupied it. Kuwaiti and Iranian forces established a cordon sanitaire between Dhahran and the Saudi Arabian forces, whose purpose was to guarantee the integrity of Riyadh. Skirmish and counter-skirmish continued, but the Soviet and UAR sea and air units had now been removed from the scene, and the 'Gulf' – no matter what the UAE might think about it – could again be called Persian. For it was Iranian sea and air power, backed by that of the USA, which called the tune there. United States land forces occupied Dhahran and secured and ran the base and its communications.

'Lieutenant-Colonel Ahmed Medilatif el Kasemy was a helicopter pilot of the Union Defence Force, the Army of the United Arab Emirates. He had been loaned by its Commander to take charge of a mixed air regiment equipped with French *Lynx* and *Gazelle* helicopters, which had itself been allotted to support the Kuwaiti forces helping to keep Dhahran free from Saudi interference. For a week they had had little to do except patrol, and he was beginning to agree that three-quarters of a soldier's life is spent hanging about doing nothing. He didn't mind hanging about, but he'd much rather do it from his air-conditioned house in Abu Dhabi than in the desert. Soon after dawn one day early in September, however, there occurred one of those incidents that made the whole thing memorable.

He was listening to the *Gazelle* patrol leader's report in his Landrover with his Operations Officer beside him. It was still being transmitted when he pressed the horn of the vehicle to alert the *Lynx* squadron for imminent action.

"At 0512 hours, at position 738492, mixed force of AMX tanks, *Greyhound* armoured cars and APC, estimated total thirty vehicles, moving east-south-east," went the message. "If they continue present direction and speed will reach minefield gap at 850431 between 0600 and 0630. Am continuing to observe, but have fuel for only 40 minutes more on station."

The Colonel heard his Operations Officer acknowledge the message, then switch channels and report it to HQ, as he seized his map and did some quick markings with a chinagraph pencil.

"Tell HQ I'm going to engage as soon as possible and suggest moving the *Scorpion* tank squadron to just this side of the minefield gap in their prepared positions. I'm going on this mission myself. And tell the *Gazelle* patrol to look out for us and guide us in!"

He dismounted from the Landrover and walked rapidly towards the twelve *Lynx* helicopters with their business-like *HOT* missiles slung three per side near the skids. The Squadron Commander, with his three troop leaders, was waiting in a group. Rotor blades were turning, mechanics and armaments-men checking. All other crews were mounted. Quickly he gave his orders, adding that he would accompany the squadron in the second-in-command's *Lynx*.

"But it's your show," he added to the Squadron Commander.

Within minutes they were off, swooping over the desert very low in four groups of three. Twenty minutes later he sighted two helicopters, soon identified as the *Gazelles* he was looking for. There was a quick interchange of information between the Squadron Commander and the *Gazelle* patrol leader, then the Squadron Commander gave his orders.

"Bearing 240, three columns armoured vehicles. We attack from north-east in two waves, my group and Alpha first, taking leading vehicles; normal drill of target choice; Bravo and Charlie attack five minutes later taking rear vehicles; return to base for replenishment immediately after attack. Acknowledge."

The time was exactly 0555 hours.

Shortly after 6 a.m. a part of the Saudi Arabian desert was a shambles of burning vehicles and dead and wounded men. There were still fitful explosions. As the *Lynx* squadron headed back for replenishment, the two relieving helicopters of the *Gazelle* patrol appeared. There was more exchange of information, more reports to base and to headquarters, which was anxious to learn whether there was any need for support from the mobile column with its guns and British *Scorpion* light tanks, now standing-to. The Colonel ended his own report with the words: "I don't think the *Scorpion* squadron will have much more to do now."

"I wonder if we will, either," he added to his Operations Officer. "Anyway, it was good while it lasted." '*

The third phase of this principal operation – aimed, as we have seen, at seizing complete control of the Persian Gulf – consisted of further reinforcing Oman with Iranian and UAE forces. These, in co-operation with the Sultan's own not inexperienced or inconsiderable army, once more began to cudgel the dissident tribesmen into obedience and to make the Yemeni 'volunteers' begin to wonder whether the game was worth the candle. But the elimination of Yemenis and the rehabilitation of the tribes was to be a lengthy affair.

In Southern Africa, the first real blows were struck with the simultaneous advance of four armies from Mozambique, Zimbabwe, Botswana and Namibia into South Africa in the summer of 1985. The expedition from Mozambique fared worst, that from Namibia best, and the two guerrilla incursions from Zimbabwe and Botswana, although destructive and elusive, had little impact on the outcome of the general battle. In its drive through the

*Taken from *Mirage in the Desert: The Overthrow of Soviet Power in its Challenge to Islam*, a collection of reminiscences by officers who took part in the fighting. Amman 1986, trans. and pub. SOAS, London 1986.

Transvaal, the composite army of FRELIMO, Zimbabwe, Cubans and Somalis deployed a respectable force of all arms with proper air, but poor logistic, support. But the attacking forces greatly misunderstood and underestimated their enemies. They had learned nothing from their easy victories over the Portuguese and their battles with Rhodesians. Not only did the South African *Volkssturm* defend their homelands with skill, savagery and success, not only did the regular South African forces operate with disturbing suddenness and speed, but, much to CASPA's consternation, the special forces of South Africa's army took the battle into CASPA's own base areas, mounting deadly attacks on its airfields and supply depots, on its lines of communication, even on the city of Maputo itself. They had not bargained for this.

The resistance both in the Transvaal and in Natal of the South African Kommandos was fanatical – but it was a fanaticism tempered with cool measuring of the military odds. The Afrikaaners fought with a ferocity which shocked and dismayed both the cynical mercenaries and the dedicated guerrillas of the invading forces. They were not always successful.

'2/Lt Pieter Van der Horst had just finished setting up his first ambush. He had received information over the radio two hours earlier that a column of some fifty mixed Mozambique and Zimbabwe guerrillas, supported by two T–34 tanks, were expected to reach his patrol area about now, and it had taken him every bit of the time available to get ready. In his platoon he had thirty-two men, four French medium machine guns, two anti-tank launchers of the Karl Gustav type and two 81 mm Malaysian mortars. They were completely mobile in eight Japanese Landrover-type vehicles and had rations for a week. Two Landrovers with trailers were separately loaded with ammunition and petrol. His men carried 100 rounds each. He had chosen a disused farm which offered excellent cover and superb ambush positions. Through it the main dusty track ran on towards Lesotho. The ambush was laid out over a distance of 300 metres: the first killing group of ten men with the anti-tank weapons and two machine-guns at the front, or southern, end; the rear group with mortars and two machine-guns at the entrance to, or northern part of, the ambush; and his own HQ and support group in the centre with some ten men and plentiful supplies of grenades. His own HQ men had the flame-throwers. Everyone was out of sight, the anti-tank and anti-personnel mines laid, the detonating charges ready for distracting or deceiving the enemy.

Van der Horst's radio crackled. It was a helicopter pilot reporting. "Column now within two miles your position, two tanks leading; remainder of force in two parties, approximate strength twenty-plus each party. Some carrying supplies. No heavy weapons." Van der Horst gave swift and low confirmatory orders through his walkie-talkie to the two NCOs in charge of killer groups. It was to be done broadly as planned. First enemy party with tanks to be allowed to proceed unmolested to Point A; then as second enemy party reached Point B or on his order or by his opening fire, this latter party to be destroyed by machine-gun and automatic rifle fire; immediately fire to be opened by own rear group, leading group to detonate anti-tank and anti-personnel mines, engage enemy tanks with recoilless launchers and destroy enemy foot with machine-guns; his own group to use flamethrowers against tanks. All enemy weapons and ammunition to be secured. If detonating charges required for deception – under his control. If for any reason enemy column does not enter ambush, further orders on radio.

When they came in sight, the guerrilla forces did not appear to be expecting any opposition. As they advanced, they barely bothered to adopt tactical formation at all, but trudged along behind the tanks, weapons slung over shoulders, talking, chewing, laughing, the gap between the two parties a mere 100 metres. As he watched them coming, Van der Horst was thinking that his plan should work.

As a plan, it was good. But military plans, as von Moltke observed, rarely survive contact with the enemy. In this case the seemingly unwary enemy suddenly took the whole affair into their own hands. When the guerrilla column was no more than 800 metres away from the ambush, the two tanks deployed to either side of the track and opened fire, first with machine-guns, then with high-explosive shells, on the derelict farm buildings. They were well out of range of Van der Horst's rocket launchers. The guerrilla foot soldiers rapidly dispersed on either side of the tanks and went to earth. Van der Horst gave a quick order over his radio: "Keep in cover and return fire with mortars and machine-guns. Leading group at five minutes' notice to move back to get behind them."

The tanks kept up a steady fire and seemed quite impervious to the machine guns now engaging them. Meanwhile, to Van der Horst's concern, the enemy guerrillas seemed to be crawling through the bush to the north of them in an obvious attempt to outflank his own position. It would be foolhardy to try to outface tank fire and allow his force to be pinned down while the guerrillas crept even closer. He still had one advantage over the enemy – speed. He spoke into the radio again. "Cancel last order. Rear group prepare to mount in Landrovers and move south in fifteen minutes; leading group prepare to give covering fire; my group will follow rear group, covered by leading group, and we will leapfrog back to agreed rendezvous Charlie. Maximum covering fire throughout move. Mortar fire to switch now to Hill 102. Leading group to withdraw when my group established at Charlie. Move on my orders.'

From a concealed position of great strength, with the expectation of gaining both surprise and success, Van der Horst was obliged to resort to defence, evasion and retreat. And all because he had no anti-tank weapons of sufficient range. It was a lesson well learned, and would not have to be relearned, as before long his unit and others like it would be equipped with the longer-range *Milan*-type anti-tank guided missiles, also now coming in from Japan. And the helicopters would have a new missile too. For the time being, it was necessary to run away in order to fight another day. After all they had plenty of space. And plenty of time. It was usually shortage of those two commodities that lost wars. Meanwhile Van der Horst, noticing with satisfaction that none of his men had been hit, used a little time to put a respectable space between his command and those T–34 tanks.'*

Even when the invading columns from Mozambique did meet with some success in their advances, they threw away their advantage by their savagery to the black inhabitants they claimed to have come to deliver. The Cuban proxy leaders of the FRELIMO bands were men to whom the death or mutilation of wholly innocent men and women was of no moment. Such was the shortsightedness and vindictiveness of the invading army's leaders that they were ruthless where they should have been conciliatory, and – in the case of their own members who revelled in excesses – tolerant where they should have been stern.

The invasion from Mozambique was held, but CASPA would not lightly give up the battle. Guerrilla forces from Botswana were advancing deep into enemy territory, reinforced by incursions from Zimbabwe. But what was rapidly becoming clear was that South Africa was holding on.

Long before it was all over, the USSR had wholly ceased to be in control of anything that was happening either in the Middle East or in Southern Africa. Orders from Moscow, growing in confusion and inadequacy in the last

* Extract from *The Veld Aflame: South Africa's Fight for Survival* by a group of participants, ed. Major-General K. E. Rymer, Cassell, London 1986.

few days of August 1985, had, by the end of the month, virtually ceased.

The United States now faced a huge new problem. This was not wholly unforeseen, but in the event it was greater, and came to a head sooner, than had been expected. Very considerable forces of all arms of the Soviet Union, disposing of immense masses of war material, with hordes of technicians, advisers and civilian operatives of every sort, were now spread over vast areas with no coherent purpose and no further reason for being where they were. Some units and formations went on fighting, for a while at least, wherever they happened to be, to whatever local end seemed to their commanders sensible. Others sought the earliest opportunity to surrender to the nearest American headquarters, at any level. One startled US captain signalled to his superiors that he had at his disposal two Soviet generals, an acre of officers and ten acres (approximately) of Soviet rank and file, all now disarmed, and he requested orders. Local belligerents made a beeline for Soviet weapons, equipment and stores, and more than one Soviet unit, compelled to defend itself against raiders, found itself in action with the support of some microcosm of the US forces to which it had surrendered. Soviet ships usually made for port and tied up. Many aircraft simply flew home, or as near to it as fuel allowed. Many thousands of men drifted away, leaving heavy weapons, equipment and stores where they lay for whoever chose to take them away.

To tell the story of the mounting of the United Nations Relief and Repatriation Organization (UNRRO), which soon took over from the United States in the concentration and maintenance of the remnants of Soviet forces deployed in Africa and the Middle East, and then set in hand the long and complex business of getting the men (and women too) back to their homes, is no part of our present task. The operation still goes on as we write, having had to face many more difficulties than those confronting the United Nations Displaced Persons Organization, set up at the

:ame time in Europe. No history of the time, however,
would be complete without reference to one of the least
ractable problems to emerge in the immediate aftermath
of the war. There will be traces of its impact in Africa and
he Middle East for a long time to come. It will be many
years, for example, before the last weapon brought by the
Soviet Union into Africa and the Middle East in the
chapter of the world's history which ended so abruptly in
1985, ceases in one hand or another to serve a purpose.

The elimination of Soviet support, direct or by proxy,
heralded the end of any further external intervention. The
security of South Africa was assured by the success of her
own armed forces in resisting and defeating tactical attack,
with some help from the efforts of the US Navy. These
efforts, though aimed directly at the peripheral operations
of the Soviet Union, also had the result that both the
Soviet proxy fighters and the indigenous guerrillas were
largely cut off from the sinews of war. The end to the
strategic external battle was far indeed from bringing to
an end the only sort of struggle of enduring concern to the
Africans – the internal one. Bitter battles between Angola
and her neighbours, and within Angola, were matched by
frontier incidents in Zaire and a renewal of the disruption
of Mozambique. South Africa, though everywhere penetrated, held firm at the core. Her front-line adversaries,
while clinging to the idea of confrontation, began to look
to their own internal welfare. Far from a Confederation of
Africa South coming into being and flourishing, a de-
federation of those dedicated to set it up was already in
progress.

The impotence of the Soviet proxies in Southern Africa
had been demonstrated. The success of Iran in the Persian
Gulf and southern Arabia had been such that even before
the nuclear exchange in Europe precipitated the end she
was already concentrating forces on her northern borders
for the invasion of the Soviet Union. The aimless man-
oeuvrings of the Egyptian Army on the shores of the Red
Sea signified little. Soviet initiatives on the outskirts of the

main battle had been stifled and a great strategic prize retained firmly in the grasp of the United States. If this success did not in itself ensure that the Western Allies would win the war in Europe against the Soviet Union and the Warsaw Pact it made two important contributions. By stabilizing a situation in the Middle East to the advantage of the West, and securing the oil flow along the sea routes the US had already gone some way to ensuring that the war, particularly if it were to be prolonged, would not be lost. By setting up a situation in which Soviet initiatives on the periphery were almost from the beginning seen to fail it hastened the general realization that the military might of the USSR was very far indeed from being invincible, and thus added to the growing weight of encouragement to its enemies nearer the centre.

CHAPTER TWENTY-FOUR

THE NUCLEAR DECISION

As the Soviet offensive ground to a halt in Europe and the war at sea emphasized not only the geographical disadvantages of the Soviet Union as a naval power but also the misdirection of its efforts to overcome them, various signs of political instability began to appear, both inside and outside the Kremlin. The purpose of the war had after all been largely political – to exploit the conventional weakness of the West in order to humiliate the US and to re-establish absolutism in Eastern Europe as the only safeguard against dissidence and fragmentation. The very statement of these war aims demonstrated the hollowness and imbalance of Soviet power. The military machine had been built up to an unparalleled size to buttress a political performance which was almost uniformly unsuccessful. The Soviet Union had been unable to take part in genuine *détente* because the appeal of Soviet communism to the masses either inside or outside the Soviet Union had proved mainly negative. Force, or the threat of force, had been necessary to counter the greater political attractiveness of the West and fissiparous tendencies within the Warsaw Pact. Political cohesion had failed to develop in Eastern Europe. Even the approach to power of communist parties in the West had not increased Soviet influence there; it had merely set an example of dissidence for communist countries in the east.

In 1956 in Hungary and in 1968 in Czechoslovakia Soviet military power had sufficed to restore political situations which were escaping from Soviet control. In 1985 the Soviet military machine proved just inadequate to extend Soviet political control in south-east Europe

and over West Germany. One of the major objectives o
this effort had been to master the general unease and
insubordination of the governments and peoples of Eastern Europe. The attainment of this objective would have
required quick and decisive victories in Yugoslavia and
in Germany. The check which in fact occurred was
enough, even without actual defeat, to allow pent-up
political forces to burst out. The leaders of the former
satellite countries, and very soon the leaders of the Soviet
Union itself, began to realize that military force no longer
provided a sovereign remedy for political dissent. Military
stalemate would not only allow the greater potential
resources of the West to be mobilized; it would also
foster revolution in the East, just as it had in 1917.

Foreseeing the dangers of disintegration in the Warsaw
Pact and disaffection at home, the Soviet policy-makers
split once more: the hawks became cataclysmic, the doves
were for return to Mother Russia. The former argued
that while the conventional battle had not gone quite
according to plan this had always been only one element
in the total strategy. The nuclear weaponry remained
intact. Better to have some mutual destruction than
creeping political decay and forcible decolonization. The
very backwardness of large areas of the Soviet Union
would allow it to survive better than the USA after a
nuclear exchange. Besides, there were enough warheads
to target some on China as well and so put off that
menace for another generation, with negligible risk o
Chinese retaliation. Also, if they were really prepared to
go to these lengths there was a good chance of a deal
with the United States before the major destruction took
place. They could, for example, carry out one or more
nuclear attacks on targets in Europe to show they mean
business, and at the same time propose to the United
States a bilateral *status quo* and the division of the world
into two spheres of influence. The two superpowers had
more interests in common than either had with its allies.
It would pay each of them for Europe to stay divided and

or the Middle East to be kept in order by both, acting
ogether. Either could deal with China, provided the
ther kept out.

It was a persuasive picture, but reports from Eastern
urope and from the constituent republics of the Soviet
nion, which were growing in volume, were already
nding support to a contrary thesis put forward by the
oves. The Poles as usual led the way. With the outbreak
f war the Soviet Union had re-imposed its own control
n Poland, working through the Polish ministries and the
pparatus of the police. This only served to stimulate
esistance, which is a natural habit of mind in a people
ho have been oppressed for 200 years by larger neigh-
ours.

Meanwhile, the Western Allies were hastily continuing
heir by no means fruitless efforts to reactivate the OSS
Office of Strategic Services) and SOE (Special Opera-
ons Executive) and improve liaison with resistance
roups. In the confusion of the turning-point battle in
ermany a Polish armoured unit in the north deliberately
et itself be overrun by the advancing Americans, which
rovided a breakthrough for Western intelligence and an
valuable nucleus for a further liaison network. The West
or some time tried to play the old themes of 1939–45,
ut in fact the grounds for revolt this time were rather
ifferent. The basic aims in Poland and elsewhere were
o get the Soviet Union off their backs, to get enough to
at, and to find their own way to whatever political future
hey might choose. This did not necessarily imply rejec-
on of a communist future, but only, and most decidedly,
f the Soviet way of achieving it. For a society aiming at
iddle-class consumer values the dictatorship of the
roletariat was in any case rather an out-of-date concept.
ut what was really intolerable was the dictatorship of
he Soviet proletariat, as represented by the Soviet Polit-
uro and the KGB.

As the more acute observers in the West had foreseen,
he phenomenon of Euro-communism was proving far

more lethal to the Soviet empire than to Western capi
talism. The oppressed nationalities of Eastern Europe
and in the Soviet Union itself, were not blind to th
defects of Western society in general. They did not a
aspire to have their economies run by US multi-nation
companies any more than by Soviet planners. The ide
which inspired them was that of a society based at on
and the same time both on national freedom and o
socialist principle. Once the Soviet offensive in Europ
stalled an opportunity began to open up for asserting th
approach. There was not much combination between th
various national movements, but the fact that so many c
them both in Europe and in Asia felt the same urge t
national independence, and started moving at the sam
time, turned a few local outbreaks into what was t
become an irresistible revolt.

Disaffection achieved a cumulative momentum of it
own. In addition to the growing resistance in Easter
Europe, the stirrings of nationalist revolt in Central Asi
fomented by the Chinese made it unsafe for the Sovie
General Staff to rely on units which contained a hig
proportion of soldiers from those areas. A larger numbe
of reliable units had to be sent eastwards from militar
districts which could be properly called Russian. This le
fewer troops for internal security in Poland, Hungary an
Czechoslovakia. There they had to watch not only th
civilian population but the local army units as well, th
loyalty of whose rank and file to the Soviet comman
became every day more doubtful. The resistance was no
as in the Second World War, that of an undergroun
movement against the authorities; the authorities them
selves began to resist the pressures and directives of th
Soviet civil and military hierarchies. This showed itse
principally in the failure to maintain communicatior
through Poland between the Soviet Union and Eas
Germany. Railways and roads were sabotaged, thu
gravely hampering forward movement of second and thir
echelon formations and of munitions, as well as th

elivery of food and manufactures from Poland to the
JSSR. The Polish authorities proved singularly unable
) find those responsible. Attempts by Soviet forces to
o so directly not only tied up still more units which
ould have been better used elsewhere, but led to the
rst incidents of urban guerrilla fighting directed against
ne billets and movements of Soviet garrisons.

Russia had been successful in previous conflicts, against
lapoleon and against Hitler, because of three priceless
ssets: unlimited space, apparently unlimited manpower
nd the willingness of Russians to be led into frightful
acrifice for the defence of the motherland. Now, every-
ning was reversed. It was no good retreating into the
ast interior space of Eurasia when this would merely
onsolidate the ring of states, not all friendly, which was
orming out of the fragments of an empire. And man-
ower was no longer wholly reliable. The men who came
om subject territories were less willing to be sacrificed
a order to maintain alien rule on neighbouring countries.
oviet manpower was at the same time intolerably over-
tretched by national revolt against the Soviet Union on
wo fronts as well as by resistance to the gathering
Vestern forces in Germany and by the requirement to
ace a potential Chinese threat.

The threat in the east was not seen primarily in military
erms. The Soviet superiority in equipment and experi-
nce still seemed enough to compensate for greater
Chinese numbers. Nuclear preponderance still lay with
ne USSR, though how long this would continue into the
uture was doubtful. The threat was once again not to
oviet Russia's military strength, but to her political
veakness. The peoples who now formed the Central
sian republics of the Soviet Union had been conquered
r absorbed in the nineteenth century in a great surge of
olonialist expansion to the east and south. Russia had
een drawn forward in an age of competitive imperialism
y rivalry with Britain, pushing north and west from
ndia, and the opportunity to take advantage of the

weakness of China. The Russians had been in some way
more successful and more ruthless than the British. The
north-west frontier of India remained a battle-ground for
the British and British-Indian armies up to the end of
British rule in India in the mid-twentieth century. Russia
had liquidated similar tribal opposition in Georgia and
the Caucasus before the end of the nineteenth. Even
more remarkably, Russian control over enormous areas
of Asia and many millions of non-Russian subjects survived not only the transition from Tsarism to Bolshevism
but also the break-up of Western empires in Asia, which
might have been expected to set a dangerous example to
the republics of the Soviet Union in Central Asia.

Now, however, there was a new factor. It was the
growing strength and prosperity of China. Up to the 1970s
China had not proved an attractive force. The Chinese
had suppressed the Moslems in Sinkiang no less brutally
than the Russians in Tashkent and Alma Ata. The material rewards of Chinese communism had been even less
satisfying than membership of the Soviet Union. Now,
however, co-prosperity was changing the material balance, and the Chinese were using the minorities on their
side of the border to infiltrate and influence those on the
other. Apart from offers of great economic well-being
there were arguments closer to the heart of Soviet doctrine which could be turned against their authors. It had
long been an essential element of Soviet policy and
propaganda that 'peaceful co-existence' included the support of movements, even wars, of national liberation.
These had up till now been far away, in Africa or South-
east Asia; but why, it was now asked, should not the same
principle apply to the nations of the Uzbeks and Kazakhs?
Had not the Soviet constitution provided for the secession
of the constituent republics if these should ever wish it?
Had not the moment come, at this time in an unsuccessful
war, when such aspirations might begin to be realized?

For the time being the Communist Party apparatus and
the secret police were strong enough to keep such move-

ments in check. But their existence was enough to add powerfully to the worries of the central authorities, and to sharpen the arguments between those who thought the crisis should be heightened as a means of restoring order and obedience, and those who wanted to draw back from the over-extension which had already led Soviet Russia into so many troubles.

The Kremlin doves, who called themselves realists, used all these facts and all these arguments against the superpower *status quo* thesis of the nuclear hard-liners. What good would it do to get the United States to recognize a Soviet sphere of influence in Eastern Europe and Siberia when the Soviet régime was no longer able to exert its influence in those areas? Even if the forces now facing NATO remained immune to reduction by agreement with the West there would still not be enough to hold down the previously subject peoples. Better to accept facts as they were, and to recognize the errors of gigantism inherited from Tsarist dreams of empire and from the illusions of world revolution of some of the early Bolsheviks. (It was still impermissible to criticize Lenin by name.) Russian greatness had always been less of material things than of the spirit. Moreover, the pure doctrines of communism had been distorted by the needs of empire. Far from withering away, the state had been obliged to intensify its presence and its pervasiveness. Russians might be better off alone, without the lesser breeds whom they were finding it increasingly hard to keep in subordination.

On the Western side another argument raged almost as fiercely, though without the personally lethal outcome common to argument in the Kremlin. To invade or not to invade was the question. US reinforcements were now flooding in, the sea routes were more or less assured, the European Allies had recovered and regrouped. French participation had been an enormous source of strength. Evidence of Soviet disarray was seen at every hand. Why not now go over to the offensive, it was asked, and finish off for ever the threat from Eastern Europe, so that everyone could live happily ever after? There was no need to repeat Hitler's mistake and go too far. No *Lebensraum* was now required. East Germany and Poland could be freed and the advance could be pushed forward in the Ukraine as far as the Dnieper. Control of the Ukrainian harvest and of the Dnieper hydro-electric installations would be enough to cripple any further war effort by Soviet Russia. It would be tempting to go on and liberate Georgia and control Baku, but that might be counter-productive in the long run as it would expose too long a line of Western communications, with the need for garrisons to secure them, and repeat in the East the Soviet error in the West.

This line of argument, propounded largely by the more influential US commanders, was supported by those who thought in terms of land masses and geo-politics. But there was one element in it which ran foul of European political instincts and political fears. The first stage in this advance would obviously be to free East Germany from Soviet control and to occupy it with Western forces, among whom West Germans would be preponderant. Could it really be believed, asked the French, the British and the smaller Western Allies, that this would not result in Germany being reunited? In the cold war years of the 1950s the reunification of Germany had been a parrot-cry of Western governments. Many Europeans had gone along with this line only because they were fairly sure that nothing of the sort would happen. It seemed at the time a useful stick with which to beat the Russians and a useful carrot to hold out to the West Germans to bring them more closely into the Western Alliance. But it was not a genuine long-term aim, except to very few. Many of the more thoughtful Germans themselves had misgivings about what a reunited Germany might be like, and what effect it would have on its neighbours. They might be fairly confident that West Germany at least had profoundly changed and would not allow a reunited

Germany to become an aggressive force again, but they saw equally clearly that others would not feel the same confidence in their pacific intentions; in contrast to the dawning hopes of reconciliation in Western Europe through the Economic Community a reunited Germany might start the same old dreary cycle of national antagonisms all over again. These views had received little expression in Germany, but there had certainly been an almost audible sigh of relief when Willi Brandt, with an act of supreme statesmanship, entered upon the *Ostpolitik* in the 1960s, and to all intents and purposes renounced reunification as an aim of German policy for the foreseeable future.

Now, with the road to Berlin more or less open, the temptation was there. So, in even greater measure, was the fear and suspicion. There were some in the West German army who would find it hard to resist an opportunity to support an East German rising against Soviet occupation, and to knock down once and for all the hated Berlin wall and the frontier watch towers. The German command were doubtful as to how far they would be able to hold back all their units if this sort of opportunity presented itself. The French, British, Belgians, Dutch and Norwegians, on the other hand, refused absolutely to agree to a move forward beyond the West German border.

In addition to their fears of a united Germany, even one dominated by West Germany, they argued persuasively that an offensive into Soviet territory would be the one thing which might not only revive the Soviet will and capability to resist, but also spur them on, out of desperation, to make use of their still intact nuclear armoury. America might count on a measure of survival in such an event; the outlook for Western Europe would be far grimmer. Let the Western forces rather stand on the side lines, the argument ran, and watch the disintegration of the Warsaw Pact, assisted by such covert stimulus as they could give, in Poland and elsewhere, to national resistance.

There was another actor in this drama which the protagonists were apt to overlook. East German opinion had long been among the most suppressed and distorted in Eastern Europe. The failure of the Soviet offensive with the subsequent ferment in Poland and the eastern republics, at last gave back a voice to those who had perforce been silent for so long. The apparatchiks of the Sozialistische Einheitspartei Deutschland (SED) were brushed aside and a real debate began to make itself heard, among academics, technicians, managers and army officers, in fact among all those professionals who, in spite of Soviet ideological interference, had kept the state running and made its industry a formidable factor in the world. Their opinions were not exactly what might have been expected in the West, or in the East. They did not clamour to join their democratic brothers west of the Elbe; they saw little joy in a united Germany controlled by West German bankers in the sole interest of economic growth. They found the conformism and hierarchies of the West almost as stifling as their own. They saw a better future in a state with some of the old Prussian virtues which they had assimilated into their own system: frugality, a certain puritanism, a feeling of superiority towards their neighbours on each side – a conviction that they were more advanced than the Slavs on the east and morally superior to the mixed economies in the West, already, in East German eyes, showing symptoms of decadence.

The West Germans became aware of these views through the increased contacts they were able to establish across the growing anarchy of the Warsaw Pact's forward areas. They were shocked and surprised that their fellow Germans in the East should be reluctant to join in the economic miracle and the political freedom of the West. Secretly, perhaps, some of them were also a little relieved to find that they would not after all have to assimilate 17 million more Germans (and probably as many socialist voters), which would have considerably distorted the German political scene. In the light of these assessments West German pressure to invade the East was significantly reduced. There was little joy in the prospect of a West German army entering the East as liberators, only to be shortly told by their liberated brothers to go back home.

This increased the difficulty for the Americans in persuading their allies to join in a counter-offensive against Soviet Russia and the Warsaw Pact through East Germany, Poland and the Ukraine. In a final attempt to resolve the argument the President of the United States called for a summit meeting to be held in London and attended by the heads of Government of the Atlantic Allies.

The discussion revolved round three topics:

1 The advantages of finishing off the job and so guaranteeing peace in our time.
2 The risk that a Western attack would trigger nuclear war.
3 The German problem.

The Americans argued that they had once again saved Europe by their exertions; three times was enough. The only way to make sure it didn't happen again was to push the Soviet Union back out of Europe. The Russians were not mad enough to prefer nuclear destruction to the loss of their East European satellites, even if they also lost some of their territory. Limited war aims would be announced, giving them the assurance of a continued secure existence in their own heartland, but not of dominion over others. The German problem was for the Germans to solve. Even if they chose to unite, there would be so much repair and reconstruction to be done after the war that they could hardly constitute a threat to the other West Europeans, whose territory had escaped comparatively lightly and so left them with less rebuilding.

The West German leaders, still divided among themselves and conscious of continuing army pressure to move forward, kept a low profile in the discussion. The British, French, Beneluxians and Scandinavians were unimpressed by the American arguments and repeated their fears of nuclear attack and of a future united Germany. Moreover, the march of events in the Soviet Union was rapidly leading to collapse even without any further Western attack. It was much easier and less costly, as the German General Staff had argued in 1917 when they smuggled in Lenin, if defeat came about from internal disintegration rather than from external invasion. Any future Soviet attempt to arouse nationalistic passions against the foreigner and regain lost positions would be much less plausible if no foreign armies had invaded Russian soil.

The Americans, with the more hawkish elements of the German armed forces, considered moving in alone. Who knows what might have been the outcome if they had? A new dramatic shift in the debate in Moscow removed the necessity to reach a conclusion.

The 'nuclear' party in the Kremlin hierarchy, recognizing that time was against them, staged a secret meeting with the President and Secretary General from which their opponents were excluded at gun point. They insisted on an immediate move towards the threat of nuclear action. A single atomic attack on a Western target would be enough to demonstrate their determination. A simultaneous message would be sent to the US proposing the immediate withdrawal of all foreign forces in Africa and the Middle East and bilateral negotiation to establish US and Soviet spheres of influence throughout the world. It would be appropriate to attack a target in England while the Western summit was in session there, to bring home to everyone the dangers of any other course than that proposed by the Soviet Union. London itself should not e the target. The effect on national feeling of the destruction of the British capital would be enormous; it would almost certainly result in a hardening of Allied opposition and determination to a degree that would render the attack counter-productive. Birmingham would do. It was a great industrial concentration and a centre of the armaments industry, and near enough to the capital or London to feel the blast without being razed to the ground. President Vorotnikov had no choice but to agree.

It was important to make it absolutely clear to the Americans that this was a single attack to demonstrate what might happen if they refused Soviet demands. It was not to be seen as an immediate prelude to a general nuclear offensive. It had to be expected that some retaliation would occur, but if the signals were understood this should be limited to a more or less comparable strike. In spite of hostilities, the Moscow–Washington hot-line had never been closed down. The plan was worked out in detail. The timing had to be very precise. The ballistic missile early warning system (BMEWS) would give only a few minutes' warning of the missile launch before its impact. The American President had to know just before this that there was only one missile on its way, and where it was going, but not long enough before for any counter-measures to be taken.

A warning message was sent via Washington to the President in London that the Soviet President would speak on the hot-line at 1020 hours GMT on the following day, 20 August. In London and Washington the intervening hours were spent in a fevered guessing game on what the message would be. One thing was fairly clear and brought relief. It could hardly be to announce a full-scale nuclear offensive, since surprise would be an essential element in any such action. Most views were fairly near the truth so far as a proposal for negotiation was concerned, but few guessed that this would be accompanied by a Hiroshima-type demonstration, or that the timetable would be as narrow and as threatening as it turned out to be. For when the Soviet President spoke, after announcing the single missile launch, he demanded that the US should send representatives within one week to negotiate on the Soviet proposal, failing which further selective strikes would be carried out. If there were any thought of preventing this by a pre-emptive general nuclear attack, President Thompson was reminded of the Soviet Union's significant second strike capability.

The superlative USAF F-15 rejoining the high altitude battle after replenishment

An American F-16 aircraft with a full ground attack munitions load. This aircraft was in use in a number of Allied air forces.

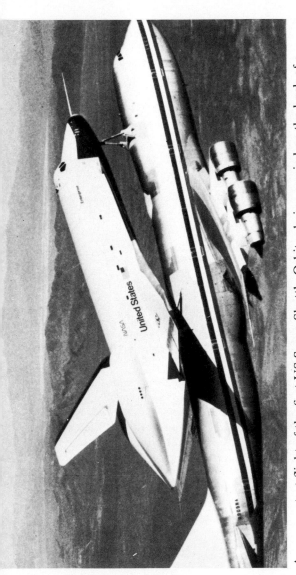

A pre-war test flight of the first US Space Shuttle Orbiter being carried on the back of a Boeing 747 to altitude for launch into space. The upper dorsal area of the Orbiter opens to carry or retrieve satellite vehicles on their space missions

A convoy of US Army armoured vehicles rolls
into a C-5 waiting to join the air bridge

S airborne infantry fighting to recover Bremen

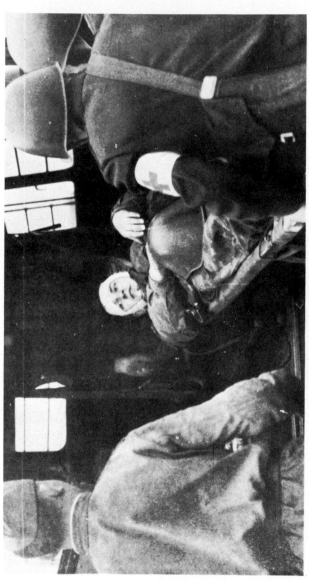

Warsaw Pact casualties: a Soviet casualty evacuation

The ballistic missile warning station on Fylingdales Moor, Yorkshire

A devastating response

CHAPTER TWENTY-FIVE

THE DESTRUCTION OF BIRMINGHAM

In the main control room of the great BMEWS station on Fylingdales Moor in Yorkshire the day watch had been on duty for a couple of hours and it was just coming up to ten o'clock in the morning. The station looked out over beautiful misty moorland, but the controller and his staff did not – there was plenty else for them to do as the giant radars swept some 3,200 kilometres out into space. They were searching and sifting the 7,000 pieces of orbiting debris and satellites that man had projected into inner space since his first invasion of it in 1957.

The control staff were of course well abreast of the war situation and they knew that, in political terms anyway, the threat of a nuclear attack was small. But they were not there to make judgments of that sort. Warning of an attack rested with the automated system coupled to the scanning and tracking dishes in the great radomes. Anything detected that was not immediately reconciled with the ever-growing catalogue of known objects was subject to an instantaneous analysis in spherical trigonometry by a battery of computers. These would assess the probability that the radar return indicated a missile and, as further radar tracking information came through, discard, decrease or increase the assessed degree of probability in the threat. If things ever went as far as that, the computer and the cathode ray consoles would show, in a somewhat academic way it might be thought, the estimated point of impact of each missile and the seconds to go before its strike.

A system that had to have the highest reliability that

man's ingenuity could devise was inevitably hyper-sensitive, and operators highly trained in monitoring the auditory and visual responses grew instinctively to feel the computer's mood. Occasionally, even in peacetime, the alerting bell would sound as particles or atmospheric conditions produced a response from space that the computer took longer than usual to analyse. When it was identified as innocuous the computer would apologize seconds later and explain its over-eagerness.

This was the way it was meant to work, and it was the pattern to which the controller and his staff were accustomed. During the last two weeks at Fylingdales and its sister stations in Alaska and Greenland bells had sounded frequently as the Soviet rockets launched more satellites into orbit to maintain their space activities. There had been plenty going on.

The station was a sitting-duck target for an air attack but no guided weapon had come anywhere near it. This was not surprising – indeed it was to be expected – because it was very much in the interests of the Russians, in their non-nuclear war policy, not to risk anything that might so much as vibrate the hair-trigger of the Allied nuclear response. For the same reason the persistent jamming to which the other electronic warning systems had been subjected from the sea and air had not been directed against BMEWS. There was an occasional indication from badly tuned airborne equipment to remind the crew that the electronic battle was still in progress, but otherwise the displays were clear.

At 1005 hours a neighbouring air defence radar warning station rang to say it was no longer affected by jamming. Wing Commander Warburton, the Controller, entered this in his log and thought it curious enough to tell his controller colleagues in the other operational centres. An airwoman brought round the tea. It was all very different from the smoke, dust, blood and horror of the battle raging in the Central Region – but they were concerned here with a different kind of war. Warburton had finished his tea when an American controller from the Detection and Tracking Centre at Colorado Springs called to say that they had detected a launch via a warning satellite over the Indian Ocean. It had come from a distance, west of Baikonur, the site from which the satellite launches had been flying during the last sixteen days, and they had not reconciled it. It would not be visible within the Fylingdales detection range for a while, and he said he would call back as soon as they had any tracking information on it.

The line to the Springs was crystal clear. The whole watch had strained their ears to piece together the message and they had all mentally worked out where the response would appear on the display before the American controller had finished what he had to say. There was a scraping of chairs as each one took up a position so that he could see over the observer's shoulder. The seconds ticked by and the radar movement seemed more sluggish than it had ever been before. Suddenly there it was: the next scan of the radar confirmed it and the computed display gave a very firm digital threat assessment on one missile on an approaching path. Instantaneously the threat light flashed and the tracking radar slewed.

The Royal Air Force control staffs were well used to calming their adrenalin flow, both through exercises simulated on magnetic tape and by the frequency with which bells punctuated the various steps in the computer process, but this had a very different feel about it. A single missile launch against the UK or the US was a highly improbable event, but the confident mood of the computer had come through to them, and with war raging in Europe anything could happen. Very definitely something was happening now.

It was twenty-four minutes past ten when the digital display abruptly upgraded the threat as the tracking radar picked up the missile soaring out of the atmosphere into space. The computer instantly calculated that it was on a sub-orbital trajectory with 353 seconds to impact. The whole watch was galvanized: if this was a real nuclear attack how could a single missile on its own make any sense? The digital warning display had gone instantaneously to all the other operations centres, including the Government Situation Room, but the Controller pressed the switch which connected them all on the voice circuit to confirm, even though they could make no sense of the alarm, that the BMEWS was 100 per cent serviceable and that the computers were continuing to upgrade the threat assessment.

While he spoke one of the plotters called out 'impact somewhere in UK, sir', and the computer print-out typed that before his eyes. The digital time-counter had now spun down to 317 seconds to impact. Warburton kept the voice circuit open to his fellow controllers with an additional hand-set to his ear connecting him directly to the Controller at Strike Command, High Wycombe, where he knew his commander-in-chief would be standing behind the control desk.

The Polaris Executive was the man in the system who would have the most to do if the President and the Prime Minister decided that a nuclear response was to be made, but it seemed hardly likely that they would agree to let sixty-four submarine-launched megaton missiles fly to the heart of Soviet Russia in response to this one baffling radar trace. 'We still don't understand it,' said Warburton as he confirmed the amplification of the threat which had just gone up on the display, showing the Midlands as the impact area. The two plotters were poised over the print-out waiting for the next mathematical refinement of the target information as the seconds to go slid down to 227. It was the RAF Strike Command Controller who had the news first: 'It's real – it's the real thing,' came over the voice system. 'The Government Situation Centre have just told us that a message has come in on the hot-line. Acknowledge – acknowledge – and Fylingdales have you any better estimate of the point of impact yet?'

The print-out started up again and in a split second it had written 'Lat/Long 52° 23′ N. 001° 49′ W.' As this appeared simultaneously on the main display there was no need to plot it on a map, for by one of the miracles of electronic automation a luminous green circle with a cross in the middle had appeared on the cathode ray map of the British Isles. It was over Birmingham. 'It's Birmingham – repeat Birmingham,' Warburton called into the voice circuit. The other controllers acknowledged this grim news in the disciplined and mechanical way in which they had been conditioned for so long to think about the unthinkable. But on the other hand-set at his ear Warburton detected more than a tremor in the voice of the Strike Command Controller when he overheard him say, after his acknowledgement, 'Oh my God!' At High Wycombe only his squadron leader assistant knew that when mobilization was ordered the Wing Commander had sent his wife and their three children to stay with her family on the outskirts of that now hapless city.

The time-counter showed 114 seconds to go as the Fylingdales assistant controller exchanged and cross-checked data on the line to his opposite number in the Detection and Tracking Center at Colorado Springs. A US Air Force major was repeating back the facts and factors as he verified them with the information at the master control centre. All the space satellite and ground radar information was now integrated in the main computer at Colorado Springs, and as he logged the details from Fylingdales he said, 'Yeah – yeah, that all checks with our data here' – and then, with more than a touch of melancholy in his voice, as the counter slid down to sixty-three seconds, 'It sure is going to be hot in Birmingham England.'

The SS–17 missile detonated its nuclear warhead 3,500 metres above Winson Green prison at 1030 hours on the morning of 20 August. Within a fraction of a second the resulting fireball, with temperatures approaching those of the sun, was over 2,000 metres in diameter and reached down towards the centre of Birmingham. The incredibly brilliant flash which accompanied the detonation was visible in London. Even at that range, individuals looking at the fireball suffered temporary blindness and felt a faint flush of heat on their faces.

The tremendous heat given off by the fireball had a more significant effect upon people and materials within a range of twenty kilometres. Lightly clad yachtsmen on Chasewater about nineteen kilometres from Winson Green felt their skin begin to burn as the lasting pulse of heat from the fireball hit them. The thoughtful ones dived into the water to escape the burning heat. Those who did not suffered blistering burns on all exposed skin. The varnish on their boats bubbled, nylon sails melted and newspapers lying in the boats burst into flames. Only those who were protected from the pulse of heat by their clothing, or were shielded in some way, escaped severe burns.

Closer in towards Winson Green the effects of the heat from the fireball were more pronounced. The foliage in the countryside had crisped as if autumn had arrived. Smaller brushwood was smouldering. Haystacks were burning and paintwork on buildings and vehicles in the path of the heat-wave blistered. At Aldridge, and at other places within about twelve kilometres of the fireball, people caught in the open received burns which needed immediate hospital treatment. At this range curtains and other materials inside rooms that were exposed to the heat pulse began to smoulder and in some cases burst into flames. Any lightweight objects such as newspapers, canvas and empty packaging in the open soon caught fire.

Closer to the fireball heat levels became even more intense, so that almost any lightweight material subject to the heat-wave burst into flame while metals and other objects were scorched and distorted. At these ranges the clothing worn by individuals no longer gave effective protection against the heat. Clothes burned off, and people in the open received such extensive burns that their prospects of recovery, even with first-class medical assistance, were negligible. Fires were started inside and outside buildings to an increasing extent as the epicentre was approached, with apparently almost total conflagration occurring within three to four kilometres of Winson Green.

The enormous blast pressures released by the nuclear device followed the heat-wave within a matter of seconds. Those in the open who had suffered severe burns had no more than a few seconds in which to register shock before the blast-wave hit them. Those inside buildings who had already experienced the overpowering flash of light were now subject to the effects of blast. Within a second or so of the detonation the blast-wave hit the city centre beneath the fireball. The enormous pressures had the effect of instantly crushing all buildings below it so that what remained was only a levelled mountain of rubble. The blast-wave then roared and crushed its way outwards from the centre utterly destroying everything in its path. No structures above ground level were able to withstand the tremendous pressures and the coincident wind speeds resulting from the blast. Within three kilometres of Winson Green nothing survived, every building and structure being reduced to rubble and strewn across the roads so that the entire area looked like a gigantic rubbish heap. The effects of the blast-wave began to decline as it travelled outwards, so that between three and six kilometres from the centre a few of the smaller and more strongly constructed buildings remained standing, some at crazy angles and missing many portions of softer construction around reinforced concrete or steel skeletons. Even these few remaining buildings were in such a twisted and derelict condition that they were hardly recognizable as the original structures. They were surrounded by the gutted remains of lighter buildings of modern construction such as hospitals and schools; demolished beyond recognition. All domestic structures within this area suffered similarly, with most brick houses collapsing under the effects of the blast-wave.

Those who had suffered the most agonizing effects of the heat-wave were mercifully killed by the blast-wave that followed. People who had been indoors were now buried beneath mountains of rubble and suffered a similar fate. Within three or four kilometres of Winson Green very few people survived the immediate effects of the detonation. Outside this range, and up to about seven or eight kilometres away, the collapse and destruction of most buildings trapped people in hundreds under fallen masonry. There were many deaths and severe injuries beyond counting. The air was full of flying objects, picked up by winds moving outwards from Winson Green at speeds which, even at ranges of four or five kilometres, approached 500 kilometres per hour. The wind drove along objects standing in its path like confetti. Motor cars and other vehicles were bowled over and over, carried tens and even hundreds of metres from where they were. People caught in the open were picked up, flung through the air and dashed against any solid object in their path. Roof tiles, pieces of masonry and any loose objects were projected through the air like missiles, smashing their way through obstructions and causing injury to many. At distances greater than seven or eight kilometres from the centre damage levels began to fall off, but even so all lightweight structures were blown over, roofs were blown off and higher masonry buildings suffered extensive damage. Large amounts of rubble and masonry fell into the streets and all windows were blown out, much of the glass being converted into missiles with much injury to people in the way.

A minor benefit of the blast-wave was that some of the innumerable fires started a few seconds earlier were blown out and did not rekindle. This was small mercy, however, compared with the even larger number of fires which were effectively fanned by the outward moving winds.

Birmingham airport, twelve kilometres from Winson Green, suffered relatively light damage, but wind speeds at the airport were of the order of 160 kilometres per hour and many aircraft lost wings and tailplanes or were turned on their sides by the blast-wave. Outside this range the effects of blast fell off rapidly, damage to buildings being confined to broken windows and shifted roof tiles.

The blast-wave had rolled outwards from the centre at something like the speed of sound, arriving at Birmingham airport approximately thirty seconds after the detonation of the weapon. Even at this point the roar of the explosion was stupendous, lasting for ten to fifteen seconds. The same roar was to be heard in London, approximately eight minutes later, as a rumbling, roaring noise from the direction in which the blinding flash of the fireball had been seen eight minutes earlier. Those in London with any knowledge of nuclear weapons were in no doubt as to what had happened.

Within one minute the stupendous activity of immediate damage from the detonation had ceased. The enormous mushroom cloud above the totally devastated centre of Birmingham had risen to a height of fifteen kilometres and had spread across a diameter of approximately twenty kilometres. It cast its shadow over a scene of extraordinary destruction, where everything was still except for the occasional crash of falling masonry and the crackle of multitudinous fires. Within a radius of five kilometres of Winson Green everything seemed to be on fire. Outside this area, to a range of about eight kilometres, hardly any building, or what survived of it, seemed to be free of a fire of some sort. Fires occurred less frequently outside this range though there were buildings on fire at ranges of up to fifteen kilometres. There were fires in towns as far away as Wolverhampton, Stourbridge, Halesowen, Solihull, Sutton Coldfield, Walsall and Brownhills.

The devastation within the centre of Birmingham was so intense that the road system had ceased to have any meaning, most roads having totally disappeared beneath the rubble of the buildings once standing along them. Outside this area, and to a range of five or six kilometres, all roads were totally blocked by fallen masonry. The only means of movement around the area was provided by the M5 and M6 motorways which encircle the centre of Birmingham. These roads, being wide and not hemmed in by buildings, remained relatively free of obstruction. The bridges along them had also survived remarkably well. Outside the motorway route the degree of devastation began to tail off, although most buildings still appeared to be unusable. Almost all roads were so littered with rubble that no immediate movement of vehicles was possible. The centres of Dudley, Walsall, Sutton Coldfield and Halesowen were impassable, though in these towns the outline of the road system was still visible and the overall extent of the damage, though still enormous, was considerably less than in the centre of Birmingham. Fires were prolific, particularly in commercial premises in high streets and commercial centres, holding large stocks of inflammable materials. In many places the gas distribution network had been broken and fires were being fed by escaping gas.

The fires which were now alight across a circle with a radius of approximately fifteen kilometres centred on Winson Green were beginning everywhere to take hold. In particular the fires amongst the devastated remains of the centre of Birmingham were beginning to burn fiercely. As the flames rose higher into the sky air was drawn in from outside, with the result that winds began to blow inwards towards the flames. This further fanned the conflagration so that, within twenty minutes of the original detonation, an area of approximately thirty square kilometres in the centre of Birmingham was totally engulfed in a fire-storm. The flames and smoke rose hundreds of metres into the sky as the in-rush of air fed and fanned the fires. The in-blowing air prevented fires moving outwards but everything within the fire-storm area was now engulfed by it. Outside the area of the fire-storm thousands of other fires were burning furiously. In peacetime many of these would have been regarded as serious fires requiring the attentions of a significant proportion of the fire-fighting effort available locally. As it was there were so many such fires burning at once over a total area of about 600 square kilometres that conventional fire-fighting equipment could have little or no effect upon them.

The human casualties resulting from the detonation of the nuclear weapon were horrific. The day had been a sunny one, so that many people were lightly dressed and therefore susceptible to burn injuries on their exposed skin. The centre of Birmingham had been crowded with shoppers and others going about their normal business. Fortunately, schools were empty and some people were away on holiday. Nevertheless, a population of approximately 2 million, including that of Birmingham and its surrounding towns, was exposed to the holocaust. Of this population approximately 300,000 were killed within minutes by the heat and blast effects of the weapon or were subsequently to die unattended by any medical or rescue team. A further 250,000 received blast or burn injuries of a very serious nature, in need of urgent hospital treatment. Another 500,000 received lighter injuries which could conceivably be treated either by themselves or with first aid. Only a very small proportion of the population within the Birmingham area was entirely free of injury. The medical and hospital facilities available to support this catastrophic level of casualty were themselves savagely weakened. Half the hospitals in the area were either destroyed or rendered totally unusable by the explosion. Of the remainder only a quarter were able to function as normal whilst the rest had suffered damage which severely limited their ability to cope with more than their original patient load. Doctors and ambulance services had suffered casualties in proportion to that of the civil population and so were hardly able to cope with an emergency. By any measure the enormous numbers of people requiring medical assistance so swamped the remaining medical facilities that the help these were able to give was almost negligible. In addition to the physical and human destruction, many of the survivors within the area were suffering from severe shock. They were helpless and in no position either to help themselves or to organize any form of co-ordinated help for others.

The fire-fighting services had also been severely disrupted, almost three-quarters of the fire-fighting equipment within Birmingham itself having been destroyed. Most of the firemen who responded to the emergency by making their way to their fire stations found that their equipment was either buried or so damaged as to be unusable, while those who were able to get their appliances out found that they were quite unable to move them along the roads. Additionally, there were so many fires burning that any sort of priority was almost impossible to decide upon. Those nearest to the fire stations received what little effort was available. Within Birmingham and its close environs the firemen who were able to deploy equipment found that the water distribution system had suffered so much damage that hydrant pressures were inadequate to support any real fire-fighting capacity. This was not the case in the surrounding towns, however, where subterranean water systems had remained undisturbed and where effective pressures were available.

Within the city of Birmingham central administration and organization had virtually ceased to exist. Normal telephone communication systems linking police, fire-fighting services, medical facilities and local administration had all been destroyed. In the preceding week a Sub-Regional Headquarters had been established at the government offices in South Yardley. These offices were approximately nine kilometres away from the centre of the explosion but they were of modern infill construction and had suffered considerable damage as a result of the blast. As offices they were generally unusable and, more important, all telephone communication had been destroyed. The personnel manning the headquarters were relatively unscathed but, having at first no form of communication with outside agencies, even by road, they were unable to co-ordinate any activity. It was some time before emergency radio communication, from what was left of local and public utility radio, together with RAY-NET Ham Stations (the net of amateur or 'ham' radio stations), could begin to help.

A further problem was the total failure of electrical power in the Birmingham area. The widespread destruction of electrical distribution systems had led to the automatic cut-out of supply, and destruction was so widespread that the distribution system throughout that area of the Midlands centred on Birmingham had been affected. Many of the power stations supplying the area had automatically shut down as their imposed load had ceased to exist. Thus the whole of Birmingham, with its surrounding towns, was without electricity.

Spontaneous attempts at fire-fighting, rescue and the giving of medical attention to the injured developed within minutes of the detonation. But, being spontaneous and limited, the efforts were soon totally disorganized as calls for assistance flooded into whatever remained of the emergency service co-ordination centres. It was some hours before the initial shock had subsided sufficiently for any attempt at local organization to take place. In Wolverhampton, Stourbridge, Solihull, Walsall and Halesowen public utility communication systems had survived to some degree and were at least able to report the extent of local damage and casualties. These towns had been hit hard, with very extensive damage to buildings and with large numbers of fires. A great many of their inhabitants had suffered extensive burn or blast injuries and needed urgent medical attention. Their fire-fighting, ambulance and medical collection services had survived reasonably intact and were available to the local authority. The biggest problem these services faced was that of moving their equipment around streets blocked with rubble. In addition, the extent of fire was sometimes so great that entire areas had to be completely avoided. Most of these towns had taken some elementary precautions of a civil defence nature during the first days of war, even if they had not done something earlier, including the stockpiling of earth-moving machinery capable of clearing rubble off the main roads. They were thus able to clear routes through the centres of the towns so that emergency services equipments could be deployed, generally to the town or city centres, where the worst devastation had been caused, where fires were burning most fiercely, and where the majority of casualties had also occurred. The vast numbers of fires elsewhere in these towns had to go unheeded. So did most of the casualties, lying unattended. The extent of damage and casualty in these towns was so great that the local authorities were overwhelmed by their problems and could spare no thought for assistance to areas outside their own.

Towns closer to the centre of Birmingham, such as Dudley, which was approximately nine kilometres away from the centre of the explosion, had fared much worse than the towns in the outer ring. Dudley's town centre was ablaze in many parts, while movement of fire and rescue appliances along its roads was severely handicapped and in many cases impossible. Again, a few items of earth-moving equipment had been assembled before the war and these now attempted to clear their way through the worst of the rubble. Many buildings had collapsed. People were trapped but little rescue effort was available. The local authority emergency services had remained reasonably intact but most of the telephone communication system had broken down; it was thus impossible to organize centrally any form of rescue effort. Rescue work continued on an *ad hoc* basis but was hopelessly inadequate to meet the town's needs: this was also the case in other nearby towns like Halesowen, Walsall, Sutton Coldfield and Solihull. These towns were in the worst state of any in the area. Large numbers of those still alive had suffered severe injuries. Emergency services existed in some form or other but without organization. The towns struggling for survival in surrounding areas could provide no form of help to those in the inner ring. Still closer to the point of detonation conditions were so bad that no help was available at all. Thus the towns in the worst condition of all were left to their own devices. This was where help was most urgently needed. As it was, there was none.

Within the motorway boundaries the position inside the city of Birmingham itself soon became quite unmanageable. Movement was virtually impossible. Although the fire-storm itself had abated, fires still raged throughout the area. The area was a wilderness in which no help was to be had, surrounded by towns quite incapable of providing any.

As the day wore on Wolverhampton and Solihull continued to struggle with the impossible task facing their rescue and fire-fighting facilities. Most of the fires had to be allowed to burn themselves out. Rescue attempts were made where resources were available and where it appeared that some benefit would result. In many places no attempt could be made to rescue people trapped inside fallen buildings or to provide medical attention to the injured. Inevitably this meant that many people trapped in buildings died either as a result of the spread of fire or from the injuries they had received earlier.

By the end of the day on 20 August an area of 600 square kilometres centred on Birmingham was a scene still lit by innumerable fires burning themselves out, with pockets of activity where fire-fighting and rescue operations were going on and groups of people had formed themselves into rescue teams to try to extricate those buried beneath rubble. A small number of people had been able to obtain medical assistance but thousands were totally unable to get near a hospital because of the large numbers of injured requiring attention. By the end of the day almost all organized endeavour within the areas hit by the nuclear explosion had to be concentrated on attempting to cope with the enormous numbers of casualties. Hospitals were being inundated with requests for help and submerged by the wave of people appearing for treatment. Many were still lying where they had been injured; there was no way of collecting them up. The numbers of people appearing at hospitals were such that physical protection of the premises was required from the police. Even so, the anxiety of people to receive treatment themselves or have others treated was so great that violence began to develop and there were disturbances outside some of the surviving hospitals.

The movement of survivors out of the area, by vehicle or on foot, soon began to clog the remaining passable roads and severely hampered the emergency services. Further police effort was required to control this. The police manpower available for this task, and also for the protection of the hospitals, even with the help of reserve army units, was simply insufficient. Chaos began to develop on the roads, chiefly near hospitals and in areas which had suffered less damage than others and where people came to find food and shelter. As the night wore on the absence of electricity made matters worse, so that the day ended in a shambles of unco-ordinated activity by fire-fighting and rescue teams doing what they could against the mountain of disaster facing them, in an environment where hundreds of thousands of people were seeking food and shelter and attention for severe injuries. The extent of the disaster and its aftermath was such that the local authorities were quite unable to control events.

During the day the situation in Birmingham had been in the minds of the entire country. Everyone was aware that a nuclear device had been exploded and most were convinced that it was only the first of many. This caused an element of panic everywhere as individuals sought either to protect themselves within their own homes or to move from urban areas out into the country, where they imagined they might be safer. The potential mass exodus of people was of great concern to the government, who strove to check it through broadcast messages. Fortunately no further nuclear attack took place. Nevertheless, local authorities everywhere were making preparations to ensure their own survival and might not have been receptive to requests to provide Birmingham with assistance, had these been made.

The government had ordered Headquarters United Kingdom Land Forces to take whatever action in support of Birmingham was possible without detriment to its ability to withstand further nuclear strikes. Headquarters West Midland District was ordered within minutes of the strike to provide what assistance it could in the Birmingham area.

By mid-afternoon that day twelve major units from the regular and volunteer armies, together with units of the RAF Regiment, amounting to some 10,000 men, with logistic and medical services and some fire-fighting equipment, were being deployed on emergency relief operations. Units drawn from West Midland, Eastern and Wales Districts, including the Mercian Yeomanry and men from the Light Infantry Depot at Shrewsbury, were deployed to Wolverhampton, Stourbridge, Halesowen, Solihull, Sutton Coldfield, Walsall and Brownhills. Here the local authorities had retained some semblance of local control and rescue and relief operations were therefore already under way in some form or other. The military units brought with them vehicles, communications, tentage, blankets, medical assistance, engineer equipment and fire-fighting equipment. Most important of all, they were organized bodies of men, capable and under disciplined control.

By the evening of the same day the emergency committees nominated in peacetime had come into operation. These committees included representatives from the police, fire-fighting services, ambulance services and medical authorities. With liaison officers from military relief units the emergency committees now took control of the deployment of rescue and relief operations during the recovery phase. It was evening before troop deployments were complete and before the emergency committees had a chance to take stock of the situation within their areas. With no electricity and fires still freely burning almost everywhere, little could be done other than attempting *ad hoc* rescue and relief operations with existing facilities, while plans were made for a major effort at recovery from dawn next day.

By the early morning of 21 August the Sub-Regional Headquarters at South Yardley had managed to establish radio and land communications with central government and with emergency committees in the surrounding towns. It was thus able to co-ordinate the activities of all the emergency committees, which were by now backed by their own surviving emergency facilities and military help.

All surviving hospitals were still being besieged by crowds of casualties needing treatment. There were few doctors available either in the hospitals or in the surrounding areas. Most of the roads were still impassable to vehicular movement, so fire-fighting, rescue and ambulance teams could not approach the scenes of worst damage. There were no telephones and no electricity. Gas supplies had by now been cut off. The water distribution system had failed in many places, which made fire-fighting more difficult still. There were many thousands of slightly wounded people with no accommodation and no means of feeding themselves. Looting of damaged commercial premises was becoming widespread as some looked for food while others hoped for material gain.

Many people were trying to leave the area, clogging the roads with their vehicles and preventing the effective deployment of emergency services. Fires were still burning in many places, and the thousands of bodies littering the streets and lying amongst the destroyed buildings threatened a future hazard to health.

The weapon had fortunately exploded at such a height as not to cause extraordinarily high levels of radiation over the area. Emergency teams were able to operate wherever they could be deployed without concern for radiological hazard. There would have been extensive and dangerous radioactive fallout if the device had been exploded closer to the ground. A very large area downwind of Birmingham which might have been significantly affected by radioactive fallout was thus not placed at risk.

As the day of 21 August wore on the emergency services, with military support, began to make some headway in restoring order to the devastated area. Emergency committees established road blocks at many places throughout the towns to reduce the movement of refugees. Specific evacuation could now be mounted to move casualties into other hospitals in the Midlands. Reduction in refugee movement also allowed the emergency services access to the roads, where these had been cleared, so that further rescue operations could be carried out. Relief centres were set up in suitable surviving buildings such as schools, assembly halls, community centres and cinemas. Emergency supplies of food were established at the centres so that those being sheltered could be adequately fed. Strong police and military guards were mounted at all hospitals to control the access of injured people. Patrols of police and military also operated throughout the area, wherever movement was possible, to check looting, which was widespread. Emergency teams, reinforced by military and *ad hoc* groups of local citizens, were organized to carry out further rescue operations and to gather in all those casualties who had remained unattended so far. Casualties so collected were passed through control centres where they were allocated to categories of treatment, including first aid, attention at local hospitals where possible, or evacuation to other hospitals in the Midlands. Military communications greatly improved the co-ordination of operations. Some headway began to be made at last in assessing the extent of the disaster and in allocating priorities.

The task of restoring order and of rescuing and providing succour to the injured was still enormous in relation to the resources available. Fires were still raging, thousands were still dying where they lay, many people remained buried alive. Scattered crowds wandered about in a state of shock and there was frequent violence amongst those who thronged around the hospitals, relief centres and food stores, all of which were now under police and military guard. Police and military were armed and in many cases had to use force, sometimes even with weapons, to maintain control.

By the morning of 22 August some semblance of order had been established in neighbouring towns such as Wolverhampton. Here all fires had now been extinguished or had burned themselves out, and the combined efforts of police and military were at last able to maintain some degree of law and order in the streets, while rescue operations went on in damaged buildings and the further evacuation of homeless and injured to other areas was arranged. Compulsory billeting had allowed shelter to be found for most of those still wandering the streets. Some military effort was now becoming available to probe further towards the centre of the devastated area and to carry out rescue and relief operations in the innermost ring of towns surrounding the city of Birmingham. Most of the surviving populations of these towns had already left them and had arrived in the outermost ring of towns. There they had been given shelter and such medical help as existing facilities allowed. Nevertheless, within the innermost ring of towns, in places like Dudley, many thousands of injured people still lay amongst the rubble of their homes and countless others were buried beneath the ruins. The extent of damage in this area was so great that only minor relief was possible.

The Sub-Regional Headquarters within the city of Birmingham had by now realized that little could be done for most of the city area. Fires had largely burned themselves out but the devastation had extended over such a wide area that the capacity of rescue teams, already engaged in rescue attempts in the towns of the inner periphery, was severely limited. It was evident that the resources in the area were hopelessly inadequate to begin to attempt rescue operations in what remained of the city of Birmingham itself. This would have to wait until national resources became available. The city was therefore cordoned off along the line of the motorways to the north and west and along the line of the River Cole and the Stratford-upon-Avon Canal to the south and east. It was ordered that no rescue or relief operations would be mounted within this area for the time being. The cordon was strongly manned by police and military units and access into the city area was forbidden.

By limiting the deployment of available relief resources in this way the Sub-Regional Headquarters was able to make some headway in organizing and administering the area outside the cordon.

Many thousands of seriously injured were now dying daily and sanitary conditions had deteriorated to such an extent that there was widespread danger of disease. Police and military units were forced to the frequent use of firearms in maintaining law and order amongst the droves of injured and often dispirited people who overcrowded the limited accommodation and swamped all medical facilities. Evacuation of the injured was proceeding as fast as possible but the numbers were so great that it was becoming increasingly difficult to find suitable destinations for them. Further attempts were being made at clearing major roads around the city of Birmingham, but with the resources available only those in and out of the towns concerned could be cleared. It was obvious that a major evacuation of the entire area would have to be carried out, leaving behind only personnel essential to further rescue operations.

Londoners had seen the flash and heard the detonation of the nuclear explosion over Birmingham. While they watched the high mushroom cloud gather and disperse the government was already taking action. Civil and military staffs started immediately to put into operation contingency plans for nuclear attack. It was announced that the Prime Minister would speak to the nation on television and radio at midday.

Central government was already established away from London. On 4 August the first stages of the plans for evacuation had been carried out, with token staffs setting up in underground war locations. The main bodies of civil and military headquarters soon followed. Everywhere throughout the country the regional centres for joint civil and military control, located underground and well-protected, and subordinate sub-regional centres, had from the outset been fully operational. At the head of each was a minister of Cabinet rank, with representatives of all essential military and civil authorities. Procedures were well-practised. Communications had long been hardened against bomb damage and interference, even from the electro-magnetic pulse generated by a nuclear detonation.

Conventional air attack on many parts of the country had already been heavy, particularly on ports, power stations and communication centres, with severe damage and heavy loss of life. Fears of further nuclear attack were widespread. As a result, it was not immediately possible to divert to the stricken cities and towns in the vast circle of damage more than a comparatively small proportion of the units of United Kingdom Land Forces. Police and civil defence forces were under heavy strain. The voluntary groups trained by local authorities to cope with civil emergency, as well as conventional or nuclear attack, and the RAYNET Ham radio communications linked to the local authority and public utility radio networks were invaluable. Equipment stockpiled by local authorities, acquired by grant-aided purchase in the recent past or more recently still by requisition, was a godsend. Against the background of the damage done in Britain in the past few weeks by conventional air attack the Birmingham disaster could have pushed the national situation out of control. What had been done for civil defence in the preceding few years was just enough to prevent this.

Delegation of power over military and civil defence resources had become the responsibility of the Headquarters of UK Land Forces. Representatives of the Prime Minister, the naval, air and military commands and the civil agencies controlling essential services were assembled there, in well-defended underground bunkers, hardened against attack or interference to communications, containing all necessary equipment.

The news media had used all their resources to cover the Birmingham disaster – though for the first twenty-four hours after the detonation all pictures from the scene were banned. Approach by road to the towns of the countryside surrounding Birmingham was impossible. Visual cover was therefore only obtainable through oblique scanning from the air. There had been commentary all day on television and radio. When the Prime Minister broadcast, she explained what had happened in the first nuclear attack on a British city – indeed upon any city in the Western world – and outlined what was being done to provide relief. She repeated urgent advice that all people outside the disaster area should stay where they were; no one could yet know whether, or where, in the United Kingdom there might be another attack.

The Prime Minister then went on to announce that the enemy had in his turn been struck by nuclear attack, with even greater force than that used on Birmingham. This was the first official intimation in the United Kingdom that the Soviet city of Minsk had been destroyed.

Her Majesty the Queen with her family, said the Prime Minister, would remain in London, and she, the Prime Minister, herself would, of course, do the same.

CHAPTER TWENTY-SIX

A DEVASTATING RESPONSE

A few minutes after the detonation of the nuclear weapon over Birmingham, as the huge damage from blast was being followed by swiftly spreading fire, and as millions throughout the British Isles reacted in dumb horror to the emergency transmissions on their television screens and on the radio, the President of the United States was speaking to the British Prime Minister. The time was 1035 hoærs Greenwich Mean Time, 0535 Eastern Standard Time. It was at once agreed that immediate retaliation was necessary, if only to avoid a catastrophic decline in civilian and military morale. The French President was called and gave his instant concurrence. As the other Allies were being informed instructions were on their way to two SSBN, one American, one British, to launch two missiles each, targeted on the city of Minsk. The epicentre was to be directly over the middle of the city, at 3,000 metres. Each submarine reported a trouble-free launch, exactly on time, and the multiple warheads from the four missiles, tailored exactly to their task, detonated on target in quick succession. The effect was cataclysmic. It was the horror of Birmingham repeated, only many times worse, scarcely mitigated at all by civil defence precautions. There was no TV or radio reporting of the attack. The news spread nonetheless like wildfire round the world. Its impact was everywhere enormous but nowhere more so than within the Soviet Union and its satellites.

The hot-line was used again, to tell the Soviet leaders that this was a limited attack ordered as an inevitable reprisal and that a reply about negotiation would be given in three days. In the event this proved unnecessary.

This nuclear exchange, carried out on the Soviet side

391

with no pretence of consultation with their subject allies let alone with the regional republics of the USSR, proved to be the trigger which set off the smouldering nationalist explosion. The growth of disaffection and resistance in Asia and in Eastern Europe has already been described. Its causes were the check to Soviet arms in Europe and elsewhere; the fundamental contradiction in the Soviet system as a revolutionary empire – forcing its own subject nations to fight wars of national liberation in Africa while denying them national freedom at home; offers of external help, from China to the Central Asians and from the West to the European satellites; now finally the realization that Russia might well have initiated a nuclear war which could engulf them all unless they immediately separated themselves from Russian control. The outbreaks were quicker and more violent in the East, more subtle but more decisive in Europe.

The Council of Ministers of the Kazakh Soviet Socialist Republic started the ball rolling by securing the adoption by their local Supreme Soviet of a proclamation of secession from the Soviet Union and of independence and non-commitment. The new régime was at once recognized by China, who instituted large-scale military manoeuvres on the frontier. The Soviet commander at Alma Ata prepared to attack the Supreme Soviet building, now guarded by the local police and militia, but, being unaccustomed to taking local initiatives, asked Moscow for instructions and authority. The Kremlin, plunged into preparations for nuclear war and still torn by internal disagreement, was too busy to reply, and the tactical moment was lost. Enthusiastic crowds filled the streets carrying banners proclaiming their friendship for the Russian people and calling on the Russian troops to return peacefully to their own country. The Chinese threat appeared even more dangerous than the local 'disturbance', and the general took himself and most of his garrison off to reinforce the frontiers.

Proclamations of independence were equally successful

in other republics which bordered on Chinese or Iranian territory and where military activity on the frontier diverted Soviet troops from their internal security role. In the Uzbek republic, which did not have this advantage, however, the Soviet forces in Tashkent took bloody reprisals against the nationalist leaders and temporarily halted the independence movement. They might in the end have been able to re-establish the situation in other territories, but meanwhile there was more serious trouble in the West which finally gave the *coup de grâce* to the crumbling edifice of Soviet rule.

The annihilation of Minsk also precipitated events on the western borders of the Soviet Union. It was a well-chosen target, close to Poland on the west, capital of the theoretically autonomous republic of Byelorussia, and Ukraine's neighbour on the north. Both Poland and Ukraine were quick to draw the necessary conclusion that it could be their turn next unless they took steps to change the course of history. In preparation for such an occasion the Polish defence authorities, still able to call on great signals expertise such as the Enigma disclosures had revealed, had secretly arranged direct links to their commanders, separate from the Soviet-controlled Warsaw Pact network. They now activated these links and instructed all Polish units to stand firm in their positions and resist any, repeat *any*, other orders to move and any attack on their positions, from whatever quarter. At the same time they made contact with the underground (in typical Polish fashion the authorities and the underground had known perfectly well how to get in touch with each other for some time past) and arranged for them to send urgent messages on their clandestine radio to London, reporting what had been done, asking for confirmation that no Allied attack would be made on Polish positions, and requesting air drops of supplies of essential foodstuffs and communications equipment. A positive and encouraging reply was received and the Polish government quietly prepared a declaration of withdrawal from the Warsaw

Pact and the isolation of Russian units still on Polish territory.

The really crushing blow came from an unexpected quarter, however. Soviet policy had always been at pains either to suppress or to appease any symptoms of independence of mind on the part of the Ukraine. Its enormous contribution to Soviet food supplies, its position in the front line of Soviet territory facing the West, bordering on Poland, Czechoslovakia, Hungary and Romania, and its vast hydro-electric potential, had made it, after Russia proper, the most vital component of the Union. It had suffered more than any other republic from the actions of the Soviet state to obtain food supplies by force after the Revolution and from the subsequent persecution of the wealthier peasants. It had been rewarded after the devastation of the Second World War by being given, with Byelorussia to the north, a privileged but fictitious autonomy as a separate member of the United Nations.

Ukrainian nationalist sentiment had been repressed in 1966 in the Kiev trials of the intellectuals and members of the Ukrainian Workers and Peasants Union. Their main crime had been to promote the idea of secession from the Soviet Union, a right enshrined in the Soviet Constitution. Repression had only diverted this sentiment into more powerful channels underground. Its modern exponents understood the axiom that successful revolutions begin at the top. They determined to make use of the one important freedom left to the inhabitants of the Ukraine – the access of individual Ukrainians to positions of power in the central apparatus of the Soviet Union. There had been several successful generals; now the favourite son of the Ukrainian nationalists was in the unlikely guise of a secret policeman.

After graduating from the police academy at Kiev in 1960, Vasyl Duglenko had been recommended to Khrushchev by some of the latter's Ukrainian cronies, and transferred to the KGB headquarters in Moscow. Being still in a junior post he had managed to survive Khrushchev's fall, and climbed up the precarious ladder of power to be Deputy Commandant, with special responsibility for the security of the Kremlin. He had retained close links with the nationalist cells in the Communist Party of the Ukraine and he had naturally placed a good number of fellow Ukrainians in suitable positions in the KGB, particularly in the Kremlin section.

So a powerful mechanism was in place, and the Minsk explosions provided the opportunity, and the necessity, for its use. Duglenko and his friends in the Ukrainian Party machine had no wish to take part in the last act of a Russian *Götterdämmerung*. Although they vaguely knew what was about to happen in Poland they saw no sure future in a separatist movement confined to the Ukraine. The central keep of the Soviet system had be attacked.

At the centre they could join forces with the group of 'doves' already referred to in Chapter 24, whose influence had spread, with the worsening news from East and West, even among sections of the command of the armed forces. It would be vital to have some friends there if a coup was to survive its first dangerous hours.

This army group, small at first and of necessity conspiratorial, had decided even before the attack on Birmingham that nuclear war was not going to achieve Soviet objectives in the West, nor restore order in the East. Moreover, in the ensuing destruction of organized life in the Soviet Union the armed forces themselves were likely to disintegrate. A deliberate return of army units to the Russian heartlands offered better hope for a future system of orderly government in which the armed forces would have an effective role, and its commanders a tolerably secure life. Their ideas probably did not include so radical a break-up of the Soviet Union as the Ukrainians secretly envisaged. They would have been in closer agreement on the need to relax the dead hand of centralized control on the economic life of the country, not in the interests of *laissez-faire*, but in order to restore efficiency and come nearer to matching the agricultural and industrial productivity of the West, not to speak of China–Japan.

As it turned out, both parties, keeping their ultimate objectives to themselves, were able to establish discreet links for the tactical purpose of overcoming the probable insistence of the hard-liners in the Central Committee on committing nuclear suicide.

There was in any case no time to be lost. The Politburo was due to meet on 22 August to decide on further action in the event that the Americans did not comply with the ultimatum to join in talks on maintaining the *status quo*.

On the morning of the fateful meeting, Duglenko's boss, the KGB Chief, met with a fatal 'motor accident' on his way into Moscow. Duglenko, already in the Kremlin, could now be satisfied that he would have access to the Politburo session. He relied on two things: complete surprise, for which reason no one knew of the details of his plan except the dozen secret policemen required to carry it out, mostly fellow Ukrainians; and the willingness of the Soviet administrative machine of that time to accept orders from the top, whatever they might be – a characteristic which he in fact was determined to change but which on this occasion was to serve him well. When the meeting had assembled and he was summoned to report on the accident to his Chief he drew from his pocket not a sheaf of paper, but a pistol, with which he shot dead President Vorotnikov, and on this signal his fellow conspirators, already on guard outside the room, broke in and disarmed the rest of the Politburo. Duglenko announced that he was assuming the offices of President and Party Secretary; he ordered the removal, under guard, of the leading hard-line members, and received the allegiance of the rest, who had little choice, with guns still drawn all round them.

The next few hours were a feverish race against time, to assume effective command of the armed forces before any counter-move could be made and before any wild orders could be given for nuclear release, to reassure the population, and not least to reassure the Americans and dissuade them from any idea of a pre-emptive nuclear strike. Some of the Soviet commanders were, as has been said, generally favourable to the idea of salvaging what they could from the present unhappy situation, as the only means of keeping the armed forces in being, but very few of them were privy to the details of the conspiracy. It had, of course, been necessary in advance to place one of these few in the post which handled the transmissions of presidential orders to the strategic nuclear forces, so that when Duglenko, having done what was immediately necessary in Moscow, finally got on the hot-line to President Thompson, he was able to assure him confidently that the Soviet nuclear forces had been ordered to stand down, and to ask President Thompson kindly to give corresponding orders on his side. Duglenko proposed in addition a complete ceasefire within twelve hours, and the opening of an early conference in Helsinki to draw up terms of peace.

Even the most expert Kremlin-watchers on the Western side were taken by surprise. In the confusion of the next few hours, while the American answer was being prepared, some voices were heard urging that it was a trick, or that if there were a real upset in Moscow, now was the time to push ahead and finish the Russians off. More accurately, some others argued that this was no more than a change of Russian tactics; the new, more open and more decentralized communism, of which they were getting the first news by monitoring Moscow broadcasts, would in the long run be more dangerous to the West than the brutal obscurantism of its predecessor. Therefore no concessions should be made, the guard should be kept up, and so on. But it was eventually agreed to be thankful for a large if not necessarily permanent mercy, to reciprocate the downgrading of nuclear alert, to accept the ceasefire, and to prepare, with all due caution, for a conference.

Duglenko had to contend with far more arduous decision-making, on no less a subject than the future of the Soviet Union. At a hastily-summoned meeting of representatives of all the constituent republics there was not really much choice but to accept that the Union was in dissolution; independence was now openly proclaimed as the objective of the Ukraine. It had already been achieved by many of the republics of Asia. The Russians now clearly had to accept that whether they liked it or not they were on their own.

It was generally agreed that they would all form a joint delegation to the Helsinki Conference, and at the same time work out the modalities of separation. Needless to say, the violent transition from a centralized autocracy to multiple nationhood was not everywhere achieved in an orderly manner. Not all the republics were geared to establish their own administrations, and many had deficient economic resources. The enormous problem of disposing of the former Soviet forces, in Europe and Africa and the Middle East, was being handled by UNRRO.

The Conference, as is the way of conferences, proliferated into a whole series, some of which are still continuing, and it would require another volume of this history to do justice to all these deliberations. The collapse of the USSR meant the end of large-scale hostilities in Europe. It did not mean universal peace.

CHAPTER TWENTY-SEVEN

REFLECTIONS ON A WAR

Conflicts which the Soviet Union did not start, but which it studiously sought to sharpen and exploit, have yet to be resolved. Fighting still goes on. The pattern of the successor states into which the USSR seems now to be dividing has yet to be fully determined. There are differences between the countries which, under their former régime, were all members of the Warsaw Pact. There are also differences between each one of them and the member states of the Western Alliance, with which they have so lately been at war. To settle all these differences will take time and will be far from easy. Meanwhile, there is still warfare outside Europe. No doubt it will continue, in one way or another, for some time, with whatever resources (and much material has been left behind by the Russians) the belligerents can find.

The Third World War, however, can be fairly said to have ended with the collapse of the Warsaw Pact in late August 1985 and the cessation of direct hostilities between the major powers. We have already taken a brief glance at how the world then looked, and in the concluding chapter we look a little into the future. Something more should now be said about what might have happened and did not, about certain contributory factors to the outcome and about some, at least, of the conclusions that can be drawn from these events.

What especially distinguishes the scene we now see about us – and this is something to which we shall only be able to grow accustomed with the passage of time – is the absence from it of the powerful, restless, baleful, expansive, intractably dogmatic imperialism of Soviet Russia.

The world has come out of another bad dream, just as it did out of the Nazi nightmare. This one lasted rather longer. The myth born in the Bolshevik Revolution of 1917 persisted, before it was dispersed, for nearly three-quarters of a century. It was the myth of the emergence of true democracy from a proletarian explosion, when what had really taken place was the murderous overthrow of a democratically elected government by a fanatical authoritarian minority.

It is argued by some that the basic contradictions of Marxism-Leninism would inevitably have caused, in time, the downfall of any state built on it. Whatever Karl Marx may have contributed to nineteenth-century thought his political philosophy is held by many today, a century later, to be unscientific, romantic and obsolete, no more useful as a guide to government in the twentieth century than the novels of Charles Dickens as a reflection of life today in England. Indeed, if the revolutionary genius of Lenin had not harnessed to the advancement of Marxism a huge and backward group of peoples accustomed to absolutism – most of them Asiatic and some still semi-savage – it might have been consigned to the dustheap of history long ago, and this particular nightmare might never have occurred at all. The nightmare is now over, and we shall never know if the USSR, given time, would have fallen apart by itself or not, without the war it brought about. There may be other nightmares still ahead.

It has been suggested with some plausibility that in addition to the conjunction of miscalculation and mischance which triggered off the explosion of August 1985 there had long been a growing awareness among rulers of the USSR of increasing strains within the Warsaw Pact, and within the Soviet Union itself, which could hardly be contained without a signal military victory over the capitalist West. There had also been, among the top people in the régime, a very real fear of Germany. There had even been some fear of the capacity of the Federal Republic to lead the West (and above all the United

States) into an aggressive war against the communist East. This was a fear which West German insistence on 'forward defence' (whatever that might mean – and it clearly meant different things to different people) did little to abate. It was for all that little but the product of the Soviet Union's own propaganda.

The real causes of this war between the Eastern and the Western blocs will long be matter for debate. Whatever they were the fighting could not, it now seems, find its resolution (if it did not move into the strategic exchange of weapons of mass destruction, which would have emptied the concept of 'resolution' of all meaning) anywhere but in Europe. Its focal point could be nowhere but in the Federal Republic of Germany.

The critical point in the military action was therefore bound to be, at least as far as the battle on and over the land was concerned, in what was designated in NATO as the Central Region of Allied Command Europe.

What also seems beyond doubt is that the Soviet plan to penetrate the Northern Army Group, cross the Rhine in the Low Countries, and roll up AFCENT by an offensive thrust from north to south along the west bank of the Rhine, which would have taken CENTAG in the rear, came very close to success. It was well conceived and well prepared, with a not unreasonable assessment of the difficulties involved. This particular plan was an element in a general structure of contingency planning, any one part of which was valid in itself though none was likely to be implemented in isolation. It was the unexpectedly strong Western response to the Soviet intervention in Yugoslavia which pulled the chocks out, as it were, and set the plan for the invasion of the Central Region rolling down the slipway to the launch.

What might have happened in the long run if this plan had come off is quite incalculable. It can be said with complete confidence that in the shorter term it would have brought about the total destruction of the Federal Republic of Germany, and that the Atlantic Alliance would in consequence have lain in ruins. The possibility of a counter-offensive by the United States, in these circumstances, can hardly be conceived. The situation would have been beyond repair.

The bogey of an all-out attack on Allied Command Europe by forces of the Warsaw Pact, planned in total secrecy and carried out with complete surprise by forces already in place, with the aid of massive under-cover operations prepared with absolute security, was not the sort of thing to give sensible men sleepless nights in the years before the war – though it might not have been sensible wholly to disregard the possibility. Much more likely, Allied planners thought, was what actually happened: the implementation of well-prepared contingency plans, involving a high degree of preparation, as crises developing elsewhere showed signs of moving out of control.

Unlikely though it may have been, a surprise attack in the late seventies by in-place forces of the Warsaw Pact would have found Allied Command Europe so ill prepared that its early success could hardly have been in doubt, whether the French came in on the Allied side or not. The US Army in Europe had not yet fully recovered from the Vietnam experience. It was becoming accustomed to the absence of the draft but was already running into serious and unexpected difficulties over reserves as a result of ending it. Stocks which had been run down for the Israeli war were only slowly being replaced. The 'Reforger' system, by which formations would be flown in from the continental United States to marry up with equipment pre-stocked in the Federal Republic, though already showing great promise, had not yet been as fully developed as in the years to come.

The *Bundeswehr* was improving, but although its units were rated by the Russians as the best of the Allied bunch it was still only in moderate shape by the exacting standards of German professional soldiers, while the

German Territorial Army was scarcely more than embryonic.

The British Army of the Rhine was again in the throes of reorganization, with the level of provision (and the state) of its equipment causing concern to its officers and with several battalions of its invaluable infantry still in Northern Ireland. The forces for defence in depth in NORTHAG, when the inevitable breakthrough occurred and there was no release of Allied nuclear weapons (which would almost certainly have been withheld), were wholly inadequate.

Belgian and Dutch forces were heavily – and dangerously – reliant on reservists with no more than short conscript training behind them, and were still reluctant (particularly in the case of the Dutch) to maintain any considerable strength in proximity to their forward battle stations in the Federal Republic. There was very little hope that in the event of a surprise attack Dutch forces of any real significance would have been able to reach their emergency positions before these were overrun.

The Allied air forces were still ahead of those of the Warsaw Pact in quality of equipment, though the gap was closing. They were also well ahead in the quality of their aircrew, but among the European Allies air forces had been ruinously run down. Air defence with surface weapons, even in Allied Command Europe, was nowhere strong. Some of the equipment was good. The British low-level *Rapier*, for instance, was outstanding. There were in 1977 only two *Rapier* regiments in BAOR, however, neither of which was armoured or even tactically mobile. The air defence of Great Britain, upon which so much would depend, was particularly weak. It was almost as rundown as the UK's civil defences against air attack, whether by conventional weapons or nuclear.

Invasion from a standing start in the late seventies, if it had ever been tried, would almost certainly have brought the Russians to the Rhine in a very few days – unless NATO employed nuclear weapons. What would have happened then is anyone's guess. A high probability would have been swift escalation into the strategic nuclear exchange which would very soon have rendered the land battle in Europe largely irrelevant.

Deliberate all-out attack with complete surprise from a standing start, it must be repeated, was always unlikely. The more probable way in which it was thought in the West that a war in Europe would be likely to break out was just the way it did. What happened to start it off in 1985 could have happened, in one way or another, much earlier.

If the crisis of 1985 had occurred in 1977, say, or even in 1978, it is, as we have seen, scarcely conceivable that the Soviet plan for an advance to the Rhine, the dismemberment of the Alliance and the total destruction of the Federal Republic of Germany could have failed given the state of preparedness of the Allies at that time.

What was done in the years between 1978 and 1984 was enough to prevent this. The tale of it has already been referred to in outline. It is told more fully, using Britain as a test case, in Appendices 1 and 3.

The advantages of the military structure formed to function in peacetime – a quite unique feature of the Atlantic Alliance – have become ever more abundantly clear. Without NATO as a framework the individual efforts of the Allies would have been of little account and much less effective in the aggregate. Within NATO the contributions of the Allies, though incompletely co-ordinated, added up to far more than the sum of the parts. In those years the United States came out of its post-Vietnam trance. Great Britain threw off some of the illusions which had flooded into the vacuum left by the disappearance of an empire. The Federal Republic ceased to be mesmerized by the success of its economic miracle and the allure of a welfare state. Even Belgium and Holland, though late and incompletely, began to show some awareness that the Soviet Union was already in a position to meet and master a real crisis and would welcome a showdown with the capitalist West, and sooner rather than later at that. Throughout NATO there was a growing tendency to face and accept defence responsibilities, nowhere more clearly shown than in a steady rise in readiness, an improvement in reinforcement capabilities and a striking advance in anti-tank and air defence.

The miscalculation over the possible participation of France was a major blunder on the Soviet Union's part at the very outset. In the sphere of grand strategy the Soviet Union was soon to be in deeper water still. It was attempting to handle an almost worldwide problem of war command, with operations proceeding simultaneously from Bodo in Norway to Berbera in North-east Africa, from the Caribbean to the Caucasus. This was beyond the powers of the centralized system of control on which the régime depended. Only a degree of independence in command which was wholly foreign to it, and to which Soviet commanders themselves were completely unaccustomed, could have enabled peripheral commands to retain the initiative without which they were bound to fail.

At the tactical level, a very similar point applied. The Russians were attempting to apply a battle-fighting method which demanded a degree of independence in junior leaders which it had been a major interest of the Marxist-Leninist system to discourage.

The battle-fighting method itself was on the whole unremarkable. What was hailed in the West by some in the late seventies as a tactical revolution in the Red Army, the conversion from mass attack to manoeuvre, from the shock of frontal assault to the 'deep thrust' and the 'daring raid', was neither so novel nor so radical as was thought. What was being developed in Red Army tactical practice was the action of combined arms, co-ordinated and commanded at a lower level than was customary. This marked a shift of emphasis which showed up weaknesses none the less. The BMP, designed for the nuclear battlefield, was found not to be the best combat vehicle for the carriage of infantry supporting armour in a non-nuclear battle. It was in the process of being somewhat hesitantly replaced by a better vehicle, the MTLB, when war broke out. The problems of interrelating combat elements with different speeds and other characteristics remained unsolved.

So did the difficulties of combining many widely differing parts into a composite tactical whole in a fluid situation, where initiative, inventiveness and a bold independence of mind in junior leaders were what counted. The Red Army had made much over the years of the importance of free and lively debate among junior officers, particularly in journals available to the public and to foreigners – much more, in fact, than the armies of the West where such things were taken more for granted. In action on the battlefield, however, the young Red Army officer – who almost certainly expected nothing else – found himself as usual under the deadening hand of total conformity. It was this which made the command posts, control structures and communications systems of the Warsaw Pact such rewarding targets for attack.

It must here be strongly emphasized again, however – and it cannot be too often repeated – that the forces of the Western Allies were only in a position to survive the onslaught of the Warsaw Pact because, though heavily outnumbered from the outset, they were able to remain in being. Without the sort of improvements effected in the years between 1978 and 1984 this would have been impossible.

The war on land in Europe was a short one. Deprived of the swift victory that could have been so confidently predicted only a few years before, the Warsaw Pact, once checked, could not recover momentum in time to achieve and stabilize a decisive advantage before the arrival of the first of those Western reinforcements, with their great weight of weapons, which could soon be expected to flow so plentifully.

The fighting could hardly have gone on for very long in any case. Neither side could have sustained for more than a few weeks the expenditure of aircraft and of missile and other stocks – of fuel, for example, and of all manner of warlike stores and equipment – demanded in the modern battle. Even if the production of munitions of war in the home bases had been possible at the rate at which they were used up on the battlefield, it is doubtful whether, with hostile interference to the lines of communication, supply could ever have kept up with consumption.

The Soviet concept of the application of armed force for the purpose of securing a political advantage, in the state of the art in the last twenty years of the twentieth century and in the circumstances of the time, was thus wholly rational. It was facing an adversary relatively weak in the first instance but disposing of potentially overwhelming resources. Late twentieth-century war consumed material in such enormous quantities as to put very long drawn-out operations out of the question. It was imperative, therefore, to secure a position of great political advantage in a short, sharp, violent encounter, starting with the offensive initiative, exploiting as far as possible the advantages of surprise and of a somewhat longer period of preparation than the enemy's, and reaching a chosen strategic objective before the enemy could bring his superior resources to bear and while stocks were still sufficient to sustain intensive action.

We have seen what happened. In the last few years before the outbreak of war the West began to wake up to the danger it faced, and in the time available did just enough in repair of its neglected defences to enable it, by a small margin, to survive. The Allies had better luck, perhaps, than they deserved. The Soviet Union was guilty of an important misjudgment in the matter of the American response to intervention in Yugoslavia, and of a critical blunder in their assumption that the French would

not come in on the Allied side. A check to the forward
impetus of the Warsaw Pact's invasion of the Federal
Republic of Germany followed by a single, catastrophic,
strategic nuclear exchange, triggered off the dissolution
of the Pact and started the disintegration of the Soviet
Union itself into its national components. The Marxist-
Leninist empire, as hated and feared, perhaps, as any
régime the world has seen, collapsed in total ruin, and
the world is even now engaged, in many different ways,
in picking up and sorting out the pieces.

The immediate tidying up which engaged the Allies, as
soon as the USSR ceased to be able to prosecute the war
and hostilities in Europe came to an end, contained
operations that were already more or less familiar from
experience of other wars but also one that was both
highly important and quite new.

The presence of large numbers of nuclear warheads in
Europe presented the Allies with a new and very difficult
postwar problem. Many remained firmly in Allied hands,
though a considerable number had been in Special
Weapons Stores overrun in the offensive and could not
now be accounted for. Very many more were dispersed
and lost on the other side, amidst the confusion in which
hostilities ended. Much of the deadly content of these
weapons had disappeared and so far has not been traced.
The United Nations Fissile Materials Recovery Organization (UNFISMATRECO) is seeking urgently to recover
all it can. Some will almost certainly find its way into
hands from which, in the interests of peace and security,
it should at any cost be kept.

One last lesson is worth drawing from the war itself.
Not inappropriately in an age of high technology, it lies
in a technical area.

The period of full-scale hostilities between the forces
of the Atlantic Alliance and the Warsaw Pact was short
– no more, in fact, than a few weeks. It was still sufficient
to show in quite astonishing fashion how far the electronic
technology of the West had outstripped that of the

Eastern bloc. The reason was very simple and beyond dispute. The advantage of the West lay in commercial competition. No state-controlled activity, no collective operation, in a field wide open to scientific inventiveness and industrial enterprise, could have produced developments as staggering as those in the electronics industries of the non-communist world. The reduction in size, weight, power consumption and cost of electronic components in a competitive market had been quite phenomenal. The evolution of micro-electronics and of micro-processing had been nothing less than a technological explosion.

Let a short example suffice. In the 1950s the transistor began to replace the vacuum tube. In the 1960s circuits of ten transistors were in use. Within ten years transistors numbering several hundreds could be mounted on one small chip of substrate two centimetres square. What was called medium-scale integration (MSI) was then possible. By 1977 large-scale integration (LSI) had come in, employing 1,000 or more transistors mounted in the same space. When war broke out very large-scale integration (VLSI) was already in use, with *10,000* transistors mounted on a chip still only the size of a postage stamp. The work of a computer whose equipment in the forties, using vacuum tubes, would have filled a barn could now be done by something the size of a wrist-watch.

The impact of this on the development of military hardware was incalculable. The equipment for communications, control, guidance, the detection and location of weapons and emitters, the means of jamming, interception, interpolation, diversion and a thousand and one other functions, was flowing in such profusion that there was much more, and in much greater variety, than could be used. The irony for the West, in the shortness of the war, welcome though it was, lay in the inability of military men to find the questions to which the electronics men already had the answers.

They were only beginning, when the fighting ended, to get the best out of the equipment and techniques already in service. They had not yet begun to explore, in a technology developing at an almost frightening rate, the applications of techniques already far advanced and being improved on daily.

The wars of the late nineteenth century – the American Civil War, for example, and the Franco-Prussian War – were wars of the railway, the telegraph, breech-loading small arms and tinned rations. The seas were dominated by the ironclad. At the beginning of the twentieth century the Russo-Japanese War showed to any who cared to learn the dominance on the battlefield of the spade, barbed wire and automatic weapons. The First World War rammed home the same lesson, in a war in which the internal combustion engine, artillery, the submarine, air power and armoured vehicles became the dominant features. The Second World War was one of worldwide mobility on land and sea and in the air, of total mobilization of population and industrial reserves, of seapower and of air forces. It ended in the shadow of the nuclear weapon. The Third World War was widely expected to be the first nuclear war – and perhaps the last. It turned out in the event to be essentially a war of electronics.

To end these reflections on the Third World War upon a technological note may appear odd. It is unlikely to seem so to some future reader. Wars commonly produce an acceleration of technical advance. This one did more: it took the lid off Pandora's box. We are now moving forward into a world which will be more and more dominated by electronic technology. It is likely to prove a very different world from the one we knew, the one which came so near to destruction in the Third World War. That war was fought, it is true, under the shadow of the threat of nuclear devastation. On the basis of NATO's rediscovered confidence and hastily repaired defences it was largely won by electronics. We cannot begin to guess how our lives, and even more our children's lives, will be influenced by the possibilities which these swiftly developing techniques are now opening up. An unfamiliar, perhaps uncomfortable world awaits us, very strange and new. We can only be thankful to have survived, and wait and see.

CHAPTER TWENTY-EIGHT

THE BEGINNING OF THE FUTURE

We believe that later historians who write the history of the Third World War will not drastically alter our conclusions about its causes. However, we are writing very shortly after the end of the war and can only provide the best predictions we have about its effect – and we are very mindful of the anecdote with which this chapter concludes. History is not an exact science. And 'the historian of the future' is as much artist as scientist or academic. But the futurologist cannot be taken lightly. He bases his conclusions on perceived trends, and his predictions themselves may possibly have some effect on the future: in helping either to prevent his predictions coming true or to realize them.

Nobody can be sure which of the many meetings and international position papers of the first three months of 1987 will prove of lasting significance to the world. At least one of these papers, we suspect, may have begun to paint the picture of the future.

It was prepared for the meeting of the EEC heads of government at Copenhagen. It had been collated in the Council of Foreign Ministers. This had not been a recipe for meaningful documents in the past, but this document may be destined to play a role in the history of Europe more significant than the past treaties of Rome, Versailles, Vienna and Utrecht put together. What it embodies has already become known as the Copenhagen doctrine. It is a lengthy document, legalistically expressed. A detailed summary of it appeared in *The Times* of 15 February 1987, and we quote this in full:

1 At the end of the 1939–45 war there were two superpowers: the United States and the Soviet Union. At the end of the 1985 war, there are again two superpowers: the United States and the China-Japan co-prosperity sphere. The difference for us this time is that Europe does not lie between them.

2 America and China-Japan will face each other – we hope in amity – across the Pacific Ocean. The Pacific basin will become more important to each of them than the Atlantic is.

3 The most extreme version of this emerging Pacific superpower isolationism is already being expressed in the Schneider memorandum, from the American General Art Schneider, who was most angry when President Thompson allowed European political instincts and fears in 1985 to delay the invasion of East Germany which Schneider (popularly known as 'young blood and guts') had expected his own army group to spearhead. Schneider, who may be the Democratic candidate against President Thompson in next year's 1988 presidential election (and failing that will almost certainly win the now almost as important office of Governor of his native California), has written:

'Henceforth we should let Europe and Africa stew in their own tribal wars. It will not be worth the death of a single American soldier to prevent them, especially as (a) the Birmingham and Minsk bombs have shown that the whole world is not contaminated by single N-blasts and (b) it will be possible for China-Japan and the US to quarantine smaller countries' N-wars from afar by saying that any country which launches an N-weapon will immediately have a neutron bomb from us homed in by missile to its president's palace.'

It is possible that within ten years an even more tempting weapon for such quarantining may become available to countries with the technological capability of the US and Japan. They may be able to announce the setting up of a telecommunications 'ring fence', for the state of the art will then permit those capable of developing the appropriate technology to take charge by telecommunication of the guidance system of any missile in flight and redirect it at will. This would mean that any country launching a missile could find it reversed upon a reciprocal course and turned back to land and detonate at its point of launch. The advance in telecommunications during the technological spurt caused by the threat of war, even more than in the brief duration of the war itself, has been greater than in any other technology except that of energy.

4 It is therefore important for us in the EEC to see that the sort of Europe we rebuild during this peace should not be one liable to 'tribal wars'.

5 The rest of Europe, both East and West, will be frightened if the two Germanies unite. They would then form too dominant a European power. It is therefore important that each Germany should be a member of the EEC, and be united within the EEC to the same degree as France and West Germany are, but no more than that.

6 The same applies to all the former communist states, including the European states of the former Soviet Union. The EEC now needs to extend its boundaries in the way that Charles de Gaulle once envisaged. The European Economic Community should become a Europe from the Atlantic to the Urals.

This document was accepted at Copenhagen with some relief by the governments concerned, including that of the Federal Republic of Germany. Charles de Gaulle was now seen in retrospect as a prophet, where in life he had more often been regarded as a prickly and tiresome man. Two new issues were strenuously discussed at Copenhagen. One concerned the best rules and aims for the new, enlarged EEC; on this there was a note of innovation, excitement, enthusiasm and intellectual daring – an attractive throwback to the European spirit of the late 1950s which had seemed to be sleeping since. The second issue was what on earth to do about the politico-strategic problems on the long southern border of the new EEC; on this there was a note of near-despair.

First, the governing mechanism of the new EEC. It was recognized that free trade in goods, though to be continued, was likely to be much less important to rich countries in the future than freedom for international and transnational telecommunications. Now that factories (except in low wage areas) were bound to become more and more automated, people in the rich northern one-third of the world would mostly be in white-collar jobs where they would be working with their imaginations rather than their hands. But people in such jobs would not necessarily need to live near their workplaces. What should be the nationality and tax position of a Belgian dress designer who lives in Monte Carlo and St Moritz in the winter, at Stratford-on-Avon in the spring, and Corfu in the summer, and does his work by daily telecommunication through a portable console to colleagues and computers at the largely automated textile factory at Volgograd where he works – who becomes, in fact, a telecommuter?

The EEC ministers at Copenhagen began to grope towards the concept that the European citizen of the future would need what the West German Chancellor called 'triple nationality', but the Luxembourg Prime Minister significantly called 'triple tax status'. Let us use the Luxembourg terminology; it is more novel and, for that reason, in this fast-changing world, easier to understand.

First, each citizen would have to pay some taxes to the area in which he lived; this would maintain purely local government services there. There is here the obvious danger that all the rich might then choose to live together in areas with low social security costs (because there were few local poor around) and thus low tax rates, while the poor might find themselves huddled together in areas which needed a lot of social expenditure but with no local rich to pay the taxes. In order to avoid this 'ghettoization of continents' in the telecommuting age, the ministers at Copenhagen were beginning to realize that much wider governments (in this case, a central government of the EEC itself) would probably have to become responsible for what might be called the 'welfare' or 'transfer incomes' roles performed by national governments in the pre-telecommuting era.

Otherwise, rich folk would all take off to tax havens, and telecommute from there. So there would probably have to be a set schedule of income tax rates across Europe: perhaps a maximum marginal rate of not more than 55 per cent for the richest and a negative income tax for those falling below a minimum level, so as to set a floor income for the poorest Europeans.

It would not be sensible for Monte Carlo to be able to declare itself a tax haven and for all rich telecommuters to congregate there, while the poor of Europe congregated in some decaying old city like, say, Warsaw, which might then become the 'welfare capital' or 'muggers' capital' of Europe.

It would therefore be advisable to have a European regional policy. One object: to attract more rich telecommuters into the troubled old cities like Warsaw so as to get a better social mix there (therefore, allow the inhabitants of Warsaw to pay a lower top tax rate on incomes above a certain size). Concurrent object: to persuade some of the poor to scatter from Warsaw to other areas. This would involve a direction that unemployed youngsters going on to social security would after a certain period get lower social security benefits in Warsaw than if they moved to seek jobs outside it.

Already in the 1970s New York City was suffering from not being able to implement a policy of this sort. High local taxes and crime rates meant that richer taxpayers were fleeing the city, leaving behind a city electorate that

ecame poorer and so more left-wing, and voted itself
arger welfare benefits which it could not pay for. The
igher welfare benefits in New York City then attracted
nore welfare families in. There would be a spreading of
his sort of vicious circle right across the world in the
elecommuting age (and also of the twin problem of rich
ax havens) unless regional policies of this type could be
ut in train.

The third leg of the European citizen's 'triple tax status'
vould then be the leg of the nationality on which he chose
o stand. There is the advantage that each person could,
vithin reason, choose which this should be. National
;overnments need no longer rule over purely contiguous
,roups of people. The problem of Belgium has long been
hat one part of the people has regarded itself as Flemish,
he other as Walloon. With the tripartite system it should
e possible for the Flemish to elect their own governments
for systems of family law, for cultural issues, including
ducation, and for other representational matters) even
vhile living amid the Walloons, who could similarly elect
heir own government. The same would apply to Catholics
nd Protestants living together in Northern Ireland and to
he provinces of Yugoslavia, and, so long as national
;overnment diminishes in importance in this way, it might
ventually be possible for the two Germanies to have a
oint unimportant national government of the same kind.

It is probable that in the telecommuting age all areas of
he world will eventually have to move to tripartite
ystems of this sort: with (a) continental-sized govern-
nents to pursue regional central tax policies in order to
revent some tax havens becoming ghettoes of the rich
nd some inner cities ghettoes of the poor; (b) very local
;overnments, which could eventually become as small as
articular groups of citizens wanted them to be (so that
eople who wanted to live in a commune and telecommute
rom it could set that commune up as a unit of administra-
ive local government if neighbours agreed, while at the
ther extreme other groups might prefer to employ a

commercial company on a performance contract to carry through administrative local government tasks rather than pretend that, for example, voting Republican or Democratic was the right way of getting a mayor who would be best fitted to find the most successful changing technology for operating New York's drains); and (c) national governments that would have a diminished role over their peoples, who would not necessarily live contiguously.

The EEC at the end of the Third World War seemed lucky in being well placed to set up a prototype for this tripartite system, when it should be needed. One problem concerned the capital city or cities for the new Europe. It had been argued even before the war that the existing city of Brussels was too crowded for this purpose, and also, strangely, too central. A central city as a capital now means that centripetal forces become too strong, so that the central area grows richer and the flanks too poor. Even by the 1970s there had been grounds for arguing that the best scheme would be to have twin cities nearly a continent apart as capitals, joined by close telecommunication links and with great data banks planned from scratch for the new information age. A sentimental opportunity now presented itself. It was the Dutch Prime Minister who suggested at Copenhagen that the custom-built capitals of the new Europe should be Peace City West and Peace City East, built on the former sites of Birmingham and Minsk.

One of the most important functions of government is the organization of military preparedness and defence. Much of this should be organized on a continental scale. The new Europe felt reasonably confident that it could avoid internal tribal wars. But it regarded the chaos emerging on its southern boundaries with sickened alarm.

The two most worried reflections at Copenhagen were: 'the world is now divided into three parts, and the EEC is perched on top of the wildest south'; and 'unfortunately, the earth is round'.

Many people expect the China-Japan co-prosperity

phere (including Australasia) to be the future centre of he world. Japan is rapidly becoming the most advanced ountry technologically. China has the largest literate abour force, and as this is still relatively underpaid in omparison with its ability and entrepreneurial drive it herefore has the fastest early capacity for growth. Aus-ralia and the islands to its north will be among the pleasantest places in which to live during the telecom-nuting age. No part of this area was invaded in the Third World War, though a great many Australians and New Zealanders fought as volunteers on the Allied side and in southern Africa, and many more were on their way to Europe when the few weeks of full hostilities came to an nd. The parts of the China-Japan co-prosperity area that nay still be ravaged by *coups d'état* and urban guerrilla-lom (Indonesia? Thailand?) are relatively small, and hould prove controllable – especially (and this is worry-ng) as Japan and China may be more willing than others o 'cure' or 'control' violent individuals with personality-hanging tranquillizing drugs.

The second main area of the world is the Americas. North America was undamaged by the Third World War ust as it had been by the First and Second. The main economic effect of war and post-war reconstruction has been (as in 1941–45) to restore it to full employment. South America has prospered, and communism has been overthrown in the Caribbean. It is about as popular to advocate Soviet-style communism in the Caribbean (including Cuba and Jamaica) in the late 1980s as it was to advocate Nazism in continental Europe in the late 1940s. For a time, at least, urban guerrilladom in the Americas s likely to be on the decline.

The problem area is the territory to the south of the new EEC. On the western side of its long southern border, Africa has become a dumping ground for every sort of surplus military weapon used in the late war; its tribal hatreds are still seething; it may be entering a new dark age. Perched on its southern rim are the triumphant white

homelands of South Africa. During the years 1988–201
they may feel as self-confident after military success a
Israel did in 1948 and 1967, offering some of the sam
attractions but posing some of the same problems.

China-Japan is likely to co-operate with Australasia t
its south, in order to help bring humane and sensibl
telecommuter-era government to the troubled area
between them. Some of their joint methods of neo-gunboa
diplomacy will be called neo-colonialism; but as they wi
be a multi-racial partnership they will get away with a lo
North America may co-operate similarly with Brazil, t
create its own north-south axis and an area of prosperit
between them.

There will be a school of thought that thinks that th
new EEC should ally itself with white South Africa, a
China-Japan with Australasia, and the United States wit
Brazil. But the EEC might then find that it had made racia
problems in its 'wild south' even more likely to bring ric
upon itself.

At the eastern end of Europe's southern border, non
of the problems of the Middle East has been resolved. A
EEC's south-eastern border would lie on the Caspian Se
including a short land frontier with triumphant Iran.

As Iran has been on the winning side, it may hav
temptations to extend a new Persian empire across Araby
There will be fierce resistance if this is attempted. Thi
uncovers two other problems: first, the fact that Iran i
now the cockpit between the China-Japan and EE
spheres of interest; second, the question of how lon
Middle Eastern oil is likely to remain important.

While Iran's western border is with Iraq and the Gul
its north-eastern border is with the Asiatic republics c
the former Soviet Union, now under Chinese influence
and its south-eastern border is with Pakistan. India
Pakistan was not a scene of fighting in the war; the ne
generation of youngsters coming out of its schools is th
first generation to be almost entirely literate (like the firs
generation of literate Chinese to emerge from their schoo

ifteen years ago, and look how they've progressed); some people therefore expect rapid economic development in India-Pakistan at last. Some trends suggest it may become the manufacturing area for the China-Japan co-prosperity sphere, the place to which that rich area devolves its pollutant heavy industries. This may be especially likely if nearby Middle Eastern oil remains an important industrial fuel.

There could be a paradox here. The Japanese remember all too well that, on the day in 1941 when they started their war with the United States, a paper before the imperial government had said that war was necessary because of the coming shortage of oil. In that December of 1941 Japan had a reserve of oil sufficient for its needs for a few months ahead; the Japanese government believed that it would never have so much oil again unless it seized control of the oilfields of Indonesia and perhaps Burma. Thirty years later oil supplies from Indonesia and Burma were much less important than anybody had forecast. Though Japan had been defeated, Japanese industry was using every six hours an amount of oil equal to the entire stock that Japan held on Pearl Harbor day. It was buying it easily from temporarily glutted supplies in the Middle East.

The 1985 war also owed its start partly to fears on the part of the great nations that they would face penury unless they could secure physical possession of oil-producing areas. One remembers the competition run in 1920 by an Austrian newspaper for the most dramatic conceivable newspaper headline. The winning entry was 'Archduke Franz Ferdinand alive. World war fought by mistake.'

The history of energy supplies during the recent conflict has raised some question as to whether, in relation to the oil shortage', that sort of headline may not now be proved apposite.

The areas that have increased their industrial production most in recent years (Japan-China and South America) were cut off from imported supplies of oil when the 1985 war broke out. Each had accumulated large reserve stocks before the war and the war was far shorter than they expected. They got by with ease. The Japanese, who are now the world's most advanced technicians and who had feared that the impeding of oil supplies from the Middle East might prove much longer-lasting, have progressed dramatically with experiments on the thousands of possible other ways of releasing energy from storage in matter. This does not apply simply to nuclear, solar, wave and geothermal energy, but also to, for example, creating artificial rain in large tanks by allowing warm air above sea water to rise through deliberately cooled upper air and getting hydro-electric power from that. Also, the protests of environmentalists against nuclear fission have diminished since the war, and nuclear fusion is at hand.

One must beware of any forecasts about fuel supplies now the war is behind us. In February of 1947, during the Shinwell fuel crisis, Britain's Prime Minister, Clem Attlee, said that no coal miner need fear for his job for the rest of the century. Within twelve years, a majority of the then existing coal mines in Europe and Japan had closed down. The forecast 'oil-short 1990s' may prove like that. The Middle East may, like the coal-mining districts at the end of the coal age, have tragically priced itself into standards of living it will no longer be able to afford. Or it could still prove for some years (as many people suppose) to be the main supply area for a valuable and depleted natural resource.

In either event, the Middle East is not going to be a comfortable southern neighbour for the new EEC. If oil is still scarce, there will be a jockeying for positions there. If the area is going to be poorer than it has grown accustomed to thinking it has a right to be, there may be constant *coups d'état*. It became fashionable in the 1970s and early 1980s to suppose that a main object of diplomacy would always be to make good friends of the rulers of Iran and the Arab oil countries. But billionaire shahs and sheikhs are not likely to be the most popular folk heroes for the last decade of the twentieth century.

After each major war this century, a great empire has melted away. After the 1914–18 war, the defeated Austro-Hungarian empire. After the 1939-45 war, the victorious British empire. After the 1985 war, the defeated Soviet Union. That last is the only result of the late war that can be accounted as certain so far. For the rest, the most accurate prophecies could prove to be the ones that seem least likely now.

There is a nice story of a political prophet in Munich in 1928, who was asked to prophesy what would be happening to the burghers of his city in five, fifteen, twenty and forty years' time. He began: 'I prophesy that in five years' time, in 1933, Munich will be part of a Germany that has just suffered 5 million unemployed and that is ruled by a dictator with a certifiable mental illness who will proceed to murder 6 million Jews.'

His audience said: 'Ah, then you must think that in fifteen years' time we will be in a sad plight.'

'No,' replied the prophet, 'I prophesy that in 1943 Munich will be part of a Greater Germany whose flag will fly from the Volga to Bordeaux, from northern Norway to the Sahara.'

'Ah, then you must think that in twenty years' time, we will be mighty indeed.'

'No, my guess is that in 1948 Munich will be part of a Germany that stretches only from the Elbe to the Rhine, and whose ruined cities will recently have seen production down to only 10 per cent of the 1928 level.'

'So you think we face black ruin in forty years' time?'

'No, by 1968 I prophesy that real income per head in Munich will be four times greater than now, and that in the year after that 90 per cent of German adults will sit looking at a box in a corner of their drawing rooms, which will show live pictures of a man walking upon the moon.'

They locked him up as a madman, of course.

BRITISH DEFENCE POLICY

Reorganizations of the British contribution to the land forces of Allied Command Europe – of which, over the years, there had been several – had always been represented by the British government of the day as improvements to BAOR's effectiveness, even when their actual result could only be a reduction in combat capability. The 1974 reshuffle was no exception. The Northern Army Group (under British command, it should be remembered, and containing almost all the British ground troops assigned to NATO) had never at any time been fully adequate to its task – to repel a Warsaw Pact incursion into northern Germany. No one really believed that NORTHAG, even given time for its four constituent corps (Belgian, British, Dutch and German) to be brought up to war strength and moved forward to battle locations from barracks far in rear, would be able to hold up indefinitely a conventional attack on the scale to be expected, and there were virtually no reserves in depth to deal with a breakthrough. The 1974 reorganization of the British Army made a weak position weaker.

It was this lack of forces in depth which had led to the stationing of two US brigades in northern Germany – most valuable but still far from sufficient to restore tactical control once the NORTHAG front was pierced. The main significance of this move on the part of the Americans, though its purpose was essentially military, can be seen as *political* rather than tactical. It showed simply that the US did not accept the clear implication of British defence dispositions in Germany: that a failure to hold an invasion on the Demarcation Line must very soon be followed by nuclear action, which could lead to a strategic nuclear exchange; that provision for a land battle in depth was unnecessary. The Americans, in rather pointedly providing two combat brigades for the very purpose of defence in depth, in an area of mainly British responsibility, demonstrated that in a matter directly affecting the security of the United States under threat of strategic nuclear attack, they were not prepared to allow their choice of options to be dictated by British defence policy.

This did not pass unnoticed in Britain. The suggestion, given a generous airing in the British press, that Britain was continuing to rely on the US to do what Britain should really be doing for itself, was not particularly pleasing to the British public in a time of reviving national confidence. It was to play a small but not unimportant part in securing public approval for the increase in Britain's contribution to the NATO ground forces, which will now be explored.

The principal features of the restructuring programme for the British Army carried out under the Defence Review for 1974, to which reference has already been made, were as follows: divisions would be made smaller and one level of command, the brigade, would be eliminated. The span of divisional and unit command would be increased, with the result that there would be fewer HQ and fewer but larger combat units. The fighting capacity of the British Army of the Rhine, it was claimed, would be maintained and in some respects enhanced – though if anyone believed this to begin with no one did for long, not even the politicians who made the claim. Certain specialist functions (such as the flying of army aircraft, the manning of the larger anti-tank missiles and the driving of supply vehicles) would be concentrated in the hands of a single branch of the army.

For the army as a whole, the aim was said to be to reduce manpower while maintaining combat effectiveness. It was true that the numbers of equipments in service were kept at about the same level, which was dangerously low. What was described as 'cutting the tail and keeping the teeth', however, only meant that even in the inadequate numbers to which these equipments had been reduced, there were insufficient men to man, maintain and move them. The real purpose, of course, was economy at almost any price. Within three years of the 1974 Defence Review BAOR was at its lowest level of operational efficiency ever.

Not everything that was done was wholly bad, however. The regular army logistic reinforcement which the army at home (United Kingdom Land Forces – UKLF) was to provide for BAOR was drastically reduced, but to help fill this gap units of the Territorial and Auxiliary Volunteer Reserve (TAVR) were integrated into newly created regular combat formations. These, though brigades in all but name, could not be called brigades without contravening one of the declared principles of the exercise. They were therefore given the imprecise but otherwise inoffensive title of 'field forces' instead. This was at least one step towards a much needed improvement, the better use of reserves.

The effect of the restructuring plan on NATO reinforcement plans was one of nomenclature and source rather than of numbers. Before it, UKLF had undertaken to despatch to BAOR in support of NATO a total of some 60,000 to 70,000 troops, consisting of complete formations – 3 Division and 16 Parachute Brigade, for example – and a whole series of unit and individual reinforcements of great variety. Some were TAVR Signal Groups to activate the NATO and BAOR communications systems; some were so-called Yeomanry Regiments, fully equipped with armoured reconnaissance vehicles, to thicken the covering force troops available to I British Corps; others were units or individuals to strengthen either the structure or total numbers of BAOR formations, regiments, companies and squadrons. Leaving aside those who might be sent to the so-called flanks of NATO (Scandinavia, Italy, Greece, Turkey), the operation was designed to bring BAOR on to a war footing, which involved more than doubling its peacetime establishment. It was essentially a reinforcement which combined regular units, regular reservists and units of the TAVR.

After the army's restructuring programme had been completed in 1978, the plans for reinforcement were substantially the same, but it was of course a reinforcement of a BAOR which had itself been restructured. By then I British Corps contained four armoured divisions (which were little more than large brigades) and one light infantry formation, called 5 Field Force. Two other field forces, 6 Field Force from Aldershot and 7 Field Force from Colchester, were part of UKLF reinforcements for BAOR and were themselves composed partly of regular units and partly of TAVR, the latter providing the bulk of the logistic support. Otherwise the reinforcement plan conformed to the previous pattern. As far as equipment was concerned BAOR remained as poorly provided as ever, though some new ATGW were promised soon.

Public dissatisfaction in Britain with its contribution to NATO, as Soviet military preparations still showed no sign of slowing down while pressure within the Alliance upon its members to do better steadily increased, caused the British government to introduce in 1979 a new Army Reserve Act, whose main purpose was to tap unused sources of trained military manpower. This Act laid down the means by which a liability for annual training and for embodiment in a national emergency would be given to those officers and men leaving the army each year (some 20,000 in number) who had hitherto not had any such liability. There were two main categories: first, those who served on short regular engagements, that is, officers who had completed a three-year Short Service commission and soldiers who had served for three, six or nine years with the colours. The second category (for it was decided to disregard Long Service men who retired at the age of fifty-five) comprised officers who had served on Special Regular commissions of up to sixteen years and soldiers who had completed twenty-two years. Although this second group already had certain reserve liabilities in an emergency, they were not required to do annual refresher training. The new law would therefore enable the government to call on both junior officers and soldiers and also on more senior ones, such as majors and warrant officers. All those in these various groups would for three further years have a training liability for two months' annual embodiment, including overseas training, and their reserve liability in times of national emergency would continue until their forty-fifth birthday. The necessary safe-guards of employment and so on were included in the legislation. Thus some 20,000 officers and men, well trained in existing equip-ment and techniques, from all corps of the army, became available each year from 1980 onwards.

Four things would be required to turn this availability of men into a really valuable NATO contribution – weapons to equip them, the structure to absorb them into units and formations, training exercises both at home and in their NATO role, and all the administrative, ammunition and transportation support necessary to make them operationally effective. Extra equipment came to hand in two ways: first, a modification of regular infantry and armoured units reduced them once more from four companies/squadrons to three, which was all their authorized manpower could properly support anyway; second, re-equipment programmes for regular units on a rather more generous scale made it possible to transfer weapons and vehicles to the newly forming reserve units. These were themselves formed by the expansion of existing TAVR organizations. The Artillery and Engineer Groups were trebled, each regiment forming a group; the dismounted Yeomanry Regi-ments were remounted on armoured vehicles; the two fully equipped Yeomanry Regiments quadrupled in size, each squadron forming a complete regiment; fifteen more of the TAVR Home Defence battalions were given a NATO role and equipped accordingly. There were similar expansions and re-equipment programmes for signal support and logistic units, and all was fitted into the existing organization of UKLF. At the same time, what was known as TAVR II was again, after some years in suspense, brought into being. It was a force resembling a militia, mobile and lightly armed, with an important role on the home front.

By 1984 the whole position had been transformed: 5 Field Force stationed at Osnabrück had become a division, which, with its TAVR and regular reinforcements, could be made fully up to strength. Both 7 Field Force and 8 Field Force (which was stationed on Salisbury Plain and which had had a home defence role), with their TAVR components, became fully-fledged armoured divisions on the same pattern as those in I British Corps. Their despatch to Europe meant that a second corps would be available to NORTHAG, a corps HQ having been formed at Bulford from resources thrown up by the reduction of HQ UKLF and the former HQ South-West District. In addition to these increases, 6 Field Force became a full light division with a limited regular and TAVR parachute capability, to be employed either on the flanks of NATO or in the Centre.

The Home Defence units of the TAVR, together with certain regular units formed from the Training Establishments and Base Organization, numbered in all some 30,000. Thus C-in-C UKLF was able to retain a sufficient fighting strength to ensure the security of so-called key points, and have a mobile reserve for emergencies, provided initially by 6 Field Force, and later from mobile columns from the Training Establishment.

It was planned that from 1985 onwards II British Corps, with its headquarters normally located in Britain and with a wartime location near Rheine on the Dortmund-Ems Canal, would carry out manoeuvres in BAOR once a year. The extra divisions would at last give the Commander of NORTHAG what had been lacking for so long – some degree of depth. He would now have in consequence a better chance of containing an incursion without very early recourse to nuclear weapons.

During this time of awakening interest in defence, perhaps no question in any Allied country (except possibly the truly critical problem of reserves in the United States, to which we shall return) raised more domestic difficulties than that of the air defence of the

United Kingdom. The nakedness of NATO, once the nuclear shield was seen to be so brittle, was nowhere more brutally exposed than in the vulnerability of the British Isles to air attack. The comforting assumption of the short, sharp war conducted in someone else's country had vanished once it had been realized that in the present condition of NATO a war with the Warsaw Pact was most likely to be short and sharp if it were to end in victory for the other side. To prevent this would need a capacity for sustained intensive conventional operations, and in these the position of the United Kingdom as a rearward base for Europe and a forward base for the United States made heavy air attack inevitable.

Rueful looks were now cast back at the baleful consequences of the 1957 White Paper, of which one had been the concentration, in the interests of economy and ease of management without operational penalty, of RAF installations in vulnerable patterns offering responsive and rewarding targets to penetrating aircraft. The recovery and rehabilitation of airfields disposed of to the army or to civilian use, the construction of further airfields to relieve dangerous congestion on those used by the USAF (which already in 1977 had more than 200 F–111s in Britain), the hardening of operational control centres and the provision of mobile alternatives were all only parts of a very big construction programme demanding the expenditure of something like £1,000 million in a three-year plan.

It had soon become apparent that the permanent stationing of further USAF squadrons in the UK, probably on the west coast, would now be unavoidable. This brought at least partly into public view a matter which had long been under confidential discussion: the question of the distribution of responsibilities between British and American air forces in an emergency.

There had long been little doubt that the USAF would generally play the dominant part in air operations based in the UK. There was equally little doubt that, although the USAF would assume the chief responsibility for the security and air defence of its own installations in the UK and a high degree of responsibility for the defence of the UK base as a whole, the RAF would have to play the chief part in the defence of national territory. It was, indeed, a sign of the reviving national self-respect evident in Britain at the end of the seventies that in the matter of air defence, as well as in other respects, total reliance on the United States was being increasingly replaced by a robust determination in the British people to play a full part in their own defence – and to pay for it.

A growing public willingness in Britain from the end of the seventies to see a higher proportion of a rising GNP devoted to defence can be said to have been truly indispensable to the survival of the Western Alliance in the years that were to follow. There was a limit to the share of other people's burdens which would be borne by the United States. There was also no lack of latent support on the western side of the Atlantic for the dangerous argument that the US should disengage itself from the Alliance.

At sea, the rundown of the Royal Navy had thrown a heavy additional load on the US Navy in maintaining the flow of fuel, food and raw materials into Western Europe, which would be vital in an emergency. Contraction of the RAF had gravely impaired Britain's ability to give air support to BAOR ground troops and keep the air forces of the Warsaw Pact off their backs, and above all had removed the capacity to defend the UK base. The reduction of Britain by blockade at sea, the collapse of the Northern Army Group on land, the neutralization by air attack of Allied forward bases in the British Isles – together these would spell ruin for the Alliance as a whole. This was in the event only prevented by the reversal of the rundown in Britain's defences forced by public opinion on politicians from the end of the seventies. It was costly but the money had to be found, if necessary – if, that is, a growing GNP could not cover the increase – at the expense of other programmes. The reconstitution of UK air defences was at least labour-intensive and thus useful in the continuing fight against the obstinately high level of unemployment in Britain.

Important though the problems of the British contribution to NATO ground forces might be, the situation of the RAF and the needs of air defence could be said to be marginally even more critical. Britain could survive, in some form, if only for a while, the collapse on land of Allied Command Europe. It could probably get along somehow under severe blockade at sea. What it could hardly be expected to survive, given the state of technology today, was devastation from the air. To prevent this, then, was the task of highest priority. It was also the most costly. Because of its impact on so many different aspects of life in Britain, and its widespread requirement for the diversion of effort and resource from other uses, the re-creation of the air defences of Great Britain was also the most difficult part of the defence programme.

The programme got off to a relatively slow start in the financial year 1979–80 and gathered strength in the following years, as the percentage of the GNP devoted to defence moved upwards from 5 per cent and began to approach – though it never quite reached – the 11 per cent it had touched during the war in Korea at the turn of the fifties. It never, in fact, until the outbreak of war, exceeded 9 per cent, but since this was a percentage of a greatly increased GNP, the rise in expenditure in real terms was very considerable. Vulnerable points, such as main ports, airheads, defence and other key industrial installations and command and control centres, against any or all of which attack by precision-guided weapons could be expected, were furnished with point-defence surface-to-air missile systems supplied by the United States. Airfields were extended and hardened to 2 ATAF standards, like those in Germany, and light and easily concealed operational control centres were established. The lack of ordnance for operations sustained for any more than a very few days – one of the gravest weaknesses in all aspects of Britain's defences – began to be made good by the reactivation of production lines allowed to lapse, and where this was not possible (as was sadly all too often the case) the setting up, at great expense, of new ones. The training machine began to be rescued from the poor condition to which successive defence cuts had reduced it and a vigorous recruiting drive opened in the schools and universities. The Auxiliary Air Force was expanded with a non-combat role of weekend instruction, thereby developing a nucleus capable at the appropriate time of taking on a full-time function and releasing flying instructors for combat duties. Even so, with the training time for pilots to front-line standards approaching three years and a grave shortage of instructors it was to be a long haul before the new cockpit seats arriving in the front line would be filled with competent combat pilots. As was also happening for the other two services, legislation was amended to permit the embodiment of volunteer reservists in advance of Royal Proclamation. At the same time provision was made for the utilization of reservist RAF general duties personnel without high specialization but with an invaluable initiation into service under arms. These were absorbed into Home Defence units of the land forces.

In the matter of equipment, as a top priority, orders for the MRCA (multiple role combat aircraft) – the *Tornado* – in the air defence variant were increased, but lack of elasticity in the production line compelled the RAF to run on their existing F–4 *Phantoms* to achieve the 100 per cent increase now sought in air defence aircraft. Radar cover was provided around the west coast, and a tanker force augmented by aircraft from the United States to sustain long-range interception of enemy aircraft operating in the Western Approaches. Real progress, hitherto stalled for lack of funds, was made in exploiting over-the-horizon radar techniques and satellite information; organic aircraft radar was steadily improved and increasingly relied upon; airborne early warning (AEW) became available to the extent that it could be relied upon as a mainstay and the ambition of the RAF to be largely independent of ground radars by 1990 looked like being realized as much as five years sooner.

A bid for a 100 per cent increase in maritime patrol aircraft was agreed, but it was already too late to save the jigs for *Nimrod* production, and the American Lockheed *Orion* had to be purchased instead. Finally, proposals to station further USAF air defence forces in the UK, both to afford further security in the Western Approaches and to strengthen UK air defence as a whole, proposals which had only received lukewarm support in Britain in the early seventies and had encountered stiff resistance in Congress, were now, as it became evident that Britain was at last beginning to do something for herself, looked on with favour.

On the side of offensive air operations, it was not quite so easy to secure funds for expansion. An increase in front-line strength of 30 per cent was eventually negotiated, to be taken in a combination of *Tornados, Jaguars* and *Harriers*, with an option on the F–16 and F–4 *Phantom* if *Jaguar* and *Harrier* production should prove – as turned out to be the case – to have been run down too far to meet the requirement. A long and keenly debated decision as important as any in the development of air power was taken to bring the cruise missile into service with the RAF in its air-launched version. This, in its high-explosive mode, was seen as a quantum jump in the capability for counter-attacking enemy air bases and attenuating the weight of effort which might be mounted from them against the British Isles. This was a complex and expensive programme which had to follow in the wake of the American re-equipment with these weapons, and it was not expected to be available to the RAF until the middle, possibly late, 1980s.

GORSHKOV AND THE RISE OF
SOVIET SEA POWER

'The flag of the Soviet Union flies over the oceans of the world,' observed Admiral of the Fleet Sergei G. Gorshkov in 1974. 'Sooner or later the United States will have to understand that it no longer has mastery of the seas.' Throughout the 1960s and 1970s, even after Admiral Gorshkov's retirement from active service, successive Politburos had accepted his well and persistently argued thesis that world peace, that is to say the triumph of Marxism-Leninism throughout the world, must be, and could only be, based upon mastery of the seas.

To gain this it would be necessary to allocate an exceptionally high proportion of Soviet resources of men and material to naval and maritime purposes, and to apply these scientifically. The classical sea power doctrine of Mahan had to be reinterpreted in the light of Marxist-Leninist theory and the socio-political and technical conditions prevailing in the last quarter of the twentieth century. These included the continuing credibility, and therefore necessity, of the submarine-launched strategic nuclear missile system, with matching general-purpose naval and air forces in support, and to counter, as far as possible, the opposing submarine strategic systems. Necessary, also, was the evolution from Mahan's theory of general command of the sea of a doctrine of local and temporary command appropriate to the support of 'state interests'. Additional general-purpose naval and air forces would be needed, in consequence, for use in situations involving a limited number of participants, in a limited area, using limited means to realize limited ends.

This line of reasoning was not only persuasive in itself, and accorded almost universal agreement by the naval hierarchies of the non-Soviet world. It also seemed to be fulfilling, when put into effect, the promise of its progenitor. The activities of the new Red Navy began to hit the headlines just after the Six-Day

Arab–Israeli War in 1967, when Soviet naval forces entered Port Said and Alexandria 'ready to co-operate' with the Egyptians to repel any aggression.

Indeed, the hitherto self-evident asymmetry of the superpower confrontation as it had developed since the end of the Second World War – maritime coalition versus continental colossus – began to be questioned. Between powers of a different nature a *modus vivendi* could be reached. It did, in fact, exist. When Alexis de Tocqueville predicted of autocratic Russia and democratic America: 'Their starting-point is different, and their courses are not the same; yet each of them seems to be marked out by the will of Heaven to sway the destinies of half the globe,' he did not prophesy war. between them. Yet might not the projection of autocracy over the sea, by calling forth the projection of democracy on to the continent, eliminate the differentiation between the respective destiny-swayers upon which their peaceful co-existence, being an agreement to differ, had rested?

Whatever dangers Soviet determinism might hold for the peace of the world, American pragmatism had already compounded the risk by her involvement in the war in Vietnam. The contribution made to her national security by this mistimed, misplaced and misconducted intervention in South-east Asia was almost totally negative. A far more fruitful, less politically sterile and less socially disruptive policy would have been to bring the Persian Gulf and Indian Ocean into the orbit of statecraft and naval policy, as urged by Admirals Arleigh Burke, Chief of Naval Operations, and John S. McCain Jr, Commander-in-Chief Pacific Fleet, in the 1950s. Better late than never, Drew Middleton, the military correspondent of the *New York Times*, wrote on 20 April 1973: '. . . the strategic interests of the United States and global strategy in general will pivot on the Persian Gulf late in this decade as a result of competition for the area's oil.'

The rapid growth of the Soviet (and satellite) merchant and fishing fleets throughout the 1960s and 1970s, while not directly associated with the Gorshkov naval expansion, coincided with it. Apart from specialized shipping used for oceanographic research, hydrography and space programme support, the Soviet Union sought, as many a nation had in the past, the political, strategic and economic benefits of self-sufficiency in maritime transportation: prestige, conservation of currency, control over shipping, maintenance of employment in the home shipbuilding industry, and, in addition, a specifically

Soviet requirement, the ability to carry economic and political war-fare into the capitalist camp. Fishing (and whaling) fleets, operated industrially and on a huge scale, also provided protein to help make good deficiencies in agricultural production.

That a serious contradiction existed near the centre of Soviet maritime policy-making had become apparent during the series of United Nations Conferences on the Law of the Sea (UNCLOS) which took place during the 1970s. While the Soviet navalists were at one with those of the United States and the other 'traditional' maritime states in seeking to maintain the freedom of movement so far enjoyed by ships of all nations upon the high seas, and through the straits that connected them, the Soviet foreign relations experts, hoping for political advantage, favoured the claims of 'Third World' nations, some old, some new, who wanted to extend their sover-eignty over wide expanses of sea and ocean off their coasts, and the sea-bed beneath, thus severely eroding the whole concept of free-dom of the high seas. Of course, historically, the freedom of the seas has always been in the gift of the dominant naval power. The granting or withholding of belligerent status and of the rights of neutrals in war, whether declared or undeclared, remained in 1985 something rather more than a folk memory but less than a governing factor in the determination of national and international responses to hostil-ities at sea. But the Soviet Navy had conducted itself with propriety as it extended the scope and intensity of its peacetime missions. It was not until the shooting started, and political guidance had to be sought from Moscow, that failure to harmonize the political with the operational requirements in taking account of the international law of the sea began to have its effect.

It can now be seen that to meet a number of pressing requirements, including the need to relieve pressures in the Soviet Union no less than in the satellites, the Soviet leadership had brought to an advanced state contingency plans which, directly or indirectly, would put the Soviet Navy to the test. The time was coming to cash Gorshkov's cheque. The plans involved in the first instance the use of naval and air forces in support of political operations designed to offset American reaction to savage, repressive measures within the Soviet empire and to secure advantages over the USA while it was still under a new and untried Administration. One of these plans hinged upon upsetting violently the political stability of the Persian Gulf; another on delaying the establishment of· a stable political settlement in Southern Africa. Thus, the supply of Middle Eastern oil to the United States would immediately be in jeopardy, both at its source, in the Persian Gulf, and en route in tankers via the Cape of Good Hope.

On 29 December 1984 came news which electrified the world. An Iranian troop transport had been torpedoed and sunk, with heavy loss of life, by a Soviet submarine in the Strait of Hormuz; and an American intelligence ship had been subjected to missile attack off Aden.

Had Fleet Admiral Gorshkov still been in charge of the Soviet Navy it is doubtful whether things would so soon have begun to go wrong for the Russians. In the first place, he would have had sufficient prestige, courage and professional acumen to have demurred when given orders to send a submarine into the Persian Gulf approaches to sink an Iranian troop transport and immediately report the successful attack. The depth of water being insufficient for nuclear-powered submarine operations to be fully effective, the submarine had to be one of the diesel-driven 'patrol' type. But the Iranian Navy was known to have been equipped with up-to-date ASW forces, mainly of British origin, and to be well trained in their use. The prospect, therefore, of a successful submarine attack, followed by the safe withdrawal of the submarine and receipt of the all-important attack report, would not be good. By the same token, Gorshkov would have been unlikely to countenance a surprise missile attack upon an American intelligence ship. He would have reasoned that such an attack might invite reprisals against the Soviet Union's own intelligence-gathering ships upon which so much depended; and that the US Navy could quickly concentrate a powerful force to escort the damaged ship to safety.

These dramatic events, when reported to the Soviet naval high command, had the effect of concentrating the comrades' minds wonderfully. Despite the careful planning which had preceded the challenge to the United States, there was suddenly a feeling that events might get out of control. It was central to Soviet politico-military doctrine that military measures must directly and effectively serve some chosen political objective, whether on a worldwide or on a regional scale. Operations in the Middle East had been continuing, short of actual shooting by the great powers themselves, for many years – ever since the 1960s, in fact, soon after the failure of British nerve, French colonialism and American leadership became manifest at Suez. The rapid growth of the Soviet Navy under Gorshkov had been in response to two quite separate requirements, reflecting, as do so many aspects of Soviet policy, its dyadic nature. The first of these, as could be deduced from the Peace Programme promulgated at the Twenty-Fourth CPSU Congress, accepted as inevitable a degree of watchful co-operation between the Soviet and the Western blocs. The strategic balance would be maintained, nuclear war averted and *détente* promoted. The second need was competitive. In the Third World the Soviet Union had to compete strongly with the West for political influence, by supporting its friends and denying to the West any advantage that might be detrimental to the interest of the USSR or its clients. The Soviet Navy had to support both aspects of Soviet state policy. In theory this had seemed not only feasible but the strongest argument for naval expansion. In practice, how was it going to work out?

The more recent Soviet naval activities in the Middle East formed part of the grand strategy formulated in 1983, when the probability had been foreseen (in a planning document given strictly limited circulation within the Kremlin) that the necessity would arise 'to remove, by force if necessary, the NATO threat to the security of the USSR in Europe'. The intention of the Soviet Union to continue to take part, either directly or indirectly (but without inciting conflict with Western forces), in 'fraternal wars' had been reaffirmed. This policy, sanctified by Communist Party doctrine, could contribute to the achievement of two complementary strategic aims, one political in nature, the other military. Given the increasing dependence of the USA and her NATO allies on petroleum imported from the Persian Gulf, both its denial at source and its interdiction en route would be of great – perhaps decisive – advantage to the Soviet Union. The 'fraternal' aid currently being provided to the new United Arab Republic, and to the 'People's Liberation Armies' in Southern Africa, supported these two objectives. But now the shooting had started. It was essential to retain the initiative. The closest possible co-ordination of diplomatic and naval activity was essential; and the responsibility had to be placed firmly where it belonged – with the Politburo. The Soviet Minister of Defence, Raskolnikov, was in complete accord with the Commander-in-Chief of the Soviet Navy, Admiral Starsky. There had to be an immediate plenary meeting of the Main Military Council.

When this meeting took place, twenty-four hours later, it was attended by all the First Deputy and Deputy Ministers of Defence; also by the commanders-in-chief of the ground forces, air forces and strategic rocket forces, and, of course, of the main fleets. The ministers responsible for supplies, production of war materials and transport were present, and the Soviet Foreign Office was represented. Opening the meeting, the Minister of Defence briefly outlined the recent events. He then emphasized the need to keep the Politburo, and especially the Chairman of the Central Committee of the CPSU, fully informed and properly advised. Second, the co-ordination, command and control of diplomatic activity and naval operations had to be fully effective. The balance had to be kept between actively supporting 'fraternal' forces and avoiding general war with the imperialists. To this end the Council ordered a number of studies to be made, for presentation within forty-eight hours. One of these studies, to be made by the naval staff, was 'The Correlation of Naval Forces in the Red Sea, Arabian Sea and Persian Gulf'.

The naval paper, completed two days later, was predictable, not only in its comprehensiveness but also in its complexity. Despite Gorshkov's single-minded advocacy of Soviet sea power throughout a quarter of a century as commander-in-chief, and the implementation of most of his major proposals, there remained many in high places who had never been fully convinced. Several influential members of the Military Council were civilians, landsmen of Russia to whom sea power remained an alien concept, and one not easily accommodated within Marxist-Leninist doctrine. Nor had the generals, as a body, ever been fully reconciled to what they saw as a disproportionate diversion of resources to naval expansion. The Soviet naval staff, therefore, took nothing for granted in reviewing the naval situation in the Middle East. The summary of facts, conclusions and recommendations which accompanied the paper was commendably terse, but the paper itself was not. It began with some 'General Considerations'. These affirmed that:

1 The seas and oceans of the world remain, in spite of air, and improved land, transport, the 'broad highway' over which 90 per cent of the world's commodities, minerals, manufactured products and petroleum are moved. In addition, 70 per cent of the population of the world live within thirty miles of the sea coast.

2   Economic necessity has forced the Soviet Union to develop, first, large fishing fleets [whaling fleets, also, until there were no more whales], then a large, and still increasing, merchant fleet. The former provided indispensable protein, the latter foreign currency, essential transportation between widely separated parts of the Soviet Union, and political influence worldwide.

3   Oceanographic research has enabled Soviet scientists to understand the sea and the exploration of the sea bed.

4   National security has demanded, first, naval defence of Soviet territory against the nuclear power of the US carrier strike fleets, together with the capacity to interdict seaborne military reinforcement of Western Europe from North America. Later, the development of submarine-launched strategic nuclear ballistic missiles, both by the Soviet Union and the United States, placed upon the Soviet Navy the main responsibility for the retaliatory and damage-limitation rocket forces, indispensable to the preservation of a strategic nuclear posture that would at least not be unfavourable to the Soviet Union in the event of nuclear war.

5   The Soviet Navy must also play its part in the combined armed forces of the Soviet Union by supporting the seaward flank of the ground forces with amphibious operations, defence against attack from seaward, and supply.

6   'State interests' frequently require the support of the Soviet Navy in peacetime. The historical mission of Marxist-Leninist theory calls for the projection of Soviet power beyond the confines of the Eurasian land mass. To this end, it is necessary to contend with, and eventually overcome, the sea power of the United States and her imperialist allies, so that the supremacy of the Soviet Union, at sea as on land, will be acknowledged.

The next section of the Soviet naval staff paper was headed 'The Comparison of Naval Force'. Pointing out that navies were not in themselves to be regarded as synonymous with sea power, but rather as the instruments of sea power, it went on to give the historical context. Shortly after the end of the Great Patriotic War in 1945, it had been objectively true to say that the Soviet Union was predominantly a continental power, facing a predominantly maritime coalition, in which the United States and Great

Britain provided the main naval elements. In addition, the vast majority of the world's shipping was owned and operated by the maritime coalition, which also occupied or controlled almost all the main ports, harbours and sea routes throughout the world.

During the past three decades this asymmetry had been transformed, by the forces of history and the peace-loving exertions of the Soviet Union, in three ways. First, the Soviet Navy had grown, both actually and relatively, so that it was now in many respects 'second to none'; second, the Soviet Union had provided itself with a large ocean-going merchant fleet, as well as fishing fleets of great capacity; and third, the failure of the imperialists and colonialists to retain political authority over their subject peoples had led to a large increase in the number of independent states, and these states between them now possessed navies of their own, and many of the ports and harbours which formerly were controlled by the old maritime coalition. Fortunately, the Soviet Union, as the friend of all liberated peoples, now had access to their ports; could utilize their naval forces in the struggle for peace; and could in some cases deny their use to the imperialists. The Soviet Union was now, therefore, a maritime as well as a continental power.

It was still true, however, that in comparing the two blocs, geography, so important a factor in sea power, did impose constraints. The advantage of unified political control enjoyed by the Soviet Union, as compared with the autonomy of the countries comprising the Western coalition, was offset by the continued existence of four major threats to the freedom of Soviet movement by sea. The British Isles could act as an unsinkable aircraft carrier in the north-west approaches to Europe. The exits from Murmansk to the Atlantic, and from the Baltic to the North Sea, could not be regarded as secure. Nor could the Dardanelles, so long as Turkey was imprisoned in the capitalist camp. In the Far East, Japan was so placed as to be able to impose serious limitations on the use of Vladivostok. Soviet policy would sooner or later have to eliminate these four constraints upon her sea power.

Turning now to the comparison of actual naval forces, the paper first referred to the criteria of relative capabilities which had been used in determining the shape and size of the Soviet Navy in accordance with its various missions. Formerly, 'like fought like' at sea; a direct comparison of the numbers of similarly armed ships which could be brought into action at a given place and time had always formed the basis both of strategy and of tactics. Now, the balance of naval capability had to be calculated by mathematical systems analysis, solving multi-criteria problems for various adversary situations and different combinations of heterogeneous forces and means. Objective analysis of this kind permitted determination of the necessary and sufficient composition of forces and their combination into balanced groups. Because the application of such methodical, indeed scientific, analysis was indispensable to a proper assessment of the naval-air situation in the Middle East, it was deemed essential to explain it in some detail.

The central concept in modern naval force comparison, the paper affirmed, was the weapon system, not the ship, the submarine or the aircraft, though these were considered as targets for the various weapon systems. In defining a weapon system a choice had to be made. At one end of the spectrum, a club in the hand of a caveman could be called a weapon system; at the other, a ballistic missile submarine. In the present context, the elements of a weapon system were:

1   A means of detecting and identifying a possible target.
2   A warhead capable of destroying or neutralizing that target.
3   A vehicle to carry the warhead to the target.
4   A launcher for the vehicle.
5   A means of controlling the vehicle so that it will hit the target.
6   Protection for the vehicle and warhead against counter-measures designed to prevent either or both from hitting the target.

Certain features of the operational environment profoundly affected weapon systems, the paper went on. If the target was under water the system would be dependent upon the acoustic properties of seawater; if it was above water, it would be dependent upon electro-magnetic radiation. Weapon systems which required a homing device of any kind for target acquisition could always be decoyed or otherwise countered. Those guided by radio command were susceptible to electronic jamming. The tactics used in bringing weapon systems to bear were governed by their characteristics. The principle of concentration of force required continuous reinterpretation in the light of complex and varied weapon systems.

Taking the targets in turn, studies had shown that:

1 Surface ships are vulnerable to surface-skimming, submarine-launched, horizon-range missiles; to tactical surface-to-surface missiles; to air-to-surface missiles; and to torpedoes and mines.

2 Submarines are vulnerable to submarine-launched, wire-guided torpedoes; to aircraft-launched torpedoes and nuclear depth charges; and to ship-launched torpedoes.

3 Aircraft are vulnerable to surface-to-air short-range missiles; to surface-to-air medium- or long-range missiles; and to aircraft-launched missiles.

It had been established, the paper continued, that the latest Soviet weapon systems performed as well, if not better, than their equivalents in service in the US Navy. Soviet strategic deployments and tactical dispositions, therefore, must always aim at bringing to bear a superior concentration of appropriate weapon systems, while denying to the enemy the opportunity to do so. In the field of underwater warfare, two special factors had to be borne in mind. First, owing to the relatively low speed of sound waves in water, it was not feasible for submarines to operate in close formation with each other in order to bring to bear a concentration of weapon systems upon a hostile submarine or surface target. In a submarine versus submarine action, therefore, victory was likely to go to the one which first detected the other. And because noise levels depended mainly upon speed, the submarine whose mission required it to move rapidly would be at greater risk of being surprised. Second, mines could be used with great effect in certain circumstances.

A reminder was then given of the effect upon naval operations of the almost continuous reconnaissance, by satellite or aircraft, now available. The movements of all major surface ships, whether naval or merchant, were now known, and could, if required, be shown direct on TV screens anywhere in the world. Only the submarine forces remained secure from observation, and even in their case good estimates could often be made of the number and types at sea in various areas. But one very serious constraint remained in regard to submarine operations: the need to avoid mutual interference between friendly submarine and anti-submarine forces.

The final section of the Soviet naval staff paper reviewed the situation in the Red Sea, Arabian Sea and Persian Gulf. In comparing the naval and air forces, it assessed the available weapon systems on both sides as approximately equivalent. The Soviet naval object was to support Soviet foreign policy, in exerting pressure on the United States forces in the area, and assisting the fraternal United Arab Republic forces to deny full control of the Persian Gulf to Iran. The course of action recommended was to reinforce the Soviet naval air squadron re-established at Aden with an additional squadron of *Backfire* bombers, and one of *Foxbat* fighters. The task group based on a *Kiev*-class anti-submarine carrier, now visiting Mauritius, should proceed to the Red Sea, preparatory to the declaration of a War Zone there, should this become necessary. Under the heading 'Command Communications and Control', the naval staff advised the establishment forthwith of a Flag Officer Soviet Middle East Forces (FOSMEF), with headquarters ashore at Aden. The agreement of the People's Democratic Republic of Yemen (PDRY) government should not be difficult to obtain. FOSMEF would require a full operational staff, an air deputy and a political adviser. A communications echelon would be set up, with an organization appropriate to the major operational task envisaged. FOSMEF would, for the time being, be responsible administratively to the Commander-in-Chief Soviet Black Sea Fleet, at Sevastopol. Operationally, he would be directly responsible to the Commander-in-Chief Soviet Fleet.

When the Soviet naval staff paper was taken by the Main Military Council, together with several other important papers, the Conclusions and Recommendations were approved.

NATO NAVAL COMMAND
STRUCTURE

It was natural in 1951 to create first an Allied Command Europe, in order to establish US forces on the ground, where they would discourage the Soviet Union from any further westward advance. It was also natural to create an Allied Command Atlantic, in order to ensure the reinforcement and re-supply of the US ground forces. It was inevitable, also, that both supreme commanders should be US officers. It was, perhaps, equally natural, and inevitable, that Great Britain, especially with Winston Churchill once again returned to power as Prime Minister, was not ready to subordinate the Royal Navy entirely to an American admiral with his headquarters on the far side of the Atlantic. Not until it had been agreed, therefore, to set up an Allied Commander-in-Chief, Channel, with supreme commander status, and a British admiral in the post, would Churchill agree to the activation of SACLANT. The Channel command was confined to the southern North Sea and the English Channel; and it was hoped that the worst possibilities of operational misunderstanding, at the command boundaries, would be eliminated by ensuring that the same British officers who exercised certain British national commands, and appropriate subordinate commands in Allied Command Atlantic (ACLANT), would also hold the subordinate posts in the Channel Command. The wartime mission of SACLANT would be to maintain intact the communication lines of the Atlantic Ocean, to conduct conventional and nuclear operations against enemy naval bases and airfields, and to support operations carried out by SACEUR, while the Commander-in-Chief, Channel (CINCHAN) was 'to control and protect merchant shipping, to endeavour to establish and maintain control of the area, and to support operations in adjacent commands'.

Since 1951, a number of important developments had taken

place, both political and strategic. Although no single one might have justified a change in the command structure, their cumulative effect would do so. The developments were these: the postwar recovery of Western Europe, despite severe economic setbacks, which had transformed the relationship with the USA from dependence to interdependence; the advent of submarine-launched ballistic missiles, which had relegated the US Strike Fleet from being the primary naval strategic force, and only secondarily a general-purpose force, to being primarily a general-purpose force, with a nuclear strike capability; the rapid increase in the number of nuclear-powered general-purpose submarines in both the Soviet and the US Navies; the continued failure of scientific research and technological development to provide an effective means of detecting and accurately locating submerged submarines (while this failure preserved the second-strike capability of the SSBN forces, and hence contributed to the maintenance of strategic nuclear stability, it augmented the threat of submarine attack on shipping and surface warships, already far more serious than in the worst period of the Battle of the Atlantic in the Second World War); the discovery and exploitation of oil and natural gas in the North Sea and the Norwegian Sea; the withdrawal of British naval forces from permanent stations outside the NATO area, and full dependence upon NATO for national security; the closer political association of the Western European members of NATO, and their desire to have a greater say in the conduct of the affairs of the Alliance, *vis-à-vis* the United States; the adoption of communication networks, data exchange systems, warning systems and air defence systems which needed to be matched by appropriate command and control arrangements if full advantage was to be taken of these techniques; the fact that nuclear-powered general purpose submarines operate with so much less effectiveness, and are indeed much more susceptible to detection, location and destruction, in the shallow waters of the Continental Shelf (200 metres or less) than in the deep ocean beyond; finally, and most important, the adoption of a strategy of 'flexible response' in place of the originally declared strategy of 'massive retaliation' against the first identified aggression.

Thus, while the basic requirement remained, that the NATO ground forces in Western Europe should be reinforced and supplied across the Atlantic, almost every other condition which governed the original NATO command structure had altered. What was, in effect, a continuation of the Second World War-winning set-up would no longer serve. A flexible response strategy meant nothing if it did not mean the demonstration, in peacetime, of both the determination and the capability to engage major enemy forces by land, sea and air, if put to the test. Given the speed of movement and scale of attack which had to be expected, as well as the range of tactical missiles, the whole land and sea area of the north-west European Continental Shelf would have to be regarded, from the outset, as part of the central front battlefield. True, the nature of the operations thereon would be three-dimensional; and the area would retain its character as the terminal and *entrepôt* for transatlantic support. But one thing was certain: the purely political character of Channel Command, squeezed between a subordinate command of SACLANT, who was far away in Norfolk, Va., and the presumably hard-pressed SACEUR, across the Channel, could not be expected to meet the requirements of war.

To abolish CINCHAN, and incorporate his command in ACLANT, would merely invite that well-known over-centralization syndrome known as 'apoplexy at the centre and paralysis at the extremities'. To subordinate CINCHAN to SACEUR, with whatever title, would cause the latter to be continually looking over his shoulder. There remained a third alternative, namely to create, out of CINCHAN, a new Supreme Allied Command, which would comprise the existing Channel Command, and part of the existing Eastern Atlantic Command, adjusted so as to be approximately contiguous with the United Kingdom Air Defence Region. The new command, which it was decided to call the Joint Allied Command Western Approaches (JACWA), would be a joint sea-air command, held by the British Naval and Air Commander-in-Chief. The British Flag Officer Submarines, and a US flag officer, would be deputies, and the chief of staff a NATO admiral of another nationality. The EASTLANT-Channel naval-air headquarters became the home of JACWA, and fairly soon the structure of subordinate commands, based upon retention of national command, but flexibility of operational command and, to an even greater extent, of operational control, was in being and working well.

The Commanders-in-Chief of JACWA discovered first that, whether they liked it or not, they would become, early on in a typical 'invasion from the East' situation, engaged in a battle for the Baltic Exits; they might also find themselves arranging for the withdrawal from West Germany and the Netherlands of warships and submarines nearing completion, or refitting, lest they should fall into enemy hands. In fact, had they not existed at the outbreak of the Third World War, Cs-in-C JACWA would have had to be created. Their task included the entire planning and operational responsibilities which had fallen to the Admiralty during both the previous world wars, in its capacity as a command post for operations in home waters and the North Atlantic. It was still in his capacity as C-in-C Fleet, however, and not as Naval C-in-C JACWA, that the British admiral set in train the NORSECA plan (see pp. 78–9).

THE HOME FRONT

I: A summary of events in civil defence in the seven vital years 1978–85

1978
Government allocation for civil defence at approximately £2 million (in real terms about one-twentieth of the 1968 budget) is totally inadequate. Government directives and plans for dealing with emergencies are out of date and irrelevant. Except in a few counties there is little or no interest in civil defence or emergency planning.

1979
Formation of National Emergency Volunteers (NEV) – a voluntary, self-financing organization formed to recruit, train and equip civil defence workers at parish/community level and to encourage parishes and urban communities to plan and organize as survival units in an emergency – with the emphasis on self-sufficiency.

In a period of massive unemployment and uncertainty the NEV rally strong support. Under imaginative and forceful leadership it begins to impress government and local government with the urgent necessity of taking positive action to restore a civil defence capability.

In late 1979 the government passes legislation facilitating the embodiment of TAVR in an emergency.

1980 and 1981
The NEV increase rapidly in all counties. Fifty per cent of all rural parishes now have workable emergency plans and are equipped with radiac instruments and chemical detector papers, and 65 per cent have one or more civil defence advisers. In urban communities the proportions are 12 per cent and 18 per cent.

1982
In March 1982 a US bomber carrying five 10-megaton nuclear

weapons collides in mid-air with a Jumbo jet over Hampshire and crashes in flames on Fawley oil refinery. There is no nuclear explosion, but a substantial escape of radioactive cloud which blows across Southampton Water. Radiation is detected by a NEV operator in Warsash. His early warning makes possible rapid evacuation of population in the path of the fall-out as far inland as Petersfield. Casualties treated number 631 and include five deaths. Population in southern counties alerted.

Later in the year the IRA threaten to detonate a nuclear warhead in the Bristol Channel. The partial evacuation of Bristol is started before the threat is disposed of. The public is now aroused to demand that the government provide proper protection in an emergency with a faster reaction time.

1983

The government passes the Civil Protection (Emergencies) Act, giving statutory recognition to the NEV with an annual allocation of £2 million per annum for the purchase of civil defence equipment at parish/community level, and to defray administrative and training costs.

The total grant for civil defence and emergency is increased by £30 million per annum; this includes provision for the hardening of essential communications systems against EMP (electromagnetic pulse).

This Act sweeps away the former emphasis on secrecy, and introduces a new two-stage emergency warning – Phase 1, 'Warning Stand-by'; Phase 2, 'Action' – and stresses that each level of authority in an emergency – region, county, district, parish, ward, street association, etc. – must plan and equip to be self-contained at immediate notice and to survive for at least a week without help from outside.

All authorities down to and including parish/community level are directed to prepare and update emergency plans for approval by government inspectors. These plans should provide for the appointment of a controller and emergency committee with the necessary powers to run the parish/community and co-ordinate survival measures in emergency for a considerable period.

1984

International tension is growing. There is talk of a possible world war. NEV step up recruiting and training. Most rural parishes are equipped and ready. Less than 40 per cent of urban communities are prepared.

The government holds a national civil defence exercise in August with simulated emergency alerts and trial evacuations. Existing evacuation plans are modified to a more flexible system. The lessons of the exercise are that law and order may be a major problem.

A new government booklet, *Civil Protection in an Emergency*, is issued to local authorities down to parish/community level, to government and local services, and to the NEV and voluntary bodies.

1985
In the summer international tension, less in the early part of the year, is again acute.

20 July. In response to its recognition that the Warsaw Pact is mobilizing NATO begins to put Allied armed forces on a war footing. The USA prepares to airlift troops to Europe and loads war equipment on to shipping.

The UK government issues Emergency Phase 1 warning and distributes a *Civil Protection* booklet to all householders. Radio and TV broadcasts and newspaper articles advise the public how to behave and survive under attack. Evacuation plans are explained. The orderly evacuation of school children is to start on 22 July. Plans for petrol and food rationing are announced. The Stock Exchange is closed.

All community councils and local authorities convene extraordinary meetings and update emergency plans. Councils confirm appointment of controllers and emergency committee members. Final preparations are made to put emergency plans into operation.

II: Extracts from the Emergency Diaries kept by three English communities, recording the course of events in sixteen critical days, 4–20 August 1985

4 August

Branscombe, a village in Devon, pop. 400

0900* Emergency Diary opened. BBC has reported Warsaw Pact forces advancing into West Germany – only conventional munitions (incl. chemical) reported used so far. UK Govt declares State of Emergency (Phase 2).

0920 District Controller confirms State of Emergency locally.

0931 Chairman Parish Council directs activation of Branscombe Emergency Plan (BREMPLAN).

0940 Branscombe Emergency Committee (BREMCO) takes over Holt House (a private dwelling) as Emergency Control HQ. Instructions issued to establish Feeding and Rest, and Hospital and First Aid Centres.

0950 Report received that already 4,000 holiday-makers and refugees are in the parish and more arriving at approx fifty per hour. Controller asks police in Seaton to divert refugees. Reply negative (have no authority and we are already overwhelmed with problems in Seaton and Beer).

1005 In agreement with Chairman Parish Council, Controller blocks roads into Branscombe with bulldozers leaving Gatedown Lane open with Control Post at northern end.

1200 PM broadcasts to the nation. State of War exists but we will not be first to use nuclear weapons.

1400 Meeting in Village Hall. Chairman Parish Council and Controller speaks to villagers and visitors. Parish ration/identity cards issued.

1500 BBC reports NATO troops withdrawing.

1600 Survey team starts continuous radiac monitoring watch.

1700 Govt broadcast advising population to remain calm and all except key personnel to · remain at home and await further instructions; meantime to carry out directions of Govt booklet.

Buxford, a town south of Manchester, pop. 8,000

1700 Buxford Emergency Committee activated, Emergency Control HQ established and Control Staff closed up at full

* All times are according to British Standard Time.

strength. Continuous watch opened with radiac equipment and chemical detector papers. Large numbers of refugees moving south from Manchester by car and on foot, but passing through.

Sparksley Green, an urban community in central Birmingham, pop. 2,075

1810 Emergency Control HQ established at the 'Red Cow'. Only Controller and two Communications Officers have reported. No radiac or other equipment. HQ organized on reporting basis only. Rapid exodus of population, roads blocked. Some looting of food shops and liquor shops. Few police in evidence.

5 August

Branscombe

0915 All private cars moved to parks in fields and tanks drained. Hospital operating Edge Hill. Feeding arrangements going well. Emergency latrines being dug at Rest Centres and at all Billeting Centres on main drainage.

1000 All refugees reported under cover. Emergency water scheme operational.

1100 Stocks of detergents, lavatory paper, pharmaceutical and medical supplies received from District Controller.

1200 Steady stream of US transport planes flying overhead since 0900.

2300 Signal from District that enemy bombing can now be expected at any time – probably from aircraft using HE and chemical weapons.

2400 Electricity supply failed. Switched to own generator.

Buxford

1200 Emergency plans operating well. Refugee stream to south continues. US planes arriving in some numbers Manchester Airport. Buxford population fear they will attract Soviet attack and 20 per cent have already left. Control Staff at 90 per cent strength.

2300 District warn that enemy are expected to start bombing our airfields at any time.

2400 Electricity failed. Stand-by candles.

Sparksley Green

2200 Still on reporting watch only with Controller and two Communications Officers – no equipment. Approx half population seem to have left. Armed police are bringing looting under control. Two looters shot, one policeman murdered and two injured. A number of fires which a depleted fire brigade have difficulty in controlling.

2300 Signal that bombing attack expected. District sending two spare Communications Officers with radiac and chemical detectors. Two Emergency Committee members reporting at 1000 tomorrow.

2400 Electricity cut.

6 August

Branscombe

0350 Air raid alert.

0415 Sound of A/C overhead. Bombs falling to east and west.

0430 Signal that our airfields under heavy bombardment.

0730 'All Clear' sounded.

1000 Signal received that bombs dropped during night had contained HE, incendiary and nerve gases (tabun, sarin and VX).

1700 Air raid alerts and All Clears have followed each other all day. Controller directed that no further air raid warnings would be sounded in the village unless bombs were seen to be dropping or there was threat of a nuclear attack. Hot meal ordered for all at 1830.

1930 US transport A/C flew over Parish at 2,000 metres on fire – parachutes emerging as A/C flies off west. Reported to District.

1935 Enemy A/C flew low across Parish west to east. Reported.

2300 Electricity restored.

Buxford

0350 Air raid warning.

0400 to 0600 Heavy air raid high level A/C – 100+ bombs land Buxford area. Survey team make short recce at 0500 during lull – report much damage and many fires, and chemical detector papers show positive readings. Police, ambulance, fire brigade and rescue squads working in respirators and protective clothing.

0615 All Clear. Survey team report bombs still exploding intermittently – presumably with delayed action fuses. As some contain nerve gas it is agreed with police to re-sound Alert to get everyone under cover while unexploded bombs are dealt with.

0800 Survey report shows approx 1,200 casualties of which 15? are dead.

0900 Two enemy A/C attack airport. No bombs on Buxford. US transport planes continue to come in in spite of bombing.

1006 One US and one Soviet A/C come down in flames over Buxford. Both crash to south.

1138 Five A/C attack airport – 50+ bombs on Buxford including nerve gas.

1400 District Controller agrees all civilians except key personnel be evacuated. Control Staff to stay.

Sparksley Green

0550 Air raid warning.

0600 A/C overhead, bombs falling and exploding to east. None in our area. Reported.

0615 All Clear.

0700 District advise water will be cut off at 1200. Police agree to tour area with car loud-hailers to advise householders to fill baths and containers before 1200 and to use plastic bags etc for toilet purposes.

1500 Police are withdrawn. Looting and fire-raising starts again. Three murders in streets and some inter-racial fighting. All food shops run out or looted. Communal meals supplied by District at school. Less than 25 per cent of population remain.

7 August

Branscombe

1200 Much A/C activity all morning. Villagers and refugees continue to work on farms and at allotted tasks.

1341 Electricity fails. District advises water will be cut off at 1600. Emergency water and hygiene plans activated.

1400 At BREMCO Conference with Parish Council a reserve Controller and four Committee members chosen to replace existing BREMCO team should they become casualties. The Parsonage House chosen as an alternative Control HQ if Holt House destroyed. Directed that second copies of Emergency Diary and Financial Records be kept there.

Buxford

1000 No air raids for 20 hours; area declared clear of bombs and contamination. Buxford Controller suffered nervous breakdown – his 70th birthday. Cncllr Deschet appointed as new Controller.

1115 Gang of four armed youths reported looting liquor warehouse – no police or troops available. Controller with armed posse goes to restore order.

1330 Controller returns with posse and police Inspector, who has charged Controller with murder and malicious wounding. He charges that after the youths had been disarmed in the warehouse the Controller held a summary court martial and sentenced the four youths to death. When he ordered his armed posse to carry out the sentence and shoot the boys they refused, whereupon he took one of the guns himself and opened fire, killing one and wounding three. At this point the Inspector arrived. Chairman of Buxford Council arrives, relieves Cncllr Deschet of his appointment and replaces him with Cncllr Burt-Rand.

Sparksley Green

1200 For mutual protection and support most of remaining inhabitants have concentrated in the area round the school and the 'Red Cow'.

8 August

Branscombe

0600 Signal ex District – enemy concentrating attacks on power stations, oil depots and ports.

0700 Farmers northern perimeter of Parish report looting of food stocks during night.

0800 Recce of N perimeter report 850+ refugees camped alongside A3052 demanding accommodation in Parish.

1000 Controller visits refugees and offers accommodation for 34 women and young children, a hot meal for all and two days'

food for the remainder if they will keep moving. Offer accepted. They are given medical supplies.
1150 Controller orders construction of strong barbed wire fence along northern boundary of Parish.
1200 Four refugees in village brought before Controller accused of raping girl. Accused and witnesses with armed escort sent to District HQ for trial before JP.
1350 District HQ signal that nuclear bomb has exploded over London. Village advised and nuclear drill rehearsed.
1430 District HQ advise previous report false. Village told.
1630 Air dogfight over Branscombe. Soviet plane shot down over sea. No parachute. Reported.
2131 Intense air activity, sound of bombs falling and heavy explosions which appear to be in area of village and are getting . . . [Entry ends here. Emergency Diary was found in ruins of Holt House.]

Buxford
0800 Heavy air raid on airport during night. Over 50 bombs in Buxford area – HE and nerve – delayed action. No water or electricity.

Sparksley Green
1200 Heavy air attacks on Birmingham Airport during night. About 30 HE bombs fell in Sparksley area, approx 170 casualties. Police, rescue, fire, etc, in control. Still no water or electricity.
1410 Epidemic of sickness and diarrhoea reported to District.

9 August

Branscombe
0800 Emergency Control HQ at Holt House destroyed by direct hit with 225 kg HE bomb at 2131 yesterday and Controller and Emergency Committee members and all Control Staff killed. All CD equipment except one dosimeter destroyed. Reserve Emergency Control HQ opened up in Parsonage House at 0400 and stand-by Emergency Committee members and Controller took over as agreed. Supply of dosimeters, survey meters, chemical detector papers, respirators and

protective clothing received from District at 0700. Priority phone connection established at 0750.

Eight killed, seventy-three injured and gassed in village in last night's raid caused by HE and nerve gas. All casualties evacuated to Axminster.

0900 120 cattle and sheep killed previous night. Buried at Holt Pits.

1015 New stand-by Controller and BREMCO members appointed. Reserve Control HQ will be at Hayes Farm.

1350 Burial service of casualties of last night's raid. Service in Parish church.

1500 Farmers report large number cattle and sheep with unusual symptoms, thought to be due to nerve gas. District asked to send vet.

12 August

Branscombe

0800 BBC report Warsaw Pact forces still advancing southwards up west bank of Rhine. Continued enemy A/C attacks on UK airfields, ports and power stations.

0900 Outbreak sickness and diarrhoea reported Rest Camp I. District asked to send doctor.

1000 Controller meets deputation from refugees who complain of inadequate food and harsh and uncomfortable living conditions, and say that many do not wish to work on farms and all have to walk too far to work and for their meals. Controller explains necessities but promises to try to improve conditions.

1800 The first of the daily evensong ecumenical services in the Parish church. Full.

19 August

Branscombe

0800 BBC reports NATO counter-attack northwards towards Bremen has made headway, and enemy's southern advance has been stopped. No air attack on UK for 48 hours.

1400 Cricket match – Village v the Rest. Village 86 all out, the Rest 87 for 4.

1900 Evening concert Village Hall.

20 August

Branscombe

1140 District reports nuclear explosion Birmingham area.

1300 BBC confirms high-yield nuclear bomb burst over Birmingham at 1130. Very heavy casualties and great damage. Villages within 50 kilometres and in path of fall-out cloud being evacuated. Govt warns there is possibility that other nuclear strikes may be expected.

1600 Controller addresses village on sports field – explains position and rehearses nuclear drill. Everyone to continue as normal with no extra precautions.

Buxford

1130 Extraordinary bright flash in southern sky, followed by ascending, expanding huge red ball of fire. Immense shock wave later. Can it be?

Sparksley Green

0028 Residents' party in Control HQ ends at midnight. Little activity in UK over past 72 hours. Many hope war will be over in few days. But who has won?

1100 Routine call to District. Signal loud and clear.

1128 Warning – all Control Posts to stand by for urgent signal.

1129 Signal – RED ALERT (air raid warning sounded): 'President USA has received Soviet warning of immediate nuclear attack on Birmingham Engla . . . [The charred remains of this log were found in the cellar of the 'Red Cow'.]

APPENDIX 5

DEPLOYMENT OF FORCES AND EQUIPMENT, 1 AUGUST 1985

Table 1 NUCLEAR DELIVERY VEHICLES*

Operated by	Intermediate/Long-range (over 2400 km)†				Short-range (160–2400 km)				Close-range (below 160 km)		Remarks
	ICBM	IRBM	SLBM	Bombers	SSM	GLCM	SLCM	Fighter-Bombers	SSM	Artillery	
USSR	1400	100	950	100	700	–	100	1000	500	500	Long-range numbers limited by SALT
Other Warsaw Pact	–	–	–	–	100	–	–	some	200	–	Warheads in Soviet custody
Totals	1400	100	950	100	800	–	100	1000+	700	500	
USA	1000	–	900	350†	–	100	300	500‡	100	500‡	Long-range numbers limited by SALT
NATO‡	–	–	–	–	–	100	–	100	100	300	Warheads in Soviet custody
Totals	1000	–	900	350	–	200	300	600	200	800	
UK	–	–	64	–	–	50	–	200†	–	–	
France	–	18	80	–	–	100	–	200	120	–	
China	50	250	–	100	100	–	–	100	–	–	

* Missile launchers with single or multiple warheads; bombers carrying multiple missiles and/or bombs; cruise missiles and artillery (dual-purpose). Carrier-borne aircraft are included.
† With ALCM.
‡ In Europe.

Table 2   GROUND AND TACTICAL AIR FOR

Country	Manpower (in thousands)	Equivalent divisions*	Tanks Medium	Light	ATGW
NATO					
Belgium	47	2	400	200	6
Britain	138	5	1050	500	25
Canada	12	1	150	–	5
Netherlands	30	2	425	100	7
West Germany	800	14	3000	350	57
United States	250	7	2150	600	35
	1277	31	7175	1750	136
France	90	5	750	250	12
Totals	1367	36	7925	2000	149
Warsaw Pact					
Czechoslovakia	165	10	3000	–	10
East Germany	100	6	1700	100	6
Poland	240	15	3000	250	14
Soviet Union In Eastern Europe	425	28	8000	600	43
In Western USSR	495	34	9000	700	52
Soviet total	920	62	17000	1300	95
Totals	1425	93	24700	1650	125

* Divisions, brigades and similar formations, aggregated on the basi
three brigades to a division.

† Multiple launchers carried on one vehicle are counted here as one AT
Launchers carried on the tanks or helicopters shown in this table
excluded.

TRENGTHS IN THE CENTRAL REGION

Artillery, rocket launcher nd heavy mortars	Armed helicopters	Tactical fighters	Remarks
80	100	150	
325	150	620	Including aircraft but not ground forces in the United Kingdom
50	50	70	
100	100	175	
1150	600	650	Including mobilised Territorial Army
1050	350	1150	Including two reinforcement divisions flown in
2755	1350	2815	
120	125	550	First Army in Germany and Eastern France
2875	1475	3365	
900	50	500	Some of these forces are
750	50	350	unlikely to be deployed
1500	50	800	outside national territory
3600	700	1300	
4500	850	1500	Reinforced and ready to move into Eastern Europe
8100	1550	2800	
11250	1700	4450	

ll figures relate to launchers, not missiles; there are likely to be several issiles for each launcher.

Table 3 MAJOR WARSHIPS AND MARIT

Category	USA	Canada	Britain	Belgium	Netherlands	West Germany	Denm
Submarines							
Ballistic missile, nuclear	51	–	4	–	–	–	
General-purpose nuclear	88	–	16	–	–	–	
diesel	10	3	23	–	6	24	
Totals	149	3	43	–	6	24	
Aircraft Carriers							
Attack: large	13	–	–	–	–	–	
medium	2	–	–	–	–	–	
ASW Light Escort	–	–	3	–		2	
ASW Cruisers	2	–	3	–		–	
Totals	17	–	6	–	–	2	
Other surface warships							
Over 8000 tons	12	–	2	–	–	–	
5500–8000 tons	63	–	8	–	–	–	
3500–5500 tons	135	5	13	–	–	5	
1000–3500 tons	18	19	78	7	23	22	
Totals	228	24	101	7	23	27	
Amphibious Ships							
Assault ships	16	–	2	–	–	–	
Landing ships	60	–	6	–	–	6	
Totals	76	–	8	–	–	6	
Maritime Aircraft							
Patrol: land-based	250	60	82	–	25	25	
carrier-based	116	–	–	–	–	–	
Strike: land-based medium bombers	–	–	–	–	–	–	
land-based fighter-bombers*	100	–	100	–	24	150	
carrier-borne fighter-bombers	1020	–	42	–	–	12	
Totals	1486	60	224	–	49	187	

*These are naval fighters or squadrons earmarked for maritime support. The Wa
Pact uses medium bombers in this role, but has a large number of fighters prim

RAFT – WARSAW PACT AND NATO

ay	Portugal	Italy	Greece	Turkey	France	NATO Total	Warsaw Pact total	Remarks
	–	–	–	–	5	60	53	US/USSR numbers limited by SALT
	–	–	–	–	–	104	150	Some with cruise missiles
	3	12	6	14	23	145	100	
	3	12	6	14	28	309	303	
	–	–	–	–	–	13	–	
	–	–	–	–	1	3	–	
						–	8	*Kiev*-class
	–	–	–	–	–	5	–	Merchant ship hulls
	–	2	–	–	1	7	4	Through-deck or *Moskva*-class
	–	2	–	–	2	28	12	
	–	–	–	–	2	16	12	
	–	–	–	–	13	84	27	
	–	9	2	3	18	190	125	
	15	27	13	11	41	293	135	
	15	36	15	14	74	583	299	
	–	–	–	–	–	18	–	
	–	2	6	10	10	100	50	Excluding smaller landing-craft
	–	2	6	10	10	118	50	
	–	30	10	–	40	527	300	
	–	–	–	–	–	116	–	
	–	–	–	–	–	–	400	*Backfire*
	12	50	24	24	50	558	110	
	–	24	–	–	36	1134	110	
	12	104	34	24	126	2335	920	

e ground role that could be called upon for maritime support under certain
mstances.

w.w.–Q

Table 4   REGIONAL AVAILABILITY

Maritime area	General-purpose submarines	
	Nuclear	Diesel
Atlantic (West and North)		
USA	40	5
Britain	12	17
Other NATO	–	20
France	–	10
USSR	60	20
Baltic/Approaches		
NATO	–	34
Warsaw Pact	20	20
Iberian/Mediterranean/Black Sea		
USA	3	–
Portugal	–	2
France	–	7
Italy	–	7
Greece	–	5
Turkey	–	10
USSR:		
Mediterranean	5	–
Black Sea	–	10
South Atlantic/South Indian Ocean†		
USA	3	–
France	–	–
USSR	5	–
Red Sea/Arabian Sea/Persian Gulf†		
USA	2	–
USSR	5	4
Pacific (East and West)†		
USA	20	3
Canadian	–	1
USSR	40	20

* The figures include ships at sea and in port, but not those undergoing re
or in reserve.
† In these waters there were also the navies of regional states; notably the

AJOR NAVAL SHIPS AND MARITIME AIRCRAFT*

| Major surface ships | | Maritime strike aircraft | | Maritime patrol aircraft |
Carriers	Others	Carrier-borne	Land-based	Land-based and carrier-borne
5	60	300	50	100
5	60	40	50	50
–	–	–	50	100
–	38	–	20	12
2	25	50	250	50
1	42	12	200	45
–	50	–	50	25
1	20	70	–	25
–	12	–	12	–
1	35	12	30	12
2	30	25	30	25
–	12	–	24	10
–	12	–	24	–
1	20	6	25	25
1	25	–	50	50
1	20	70	–	50
–	10	–	–	6
1	20	12	–	25
2	12	70	–	25
1	20	12	25	25
5	60	350	50	50
–	10	–	–	25
2	45	12	100	50

South Africa, Iran, India and Pakistan in the Indian Ocean, and of China, pan, Indonesia, Australia and New Zealand in the Pacific.

AUTHORS' NOTE AND ACKNOWLEDGEMENTS

We who have put this book together know very well that the only forecast that can be made with any confidence of the course and outcome of another world war, should there be one, is that nothing will happen exactly as we have shown here. There is the possibility, however, that it could. There is also the very high probability that unless the West does a good deal within the next few years to improve its defences a war with the Warsaw Pact could end in early disaster.

Those who argue for the reduction of defence expenditure in the countries of the West not only seem to live in a land of total make-believe, but they refuse to give the Marxist-Leninists who govern the USSR any credit either for meaning what they say (and have been saying for a long time) or for knowing what they are doing. What they have been saying, and have not ceased to say, is that the capitalist countries of the West are doomed to go down before the inexorable advance of communism, with the Red Army playing a major part in their overthrow. What they have been doing is building up huge armed forces, far greater than what would be necessary, in any conceivable situation, for their own defence, at a cost gravely detrimental to domestic development in the USSR and in a mode essentially *offensive*.

We have been encouraged by signs around us that among the peoples of the West the point, on the strength of such indications, is beginning to be taken. We have outlined a possible course that improvement to the defences of the West might take, in full awareness that it might take others. We have assumed that enough is done to ensure that, when

466

the Soviet machine travels of its own momentum along a path of miscalculation and mischance towards an attack on NATO, the West, at some cost, is able to survive. It is possible, of course, that enough will not be done. The outcome is then likely to be different. This is not to suggest that a war is bound to happen, or even that it is likely. If, however, there could be no question that, in the event of war, the Warsaw Pact would win, the free countries of the West would be in no position to withstand political pressure from the USSR, which would enjoy the fruits of a military victory without having to fight for it.

We have had invaluable advice from a great variety of sources, including the Ministry of Defence in London, Supreme Headquarters Allied Powers in Europe, Allied Forces Central Europe, the British Royal Military College of Science, and elsewhere.

We are much indebted to a widely acknowledged expert on the Red Army, Professor John Erickson of Edinburgh University.

We are particularly indebted for advice to General M. Davison (formerly C-in-C USAREUR) and General W. de Puy, both recently retired from the US Army. They have given invaluable help on more than one aspect of our work.

Mr Julian Allason, whose own book on the defence of the United Kingdom against nuclear attack will appear in 1979, and Major J. A. Hibbert, who is much concerned with civil defence, have also been helpful, as have serving officers whose advice has helped to lend realism to our treatment of the fighting.

The events in this book have, on occasion, been presented according to our, the authors', views rather than according to the advice given to us. Any criticism of the result, therefore, should in no way be directed at those mentioned above. No contributions are signed since strict attribution would not be easy in so co-operative an enterprise.

Sir John Hackett
February 1978

INDEX

A-10 aircraft, 140, 286
Aachen, 294, 301
AAFCE (Allied Air Force Central Europe), 137, 284
Aarhus, 234
Abu Dhabi, 72
ACE *see* Allied Command Europe
Acholi tribes, 33
Active Forces Draft (US), 169, 170
Addis Ababa, 30
Aden, 73, 338–9, 436; Soviet base, 70, 443
Aegis anti-missile system, 244, 245
Aeroflot, Soviet Air Line, 308
Aerospace vehicles, 163, 255, 256
AEW (airborne early warning) aircraft, 234, 263, 267, 268, 273, 432
AFCENT (Allied Forces Central Europe), 99, 112, 116–20, 122, 125, 132, 135, 137, 171, 177, 297, 298, 301, 304, 401; airspace, 186; HQ, 186, 301
AFNORTH (Allied Forces Northern Europe), 112, 118, 120, 137, 313; and fighting in Norway, 204, 305
AFSOUTH (Allied Forces Southern Europe), 112, 120, 137; moves to Spain, 174, 205, 305; naval commitments, 218; gradual Soviet withdrawal, 313
Air defence of United Kingdom and Eastern Atlantic, 260–77, 283–4, 402, 428–31; USAF augmentation forces, 265–8, 272–3; airfields, 271; Soviet attack on airfields and key targets, 271; demolition of buildings, 271: civilian casualties, 271; combat air patrols (CAP), 272; threat to French Channel ports, 272–3; aircraft losses, 273
Air war over Central Europe, 278–93, 312; Warsaw Pact superiority, 278, 279; NATO forces, 278–9; Soviet objective, 279; Allied counters, 280–1; NATO improvements, 288; Allied technological superiority, 282–3, 290–1; RAF Germany, 283–4; US reinforcement aircraft 284
Warsaw Pact Invasion, 284–5; Allied counter-air offensive, 285–6; attrition of NATO aircraft, 288; aircraft reserved for nuclear strike released, 287–8; NATO reinforcements, 288; NATO defensive war battle, 288–9; Soviet weight of numbers and local superiority, 289; improved position for NATO, 290–1; concentration against enemy west of Rhine, 290–1; Soviet failure to achieve full

468